practical counselling and helping skills

practical counselling and helping skills

text and activities for the lifeskills counselling model

fifth edition

Richard Nelson-Jones

First published 2005

SAGE Publications Ltd
1 Oliver's Yard
55 City Road
London EC1Y 1SP

SAGE Publications Inc.
2455 Teller Road
Thousand Oaks, California 91320

SAGE Publications India Pvt Ltd
B-42, Panchsheel Enclave
Post Box 4109
New Delhi 110 017

British Library Cataloguing in Publication data

A catalogue record for this book is available from the British Library

ISBN 1 4129 0387 4
ISBN 1 4129 0388 2 (pbk)

Library of Congress Control Number: 2004093137

Typeset by C&M Digitals (P) Ltd., Chennai, India
Printed in India at Gopsons Papers Ltd, Noida

contents

list of activities

preface

Welcome to *Practical Counselling and Helping Skills*. The following are answers to some questions you may have about the book.

What is this book's purpose?

This is a practical 'how to' counselling and helping skills textbook. In this book I present the component skills for the Relationship–Understanding–Changing (RUC) lifeskills counselling model, which consists of three stages, each of which has three phases. The RUC model provides a systematic approach for clients to develop specific lifeskills to change how they feel, think, and communicate and act. The book's main focus is on counselling individuals. It is intended primarily as a text for counselling skills classes led by skilled trainers. I've designed the book for both introductory and more advanced training purposes. For example, the book pays great attention to skills of offering good counselling relationships and clarifying problems. In addition, it presents more advanced assessment skills and a large repertoire of counselling interventions.

For whom is this book intended?

I intend the book for the following audiences:

- Lecturers teaching counselling skills practical classes in colleges, universities, adult education centres and in voluntary settings.
- Trainees studying in educational settings for roles in the helping services: for instance as counsellors, psychologists, nurses, health care workers, social workers, youth workers, community workers, welfare advisers, personnel officers, career advisers, human relations consultants, pastoral care workers and teachers.
- Trainees developing counselling and helping skills in voluntary agencies: for instance Relate, church-related agencies, and agencies focusing on special populations, such as the mentally ill, the bereaved, lesbian and gay people, and those in crisis.

- Counsellors undergoing supervision as part of their continuing training and development.
- Helping service professionals and voluntary agency counsellors for skills development and reference purposes.

What are this book's contents?

The book is built around the lifeskills counselling model. It has five parts. Part One: Introduction consists of four chapters. Chapter 1 asks who counsellors and helpers are and what counselling and helping is. Chapters 2 and 3 introduce the reader to some important communication/action skills, feelings and physical reactions, and mind skills. Chapter 4 describes the stages and phases of the lifeskills counselling model and is illustrated with a case study.

Part Two: The Relating Stage also consists of four chapters. Chapter 5, on the pre-counselling contact, examines issues such as physical premises and advertising. Chapters 6 and 7 present ten skills of listening and showing understanding, then Chapter 8 looks at skills for starting the counselling and helping process, such as opening statements, structuring and making basic summaries.

Part Three: The Understanding Stage contains five chapters. Chapter 9, clarifying problems skills, examines questioning, challenging, feedback and self-disclosure skills. Chapters 10, 11 and 12 explore skills of assessing feelings and physical reactions, thinking, and communication and actions, respectively. This lays the basis for chapter 13, which describes skills for presenting and agreeing with clients on a shared analysis of their problems.

Part Four: The Changing Stage consists of eleven Chapters. Chapter 14 looks at different ways of planning interventions, whereas Chapter 15 presents skills for delivering interventions, including speaking, demonstrating and coaching skills. Chapters 16 and 17, on interventions for thinking, deal with some interventions for creating rules, perceptions, self-talk, visual images, explanations, expectations and also for creating realistic goals and decisions. Chapters 18 and 19 present interventions for improving clients' communication and actions, including role-playing, timetabling, planning sub-goals and sequencing graded tasks, and using self-reward. Chapter 20 examines skills for assisting clients to experience, express and manage their feelings and introduces the use of medication in conjunction with counselling. Chapter 21 describes relaxation procedures and how to conduct systematic desensitization. Chapter 22 discusses the importance of homework and ways of setting it that increase clients' compliance. Chapter 23 presents skills for the preparing, starting, working and ending phases of initial sessions and ends by discussing monitoring and evaluating progress. Chapter 24 examines when to end counselling and different formats and tasks in so doing. Some skills of client self-helping are also covered.

Part Five: Further Considerations consists of four chapters. Chapter 25 introduces the reader to ethical codes and guidelines as well as to some important ethical issues and dilemmas in counselling practice and counsellor training. Chapter 26 presents a range of areas for diversity sensitive counselling and helping, then focuses on multicultural and gender aware counselling approaches. Chapter 27 stresses the importance of supervision, discusses some of its forms and functions, and presents various ways of preparing for and presenting information in it. The chapter concludes with a discussion of the shadow side of supervision. Chapter 28 looks at issues of personal counselling for trainees and discusses some forms of self-help. The topic of continuing professional development is also briefly reviewed.

Throughout the book practical activities are incorporated into chapters and the final chapter ends with a review activity.

What features does this book possess?

- *Based on lifeskills counselling theory.* This book is based upon my lifeskills counselling integrative approach, which I regard as cognitive-behaviourism with a human or humanistic-existential face.
- *Updated model of practice.* Most trainees learning counselling skills find it helps to structure their interviewing round a model of the counselling process. This book presents a three stage Relating–Understanding–Changing (RUC) counselling process model, with each stage consisting of three phases. The RUC model focuses not only on problems, but on the problematic skills clients possess that sustain their problems and leave them vulnerable to future problems.
- *Emphasis on forming a good counselling relationship.* Counsellors and counselling trainees require the ability to offer supportive and caring human relationships as well as assessment and intervention skills. Good counselling relationships provide the context for using technical skills.
- *Comprehensiveness.* I offer a comprehensive coverage of the skills you require for effective counselling and helping.
- *Recency.* The book incorporates the latest theoretical, research and practitioner literature about counselling and helping.
- *Practical activities.* The book includes 79 practical activities to help you develop your knowledge and skills. As appropriate, you can complete these activities on your own, with a partner, or in a group.

- *Practical examples.* The book contains numerous case studies and vignettes as well as some counselling interview excerpts.
- *Anglo-Australian emphasis.* Unlike most counselling and helping texts, which are American, this book draws on British and Australian demographic data, books, articles and research findings.
- *User-friendly format.* Each chapter follows the same user-friendly format: chapter outcomes, text and activities.
- *Readability.* I have endeavoured to write the book in clear, simple English.

Acknowledgements

The lifeskills counselling approach owes much to others' work. For example, the emphasis on the counselling relationship and the importance of understanding clients on their own terms shows the influence of Carl Rogers's person-centred therapy. The emphasis on thinking skills reflects the work of Aaron Beck, Albert Ellis, Arnold Lazarus and Donald Meichenbaum. Among others, the emphasis on communication and action skills represents the influence of the behaviourists. In addition, Harry Stack Sullivan, Gerard Egan and Robert Carkhuff are forerunners in presenting stage models of counselling sessions and the counselling process. I express appreciation to all these writers and to the many others mentioned in this book's references.

I thank the following people who assisted in bringing this book to life. I very much appreciated the 'consultant supervisor' contribution of Professor Brian Thorne, who provided me with invaluable feedback on drafts of chapters as I was writing the book. Many thanks also to Alison Poyner, my editor, for commissioning the book and to the manuscript editing, production and design staff at Sage for their work in adding quality to the book's presentation.

Some final words

I hope that *Practical Counselling and Helping Skills* challenges you to think somewhat differently about how you help and live. In addition, I hope this book offers you an integrative theoretical framework and model of practice with which to develop your potential for effective and humane counselling.

I introduction

what is counselling and helping? 1

Chapter outcomes

By studying and doing the activity in this chapter you should:

- gain some knowledge about who are counsellors;
- gain some knowledge about who are helpers;
- have an introduction to what counselling is; and
- be introduced to the lifeskills counselling approach.

Below are concerns that people might wish to share with another.

'I get very anxious over exams.'
'I'm extremely shy and have difficulty making friends.'
'Our relationship is heading for the rocks.'
'I have a poor relationship with my parents.'
'I need to make my mind up about a career.'
'I have difficulty relating to my work colleagues and customers.'
'I want to get off taking drugs.'
'I'm just recovering from a heart attack and need to develop a healthier lifestyle.'
'I want to grow old successfully and go on having some meaning in my life.'
'I'm feeling very depressed and useless.'
'I feel under tremendous stress at work and am not coping well.'
'I get angry far too easily.'
'I put myself down for being lesbian/gay.'

There are seven main categories of people who either use or might use counselling skills to help others to cope with these concerns:

- *Professional counsellors and psychotherapists.* Specialists who are suitably trained, accredited and paid for their counselling services. Such people can include clinical and counselling psychologists, psychiatrists and social workers.
- *Paraprofessional counsellors.* People trained in counselling skills who use them as part of their jobs, yet who do not hold an accredited counselling or psychotherapy qualification. Some social workers fall

into this category, whereas others may be qualified counsellors and psychotherapists.

- *Voluntary counsellors.* People trained in counselling skills or with full counsellor training who work on a voluntary basis in settings such as Relate in the UK or Relationships Australia, youth counselling services, church-related agencies and numerous other voluntary agencies.
- *Counselling, psychotherapy and helping trainees.* Trainees using counselling skills on supervised placements as part of counselling, psychotherapy and helping courses.
- *Helpers using counselling skills as part of their jobs.* Here the main focus of the job may be nursing, teaching, pastoral work, supervising or managing and providing services such as finance, law, funerals, trade union work and so on. These jobs require people to use counselling skills some of the time if they are to be maximally effective.
- *Peer helpers.* People who use counselling skills as part of peer helping or support networks of varying degrees of formality. Such peer support networks frequently cover areas of diversity such as culture, race, sexual orientation, and focused support for women or men.
- *Informal helpers.* All of us have the opportunity to assist others, be it in the role of partner, parent, relative, friend or work colleague.

Counselling, psychotherapy and helping

Counselling and psychotherapy

'Psychotherapy' is derived from the Greek word *therapeia*, meaning healing. Attempts to differentiate between counselling and psychotherapy are never wholly successful. Both represent diverse rather than integrated knowledge and activities, so it is more accurate to think of counselling approaches and psychological therapies. In addition, both claim to be based on 'informed and planful application of techniques derived from established psychological principles' (Meltzoff and Kornreich, 1970: 6).

Ways of distinguishing counselling from psychotherapy – never wholly satisfactory – include the following: psychotherapy focuses on personality change of some sort while counselling focuses on helping people use existing resources for coping with life better (Tyler, 1961); they are the same qualitatively, but differ only quantitatively in that therapists listen more and engage in less informing, advising and explaining than counsellors (Corsini, 2005); and psychotherapy deals with more severe disturbance and is a more medical term than counselling. Probably most psychiatrists still view themselves as conducting psychotherapy rather than counselling. In addition, 'psychotherapy' is a term used to discuss longer-term and deeper work with mental disorders, though this is not always the case. However, many psychologists and counsellors work in medical settings, have clients with recognized medical disorders and do longer-term and deep work. Furthermore, the distinction between people who have mental disorders as contrasted with problems of living is not clear-cut.

Many psychologists, such as Corey (2000) and Patterson (1974, 1986) use the terms 'counselling' and 'psychotherapy' interchangeably, and Patterson concludes that there are no essential differences upon which agreement can be reached. Both counselling and psychotherapy use the same theoretical models and stress the need to value the client as a person, to listen sympathetically, to hear what is communicated, and to foster the capacity for self-help and responsibility. Consequently, even in medical settings the term counselling may be just as appropriate as psychotherapy, and increasingly it has come to be viewed as either the same as or similar to psychotherapy.

In Britain there has been a recent development emphasizing the similarities between counselling and psychotherapy. In 2000, the British Association for Counselling changed its name to become the British Association for Counselling and Psychotherapy (BACP). A prime reason for this was that many of its members already considered themselves psychotherapists. In the late 1990s the Psychotherapy and Counselling Federation of Australia (PACFA) was established. Here, as well as commonalities, some differences are still acknowledged. For instance, though work with clients may have considerable depth, the focus of counselling is more likely to be on specific problems or changes in life adjustment, with psychotherapy more concerned with the restructuring of the personality or self. Psychotherapists are more likely to work very intensively with more deeply disturbed individuals who are frequently seen over a long period of time. Counsellors are more likely to work in specific areas where specialized knowledge and method are needed: for instance marital and family counselling and school counselling. It remains to be seen, however, how long PACFA continues to make such distinctions.

Many British and Australian counsellors and psychotherapists are members of neither BACP or PACFA. Some receive their qualifications from other professional associations, such as those in counselling psychology, clinical psychology, and psychiatry, and consider this sufficient. Furthermore, in Britain, in addition to BACP there is the United Kingdom Council for Psychotherapy (UKCP), which has organizational members training people in psychotherapy.

What constitutes professional training as a counsellor or psychotherapist? Though subject to change, the following provides some idea of requirements. Courses recognized by BACP have a minimum of 450 hours' staff/student contact time, with, in addition, students undertaking a minimum of 100 hours of supervised counselling practice. Such courses can last for one year full-time or can be spread over two, three or four years part-time. Training offered by organizational members of UKCP is not normally shorter than of four years part-time duration. Such training involves supervised clinical work and usually personal therapy in the model being taught. In Australia, PACFA requires courses run by its member associations to consist of a minimum of 250 hours of training and supervision.

Regarding professional counsellors and therapists, two further points are worthy of mention. First, a number of people, such as some social workers and nurses, combine professional qualifications in their primary role with professional qualifications in counselling and psychotherapy. Second, completion of an approved course in counselling and psychotherapy training can no longer be equated with accreditation, since increasingly professional counsellors and psychotherapists are required to undertake mandatory continuing professional development (CPD) requirements by their professional associations if they are to achieve and maintain accreditation.

I agree that there is considerable overlap between counselling and psychotherapy. Nevertheless, throughout this book I mainly use the terms 'counselling' and 'counsellor' in preference to 'therapy' and 'therapist'. This is partly for the sake of consistency and partly because counselling is a less elitist term than therapy and lends itself more readily to the overall objectives of the book.

Who are helpers?

Sometimes, the term 'helper' is used as a generic term to cover all those engaged in using counselling and helping skills, whether they are counselling and psychotherapy professionals or not. However, increasingly the professionalization of counselling and psychotherapy makes such usage inaccurate. Here the term 'helper' is used in a more restricted sense to include all those people who offer counselling skills to other people, yet who are not qualified and accredited counsellors, psychotherapists or their equivalent.

Paraprofessional counsellors are trained in counselling skills, but at a level that falls short of professional counselling or psychotherapy accreditation. For example, some nurses have attended a number of counselling skills courses and may be effective at dealing with the problems of specific categories of patients. People with such backgrounds might be called counsellors in their specific work settings, for example nurse counsellors. Alternatively, they might continue to be called nurses. However, if it is intended that the term 'counsellor' in a given context be limited only to those with recognized specialist professional qualifications and accreditation in the area, nurses doing paraprofessional counselling should more appropriately be categorized as helpers, despite the quality of their skills, which may be considerable.

Overlapping with paraprofessional counsellors are helpers who use counselling skills as part of their job. For example, many social workers and probation officers are not accredited counsellors, yet make extensive use of counselling skills with their client populations. In addition, school teachers may perform counselling roles, for instance helping students to study better, deal with difficult classmates and make decisions about their futures. The range of helpers using counselling skills goes far beyond those in the so-called helping professions: for instance bosses and supervisors at work, financial advisers, lawyers and undertakers may all use counselling skills to provide the best possible professional service for their clients.

Another group of helpers is comprised of volunteers, who may be called either volunteer counsellors or volunteer helpers. Volunteer counsellors or helpers perform numerous roles: for example working with schizophrenic clients and their families, people who are HIV-positive or have AIDS and those close to them, or with bereaved people, those on drugs, people with relationship problems and with those adjusting to new cultures. Such volunteers may possess varying levels of training and sophistication in using counselling skills.

Last, but not least, counselling skills can be useful for those engaging in peer helping and in informal helping. For example, members of both women's groups and men's groups may help one another to become more effective by using counselling skills. One useful form of peer helping is known as co-counselling, where each partner takes a turn at helping the other, say for 20 minutes each way or, if thought desirable, for longer. Informal helping is often one way only, for instance parent–child.

Let's take a further look at some ways in which helpers can be distinguished from professional counsellors. So far two main distinguishing features have been identified. First, helpers perform different *roles* from those of counsellors. Counsellors have as their primary role conducting counselling, whether individual, couples, group or family counselling. Helpers often either have their primary role in another area or are using their skills in voluntary and peer support capacities. Second, related to the different roles, helpers differ from counsellors in their *training*. Counsellors are primarily trained to counsel, whereas helpers may be primarily trained to be social workers, nurses, probation officers, priests, welfare workers, managers or to carry out a host of other occupational roles. Furthermore, voluntary workers usually have primary work roles in non-counselling occupations, for which they are likely to have received the major part of their training.

The *goals* of helpers can both overlap with, yet differ from, those of counsellors. The primary purpose of counselling and psychotherapy is to help clients address psychological issues in their lives, for example becoming less depressed or anxious, and to work through decisions and crises that have a distinct psychological dimension to them. Sometimes such psychological issues are central to helping. On other occasions, helpers use counselling skills to assist people to achieve goals where the overt psychological dimensions may appear secondary, if not irrelevant, to the recipients of the services. Some examples of this almost covert application of counselling skills would include the offering of pregnancy advice or spiritual assistance.

The *settings* or contexts can also differ. Most often counselling takes place in offices, private or institutional, set aside specially for that activity. The décor of such offices is designed to support the purpose of counselling, for instance functional easy chairs with a coffee table between them. Often counselling services are located in specially designated areas, for instance student counselling services. Helpers may sometimes use counselling skills in areas designed for counselling, for instance in some voluntary agencies, but frequently they use counselling skills in locations that represent their primary work role: personnel offices, classrooms, tutorial rooms, hospital wards, outplacement clinics, churches, banks, law offices and community centres. Furthermore, while counsellors rarely go outside formal locations, helpers such as priests, nurses, social workers and members of peer support networks may use counselling skills in people's home settings.

Another distinction is that the *relationship* in which helpers use counselling skills often differs from the more formal counselling relationship, which is likely to have clear boundaries structured around the respective tasks of counsellor and client. Sometimes helping relationships may have similarly clear helper–client boundaries, though the prime agenda may or may not be psychological counselling. Frequently, however, helping takes place in the context of other relationships, such as teacher–student, priest–parishioner, line manager–worker, social worker–client, nurse– or doctor–patient. Whereas dual relationships, in which counsellors perform more than one role in relation to clients, are frowned upon in the professional counselling context, they may be built into the fabric of many helping relationships. And, as mentioned above, helping relationships may include home visits or even meetings on neutral territory such as cafés or clubs.

Using terms in this book

Throughout this book, I use the term *counsellor* to refer to both counsellors and helpers. The term *helper* is insufficiently specific to the population that I wish to define. Anybody who provides a service – including shopkeepers, electricians and plumbers – could be regarded as helpers. However, such people are much less likely to be regarded as counsellors. The word 'helper' also has connotations of placing the recipients of help in a dependent position. The helper may be doing things *to* or *for* the persons being helped rather than *with* him or her. In addition, the word 'helper' obscures the idea of self-help that I want to emphasize. The purpose of counselling and helping is to assist people to become their own best helpers. Throughout the book the term *client* is used for recipients of both counselling and helping.

What is counselling?

The term 'counselling' is used in a number of ways. One dimension, already discussed, is related to the *people who counsel.* Other considerations for defining counselling include viewing it as a *relationship*, a *repertoire of interventions*, a *psychological process*, and in terms of its *goals and clienteles*.

Counselling as a relationship

Virtually all counsellors agree that a good counselling relationship is necessary to be effective with clients. Some counsellors regard the counselling relationship as not only necessary, but sufficient for constructive changes to occur in clients (Rogers, 1957). One way to define counselling involves stipulating central qualities of good counselling relationships. Suffice it for now to say that these counsellor-offered qualities, sometimes called the 'core conditions', are empathic understanding, respect and acceptance for clients' current states of being, and congruence or genuineness. Terms like 'active listening' and 'rewarding listening' are other ways of expressing the central skills of the basic counselling or helping relationship. Those viewing counselling predominantly as a helping relationship tend to be adherents of the theory and practice of person-centred counselling (Rogers, 1961; Raskin and Rogers, 2005).

Counselling as a repertoire of interventions

Most counsellors would regard the counselling relationship as neither sufficient in itself nor sufficiently expeditious in its outcome for constructive client changes to occur. Consequently, they set store by a set of interventions in addition to the counselling relationship. Alternative terms for interventions are counselling methods or helping strategies.

Counsellors who deploy a repertoire of interventions need to consider carefully which interventions to use, with which clients, and with what probability of success. Counsellors' repertoires of interventions reflect their theoretical orientations: for instance, psychoanalytic counsellors use psychoanalytic interventions, rational emotive behaviour counsellors use rational emotive behaviour interventions, and Gestalt counsellors use Gestalt interventions. Some counsellors are eclectic and use interventions derived from a variety of theoretical positions. Corsini has come to believe that what counts in psychotherapy is who does it and how and to whom it is done, what he calls the '*whohowwhom* factor' (Corsini, 2005). He suggests that counsellor personality and counsellor–client match are also important, along with specific interventions.

Counselling as a psychological process

In this book the word counselling is used as a shorthand version of the term psychological counselling. Whether viewed either as a relationship characterized by the core conditions or as a repertoire of interventions derived from different theoretical positions, counselling is a psychological process. There are various reasons for the fundamental association between psychology and counselling. The *goals* of counselling have a mind component in them. In varying degrees, all counselling approaches focus on altering how people feel, think and act so that they may live their lives more effectively. So the *process* of counselling is psychological. Counselling is not static, but involves movement between and within the minds of both counsellors and clients. In addition, much of the process of counselling takes place within clients' minds between sessions and when clients help themselves after counselling ends. The underlying *theories* from which counselling goals and interventions are derived are psychological (Corsini and Wedding, 2005; Dryden, 2002; Nelson-Jones, 2001). Many leading counselling theorists have been psychologists: Rogers and Ellis are important examples. Most of the other leading theorists have been psychiatrists: for instance, Beck and Berne. Finally, psychological *research* contributes both to creating counselling theories and to evaluating counselling processes and outcomes.

Goals and clienteles for counselling

Counsellors may have different goals with different clients. They may assist clients, for instance, to heal past emotional deprivations, manage current problems, handle transitions, make decisions, manage crises, and develop specific lifeskills. Sometimes goals for counselling are divided between remedial goals and growth or developmental goals. However, the dividing line between remedying weaknesses and developing strengths is often unclear. Attaining both remedial and developmental goals can have a preventive function in helping clients to avoid future difficulties.

Though much counselling is remedial, its main focus is likely to be on the skills or lifeskills needed for satisfactorily handling the developmental tasks which confront most ordinary people rather than on the needs of the more severely disturbed minority. Developmental tasks are tasks which most people inevitably face at various stages of their life: for instance, becoming independent, achieving intimacy, raising children, and adjusting to old age. Developmental tasks often involve both managing negative qualities and fostering positive qualities.

At its highest level counselling's focus is on helping clients to develop skills or lifeskills in ways that assist their process of being fully human (Nelson-Jones, 2004). Maslow's description of the characteristics of self-actualizing people represents an attempt to state goals positively (Maslow, 1970). His self-actualizing characteristics include creativity, autonomy, social interest and problem-centredness. Other characteristics of the fully mature human being include demonstrating high levels of goodwill, compassion, generosity and service.

Whatever the theoretical position, counselling goals emphasize increasing clients' personal responsibility for creating and ordering their lives. Clients need to make choices that enable them to feel, think and act effectively. They require the capacity to experience and express feelings, think rationally and to take effective action to attain their goals. Counsellors tend to be most effective when they enable clients to help themselves after counselling has ended. Thus the ultimate goal of counselling is self-helping, so that former clients become their own best counsellors.

What is the lifeskills counselling approach?

The theoretical model underlying this book is cognitive humanistic. Elsewhere, in *Cognitive Humanistic Therapy*, I have presented the idea that counselling and therapy can be thought of as consisting of two broad areas: adaptation CHT and mental cultivation CHT (Nelson-Jones, 2004). Adaptation CHT aims to help moderately to slightly impaired clients to attain the mind skills and communication/action skills they need so that they can function comfortably in their societies. Such adaptation assumes that the societies are not themselves pathologically dysfunctional in terms of Western society's norms. Mental cultivation CHT aims to help clients and others to attain higher levels of functioning that go beyond the norms. Some important goals for mental cultivation CHT, for instance demonstrating high levels of compassion, generosity and service, were mentioned in the previous section. Though there is overlap between adaptation CHT and mental cultivation CHT, it is appropriate for a textbook such as this one to focus primarily on adaptation CHT. Readers who are interested in mental cultivation CHT are referred to *Cognitive Humanistic Therapy,* which mainly deals with higher levels of counselling.

Why focus on client skills?

The goals of the adaptation CHT can include providing emotional support, managing specific problem situations better, managing problems, and improving poor skills that sustain problems. In many instances, counsellors aim to attain all four goals with the same client. Adaptation CHT is appropriate for the kinds of problems that form much of the caseload of counsellors. Concerns involving feelings and physical reactions include being depressed, anxious, confused, stressed, tense, and dealing with conditions such as heart attacks or cancer. Possibly most clients come to counsellors because of relationship difficulties including shyness, difficulty in showing affection or managing anger, and conflicts with partners. Many clients also come with work-related concerns including procrastination, public speaking anxiety, problems relating to colleagues and customers, inappropriate risk-taking behaviour, dealing with negative performance appraisals, stresses attached to managerial, supervisory and sales roles, and sexual harassment.

There are at least two important ways that goals may be stated for adaptation CHT concerns. One way is to state them as overall or outcome goals. For example, the overall or outcome goal for a client who seriously procrastinates over work or study assignments is to do this much less often. Counsellor and client could work together to define how to measure the outcome of procrastinating less. Another way is to state the concerns as process, skills or lifeskills goals. For example, 'What are the mind skills and the communication/action skills that the client needs to foster in order to start work/study assignments more quickly?' These two ways of stating goals are both important. Overall or outcome goals indicate where clients want to go, whereas process or lifeskills goals indicate how clients can attain their overall goals both now and in future.

Most approaches to counselling and therapy focus more on counsellor skills than client skills. In fact, they rarely acknowledge that the role of the counsellor is to build client skills. Even in the cognitive-behavioural approaches, the concept of skills tends to be mainly reserved for behavioural aspects of social skills. Nevertheless, there are good reasons for thinking of counsellors building and helping clients to maintain their skills. First, it can encourage greater specificity as to the skills that humans require to live effectively. Any listing of such skills inevitably includes developing mind skills as well as communication/ action skills. This enables counsellors and clients to assess what poor mind skills and/or communication/action skills sustain clients' difficulties. Counsellors and clients can then work on improving specific skills. The notion of skills implies that individuals need to assume responsibility for maintaining them after counselling. Accordingly, this can be a feature of work during counselling and a continuing challenge for former clients once regular counselling ceases.

Process of counselling

All major approaches to the practice of counselling have the idea of process or progression built into them. A counselling process model is one that explicitly rather than implicitly articulates the stages of the counselling and therapy process. Adaptation CHT is structured around the lifeskills counselling model that is described more fully in the remainder of the book. The lifeskills counselling model has three major stages – relating, understanding and changing – each of which is divided into three phases. The model provides a framework or set of guidelines for counsellor choices. The lifeskills counselling model is useful not only for managing or solving problems but also for addressing underlying problematic skills.

An early version of a process model was that of Carl Jung, who cited four stages of analytical therapy: confession, elucidation, education and transformation (Jung, 1966). However, for the most part, the major theorists have refrained from stating the practice of their counselling and therapy approaches in clearly numbered stages. Nevertheless models of the counselling process abound (for instance, Carkhuff, 1987; Corey and Corey, 2003; Egan, 2002). An important point about these psychotherapy and counselling process models is that, in the main, they apply the concept of learning and using skills to counsellors rather than to clients. These problem management models may insufficiently address the task of helping clients to improve their skills for preventing and managing similar problems.

If we are to have skilled counsellors, why not have skilled clients too? It is inconsistent to teach and learn about counselling skills and then insufficiently to acknowledge that thinking about clients and their problems in skills terms can be equally useful. In the final analysis the purpose of using counselling skills is to enable clients to become more skilled in their own right. Whether explicitly acknowledged or not, arguably all positive changes from counselling involve clients in learning and using better skills. Counsellors are only skilled to the extent that they can be successful in skilling clients.

The lifeskills counsellor

Clients are much more likely to become skilled in specific ways and as human beings if they work with skilled counsellors. Lifeskills counsellors hold humanistic values either within or outside of religious frameworks (Kelly, 1995). These values include respect for each individual, acknowledgement of human fallibility, belief in human educability, belief in the human potential for reason and social living, and a sincere desire for a better world. Furthermore lifeskills counsellors subscribe to a theoretical framework that integrates elements of existential-humanistic and cognitive-behavioural psychology.

Lifeskills counsellors are practitioner-researchers who constantly make, implement and evaluate hypotheses about helping clients change. At least four sources of knowledge enlighten and inspire their counselling. First they attend to theoretical knowledge. Their underlying theoretical framework requires continuous updating in light of new knowledge about human development and change. Second, lifeskills counsellors endeavour to keep abreast of relevant research findings into the processes and outcomes of counselling. When working in a speciality area, for example career counselling or marriage and family counselling, they focus on pertinent research literature. Third, lifeskills counsellors continue to learn from their practical counselling experience. They actively seek to counsel more effectively by evaluating their counselling and, where necessary, modifying what they do. Fourth, lifeskills counsellors are alive and vibrant human beings who learn from personal experience outside of counselling. This is especially important for counsellors operating within a framework that assumes that fundamentally both counsellors and clients require the same skills of living. Counsellors who can acquire, maintain and develop good mind skills and communication/action skills are likely to be better placed to help clients.

Lifeskills counsellors are developmental educators. Taking into account the state of readiness, expectations and skills levels of each client, they flexibly use both relationship and training skills. The focus of counselling includes nurturing and healing vulnerable clients, assisting clients with specific problems and decisions, crisis management work and preventive and developmental lifeskills training. The clientele for counselling may be an individual, a group, or an organization. Lifeskills counsellors are always conscious of ways to 'seed' or disseminate counselling skills. Furthermore, they realize that sometimes 'upstream' counselling focusing on organizational policies, practices and personalities that create and sustain problems may be necessary either instead of or in addition to 'downstream' counselling with individuals or groups of clients (Egan and Cowan, 1979).

Within an educational framework, lifeskills counsellors use a range of training interventions focusing on feeling, thinking and action. They tend not to be psychological archaeologists or historians – instead they choose to focus mainly on clients' present and future. In particular, counsellors collaborate with clients to identify specific poor skills that sustain difficulties. Then counsellors assist clients in shifting the balance from deficiencies to strengths.

Another way of presenting what lifeskills counsellors are is to indicate what they are not. Lifeskills counsellors are no different from other people except that they possess better counselling skills. They still have their own struggles, imperfections and difficulties in affirming their positive potentials. They are not superficial manipulators. They genuinely care for the growth and development of clients. They are neither magicians nor snake-oil doctors promising instant cures. Clients usually come to counselling with long-established poor skills. Counsellors emphasize that relinquishing these and developing good ones requires much work and practice.

Lifeskills counsellors cannot do clients' work and they discourage dependency. Rather they quietly and sometimes more forcefully challenge clients with their existential responsibility to create their own lives. Lifeskills counsellors do not encourage conformity. They help each client to think through which choices have the highest probability of being best for them in their unique life circumstances. Furthermore lifeskills counsellors do not view themselves as having a monopoly on counselling skills. Many counselling skills are similar to skills needed for other roles such as being a partner, friend, parent or supervisor. In addition, many counselling skills can be used for self-helping. The more people who possess good counselling skills the better.

Introduction to activities

Each chapter in this book contains one or more activities to help readers develop their knowledge and skills. Though it is assumed that readers are learning counselling and helping skills in training groups, this may not always be the case. Nevertheless, they may still want to perform the activities either with a partner or, if possible, on their own. Readers will enhance the value of this book if they undertake the activities diligently. While practice may not make perfect, it certainly can increase competence.

Trainers and trainees can decide how to proceed with each activity: for instance, whether the activity should be done as a whole group exercise, in threes, pairs, individually or using any combination of these approaches. When doing the activities, all concerned should ensure that no one feels under pressure to reveal any personal information that she or he does not want to. To save repetition, I mention these instructions only once here and not at the start of each activity.

Activity 1.1 What is counselling?

Either on your own, with a partner, or in a group answer the following questions.

1. What does the term 'counselling' mean to you?
2. How, if at all, might you distinguish counselling from helping?
3. How, if at all, might you distinguish counselling from psychotherapy?
4. What do you view as the goals of counselling?
5. What do you think of applying the concept of skills to clients as well as to counsellors?
6. Critically discuss the idea that counsellors are primarily educators whose role is to develop clients' lifeskills.

create communication skills and feelings 2

Chapter outcomes

By studying and doing the activities in this chapter you should:

- understand why it is important to think in terms of lifeskills;
- understand what is a counselling skill;
- understand how counselling trainees and clients create verbal communication;
- understand how trainees and clients create vocal communication;
- understand how trainees and clients create bodily communication; and
- understand the role of feelings and physical reactions.

What are lifeskills?

The previous chapter made the case for focusing on client skills as well as on counsellor skills. A useful distinction exists between clients' problems and their problematic skills. Problem management or problem-solving models, such as those of Carkhuff (1987) and Egan (2002), are useful, since frequently clients require help to manage or solve immediate problems. However, a big drawback of such models is that they inadequately address the *repetition phenomenon*, the repetitive nature of many clients' problems. In the past clients may have repeated underlying self-defeating behaviours, or lifeskills deficiencies, and they are at risk of continuing to do so in future. An example of such repetition across time – *vertical* repetition – is that of people who keep losing jobs because of poor skills at relating to employers. In addition, clients may repeat self-defeating behaviours across a range of current situations – *horizontal* repetition. For example, the same people may be non-assertive at home, at work, in leisure activities and so on.

Often clients require assistance in developing skills strengths that last into the future and are not used just in managing or solving specific current problems. However, frequently practical considerations limit counsellor contact with individual clients: for example, heavy counsellor caseloads, and clients who are content with short-term problem amelioration. Nevertheless, counsellors who only aim to help clients to manage or solve immediate and specific problems when they could work more thoroughly to alter problematic lifeskills do clients a disservice. In reality, counsellors and clients often compromise on the amount of time and effort they take to address underlying patterns of poor skills that predispose and position clients for further problems.

The following vignette illustrates the difference between identifying a client's problem and identifying problematic lifeskills or skills deficiencies.

> Mary, age 27, and Jeff, age 28, come to see a counsellor Bruce, age 40, because their relationship is in trouble. The particular problem about which they are arguing right now is whether to upgrade their home by moving to a better neighbourhood. The decision is not just a matter of whether to move, but which neighbourhood to move to, and how much they can afford to spend on making the change. When Bruce listens to them and assesses them more thoroughly, he finds that they conduct heated arguments over many issues and this adversely affects their happiness. One of the issues in whether or not to move is whether they will still be together, given the current state of their relationship. Bruce then asks Mary and Jeff whether they want to work with him on making a decision about the problem of whether or not to move or, in addition, whether they would like to focus on the skills of managing problems and decisions in their relationship better. He illustrates that these skills involve how they think as well as how they communicate. When Mary and Jeff come back for the second session, they say they have decided to defer making the decision to move house because they want first to work on improving their relationship before committing themselves to moving.

In the above example, the counsellor Bruce uses mind skills and communication skills as he encourages Mary and Jeff to start addressing their own mind skills and communication skills deficiencies. It is evident that both counsellors and clients need skills. It is possible to think of these skills within a common lifeskills or human being skills framework, though there will also be differences in what skills the different parties need, as well as in how well they are using them.

What is a lifeskill? One aspect of the word pertains to *areas* of skill: for instance, listening skills or disclosing skills. Another aspect refers to *level of competence*, for instance, skilled or unskilled in a certain area of skill. However, competence in a skill is best viewed not as an either/or matter in which people either possess or do not possess a skill. Rather, within a skills area, it is preferable to think of people as possessing *good skills* or *poor skills* or a mixture of the two. For instance, in the skills area of listening, they may be good at understanding others, but poor at showing understanding. In just about all areas of their functioning, both counsellors and clients will, in varying degrees, possess a mixture of poor and good skills. A third aspect of skill relates to the *knowledge and sequence of choices* entailed in implementing the skill. The essential element of any skill is the ability to implement sequences of choices to achieve objectives. If counsellors and helpers are to be good at listening deeply and accurately to clients, they have to make and implement effective choices in this skills area.

In counselling and helping there are two main categories of skills: communication and action skills, or skills that entail external behaviour; and mind skills, or skills that entail internal behaviour. Readers may wonder why feelings and physical reactions are not mentioned as skills. The reason for this is that feelings and physical reactions are essentially part of people's instinctual or animal nature so are not skills in themselves. However, both students and clients can influence how they feel and physically react by how they communicate/act and by how they think.

Creating communication and action skills

There are five main ways counsellors, trainees and clients can send messages by creating communication and taking action. *Verbal* communication consists of messages sent with words: for example saying 'I understand what you are saying' or 'I don't understand.' *Vocal* communication consists of messages sent through one's voice: for instance, using volume, articulation, pitch, emphasis and speech rate. *Bodily* communication consists of messages sent by the body: for instance through gaze, eye contact, facial expression, posture, gestures, physical proximity and clothes and grooming. *Touch* is a special category of bodily communication. Messages sent by touch include: what part of the body one uses, what part of another's body gets touched, and how gentle or firm is the touching. *Taking action* communication consists of messages sent when not face to face with others: for example, sending a follow-up note to a client who has missed an appointment. Though not emphasized in the following discussion, it is extremely important to acknowledge cultural differences in communication.

Verbal communication skills

Let's look at some skills of verbal communication or talk.

- *Language.* Language consists of many elements other than whether people are English-speaking or not. For instance, there may be a formal language, words either BBC or ABC news readers might use, as well as an informal or colloquial language, words one might use with mates in the pub.

- *Content.* Content may refer to topic area, problem area or the task being undertaken, such as learning counselling skills. In addition, content refers to the focus of talk, whether it is about oneself, others or the environment. Content can also refer to the evaluative dimension of talk: for example, depressed clients may say many negative things about themselves, such as 'I'm worthless' and 'I just don't seem to care any more.'
- *Amount of speech.* 'Shy' is a common term attached to people who experience difficulty when it comes to their turn to talk. In some, but not all counselling approaches, clients talk more than counsellors. However, some clients may be talkative from the start, others warm up as helping progresses, and yet others talk haltingly throughout even though the counselling may be successful. Counselling trainees can also talk too much or too little.
- *Ownership of speech.* Thomas Gordon (1970), in his book *Parent Effectiveness Training,* makes a useful distinction between 'You' messages and 'I' messages. 'You' messages focus on the other person and can be judgemental: for example, 'You don't appreciate what I'm doing for you' or 'You're not listening to me properly.' 'I' messages use the word 'I' and are centred in a person as the sender: for instance, 'I feel unappreciated' or 'I'm experiencing not being heard correctly.'

Activity 2.1 Creating verbal communication skills

Trainees and trainer(s) can participate in one or more of the following activities where the object is to allow others to get to know you better. Observe how you create your verbal communication skills by what you choose to reveal and conceal.

- *Introduce yourself.* Spend one or two minutes describing yourself as a person to the whole training group.
- *Introduce a partner.* Divide into pairs. Partner A discloses to partner B, who listens and may ask a few questions. After a set time period, say two or three minutes, the partners reverse roles. This pairs work is followed by partners introducing one another to the whole training group.
- *Use triads or small groups.* Divide into threes or small groups and introduce yourselves to one another during a set time period.
- *Circulate with personal information visible.* Fill out either an index card or a Post-It sticker with information about yourself, and then pin or stick it on your front. Circulate and hold brief conversations with as many people in your training group as you can within a set time period.

Hold debriefing sessions at the end of getting acquainted activities. Explore skills connected with creating, sharing, and withholding verbal information.

Vocal communication skills

A person's vocal messages can speak volumes about what they truly feel and how emotionally responsive they are to others' feelings. The following five dimensions of vocal messages form the acronym VAPER – volume, articulation, pitch, emphasis and rate.

- *Volume.* Volume refers to loudness or softness. Counselling trainees need to speak at a level of audibility that is comfortable and easy for clients to hear. Some trainees let their voices trail away at the end of sentences. Some unnecessarily soften their voice to match that of their client. Though a booming voice overwhelms, speaking too quietly may give the impression that one is a 'wimp'. A firm and confident voice is a good starting point from which to make variations as appropriate, for instance by speaking more gently or more loudly.
- *Articulation.* Articulation refers to the clarity of speech. Trainees and clients who enunciate words well are easier to understand.
- *Pitch.* Pitch refers to the height or depth of one's voice. An optimum pitch range includes all the levels at which a pleasing voice can be produced without strain. Errors of pitch include either being too high pitched or too low pitched.
- *Emphasis.* A trainee uses vocal emphasis when responding to clients' feelings and nuances and when sharing feelings. Trainees may use either too much emphasis and seem melodramatic or too little emphasis and come across as wooden. In addition, they may use emphasis in the wrong places.
- *Rate.* Often speech rate is measured by words per minute. Speech rate depends not only on how quickly words are spoken, but on the frequency and duration of pauses between them. If speaking very quickly, trainees appear anxious and clients may have difficulty understanding them. On the other hand, too ponderous a speech rate can be boring or pompous. Pausing and being silent at the right times is another important aspect of speech rate.

Activity 2.2 Creating vocal communication skills

Part A: Assess your vocal communication skills

1 *Self-assessment*
Assess yourself on each of the following 'creating vocal communication' skills you use when you either participate in your counselling skills group and/or help clients:

- volume
- articulation
- pitch
- emphasis
- speech rate
- use of pauses and silences
- other important areas not listed above

2 *Obtain feedback*
Obtain feedback from the other trainees in your group and from your trainer(s) on your good and poor vocal communication skills.

Part B: Change a specific vocal communication skill

Pick a specific vocal communication skill that you think you might improve: for instance you may have a tendency to talk too softly. Then hold a conversation with a partner in which you work on improving the skill you have targeted. Either during or at the end of your conversation ask for feedback on how you are doing.

If appropriate, you and your partner then reverse roles.

Bodily communication skills

When both speaking and listening, counsellors, counselling trainees and clients disclose themselves through how they create their bodily communication. Following are some of the main kinds of bodily communication skills.

Facial expressions

Facial expressions are perhaps the main vehicle for sending body messages. Ekman, Friesen and Ellsworth (1972) have found that there are seven main facial expressions of emotion: happiness, interest, surprise, fear, sadness, anger, and disgust or contempt. A person's mouth and eyebrows can convey much information: for instance, 'down in the mouth' and 'raised eyebrows'.

Gaze

Gaze, or looking at other people in the area of their faces, is both a way of showing interest and a way of collecting facial information. Speakers look at listeners about 40 per cent of the time and listeners look at speakers about 70–75 per cent of the time. Gaze is useful for coordinating speech: for example, speakers look just before the end of utterances to collect feedback about their listener's reactions. Women are generally more visually attentive than men in all measures of gaze (Argyle, 1999).

Eye contact

Eye contact is a more direct way than gaze of sending messages, whether of interest, anger or sexual attraction.

Gestures

Gestures are physical movements that can frame or illustrate words coming before, during or after what is being said. An example of using a gesture to display and emphasize an emotion is clenching one's fist to show aggression. Gestures may also illustrate shapes, sizes or movements, particularly when these are difficult to describe in words. How people gesture can vary according to their sex. Sometimes men's gestures are larger, more sweeping and forceful, while women's gestures are smaller and more inhibited. Gestures can also take the place of words: for example, either nodding one's head up and down or moving it sideways for saying 'yes' or 'no', respectively.

Posture

A counselling trainee's posture may convey various messages. Turning one's body towards the client is more encouraging than turning away from them. In addition, whether the trainee leans forwards or backwards may indicate interest or uninterest. Height tends to be associated with status: for instance, one 'talks down to' or 'talks up to' someone. Small people may be at a disadvantage unless the other person's body posture is changed: for instance by sitting down.

Posture may also communicate how anxious a person is: for instance, sitting with arms and legs tightly crossed suggests being emotionally as well as literally uptight. However, for a woman, it is possible to appear too relaxed: some men may mistakenly perceive uncrossed and open legs as a sign of sexual availability whether a skirt, trousers or jeans are worn. Such perceptions manifest confused standards in how people decode body messages.

Physical closeness

The degree of physical closeness that is comfortable for Britons and Antipodeans is generally the same (Hall, 1966). The zones vary according to the nature of the relationship. In the *intimate zone* (between 6 to 18 inches) it is easy to touch and be touched. This zone is reserved for spouses, lovers, close friends and relatives. The *personal zone* (between 18 and 48 inches) is appropriate for less close friends and for parties and other social gatherings. The *social zone* (between 4 and 12 feet) is comfortable for people not known at all well. The *public zone* (over 12 feet) is the distance for addressing public gatherings.

Clothes

If clothes do not make the counsellor or helper, they certainly send many messages that can influence how much and in which areas clients reveal themselves. These messages include social and occupational standing, sex-role identity, ethnicity, conformity to peer group norms, rebelliousness and how outgoing they are. While maintaining their individuality, counselling trainees need to dress appropriately for their clientele: for example, delinquent teenagers probably respond better to informally dressed helpers than do stressed business executives.

Grooming

Personal grooming also provides important information about how well people take care of themselves; for instance, clean or dirty, neat or tidy. In addition, the length and styling of hair sends messages about what sort of person one is.

Activity 2.3 Creating bodily communication skills

Part A: Assess your bodily communication skills

1 *Self-assessment*
Assess yourself on each of the following 'creating bodily communication' skills you use when either you participate in your counselling skills group and/or work with clients:

- facial expression
- gaze
- eye contact
- gestures
- posture
- physical proximity
- clothing
- grooming
- other important areas not listed above

2 *Obtain feedback*
Obtain feedback from the other trainees in your group and from your trainer(s) on your good and poor bodily communication skills.

Part B: Change a specific bodily communication skill

Pick a specific bodily communication skill that you think you might improve: for instance you may have a tendency to sit with too rigid a posture. Then hold a conversation with a partner in which you work on improving the skill you have targeted. Either during or at the end of your conversation ask for feedback on how you are doing.

If appropriate, you and your partner then reverse roles.

Feelings and physical reactions

To a large extent, people are what they feel. Dictionary definitions of feelings tend to use words like 'physical sensation', 'emotions' and 'awareness'. All three of these illustrate a dimension of feelings. People are biological beings first, persons second. As such they need to learn to value and live with their underlying biological nature. The word *emotions* implies movement. Feelings are processes. People are subject to a continuous flow of biological experiencing. *Awareness* implies that people can be conscious of their feelings. However, at varying levels and in different ways, they may also be out of touch with them.

Physical reactions both represent and accompany feelings and, in a sense, the two are indistinguishable. For example bodily changes associated with anxiety include galvanic skin response – detectable electrical changes taking place in the skin, raised blood pressure, a pounding heart and a rapid pulse, shallow and rapid breathing, muscular tension, drying of the mouth, stomach problems such as ulcers, speech difficulties such as stammering, sleep difficulties, and sexual problems such as complete or partial loss of desire. Other physical reactions include a slowing down of body movements when depressed, and dilated eye pupils in moments of anger or sexual attraction. People are affected by their physical reactions. For example, in anxiety and panic attacks, they may first feel tense and anxious and then become even more tense and anxious because of this initial feeling. The subject of physical reactions is dealt with again in Chapter 10, where they are listed in Box 10.1.

Counselling trainees need to be able to experience and understand both their own and their clients' feelings. Even though feelings represent people's biological nature, this does not mean that trainees and their clients can do nothing about them. In counselling and helping, three somewhat overlapping areas where feelings and accompanying physical reactions are important include experiencing feelings, expressing feelings and managing feelings. In each of these areas, counselling skills students can work with clients' communications/actions and thoughts and mental processes to influence how they feel and physically react.

Activity 2.4 Feelings and physical reactions

1 What physical reactions might accompany the following feelings?

- anger
- sadness
- depression
- joy
- attraction
- tiredness
- any other feeling on which you wish to focus

2 To what extent do you consider that you are
   - in touch with your feelings
   - able to express your feelings well?

3 How might your understanding of and ability to express your feelings influence how well you counsel or help clients?

create mind skills 3

Chapter outcomes

By studying and doing the activities in this chapter you should:

- possess a framework for the relationship between thoughts and their consequences;
- understand what mind skills are;
- be introduced to creating rules and creating perceptions;
- be introduced to creating self-talk and creating visual images;
- be introduced to creating explanations and creating expectations;
- know about some other areas of thinking and mind skills; and
- gain a framework for the relationship between mind skills and their consequences.

This chapter explores how human beings, whether counsellors, trainees or clients, think. It starts by providing a simple framework for thinking about the relationship between situations, thoughts, feelings, physical reactions and communication/actions. Then a series of mind skills is described by which people can influence how they think. The chapter ends by incorporating the notion of mind skills into the initial framework. Throughout the chapter, I use examples of how people think, based on counselling trainees rather than clients. I do this deliberately to help readers understand the mind better by making the discussion self-referential before using examples of clients' thoughts and mind skills in other parts of this book.

The Situation–Thoughts–Consequences (STC) framework

Sometimes people react automatically, but most of the time how they think mediates how they behave. Though Ellis does not state it quite as simplistically as this, he provides an ABC framework for making this point (Ellis, 2003, 2005). Here A stands for the activating event and C for the feelings and action consequences of the activating event. His rational emotive behaviour therapy focuses on addressing B, or the person's beliefs about the activating event, which can be either rational beliefs (rB) or irrational beliefs (iB) or frequently a mixture of the two. Consequences (C) are most often influenced by what people think at B (their beliefs), rather than being a direct reaction to the activating event (A).

While agreeing with Ellis about the influence of how people think, I consider that his ABC model is too restricted, in particular in its focus on beliefs. People's thinking is much more complicated than the beliefs or rules they have. As will be seen in this chapter, thinking also includes perceptions, self-talk, visual images, explanations and expectations, among other mental processes. Consequently, I have widened Ellis's Activating Event–Beliefs–Consequences (ABC) framework into a Situation–Thoughts–Consequences (STC) framework. The simple STC framework provides the first step in understanding the relationship between what happens to a person and how they react.

S The situation
T A person's thoughts relating to the situation, including their visual images
C Their feelings, physical reactions, communication and actions that are the consequences of both S and T

Danny, aged 33, is a trainee on a one-year counselling skills training course and worries a lot because he thinks that he always has to do well. It is the eighth week of the course and Danny already perceives that he is not doing as well as he would like and that both the course staff and other trainees think less of him because of this. He keeps telling himself that he is not as good as he should be and imagines himself making a lot of mistakes when practising with other trainees. He attributes his difficulties to lack of talent and expects that he will have trouble passing the course.

Though this Danny example is probably an exaggeration, there are a number of readers who will identify with parts of the above description of his difficulties. Now let's put the above vignette into the STC format. The situation (S) that Danny finds himself in is taking a counselling skills course. Danny's thoughts (Ts) are described above. The consequences (Cs) of S and T are that Danny feels very anxious and depressed about his performance, physically reacts with tension in his head and chest when he practises interviewing, and communicates in a way that fails to pick up adequately the feelings of those fellow trainee 'clients' with whom he practises counselling.

What are mind skills?

Probably most readers are unused to thinking about how they think in lifeskills or skills terms. However, it can be helpful to break down how one thinks into component skills that one can address in one's own life and also in clients' lives. Trainees can learn counselling skills and assist clients much more effectively if they harness their mind's potential. How can they control their thoughts so that they can beneficially influence how they communicate? First, they can understand that they have a mind with a capacity for super-conscious thinking – or thinking about thinking – that they can develop. Second, they can become much more efficient in thinking about their thinking if they view their mental processes in terms of skills that they can train themselves to exercise and control. Third, in daily life as well as in their counselling skills training, they can assiduously practise using their mind skills to influence their communication. Below are descriptions of six central mental processes or mind skills. These descriptions are followed by a brief summary of some other mind skills. There is no magic to thinking in terms of mind skills, as the following passages show.

Creating rules skills

Rules are the 'dos' and 'don'ts' by which people lead their lives. All counsellors, helpers, trainees and clients have inner rule-books that guide how they live and work. Who sets the rules? Influences from the past and present have helped to create and to sustain everyone's rules: for example, family, religion, gender, culture, race, peer group, age, exposure to the media and so on.

A person may have rational and altruistic reasons for creating and sustaining their rules. In addition, they may sustain some rules through less rational factors. Habit, or persisting in communication in the same old unexamined way, is one such factor. Fear is another important factor. They may be afraid that they will lose out in some significant way if they examine and change their rules. Wanting immediate gratification is a third factor in keeping people in unproductive rules. Like a child they may demand that they must have what they want NOW, NOW, NOW, rather than balancing longer-term with shorter-term considerations.

Ellis, the founder of rational emotive behaviour therapy, uses the term 'beliefs' rather than 'rules'. He considers that people create and maintain much of their distress and unhappiness through demanding and absolutist thinking, making demands, rather than through preferential thinking, having preferences (Ellis, 2001, 2003, 2005). He asserts that people can possess healthy, productive and adaptive and rational beliefs that are consistent with social reality and generally consist of preferences, desires and wants. When thinking rationally about situations that either block or sabotage their goals, people who have rational beliefs are engaging in preferential thinking. Preferential as contrasted with demanding thinking involves explicitly and/or tacitly reacting with beliefs in realistic ways and experiencing appropriate emotional and behavioural consequences. Irrational or unrealistic beliefs are rigid and dogmatic and mostly get in the way of people's efforts to achieve their goals, and consist of 'musts', 'oughts' and 'shoulds'. When thinking irrationally about activating events or adversities (As) that sabotage their goals, people engage in demanding thinking.

Box 3.1 emphasizes the distinction between demanding and preferring. Notice that each of the demanding or unrealistic rules has been reworded to become a preferential or realistic rule.

Box 3.1 Creating demanding and preferential rules

Demanding rules

- I must be the perfect trainee.
- I must be liked by everyone.
- I must always be in control of the training group.

Preferential rules

- I'd prefer to be a highly competent trainee, but I'm learning and am bound to make some mistakes.
- I'd prefer to be liked, but it's even more important to be true to myself.
- I'd prefer to influence the training group to attain its goals, but total control is both undesirable and unrealistic.

Primary demanding rules can also have unwanted derivatives. Three common derivatives that people often create to accompany their demanding rules or beliefs are:

Awfulizing: 'If I don't have my important goals unblocked and fulfilled as I must, it's awful!' In this context, 'awful' means totally bad or more than bad.

I can't stand-it-itis: 'If I don't have my important goals unblocked and fulfilled as I must, I can't stand it!'

Damning oneself and others: 'If I don't have my important goals unblocked and fulfilled as I must, I'm a stupid, worthless person.' 'Others are bad people for blocking my important goals.'

As well as directly suffering from demanding rules, both trainees and clients can suffer and cause others to suffer as a result of these irrational derivatives of these same rules.

Activity 3.1 Creating rules skills

Demanding rules about yourself as a learner

1 Look at Box 3.1 and then list at least three demanding rules you either do or might possess concerning how you should learn introductory counselling skills.
2 What are likely to be the consequences of possessing the above demanding rules on your feelings, physical reactions and communication?
3 For one or more of your demanding rules state actual or possible derivatives, such as awfulizing, I-can't-stand-it-itis or damning yourself and others.

Preferential rules about yourself as a learner

4 Again look at Box 3.1 and restate the demanding rules you listed above as more preferential rules about learning introductory counselling skills.
5 What are likely to be the consequences of possessing the above preferential rules on your feelings, physical reactions and communication?

Creating perceptions skills

One of the most influential approaches to cognitive psychotherapy is that of American psychiatrist, Aaron Beck (Beck, 1976; Beck and Weishaar, 2005). Whereas Ellis emphasizes preferential thinking, based on realistic rules, Beck emphasizes propositional thinking, based on testing the reality of perceptions about oneself, others and the environment. Both preferential and propositional thinking are useful mind skills. This section focuses on how accurately one perceives oneself rather than on how accurately one perceives others.

The self-concept is one's picture of oneself, what one thinks of as 'I' or 'me'. It consists of a series of different perceptions of varying degrees of accuracy. Areas of one's self-concept concern perceptions regarding family of origin, current relationships, body image, age, gender, sexual orientation, culture, race, social class, religious beliefs, health, work, study activities, leisure pursuits, tastes and preferences, among others.

Centrality is one dimension of self-concept: 'What is really important to me?' For instance, a committed Christian's faith is fundamental to their self-concept. Another dimension of self-concept is that of positive and negative evaluations of personal characteristics: 'What do I like and dislike about myself?' A further important dimension is that of how confident one is. A person may accurately perceive their level of confidence or over- or underestimate it.

The self-concepts of all counselling trainees contain perceptions about their skills: for example, perceptions of their listening skills and questioning skills. They may accurately perceive their skill level in a particular area or inaccurately perceive that they are either more or less skilled than they really are.

Some trainees have a tendency to underestimate skill levels. Psychologists McKay and Fanning (2000) use the term 'pathological critic' to describe the inner voice that attacks and judges a person. While all trainees have areas on which they need to work, when in pathological critic mode they perceive their skills far too negatively. For example, negative perceptions that they may hold about their listening skills include that they are hopeless, unchangeable and worse than those of fellow trainees.

Conversely, trainees can perceive their skill levels too positively, even to the extent of becoming instant experts. Sometimes they may use self-protective habits that defend their current estimation of their ability. They may deny certain aspects of the feedback that they receive from their trainers and fellow trainees: for instance, that they are too inclined to give advice rather than listen. Alternatively they may distort and selectively filter out incoming information, only partly acknowledging the full extent of a piece of positive or negative feedback.

A principal skill of learning to perceive more accurately is being able to distinguish fact from inference. Take the statement 'All Aborigines walk in single file, at least the one I saw did.' That you saw one Aborigine is fact, that all Aborigines walk in single file is inference or factually unsupported supposition. Trainees need to guard against the tendency to jump to unwarranted conclusions. Furthermore, they need to be prepared to change or modify their conclusions in the light of emerging information.

Box 3.2 depicts Dave, a counselling trainee, who initially jumps to an unduly negative conclusion about his level of performance, and then reality-tests the perception to see how accurately it fits the available facts.

Box 3.2 Reality-testing a perception

Situation

Dave, age 28, assesses his performance at the start of the second semester of a one-year counselling skills course.

Initial unrealistic perception

I'm not very good at counselling skills and wonder whether I should continue with the course.

Reality-testing the initial perception

I know that I have a tendency to put myself down. Where is the evidence that I'm doing poorly? I started off the course not listening particularly well, but then so did just about all the other trainees. I thought that the best way to help people was to draw on my life's experience and to give good advice. In addition, I felt intimidated because some of the other trainees are already working in the helping services and are older and more experienced than me. However, the feedback I've received both from the trainer and from my fellow trainees is that they think I'm quite good and improving. In fact, on my end of semester one counselling skills assessment cassette, I received an above average grade. The trainer gave me some feedback about how I might improve, but that does not mean that I am doing poorly. My first practice interviews this semester were not as good as I would have liked, but the feedback was a bit better than for my assessment cassette. What is a realistic skills level for this stage of the course? I think I expect too much of myself too soon. So far I have had limited opportunity to practise my skills and they still do not feel natural to me. I'm very aware of thinking about what I do all the time. Furthermore, along with learning new skills I'm having to unlearn some bad old habits.

Revised realistic perception

My progress is satisfactory for this stage, I am improving and I should definitely continue with the course.

Counselling trainees perceive themselves, others, their clients and events with varying degrees of accuracy. They need to take care not to distort their perceptions of clients to fit their own needs and agendas. It is important not to jump to conclusions when attempting to identify and clarify problems. Rather they need carefully to sift fact from inference and, if appropriate, accumulate more information to build and test their inferences. Below are some specific perceiving errors or skills weaknesses to avoid (Beck, 1976, 1988; Beck and Weishaar, 2005).

- *Arbitrary inference.* Drawing conclusions without adequate supporting evidence or in the face of conflicting evidence. An example of arbitrary inference is that of a counselling trainee who, after a practice session, concludes 'I am a terrible trainee.'
- *Selective abstraction.* Selectively focusing on a detail taken out of context at the same time as ignoring more salient information. An example of selective abstraction is that of a trainee who feels threatened when a client tilts her head towards him in order to hear him better.
- *Magnification and minimization.* Evaluating particular events as far more or far less important than they really are. One example of

magnification is a trainee who thinks 'If I appear the least bit nervous when counselling, it will mean disaster.' An example of minimization is a trainee who describes her terminally ill mother as 'having a cold'.

- *Black-and-white thinking.* Perceiving in either/or and polarized terms: 'Either clients are very cooperative or very uncooperative', and 'Clients either continue having problems or are cured.'
- *Over-generalization.* Drawing a general rule or conclusion from one or a few isolated incidents and then applying the rule to unrelated situations: 'All my initial sessions go well', 'My clients never stick to the point' and 'She failed in one relationship therefore she has failed in all her previous relationships.'
- *Personalization.* Having a tendency without adequate evidence to relate external events to oneself. For instance concluding, when a client walking down the opposite side of a busy street does not acknowledge one, 'I must have done something to offend her.'

Activity 3.2 Creating perceptions skills

1 Think of a situation in regard to either learning introductory counselling skills or in your workplace, where you may be jumping to a conclusion based on inference rather than on fact.
2 Taking the Box 3.2 example of testing the reality of an initial perception, question the adequacy of your initial perception and replace it with a more realistic perception.
3 When questioning your initial perception, did you notice any of the following perceiving errors?

- arbitrary inference
- selective abstraction
- magnification and/or minimization
- black-and-white thinking
- overgeneralization
- personalization?

Creating self-talk skills

Self-talk goes by numerous other names, including inner monologue, inner dialogue, inner speech, self-verbalizing, self-instructing and talking to oneself. In any counselling relationship, there are at least three conversations going on: the public conversation and the counsellor's and the client's private self-talk.

All verbal thinking can be regarded as self-talk. However, here the focus is on a specific area of self-talk, namely instructing oneself in order to cope with specific learning counselling skills situations better. Some self-talk is preconscious or automatic, which is not necessarily bad. For instance, when learning to drive a car, a person first receives instructions which they then consciously tell themselves: this continues to the point where these self-instructions become automatic. In some instances, however, automatic self-talk may be unhelpful.

Negative self-talk can be contrasted with coping self–talk. A distinction can be made between coping, 'doing as well as I can', and mastery, 'I have to be perfect.' Coping emphasizes competence rather than perfection. In reality, most people use a mixture of negative and coping self-talk. Negative self-talk refers to anything that a person says or fails to say to themselves before, during or after specific situations that contributes to potentially avoidable negative feelings, physical reactions and communications. If a person creates negative self-statements or questions, such as 'I can't cope' or 'Will I make it?', they risk weakening themselves internally through unskilful thinking. Consequently they may become less in control of their feelings as well as their thoughts. They also put themselves at risk of communicating externally in inappropriate ways: for example, by excessive approval-seeking.

Box 3.3 illustrates two possibilities for a counselling trainee's self-talk before seeing her first client. Usually negative and coping self-talk are mixed, but here the differences are highlighted.

Box 3.3 Creating negative and coping self-talk

Situation
Angie is a trainee who is about to see her first real client under supervision.

Negative self-talk
Help! I've got this important interview coming up. I wonder whether I'm going to do all right. I'm scared the client will notice that I'm anxious and lacking in skills. What if the client has a problem that is out of my depth? How will I manage then? Also, my supervisor will listen and hear all my mistakes.

Coping self-talk
Help! I'm feeling anxious because this is my first time with a real client. Now, calm down and take a few deep breaths. I'm pretty certain I can cope with the situation. I've done a lot of practising and received good feedback. My supervisor just wants me to do as best I can and does not expect me to be perfect. I can start the interview with a good opening statement and speak calmly and clearly. Then I can use my active listening skills. I do not have to control everything that happens. Already, I'm starting to feel better.

With coping self-talk a person calms themselves down, becomes clear as to their goals, and coaches themselves in appropriate communication. Furthermore, they increase their confidence by acknowledging strengths, support factors and previous success experiences. Coping self-talk should be regarded as a necessary part of dealing with specific situations in counselling skills training and in counselling and helping work.

Activity 3.3 Creating self-talk skills

Think of a particular situation in relation to introductory counselling skills training that you might experience as stressful.

Negative self-talk
Using Box 3.3 as an example, develop negative self-talk in regard to the situation.
What would be the consequences of your negative self-talk on how you feel and communicate?

Coping self-talk
Again using Box 3.3 as an example, develop coping self-talk, focused on calming and coaching yourself, in regard to the situation.
What would be the consequences of your coping self-talk on how you feel and communicate?

Creating visual images skills

When experiencing any significant feeling or sensation, people are likely to think in pictures as well as words. Those whose most highly valued representational system is visual tend to respond to the world and organize it in terms of mental images (Lazarus, 1984, 2005a). Relationships with fellow counselling trainees, trainers and clients also take place on a visual level. Furthermore, trainees can use mental images or pictorial images to support or oppress themselves both now and later. For example, not only are others seen face to face, but pictures of them are stored in the mind.

Trainees differ not only in how much they visualize, but also in how vividly. Vividness incorporates the degree to which all relevant senses – sight, smell, sound, taste and touch – are conjured up by the visual image. Another possible aspect of vividness is the extent to which visual images either elicit or are accompanied by feelings, for instance, hope, sadness or anger.

How counsellors feel can influence how accurately they visualize clients. For instance, trainees who feel angry or insecure may be poor at using visualizing to understand a client's position and to take a balanced view of them. In addition, trainees may gain inaccurate pictures of what is going on in clients' lives. They are not actually there, so much is left to their imagination. However, they can ask questions to help them see scenes in their clients' lives more accurately.

Some trainees either possess well-developed powers of imagery or can develop the skills of visualizing vividly. In general, the more trainees can experience the senses and feelings attached to their images, the better they can use visualizing as a skill for helping others and themselves. As with self-talk, the visual images that people create can be negative, coping or a mixture of both.

Box 3.4 shows how Angie, the trainee in Box 3.3, can create either harmful or helpful visual images to accompany her self-talk before she has her interview with her first real client. The example is exaggerated in order to make the point for those who may think that visualizing skills are not important.

Box 3.4 Creating harmful and helpful visual images

Situation
Angie is a trainee who is about to see her first real client under supervision.

Negative self-talk and visual images
I can just see myself at this important interview coming up making a mess of it. I'm imagining myself with some of my anxious habits: feeling tense, speaking too quickly and too much, and not looking properly at the client. I can see that the interview is not going to go well. I picture a client coming in with a really difficult problem and my not being able to cope. Then I picture myself in supervision having my nervousness and poor performance pointed out.

Coping self-talk and visual images
First thing I need to do is to calm myself down. Calm down and breathe slowly and regularly. Imagine that peaceful place on the beach that I like to mentally visit when feeling stressed [*she conjures up the sights, sounds, smell, taste and touch sensations of the scene*]. Enjoy the calm, peaceful sensations attached to lying there and relaxing without a care in the world ... [*she stays in the scene feeling progressively relaxed*]. Now imagine calmly going to the interview room, taking time to set the room up for the client, greeting the client in a relaxed, warm and friendly fashion, showing the client where to sit, and asking her why she has come for counselling. If and when I feel any tension I can tell myself to imagine staying calm and visualize myself performing competently.

Activity 3.4 Creating visual images skills

Think of a particular situation in relation to introductory counselling skills training that you might experience as stressful (it may be the same situation as in Activity 3.3 above).

Negative self-talk and visual images
Using Box 3.4 as an example, develop negative self-talk and visual images in regard to the situation.
What would be the consequences of your negative self-talk and visual images on how you feel, physically react and communicate?

Coping self-talk and visual images
Again using Box 3.4 as an example, develop coping self-talk and visual images, focused on calming and coaching yourself, in regard to the situation.
What would be the consequences of your coping self-talk and visual images on how you feel, physically react and communicate?

Creating explanations skills

Explanations of cause are the reasons that people give to themselves for what happens. These explanations can influence how they think about their past, present and future. They also influence how they feel, physically react and act. Frequently, people make explanatory errors that interfere with their motivation and effectiveness. Let's take the example of the women's movement. When women explained their lack of status as due to male dominance, they were relatively powerless. However, when women also attributed their lack of status to their own insufficient assertion, they empowered themselves.

Counselling trainees can stay stuck in personal problems through wholly or partially explaining their causes inaccurately. Their unresolved personal problems may negatively intrude into their counselling skills training and helping work. Possible faulty explanations for the causes of personal problems include: 'It's my genes', It's my unfortunate past', 'It's my bad luck', 'It's my poor environment', 'It's all their fault', or 'It's all my fault.' Sometimes trainees succumb to the temptation of externalizing problems: they are the victims of others' inconsiderate and aggressive behaviour. Such trainees explain cause from outside to inside. Change usually requires explaining cause from inside to outside.

A trainee can strengthen or weaken their motivation to attain higher skills levels by how they explain the causes of their successes and failures. For instance, they may rightly or wrongly assign the causes for their good or poor counselling skills performance to such factors as prior experience, ability, effort, anxiety, task difficulty, trainer competence, adequacy of training environment, opportunities to practise skills, competing demands from other course subjects, financial worries, external work pressures, external relationship pressures, supportive home environment, supportive work environment, or luck, to mention but some. Assuming personal responsibility for counselling skills involves the ability or skill of explaining cause accurately and, where possible, addressing relevant considerations constructively.

Box 3.5 illustrates how a trainee, Craig, can create either harmful or helpful explanations for what happens in his life and counselling skills training group. Again, the example is exaggerated, but on counsellor training courses there are likely to be some trainees who are adept at making excuses that mask an inability to assume genuine personal responsibility for becoming more skilled. Instead they create harmful explanations for not being as successful as they would like.

Box 3.5 Creating harmful and helpful explanations

Harmful explanations

Craig, 23, blames his parents for his not being as happy or successful he wants. He grew up in a home where his parents argued a lot and were not as considerate of the needs of their children as he would have liked. On the counselling course, Craig is not doing well, but he takes little responsibility for this. Instead he blames the trainer for not teaching him properly and giving him insufficient opportunity to practise his skills. Craig also thinks that the other trainees do not help him, but he refuses to ask for help or be social in a way that integrates him into the group. Instead he concludes that his personal and professional difficulties are almost all caused by other people's deficiencies.

Helpful explanations

Craig, 23, realizes that his parents were not always able to show their love as he would have liked. Though he missed having as much affection as he wanted, rather than blame his parents Craig has tried to assume responsibility for making the most of his life. In regard to counselling skills training, Craig tries to make the most of the opportunities that are either provided or that he can create. He works really hard to keep his side of the skills training contract by giving and getting as much as he can from the trainer and from the other group members. If difficulties occur in the training group, Craig is not a doormat. He accepts what cannot be immediately changed, for example the photocopy machine breaking down, and assertively collaborates with the trainer and fellow trainees to improve matters that can be changed. Craig considers that it is ultimately up to his own ability and effort whether or not he becomes a really skilled counsellor.

Activity 3.5 Creating explanations skills

1 Using the scale below, rate the importance you attach to each of the listed factors in explaining how successful you will be in learning introductory counselling skills:

4 Extremely important
3 Very important
2 Moderately important
1 Slightly important
0 Of no importance

Your rating	*Factors*
——	my prior experience at counselling and helping
——	how able I am
——	the amount of effort I will make
——	how anxious I will get
——	the difficulty of the learning tasks
——	how competent the trainer is
——	how good the training facilities are
——	the opportunities I will get to practise my skills
——	competing demands from other elements of the course, if relevant
——	financial worries
——	the degree of support from my work environment
——	the degree of support from my home environment
——	my physical health
——	luck
——	other factors not mentioned above (please specify and rate each)

2 Summarize your main explanations for how successful you will be in learning introductory counselling skills.
3 Can you alter any of your explanations to increase your chances of success? If so, what revised explanations might you have?

Creating expectations skills

Humans seek to predict their futures so that they can influence and control them. Consequential thinking entails creating expectations about the consequences of human behaviour. For good or ill, people can create and influence their consequences, including their own and others' feelings, physical reactions, thoughts and communications.

Consequential thinking can be overdone. Harmful anxiety is a feeling generated by excessive preoccupation with dangerous consequences. In addition, counselling trainees can become frozen with indecision if they spend too much time trying to predict consequences. In both counselling contacts and daily life, all spontaneity may be lost if a person is continually preoccupied with the consequences of communication. Trainees create expectations about the positive and negative consequences of their own and others' communication. Sometimes they make accurate inferences but on other occasions they may overestimate or underestimate the probability of loss or gain.

In training and when counselling, trainees create expectations about their competence and coping ability. Such expectations influence how confident they feel and how they communicate. Communicating counselling skills competently is not simply a matter of knowing what to do. Trainees need the confidence to use their skills. Expectations about competence differ from expectations about outcomes. Expectations about competence involve predictions about one's ability to accomplish a certain level of performance, for instance in listening. Outcome expectations involve predictions about the likely consequences of one's performance: for instance that if a trainee listens skilfully then clients will probably experience and explore their feelings more fully.

Expectations about one's level of competence also influence how much effort to expend and how long to persist in the face of setbacks and difficulties. Unlike self-doubt, firm expectations of competence can strengthen trainees' resilience when engaging in difficult tasks. In addition, expectations about level of competence influence how one thinks and feels. Members of counselling skills groups who judge themselves to be insufficiently competent in dealing with the demands of their skills group may exaggerate their personal deficiencies, become disheartened more easily, and give up in face of difficulties. On the other hand, members with a strong sense of personal competence, though possibly temporarily demoralized by setbacks, are more likely to stay task-oriented and to intensify their efforts when their performance in skills training falls short of their goals.

Related to expectations about one's level of competence are expectations about one's ability to cope with difficult situations and people. A trainee's lack of confidence in their ability to cope with difficulties, crises and critical incidents can affect adversely how they handle them, if and when they occur. Ironically, at the times when they need to be most realistic and rational, their emotional brain can take over and strong feelings can overcome reason.

Box 3.6 first illustrates how Serena, a trainee on a counselling course, possesses unrealistically negative expectations about her counselling skills that can interfere with and undermine how she interviews. Then, Serena is presented as possessing more realistic expectations that support her interviewing.

Box 3.6 Creating harmful and helpful expectations

Situation
Serena, 31, a trainee, is about to interview a client, Pat, 20, as part of her supervised counselling practice.

Harmful expectations
I'm not sufficiently competent to be interviewing anybody and am afraid of making a mess of this interview. I am afraid that the session is going to be a waste of time for the client, who will see that I am not good at interviewing. I can see us having a very unsatisfactory time together with both of us feeling that I have not understood her problem. I am also afraid of the client complaining to the counselling agency afterwards.

Helpful expectations
OK, I am feeling nervous about interviewing Pat. I can expect to feel a bit nervous since I still have had very little experience in working with clients. However, let's look at the reality of the situation. First, I am learning counselling skills and should not expect to be really competent from the start. Second, Pat has been screened and so her problems should be within my present level of competence. Third, Pat knows that she is seeing a trainee rather than a fully qualified counsellor. Consequently, Pat will not be expecting a professional performance. Fourth, if I do experience difficulty I can discuss it with my supervisor and try not to make the same mistakes again. I am glad that we have moved on to the part of the course where we see real clients. I am looking forward to the challenge both of possibly helping Pat and of learning to become a better counsellor.

Activity 3.6 Creating expectations skills

Part A: Expectations about counselling skills training

1 What are your expectations about the goals and outcomes of your introductory counselling skills training group and how realistic are they?
2 What are your expectations about the processes of your introductory skills training group and how realistic are they likely to be?

Part B: Expectations about yourself

1 What are your expectations about how you will perform during the training group and how realistic are they?
2 What are your expectations about the outcomes you will personally obtain from your training group and how realistic are they?

Other mind skills

In the preceding sections, the reader has been introduced to six key mind skills. However, the mind is much more complicated than this, so two additional mind areas will now be briefly mentioned.

Creating realistic goals skills

Some counselling trainees have difficulty articulating goals and consequently relinquish much opportunity to create their futures. Goals can be short-term, medium-term or long-term and in various areas: for instance relationships, study, work, recreation, health, and finances. When in close relationships, goals may need to be negotiated so that they become shared goals. Apart from not possessing goals, errors in goal setting include not reflecting values, insufficient realism, inadequate specificity, and unclear time frames. Trainees' goals in relation to problem areas may suffer from not being expressed in skills language. Furthermore, they may not focus on how to think as well as on how to communicate or act.

Creating realistic decision-making skills

Counselling trainees may possess decision-making styles that lessen their effectiveness. For instance, they may be hyper-vigilant and try too hard by taking every possible consideration into account. Conversely, they may be impulsive and rush into major and minor decisions. Some may do their best to avoid decisions altogether. Sometimes decisions are best made in collaboration with others. In such instances, decision errors include being overly competitive or compliant. Realistic decision-making has two main stages: confronting and making decisions; and implementing and evaluating them. Trainees may have weaknesses in either or both stages. An illustrative weakness when making decisions is failure to generate sufficient options. An illustrative weakness when implementing decisions is poor planning.

Situation–Thoughts–Consequences revisited

Now that a number of different mind skills have been presented, it is time to revisit the STC framework provided near the beginning of this chapter. T, or the thoughts in the framework, can now be looked at in two ways. First, there is the original way in which T indicates the thoughts elicited by a situation. Second, is the more analytical way in which T indicates both the thoughts and the mind skills that they represent. As this book progresses, much attention will be paid not just to improving clients' thoughts, but to improving their mind skills as well. The same holds true for counselling trainees, both for their own and for their clients' sakes.

Now back to the example of Danny (see p. 28). Below are Danny's thoughts with their mind skill areas indicated. If Danny was a client instead of a trainee, the counsellor working with him might only focus on one, two or three of these skills areas, knowing that this would be sufficient to help him. The following are some hypotheses that a counsellor could make about Danny's mind skills.

- *Creating rules skills.* Danny's thinking that he always has to or must do well indicates that he is suffering from a demanding rule. While it is OK for Danny to want to do well and to prefer to do so, this is different from thinking that he absolutely must do well. Furthermore, Danny is likely to suffer from derivatives of his demanding rule, like awfulizing, I can't stand-it-itis, and damning himself and possibly others.
- *Creating perceptions skills.* Danny needs to collect evidence that the course staff and other students think less of him because he is not doing as well as he would like, rather than just assuming it. He also needs to be very careful to perceive accurately how he is doing. Because he may possess a perfectionist rule about having to do exceptionally well, he may inaccurately perceive how well he is doing: for instance, he may have the perceiving error of black-and-white thinking: 'Either I'm doing wonderfully or terribly.'
- *Creating self-talk skills.* Danny's self-talk in which he keeps telling himself that he is not doing as well as he would like is probably negative and unskilful. Instead, he could be using the calming and coaching dimensions of coping self-talk.
- *Creating visual images skills.* Danny imagines himself making a lot of mistakes when practising counselling skills with other trainees. Much better would be for Danny to visualize himself performing specific good skills.
- *Creating explanations skills.* Danny attributes his difficulties to lack of talent. Lack of talent is a fixed explanation. Danny's difficulties may extend to having some poor counselling communication skills. If so, a much better explanation is that he needs to identify these skills and practise them more. It is also possible that some of Danny's difficulties are exaggerated. He may perform in some ways reasonably well, but his poor mind skills stop him from accepting this.
- *Creating expectation skills.* Danny thinks that he will have trouble passing the course. This may or may not be accurate. Danny needs to make an accurate evaluation of his current counselling skills and, as with any trainee, work hard to improve. It is likely that if Danny can improve his mind skills, he will be in a good position to pass the course.

Activity 3.7 Examining situations, thoughts and consequences

Think of your current situation on your counselling skills training course as S. Put the thoughts you have about how well you are doing as T. Then put at C your feelings, physical reactions and communication as consequences of S and T.

Now try to identify one or more of your thoughts at T in the following mind skills areas:

- creating rules
- creating perceptions
- creating self-talk
- creating visual images
- creating explanations
- creating expectations

What are your reactions to thinking about how you are doing in terms of:
- your thoughts?
- your mind skills?

the lifeskills counselling model 4

Chapter outcomes

By studying and doing the activity in this chapter you should:

- understand the importance of looking at problems in terms of both communication/action skills and mind skills;
- know what are the stages and phases of the lifeskills counselling model;
- know some counsellor skills and client behaviours illustrating each stage and phase of the model: and
- understand some of the issues in applying the lifeskills counselling model of practice.

In Chapter 2 the distinction was made between problems and problematic skills. The previous two chapters described communication/action skills and mind skills. This discussion and description of skills lays the foundation for the Relating–Understanding–Changing or RUC lifeskills counselling model presented in this chapter. Though arguably mind skills are more fundamental than communication/action skills, counsellors and counselling skills students can view most problems that clients bring to them as consisting of both mind dimensions and communication/action dimensions.

The lifeskills counselling model shown in Box 4.1 provides a systematic framework both for addressing problems and for altering the poor mind skills and communication and action skills that sustain problems. Problems tend to repeat themselves if clients are not careful. It may be just band-aiding a problem to address it in everyday language. It may be much more preferable in the short, medium and the long term to assist clients to identify and alter the mind skills and communication skills deficiencies that create and sustain their problem or problems. On some occasions, such as immediate crises or decisions, a simple short-term view may be appropriate. However, in most instances, clients are not just concerned with getting counsellor support and suggestions to tide them through current difficulties. Instead, their focus is on gaining skills and strength for coping better after they terminate. Consequently they require self-helping skills that they understand so well that they can monitor their usage and, where possible, correct lapses on their own after counselling ends. Thus counsellors must be able to progressively augment and build clients' skills so that they become skilled self-helpers.

Box 4.1 The lifeskills counselling model

Stage 1 Relating

Main task: Form a collaborative working relationship

Phase 1: Pre-counselling contact
Communicating with and providing information for clients prior to the first session.
Phase 2: Starting the initial session
Meeting, greeting and seating, making opening remarks, and encouraging clients to tell why they have come.
Phase 3: Facilitating client disclosure
Allowing clients space to reveal more about themselves and their problem(s) from their own perspective.

Stage 2 Understanding

Main task: Assess and agree on a shared analysis of the client's problem(s)

Phase 1: Reconnaissance
As necessary, conducting a broad review to identify the client's main problems and to collect information to understand her/him better.
Phase 2: Detecting and deciding
Collecting specific evidence to test ideas about possible poor skills and then reviewing all available information to suggest which skills might require improving.
Phase 3: Agreeing on a shared analysis of the client's problem(s)
Arriving at a preliminary analysis of the client's problem(s) including, where appropriate, specifying mind skills and communication/action skills for improvement.

Stage 3 Changing

Main task: Achieve client change and the maintenance of change

Phase 1: Intervening
Helping clients to develop and implement strategies for managing current problems and improving relevant mind skills and communication/action skills for now and later.
Phase 2: Ending
Assisting clients both to consolidate their skills for use afterwards and to plan how to maintain them when counselling ends.
Phase 3: Client self-helping
Clients, largely on their own, keep using their skills, monitoring their progress, correcting lapses and, where possible, integrating their improved skills into their daily living.

The fact that the lifeskills counselling model is presented in a series of three stages, each of which has three phases, may imply a degree of tidiness inappropriate to the often more messy and unpredictable practice of counselling. Stages and phases often overlap and counsellors should not be surprised to find themselves moving backwards and forwards between them. In addition, they sometimes focus on more than one aspect of a complex problem in a single session. Counsellors always need to be sensitive to a client's degree of suffering and capacity for insight. In addition, they should remember to look for clients' strengths, and to acknowledge a shared humanity.

A brief overview is now provided of each stage and phase of the lifeskills counselling model from both the counsellor's and the client's perspectives. This is followed by a single case study – based on a real client of mine – that illustrates each stage and phase of the model.

Stages and phases of the lifeskills counselling model

Stage 1: Relating

The main goal of the relating stage is for counsellor and client to start establishing a good collaborative working relationship. Other goals are to find out why clients have come for counselling and to gain an initial understanding of their problem or problems.

Phase 1: Pre-counselling contact

The counsellor in the process

Counselling really begins from the moment the client first hears about the counsellor. Counsellors can gain or lose clients by how they advertise, the quality of information they offer about their services, how easy they are to get hold of, the kind of messages they leave on their answerphone, how friendly they sound on the phone, and whether and how they answer email enquiries.

If counsellors work for an agency, how the office staff behave towards potential and first-time clients is very important. Warmth, tact and quiet efficiency all convey positive messages to clients, some of whom may be feeling highly vulnerable. Comfortable and tasteful furnishings in reception areas can also be reassuring.

Arriving early gives counsellors time to relax, get the room ready and, if using recording equipment, time to ensure that it works. They can check the client's name and any pertinent details about them. If possible, counsellors should do all their preparation in private. Then, when they meet clients, they can devote their full attention to them.

The client in the process

Clients have different preconceptions about counselling. These ideas are not always accurate and some of the ways in which they are formed are mentioned above. Some clients will have had good, bad or indifferent experiences with other counsellors prior to coming. Clients' expectations may also be shaped by whether they were referred by previous clients or by sources who said positive things when making the referral. Some clients come for counselling reluctantly because they have been made or told to do so. Clients' pre-counselling expectations are also shaped by factors like culture, social class, financial status, age and sex.

Most often clients have a limited idea of what to expect and what their role is likely to be. Clients consider coming to counselling with varying degrees of trepidation. It can be a huge step for some clients. Reasons for this include their reluctance to face up to difficult issues, make intimate disclosures, and break barriers about talking to third parties about family and other problems. Some people find coming too difficult. Others may arrive only as a result of overcoming their fears and because they desperately want to ease their suffering.

Phase 2: Starting the initial session

The counsellor in the process

Counsellors need to develop good skills for meeting, greeting and seating clients. They should provide a warm and friendly, but not effusive, welcome. If clients are in reception areas, counsellors can go to meet them, call them by name and introduce themselves. Most counsellors are relatively sparing about small talk. A little of it may humanize the process; too much risks diverting attention from the client's agenda. Counsellors show clients into the counselling room and indicate where they should sit.

When both parties are seated, counsellors may make an opening statement that indicates the time boundaries of the session, saying something like 'We have about 45 minutes together' and then giving the client permission to talk. Counsellors may need to fulfil agency requirements that they collect basic information before giving permission to talk. Counsellors may also need to ask the clients if they can record the session. Examples of permissions to talk are 'Please tell me why you've come', 'Where would you like to start?', 'You've been referred by ——. Now how do you see your situation?'

Counsellors should try to create an emotional climate of warmth, respect and interest in which clients can feel reasonably safe in sharing their inner worlds and wounds. They use active listening skills to help clients feel that their thoughts and feelings are being received and understood sensitively and accurately. At some stage counsellors may make a further statement that describes to the client the structure of the initial session and how they work. Counsellors should be prepared to answer questions, but avoid long-winded replies. Some questions are really aimed at seeking reassurance and a counsellor's manner of responding can help dispel unnecessary fears.

The client in the process

From the moment they set eyes on their counsellors, clients start summing them up. Counsellors' vocal and bodily communication may speak just as loudly as their words. Though counsellors may feel anxious, clients probably feel far more threatened. They are on unfamiliar territory, uncertain how to behave, and know that they are likely to be asked to reveal personal information to someone they do not know.

Questions running through clients' minds include: 'Can I trust this counsellor?', 'How confidential is the session?', 'How much am I prepared to reveal?', 'Will this person like me?', 'Will we be on the same wavelength?', and 'Can this person help me?' Clients come to counselling bringing wounds and various levels of unfinished business from past relationships. It may take them some time to view counsellors as persons in their own right who differ from people who have been associated with past hurts and rejections.

Phase 3: Facilitating client disclosure

The counsellor in the process

A decision counsellors have to make is when to curtail the space they give to clients to share their internal worlds on their terms and change to being more active in collecting information. Where time permits, I generally prefer to encourage clients to keep talking for the first 10 to 15 minutes rather than to assume much direction near the beginning of the session. The main purpose of the early part of initial counselling sessions is to build good relationships. Helping clients to feel accurately understood as they share their inner worlds is a good way of achieving this objective.

In addition, I want to get clients used to the idea of participating actively in sessions and not just responding to me all the time. Another reason is that counsellors never know where clients are going to take them and by getting too focused too soon they may stay on the surface rather than access material that is more important to clients. As clients reveal themselves on their own terms, counsellors can start making useful hypotheses about the nature of their problems, their strengths, and their self-defeating thoughts and communications/actions.

During this process of client disclosure, counsellors require good relationship enhancement skills such as active listening, summarizing and asking occasional questions, which may take the form of encouraging clients to elaborate. When it seems helpful, counsellors can provide brief explanations of the stages of the counselling process.

In the lifeskills counselling model, it is advisable for counsellors to take notes discreetly in the initial session(s). They can explain that they are doing this in order to record relevant information for when they later suggest ways of viewing a client's problems differently. Memory is fallible. When attempting to agree on shared analyses of clients' problems, it is very helpful for counsellors to do this from actual material that clients have provided, including quoting back pertinent statements that the clients themselves have made.

Clients vary in the degree to which they are emotionally literate. Assuming clients have come to counselling of their own accord and that the counsellor is both confident and tactful when explaining the purpose of note-taking, most clients do not mind it.

The client in the process

Clients also vary in their ambivalence about disclosing problems and talking honestly about their lives. Many clients, while being willing and eager to talk about themselves, are selective about how much they reveal. Client and counsellor anxiety are always present throughout the counselling process and can distort the amount and nature of disclosure. During the initial session many clients' anxiety about the counselling process is at its highest. Some rationing or avoidance of disclosure is deliberate. On other occasions, as clients explore and experience themselves more, they get in touch with and reveal material of which they were previously unaware. Clients can be inconsistent in what they reveal. To maintain a safe emotional climate, it is sometimes best just quietly to notice this inconsistency rather than bring it to their attention. The time for greater consistency may be later rather than now.

Stage 2: Understanding

The main goal of the understanding stage is for counsellors to collaborate with clients to clarify and assess their problem(s) so that they can agree on shared initial analyses of how clients might change. Counsellors, with the assistance of clients, move from describing and clarifying problem(s) in everyday terms to assessing and analysing how clients sustain their difficulties. Throughout, counsellors respect clients as intelligent co-workers who are by the end of this stage entitled to a reasoned initial analysis of their problem(s). Depending on the complexity of problems and, sometimes, the verbosity of clients, the understanding stage may take place over more than one session. This stage can include activities for clients to undertake between sessions.

Phase 1: Reconnaissance

The counsellor in the process

Even when, on the surface, clients' problems seem reasonably clear-cut, it may be wise to conduct a broader reconnaissance. Together counsellor and client may identify further problems or uncover information relevant to understanding clients' presenting concerns. In stage 2 of the lifeskills counselling model, counsellors perform a more active role than in stage 1.

While maintaining a relationship orientation, counsellors adopt a greater task orientation as they help clients to review various areas of their functioning. Some counsellors also use biographical information or life history questionnaires that they ask clients to fill out either prior to or after the first session.

When conducting a reconnaissance, counsellors tactfully move the focus of the interview from area to area. The reconnaissance varies in length and depth according to what seems appropriate for each individual client. Influences on those areas covered are the context in which they meet, the client's presenting concerns, and anything the client has previously revealed.

Some of the reconnaissance may refer to clients' childhood and adolescence: for example, relationships with parents and significant others, schooling, problems experienced when growing up, traumatic incidents, their view of themselves, and anything else the client considers relevant. The reconnaissance can also review how clients function in their intimate and friendship relationships, their living arrangements, how they get on at work or in study, any health issues, and issues related to diversity such as culture and gender. Additional areas include information about their previous experience of counselling, any medication they are taking, any unusual current stress, and what clients perceive as their strengths. Further questioning can address their favourite hobbies and pastimes, their short-, medium and long-term goals, their central values and philosophy of life.

Counsellor skills for conducting a reconnaissance include helping clients to see that its purpose is to enable them to understand themselves better and not just for the counsellor's benefit. Counsellors should ask questions in ways that avoid making clients feel interrogated: for example by interspersing empathic responses with questions. Counsellors can make the process personal by letting clients know that they are interested in their experiencing and perceptions of events. The reconnaissance is an exploration of the client's subjective world as well as of external facts. Where possible, counsellors should keep the interview moving since they can later come back to areas that require more detailed consideration. In addition, counsellors should continue to look for evidence of clients' main problems and the poor mind skills and communication/action skills which sustain them.

The client in the process

A few words of caution are in order regarding the possible negative impact of a reconnaissance on clients. Clients need to perceive that the reconnaissance is of some potential benefit to them, so its scope should be tailored to their purposes and problems. Clients who come to counselling with fairly specific concerns are only likely to respond positively to questions in or around the area of their concerns. Where clients' problems are multiple, complex or long-standing, there is more of a case for a thorough reconnaissance. Clients may also have areas they are reluctant to discuss in detail, if at all, and such reluctance should be respected.

Often clients willingly collaborate in sensitively conducted attempts to understand them and their problems more fully. They appreciate the time, space and concern provided for reviewing their lives and problems. Many clients have been starved of opportunities to be the focus of attention. When helped to review different aspects of their lives aloud, they feel affirmed and can gain useful insights. In the initial session clients may feel better understood by counsellors who both facilitate their disclosure and review different aspects of their lives than by counsellors who facilitate their disclosure alone, since they feel they are treated as persons and not simply as problems.

Phase 2: Detecting and deciding

The counsellor in the process

By now counsellors have already assembled a number of ideas about clients, their problems, their strengths and potential poor skills. How counsellors handle this next phase may depend on the complexity of clients' problems. For example, if clients come with specific concerns – say, the wish to improve their public speaking skills – counsellors may perform more detailed analyses of any feelings, physical reactions, thoughts, and communications/actions that will help them to make more accurate hypotheses about how clients are perpetuating such difficulties.

In a more complex case, such as that of George provided later in this chapter (see pp. 58–62), I offer an overall definition of the client's problem rather than a detailed definition of any part of it. This overall definition consists of the main mind skills and communication/action skills the client needs to improve. Characteristic poor mind skills tend to carry across a range of situations. This should come as no surprise, since Ellis detects irrational beliefs and Beck identifies inadequately reality-tested perceptions in all of their clients.

Counsellors can collect more information to test ideas about possible poor mind skills and poor communication/action skills if they wish. When this process is over, they should pull together their conclusions for presenting to clients. Counsellors can ask clients to give them a few minutes to look over their notes and information so that they can offer specific suggestions about where clients might fruitfully work in future. When making notes, I highlight any information that may be of later importance. For example, I circle a T by any thoughts that appear to be of particular relevance for subsequently identifying poor mind skills.

Later I can quickly spot these thoughts and use them to provide evidence for, decide on and illustrate potential poor skills.

The client in the process

Clients can be very cooperative in providing additional information that helps them understand specific problems more clearly. For instance, in the example of improving a client's public speaking skills, counsellors may ask follow-up questions that elicit thoughts and feelings that occur before, during and after giving a talk. The client can also help the counsellor to understand how their distress varies across different public speaking situations. Furthermore, the counsellor can ask the client to show their actual verbal, vocal and bodily communication when, say, starting a speech.

I find that clients do not get upset if I politely ask them to give me some time to pull together the information that I have collected. What is damaging is a confusing and ill-considered assessment of their problems rather than one that is carefully constructed from what they have said.

Phase 3: Agreeing on a shared analysis of the client's problem(s)

The counsellor in the process

Most clients require some idea of where they have been going wrong. After making preliminary assessments, counsellors attempt to agree with clients on shared analyses of the mind skills and the communication/action skills that clients need to improve. Counsellors offer suggestions for discussion with clients, illustrating how they have come to their conclusions using material that clients provided earlier.

Good counsellor suggestions of skills that clients might improve follow logically from information revealed to date. If the groundwork has been laid in the earlier parts of the session, there should be no surprises. As appropriate, counsellors work with clients to explain, modify or even discard suggestions with which clients are unhappy. It is vitally important that clients not only own their problems, but also agree on where best to improve their skills, since they are the ones who need to work hard to change.

Often I have conducted counselling sessions with a small whiteboard at the side that the client and I can turn to when necessary. I do not favour using the whiteboard before the 'agreeing on a shared analysis' part of the initial session. Premature use of the whiteboard can slow the assessment process down and may divert it by getting into too much detail about a specific area too soon.

Using visual as well as verbal presentation to define clients' problems has many advantages. As in teaching, both types of communication can stimulate interest. In addition, clients' memories are fallible and by the time counsellors move on to the next topic clients may have started to forget what has just happened if there is no visual record of it. Furthermore, counsellors can use the whiteboard to modify suggestions of poor skills in line with client feedback. By the time counsellors finish, clients have a good visual overview not only of their problems, but of goals for change. Once agreement is reached on the skills clients need to improve, both parties can record this as a basis for their future work. However, as counselling progresses, counsellors need to be flexible about modifying shared analyses of problems and of the skills clients need to improve.

The client in the process

Most often clients come for counselling and therapy because they are stuck. Their existing ways of defining problems and their coping strategies are not working for them. They sustain their difficulties by underutilizing their strengths as well as by perpetuating their weaknesses. Many clients genuinely appreciate counsellors who take the trouble to break their problems down and show them how they can improve in easily understood language. Clients need to be active participants in the process. Clients should be helped to understand how important it is for them to question anything unclear. They should feel free to seek modifications of or abandonment of any of the counsellor's suggestions concerning deficient skills.

Clients like to be invited to contribute feedback. They want any suggestions of skills for improvement to be worded in language with which they are comfortable. They appreciate illustrations of how counsellors have arrived at their suggestions based on material they have shared earlier. In short, clients like to be treated as intelligent collaborators in the process of creating shared analyses of how they can change for the better. Clients who see their problems broken down often experience feelings of relief. They get glimpses of hope that problems that up until now have seemed overwhelming can be managed both now and in future.

Stage 3: Changing

The main goals of the changing stage are first for counsellors to collaborate with clients to achieve change and then for clients to maintain that change on their own after counselling ends.

Phase 1: Intervening

The counsellor in the process

Counsellors intervene as user-friendly coaches as clients develop self-helping skills and strategies. To intervene effectively counsellors require good relationship skills and good training skills. Skilled counsellors strike an appropriate balance between relationship and task orientations; less skilled counsellors err in one or other direction.

Counsellors work much of the time with the three training methods of 'tell', 'show' and 'do'. 'Tell' entails giving clients clear instructions concerning the skills they wish to develop. 'Show' means demonstrating how to implement skills. 'Do' means arranging for clients to perform structured activities and homework tasks.

Within collaborative working relationships, counsellors deliver specific mind skills and communication/action skills interventions drawn from cognitive-behavioural and humanistic sources. In instances where counsellors find it difficult to deliver interventions systematically, they weave them into the fabric of the counselling process. Whenever appropriate, counsellors help clients to acknowledge that they are learning and using skills. Frequently clients are asked to fill out 'take away' or homework sheets in which they record skills-focused work done on the whiteboard during sessions. Homework assignments form a regular part of counselling. Instructions for these are written down so that clients are clear what they have agreed to do.

The client in the process

The intervening stage focuses on assisting clients to manage current problems and to acquire mind skills and communication/action skills as self-helping skills. Clients are learners whose counsellors act as user-friendly coaches as they change from their old self-defeating ways to using new and better skills. Clients actively collaborate during counselling, for instance in setting session agendas, sharing their thoughts and feelings, participating in in-session activities to build their knowledge and skills, and keeping their own records of work covered during counselling.

Clients also negotiate and carry out appropriate homework assignments. Some such assignments prepare for the next session: for instance, clients list their demanding rules in a specific area so that time can be saved when this topic is addressed during counselling. Other assignments involve implementing skills learned during previous sessions: for example, learning to challenge demanding thinking and replace it with rational statements or trying to improve their verbal, vocal and bodily communication in a specific situation.

Phase 2: Ending

The counsellor in the process

Nearly always counsellors or clients bring up the topic of ending before the final session. This allows both parties to work through the various task and relationship issues connected with ending the contact. A useful option with some clients is to reduce contact by spacing out the final few sessions. Certain clients may appreciate the opportunity for booster sessions, say one, two, three or even six months later.

The lifeskills counselling model seeks to avoid the 'train and hope' approach. Counsellors encourage transfer and maintenance of skills by such means as developing clients' self-instructional abilities, working with real-life situations during counselling, and using between-session time productively to perform homework assignments and to rehearse and practise skills. Often counsellors make up short take-away cassettes focused on the use of specific skills in specific situations: for instance, the use of coping self-talk to handle anxiety when waiting to deliver a public speech.

In addition, counsellors work with clients to anticipate difficulties and setbacks to implementing and maintaining their skills once counselling ends. Together they develop and rehearse coping strategies for preventing and managing lapses and relapses. Sometimes clients require help in identifying people to support their efforts to maintain skills. Counsellors can also provide information about further skills-building opportunities.

The client in the process

Clients end counselling for many reasons, some negative, some neutral and some positive. Negative reasons include feeling unhappy with counsellors and their way of working and failure to make significant progress. Neutral reasons include clients or counsellors moving to another location or either party only being available for a fixed number of sessions. In the lifeskills counselling model, positive reasons for ending are that clients have evidence that they can manage with their current problems better and possess some skills to prevent and/or successfully cope with future similar problems.

Clients can ensure that ending is handled as beneficially as possible for them. For example, they can actively participate in discussions about how they can consolidate and maintain their skills once counselling finishes. Though some dependency may arise in the earlier parts of counselling if clients feel especially vulnerable, the consistent message they receive during counselling is that they have the resources within themselves to become happier and more effective people.

Phase 3: Client self-helping

This relates to what clients do on their own once counselling ends. The purpose of skilling clients is so that they become more skilled independently of their counsellors. Throughout the lifeskills counselling model, the emphasis is on giving clients the skills to help themselves. Counsellors try and help them understand how to apply the skills so clearly that they carry this understanding around in their heads once counselling has ended.

Clients can view the time after counselling as providing a challenge to maintain and, where possible, to improve their skills. When necessary, clients can revise their skills by referring back to any notes or records of skills-building activities made during counselling. They can also listen to cassettes made during counselling to reinforce their understanding and application of targeted skills or apply strategies discussed during counselling to help them overcome setbacks and retrieve lapses.

Clients can involve others to support them in their self-helping. Before counselling ends they may have worked with their counsellors to identify people and resources for assisting them afterwards. Clients can request booster sessions and keep in touch with counsellors by phone or e-mail to monitor their progress, handle crises, and become even more skilled. However, limits may need to set on such contacts.

The lifeskills counselling model assumes that there is no such thing as cure. Often, after ending, clients have to work hard to minimize the effects of their poor skills and maintain their good skills. Sometimes using good skills provides obvious rewards, in which case it is not difficult to continue using them. On other occasions clients may perceive losses as well as gains when using good skills, for instance giving up a favourite bad habit. One strategy for former clients tempted to go back to their old ways is to perform a cost-benefit analysis of why they should keep using their improved skills. The following case study provides an example of the lifeskills counselling model.

Case study of the lifeskills counselling model: George

Stage 1: Relating

Phase 1: Pre-counselling contact

George, aged 52, had been unemployed for six months after being fired from his position of managing director of a communications company. He was obsessed with getting back into the workforce and had become extremely depressed at his lack of success. He had discussed his depression with his doctor, who put him on an antidepressant that he felt terrible about taking.

As part of his termination package, George was given the opportunity to use a well-respected outplacement company for senior executives. Here a consultant had been assisting George with his job search programme and providing support and encouragement. The outplacement company hired me on a sessional basis to work with clients whose job search problems went beyond the ordinary. George's consultant notified him that I was a counselling psychologist on the staff, whom he could see as part of the company's service. George, who was quite psychologically minded, thought he badly needed to see someone who might help lift his incapacitating depression. While he felt some anxiety about seeing a counselling psychologist, he was prepared to give it a go and reserve judgement.

Phase 2: Starting the initial session

George was slightly anxious about meeting me. However, he was also hopeful that he might be helped. Since my office was on the outplacement company's premises, George was on relatively familiar territory and the office was similar to that of his own job search consultant there.

George was reassured to hear that the sessions would be confidential. He recounted that he was married to Jill, aged 50, and had two grown-up children in their mid-twenties who did not live at home. He was fired six months ago and 'ran out of puff' four months ago. He now felt extremely depressed: one of his images was of himself 'in a black swamp sinking into the depths of despair'. He had lost almost all his energy and had to force himself to do virtually everything. He was obsessed with the process of job-getting which 'hangs over me all the time'. George felt that I accurately understood what he was trying to say. At the same time as being uncomfortable at revealing his desperate situation, he later said that he experienced me as compassionate, supportive and competent.

Phase 3: Facilitating client disclosure

Encouraged by my making it easy for him to talk, George went on to elaborate his depressed feelings, thoughts and behaviour. He acknowledged he had contemplated suicide seven days previously. Currently he was not sleeping well. He staggered out of bed exhausted. He had about two hours of energy every morning, then basically he just sat, shut his eyes, dozed off or stared into space. He was eating OK and running every second day. However, he was not enjoying anything at the moment.

George was regularly coming to the outplacement company's premises, where job search 'candidates' could book offices, to escape from home. Jill, his wife, had voluntarily left work about a year previously and didn't expect or want to go back. She was feeling old and worthless and felt she had nobody to support her emotionally or financially. Jill was very concerned about what others thought and told her friends that her husband was consulting rather than admitting that he was unemployed.

Stage 2: Understanding

Phase 1: Reconnaissance

George cooperated in reviewing his life and in trying to obtain a fuller picture of his problems. In the financial area, he did not see money as a major problem for the time being. However, money concerns were a problem for Jill, who reproached him for not getting a job. George felt guilty about not providing her with the lifestyle to which she had become accustomed.

Regarding searching for a job, George said that, right now, 'I couldn't give a damn about a job.' In the past month he had written three letters. In the past six months he had contacted about 50 people and had five interviews.

Regarding his background George said that up until the age of 30 he was always trying to please everyone. As a kid he was constantly criticized by his carpet-fitter father. He particularly wanted to please his mum and saw his brother as the favourite. To gain attention he tried to be smart and funny.

Regarding his marriage, George thought that, despite public displays, there was no affection at all in it. There had been no sexual relationship for some years. He felt controlled by Jill, often did not stand up to her, and underneath seethed with resentment when she made comments like 'I'm really disappointed in you' and 'You always embarrass me in public.' Repeatedly George received the silent treatment. On occasion, his anger would overflow and he would shout to defend himself. However, George felt guilty when Jill was disappointed in him. Jill felt dependent on George at the same time as constantly criticizing him.

Regarding recreation, George ran regularly, and until recently had played golf twice a week. He had lunches with male contacts every now and then, but Jill was very jealous over any contact with other women. On the whole he was doing much less of the things he once enjoyed, and enjoying them less too. George felt unable to take a vacation because he thought he should spend all his time looking for a job.

George's self-concept was that he was worthless, inadequate and hopeless. In positions of responsibility he was a bit of an impostor and perceived others as superior. He summed up his philosophy of life as 'In hope I live, from love I give.'

Phase 2: Detecting and deciding

Though not all of it has been reproduced above, I had done a reasonably thorough job in assisting George to overview his problems. As part of the reconnaissance stage, I asked George to provide some specific illustrations: for example, how he and Jill communicated when Jill disparaged him. In addition, we explored topics like his pattern of nocturnal sleep more thoroughly: for example, the extent to which he was unable to get to sleep, experienced disturbed sleep and/or woke early. About 30 or more minutes into the first session I considered that I had collected enough evidence to offer some initial suggestions concerning skills George might address in order to feel happier. So I asked George to wait a few minutes while I reviewed my notes and drew together threads for making suggestions.

Phase 3: Agreeing on a shared analysis of the client's problem(s)

I told George I was now ready to write on the whiteboard some suggestions for how he might become happier. I wanted this to be a two-way process and invited George to make comments as I was making suggestions so that he was satisfied with the way they were stated. George and I agreed that there were three main interrelated areas requiring attention: his depression, his job-seeking impasse and his marital difficulties.

With George, I constructed the following shared analysis of skills that he might improve to become happier and more effective. Note that I illustrate each key mind skill with examples George provided earlier on. I also indicate how George might improve some of the communication/action skills other than job-seeking skills.

Mind skills I need to improve	Communication/action skills I need to improve
Creating rules 'I must be successful.' 'I must have approval.' 'I must feel guilty.' 'I must not get depressed.' 'I must provide financial support for Jill.' 'I must not take a break/enjoy myself.' *Creating perceptions* • myself 'I'm a failure, worthless, inadequate.' 'I'm always letting Jill down.' • others Inclined to put some people on pedestals 'Jill is highly dependent/vulnerable.' 'Jill is powerful/tyrannical.' *Creating explanations* 'I'm totally responsible for Jill and for her feelings.' 'My feedback hurts Jill, she is never contributing to hurting herself.' *Creating expectations* 'The future is hopeless.' 'I'm unable to influence my future positively.'	*Job-seeking skills* *Assertion skills* (verbal, voice, body) • especially when Jill disparages me *Friendship skills* • spending more time on own with friends • disclosing my feelings more *Pleasant activities skills* • taking a vacation • playing sports with friends *Managing sleep skills* • sleeping too much in day and then not sleeping well at night.

George participated actively in this process of identifying skills he might improve. He thought he had the job-seeking skills, but was just too depressed to use them properly. At the end of the session both George and I wrote the above shared analysis down. This analysis provided some fairly specific goals for our future work. George commented it was really useful to see his problems broken down and that it had been a good session.

Stage 3: Changing

Phase 1: Intervening

When George came back for the second session, he was looking brighter and said that he had bottomed out. He had done some homework examining his thought processes. He still didn't want a job and found it scary to think that he was losing his work ethic. As counselling progressed, the prime focus became George's learning to handle Jill's disparagement of him better, both inside his mind and when dealing with her. Between the second and third counselling sessions, George had stood up to Jill and taken a week's out-of-town holiday.

George and I unearthed a self-defeating communication pattern that he described using the following imagery: 'The drier the (emotional) desert, the more I am looking for water (affection, love and unconditional acceptance).' He went on to reflect that 'Deserts are full of cacti, spiky plants, scorpions – no wonder it's a bloody unpleasant place.' With my assistance, George conducted a cost-benefit analysis on whether he wanted to stay in his marriage and decided that he did, partly because it made good economic sense. He explored, challenged and restated demanding rules about needing approval, feeling guilty and having to provide a high level of income and status.

George challenged some of his perceptions about himself. For example, he made a list of over 100 people who valued him. He also listed his skills and strengths. He challenged his perception that Jill would provide him with emotional nourishment, an unrealistic perception that drove him to keep unsuccessfully looking for the approval he was unlikely ever to get from her. Despite her deep unhappiness, Jill did not want to seek professional help.

George assumed more responsibility for acting independently in the relationship. Instead of discussing his job search efforts with Jill daily and then being put down, he kept what he was doing more to himself. When Jill disparaged him, he developed better skills at either not responding or responding neutrally and not letting himself get hooked into responding aggressively.

Basically George had been starved of affection as a child and was being starved again at home. Becoming and staying unemployed had taken much of his source of self-esteem from him and highlighted the cracks in his marriage. I provided George with an affirming relationship and helped him to acquire the mind skills and communication skills not to become dragged down by Jill's own depression and negativity.

The major focus of the counselling was on assertion skills for dealing with Jill. However, among other things, time was also spent on looking at sleep patterns and I lent George a cassette on the behavioural treatment of sleep problems. There was also a focus on engaging in more pleasant activities. George completed a 320-item 'Pleasant Events Schedule' (Lewinsohn et al., 1986) and listened to a cassette by Dr Peter Lewinsohn emphasizing the importance of depressed people engaging in more pleasant activities. Never was there any great emphasis on improving George's job-seeking skills, since his depression was being sustained by poor skills elsewhere.

Phase 2: Ending

George received fourteen 50-minute sessions of counselling over an eight-month period, with sessions being more frequent at the start than at the end. In the first four months of counselling his mood and energy level gradually and intermittently improved and by the ninth session he was feeling noticeably happier. Though occasionally having blue patches, by the fourteenth and final session he felt considerably more serene and comfortable.

By the end of counselling, George's energy level was hugely improved and he was actively pursuing a number of work-related pursuits as well as coping far better at home. He considered that he could get by on his own now, especially since he understood how he had become so depressed in the first place and possessed the insight and skills to avoid this happening again. George said farewell to me on a happy and grateful note.

Applying the model

Counsellors, in the best interests of clients, need to apply the lifeskills counselling model flexibly. The task of managing problems and altering problematic skills rarely proceeds according to neatly ordered stages: counsellors may revert to earlier stages as more information or new problems emerge.

Short-term counselling

The lifeskills counselling model assumes that much counselling is relatively short-term, say 3 to 10 sessions focused on one or two main problems and problematic skills areas. However, counselling can also be very short-term - say 1 or 2 sessions; medium-term - say 11 to 20 sessions; or long-term - more than 20 sessions. Whatever the length, counsellors decide how person-oriented or task-oriented they need to be. For example, in short-term counselling an early skills focus may be inappropriate with recently bereaved clients who need space to tell their stories and experience their grief. On the other hand, an immediate skills focus may be highly appropriate with clients anxious about imminent examinations, public speeches, meetings with estranged spouses, or job interviews.

Medium-term and long-term counselling

Since different reasons exist for medium-term and long-term counselling, there are no simple answers for how best to go about it. Vulnerable clients require more gentle and nurturing relationships than robust clients and take longer to attain insight into how they sustain problems. However, it is possible to over-generalize. From the initial session some vulnerable clients may appreciate identifying and working on one or two specific poor skills.

Counselling may go more slowly if a client's starting-off point is low in specific skills areas. Counsellors may have to break down skills more, spend more time on instruction and demonstration, and offer clients more support as they rehearse and practise skills. In extended counselling, much session time is spent on working through the application of targeted skills to specific issues in clients' lives, including their fears about using the skills. If clients have multiple problems and poor skills, counsellors and clients face the issue of identifying the skills most in need of attention. In extended contacts, counsellors and clients also have to prioritize initial and emerging problems and problematic skills areas. Emerging problems may arise through clients themselves changing or through changes in their environments. Analyses in skills terms may require reformulation. Clients' progress may be either slowed down or helped by others in their environments, for example teachers, parents or spouses. If so, counsellors need to consider whether it is worth broadening counselling to include such people.

Counselling for existential concerns

Lifeskills counselling can be used to help clients confront existential concerns as well as immediate problems. Take the case of people suffering from terminal cancer. Such people may require assistance in at least four areas: confronting and coming to terms with death anxiety; dealing with problems that arise from the cancer experience, for instance changes in physical appearance and declining health; coping with problems that they have independently of their cancer, for instance a stressful lifestyle or poor communication with a spouse; and finding genuine meaning for the remainder of their lives (Nelson-Jones and Cosolo, 1994). A skilled lifeskills counsellor is alert to and prepared to work in all these areas.

Adapting to the model

Beginning counsellors are likely to find that it takes time to become proficient in the lifeskills counselling model. This training model requires counsellors to go beyond offering good counselling relationship skills to also offering good assessment and training skills. Counsellors need to possess effective inner game or thinking skills as well as effective outer game or action skills. Many beginning counsellors experience difficulty in making the transition from *talking* relationships, based on good facilitation skills, to *training* relationships, based on assessment and specific interventions designed to help clients to manage problems and problematic skills patterns.

The lifeskills counselling model requires counsellors to step outside their everyday language to conceptualize problems in skills terms. Some beginning counsellors do not find this congenial and take much time to make the transition, if they do so at all. It takes time to build up a repertoire of interventions and there is always room for improvement. Proficiency in lifeskills counselling is a lifetime challenge.

Concluding comment

Most existing counselling approaches have skilled client assumptions built into them, if not as explicitly as in the lifeskills couselling model. All the psychological education approaches to counselling and therapy, such as behaviour therapy, Ellis's rational emotive behaviour therapy, Beck's cognitive therapy, and Lazarus's multimodal therapy (Lazarus, 2005a), are training clients in skills for their outside lives. Humanistic approaches like Gestalt therapy help clients obtain useful skills outside therapy, for instance greater awareness of feelings and physical sensations. Arguably, person-centred counsellors assist clients in improving their skills of listening to their inner valuing process and being more genuine in important relationships. Even Jung's analytic therapy tries to impart skills to clients, for instance active imagination and basic dream analysis (Nelson-Jones, 2001). In sum, there is nothing particularly new in the idea of skilling clients, other than possibly being so open about it.

Activity 4.1 The lifeskills counselling model

1 Describe some counsellor skills and client processes for each stage and phase of the lifeskills counselling model (see Box 4.1, p. 47).

Stage 1: Relating

Phase 1: Pre-counselling contact
- counsellor skills

Phase 2: Starting the initial session
- counsellor skills
- client processes

Phase 3: Facilitating client disclosure
- counsellor skills
- client processes

Stage 2: Understanding

Phase 1: Reconnaissance
- counsellor skills
- client processes

Phase 2: Detecting and deciding
- counsellor skills
- client processes

Phase 3: Agreeing on a shared analysis of the client's problem(s)
- counsellor skills
- client processes

Stage 3: Changing

Phase 1: Intervening
- counsellor skills
- client processes

Phase 2: Ending
- counsellor skills
- client processes

Phase 3: Client self-helping
- client skills

2 What are some of the strengths and limitations of the lifeskills counselling model for use in the setting or settings in which you currently counsel or might counsel in future? If you consider you need to modify the model, please specify why and how.

II the relating stage

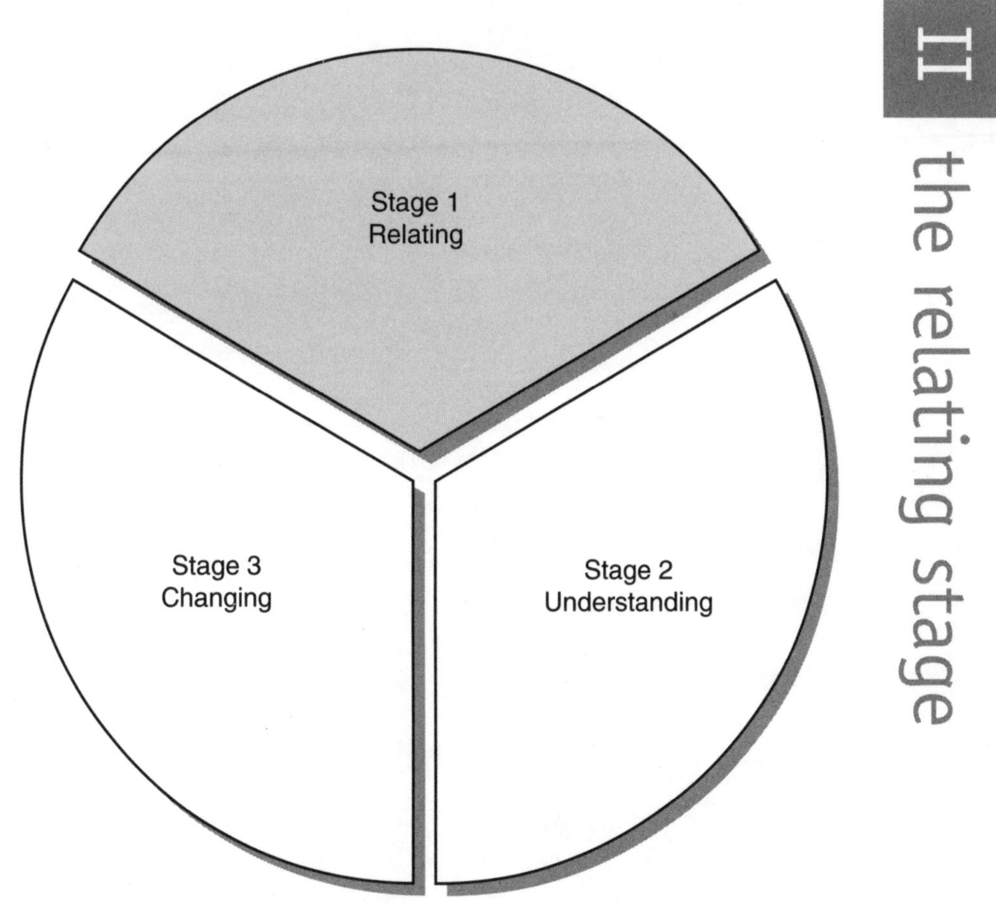

The lifeskills counselling model
The relating stage's main task: to form a collaborative working relationship
The understanding stage's main task: assess and agree on a shared definition of the client's problem(s)
The changing stage's main task: achieve client change and the maintenance of change

pre-counselling contact 5

Chapter outcomes

By studying and doing the activities in this chapter you should:

- know about orienting a counselling programme or service according to the lifeskills model;
- understand the importance of physical premises;
- have some knowledge about how to advertise a lifeskills counselling service;
- know different ways that clients can make contact with the service;
- know some ways of arranging support for counselling skills students; and
- gain some ideas about keeping records.

This chapter focuses on some important issues connected with whether or not clients come to counselling and their initial knowledge of it. Lifeskills counselling services need to be established properly if they are to be maximally effective. The goals of any programme should be clear to both counselling staff and, inasmuch as this is possible, to potential clients. Clients may not come to services that are advertised either too little or in the wrong ways. Alternatively, they may come only to find that the service is not what they thought it was. The nature of the physical premises where counselling is conducted is also important. Clients need to feel as comfortable as possible about contacting the service. If some of the considerations in this chapter seem premature for counselling skills students, this may be less the case when they embark on placement experiences.

Orientation of counselling service

One issue is whether a counselling service stands on its own or is part of a larger programme or network. For instance, the service may be part of a national organization, such as the National Health Service or Relate, or part of a regional or district programme, such as some local government career services. The counselling service might also be part of a larger student services programme, as on some university campuses. In addition, a single counselling service may have a number of different locations and ways of offering help and thus have characteristics of a larger programme.

Alternatively, counselling may be offered in smaller and possibly more informal ways. In particular, it may be offered by individuals or by small groups of like-minded counsellors and helpers. Whether counselling is offered as part of a programme, as a service on its own, or by individuals or small groups of counsellors, a key issue is always how it is funded and the degree to which the clients pay for the counselling they receive.

Counselling programmes and services differ according to their intended clienteles. The clienteles may be partners in relationships, those deciding on careers, schizophrenic clients and their relatives, people from minority populations, those with spiritual interests, and school pupils and college and university students, to mention but a few. Services vary according to the severity of problems they are equipped to tackle, though the criteria on what constitutes severity are imprecise. For example, services connected with health provision and medical centres are likely to see more severe problems than those run in educational settings. In fact, some counselling programmes in educational settings make provision for psychological education opportunities for the student body as a whole as well as providing counselling. Relate also runs preventive relationship education courses and is not solely involved in counselling partners with relationship problems. Another way that counselling services may be categorized is according to the age of their clients, though this may not be stated in their titles. Services can, in fact, be run for primary school students right through to those (usually the elderly) in hospices.

Lifeskills orientation

To date, the discussion of orientation of service has been fairly general. What gives a counselling programme or service or an individual counsellor a distinctive lifeskills orientation? Since a lifeskills orientation has varying degrees of specificity, possessing it should not be viewed as an either/or distinction. For the sake of simplicity, the following comments mainly focus on offering a counselling service and the reader is left to determine the implications for broader educational programmes or for the work of individual counsellors. The following discussion assumes that many existing services exhibit some of the characteristics of lifeskills counselling, though they are probably not labelled as such.

The counselling service is based on the assumption that all human beings need to develop psychological lifeskills. The nature of mind skills has already been outlined, with communication/action skills varying more according to people's roles. Thus the underlying model of human functioning, while allowing for medical complications connected with severe disturbance, is geared to the personal needs of the vast majority of the population. Counsellors, trainees and clients all have similar needs to develop lifeskills strengths and limit lifeskills weaknesses, though most often clients have the greater need in this regard.

The theoretical foundation of a lifeskills orientation is cognitive humanistic or a combination of cognitive-behavioural and humanistic concepts. In the last chapter, a case example of the lifeskills approach was presented. The case demonstrated work that is similar to the way in which cognitive and cognitive-behavioural counsellors operate. A basic assumption is that most psychological problems are the result of the faulty learning and maintenance of defective lifeskills. In many instances, lifeskills that have been wrongly learned and then perpetuated can be altered by learning new or revised skills. However, as mentioned in the first chapter, a description of cognitive humanistic therapy geared towards higher levels of functioning is not the purpose of this book.

Counselling service staff hold values that characterize a lifeskills orientation. Counselling is never value free. Among Schwartz's universal values, prominent values underlying the lifeskills approach include benevolence, a concern for the welfare of others with whom one is in frequent contact in everyday interaction; self-direction, an aspiration toward independent thought and action and being curious and creative; and universalism, an appreciative concern for the welfare of all people and for nature (Kelly, 1995; Schwartz, 1992). Within the overarching context of benevolence and universalism, lifeskills counselling places heavy emphasis on helping clients improve their skills in being autonomous or self-directed human beings.

Lifeskills counselling is based on the notion of an underlying mainly positive view of human nature. To a large extent, mind skills and communication/action skills are learned for good or ill and all human beings possess skills of varying degrees of adequacy or inadequacy. Given sufficient learning and environmental opportunities, virtually all people will think and behave reasonably positively towards one another. However, humans also have evolutionary characteristics that can cause them to react with primitive aggression (Beck et al., 1990). Furthermore, the individual, social and cultural learning environments of virtually everyone cause them to function below, and sometimes far below, their human potential. Acquiring and maintaining a high level of mind skills and communication/action skills requires much effort and, unfortunately, some good luck in whether one meets people who are helpful rather than harmful.

Lastly, a counselling service can only truly claim a lifeskills orientation if it is staffed by counsellors who subscribe to the above assumptions. They must be prepared to see that all humans, including themselves, need to develop and maintain good mind skills and communication/action skills. They accept the idea that clients currently hold poor skills in one or more of these areas as a result both of learning and then perpetuating erroneous ways of thinking and communicating. Counsellors wanting to help such clients need to hold values that include assisting clients to embrace self-direction. Their work is based on a mainly positive view of human nature, which nonetheless acknowledges that biological, social learning and environmental circumstances contribute greatly to people maintaining poor lifeskills.

Physical premises

The physical ambience in which lifeskills counselling is conducted is important for counsellors, trainees and clients. However, often the degree of choice is limited and the most has to be made of whatever physical premises are available. Where possible, the location of counselling services should be convenient and easily accessible for staff and clients. If this is not the case, difficulty in actually finding a counselling service may reinforce the reservations that some potential clients have about coming. Some counselling services may be offered in a number of ancillary locations to ensure ease of access, though there is usually one central or principal location for the service.

The external appearance of the location influences perceptions. One issue is the extent to which it is obvious that it is a counselling service. Debatable questions here include what to call the service and how prominently the service should have notices indicating its name and purpose. Another issue is the quality of the building or buildings, which may either confer on the counselling service the appearance of a place worth going into or be off-putting in various ways.

Reception areas can be welcoming or uninviting. This is a matter of physical appearance and layout as well as of the availability and the attitude of reception staff. Counselling services should try to make their reception areas quiet and comfortable. The décor should be clean and friendly, with soft rather than harsh colours. Suitable pictures and plants can enhance a welcoming and calming overall environment. Attention should also be paid to the layout of reception areas, to ensure ease of entry and privacy for clients as they check in, and to provide a suitably congenial area for them to wait in for interviews.

Some suggestions follow for those fortunate enough to have the opportunity to design rooms for counselling interviews. Privacy and quiet are crucial considerations. The overall atmosphere should be peaceful and comfortable, but not excessively comfortable. As with the reception area, the décor should be calm and restful. The counselling area should have at least two easy chairs with arms. The chairs should not be too close together and should be at an angle, to make it easy for clients and counsellors to engage or not engage in eye contact. A coffee table can be placed between client and counsellor chairs or alternatively there can be smaller coffee tables beside the chairs. An advantage of a single coffee table in front of the chairs is that a microphone can be placed on it for recording sessions and homework instructions. A whiteboard can be fixed on the wall behind the two interview chairs: it is better to place it here than at either side so that both counsellor and client may use it. The positioning of the furniture should ensure that neither person is bothered by the possibility of sun in their eyes. A clock can be fixed to the wall or placed on a flat surface where both counsellor and client can see it easily. A box of tissues should be readily available for clients who may cry during sessions. A glass of water may also be helpful.

Assuming that this is a personal office rather than just an interview room, in another part of the room there can be a desk and desk chair. A noticeboard may be used, for useful information. There should be a lockable filing cabinet for client records and any handouts or questionnaires that counsellors use. There may also be one or more bookshelves for professional books and journals. There should be a phone that can be put on hold during interviews. If the room is being set up for recording material for supervision, a suitably placed video camera or tape recorder and machinery for controlling the recording are needed. Counsellors may experiment with the location of furniture and equipment to produce the settings that work best for them and their clients. They can also try to ensure that the room is always at a comfortable temperature and have heaters and, where necessary, air-conditioners to achieve this. A final point is that counsellors should have some way of indicating on their outer doors that they do not want to be interrupted during interview sessions. An 'engaged' sign is an obvious way of doing this.

Advertising a counselling service

There are two overlapping issues here: how does one indicate that a counselling service has a lifeskills orientation, and how does one advertise a counselling service *per se*? It is currently rare to find a service that it called a lifeskills counselling service. It is more common to find a counselling service that states in its advertising literature that an important goal is that of developing the lifeskills of its clients. It is also possible for a counselling service to have a lifeskills orientation, but to use other terms to express this. For instance, a service may advertise that it fosters the developmental needs and skills of clients, or may refer to developing the mind skills and communication skills of clients, but without calling these lifeskills. It is even possible for services to focus mainly or partly on building clients' lifeskills without using the word 'skills' at all in their literature.

Methods of advertising

One way in which potential clients can get to know about a counselling service comes from its physical location. Is it in a place where large numbers of people will see the service, or is it hidden away, or somewhere in between? Allied to its physical location is the name of the service. For instance, it may call itself a counselling service or it may not. If not, how can people know what it does? Reputation, as in the case of Relate, will be one way that people know. The material put out by the counselling service can also clarify what it does. Then there is the question of how people know whether and to what extent the service focuses on lifeskills counselling. As indicated above, the word 'lifeskills' is unlikely to be in the title.

The following are some methods of advertising a counselling service.

- *Notices.* Notices about the availability and the basic nature of a counselling service can be posted prominently in places like college campuses. However, these may be less useful where the population for a service is spread out over an area. Furthermore, notices are little more than an invitation to find out more and are inevitably limited in how much information they contain.
- *Brochures.* Counselling services can publish attractive brochures that give the location and nature of their services. Such brochures may be handed out by people making referrals and also put in suitable places for potential clients to pick up.
- *Videotapes and audio cassettes.* Potential clients may gain knowledge about a counselling service by using audiovisual material. Such material can go further than brochures in letting potential clients know by demonstration what counselling entails.
- *Internet.* Increasingly, counselling services are advertising on the Internet. The Internet can go beyond a basic description of a service to allow potential clients to look at different written material about what is on offer, and also to ask questions.
- *Talks.* Counselling service staff can give presentations at places where potential clients are likely to be. Talks can also be given to the

kinds of people who may refer clients, for example, doctors and teachers.

- *Local radio.* In some settings it may be possible to give talks and to advertise a counselling service on local radio.
- *Word of mouth.* Counselling services build up a reputation through what people say about them. Staff can tell those whom they meet about the service. Furthermore, they can educate significant people, for instance teachers in schools, and let them advertise the service and refer clients. Current and former clients may also have favourable things to say about a service that may encourage others to use it.

Activity 5.1 Advertising a counselling service

1 What do you think it is important to convey when advertising a counselling service? Are there any special considerations for the types of clients with whom you work or may work in future?
2 Assess each of the following methods for advertising a counselling service:

- notices
- brochures
- videotapes and audio cassettes
- Internet
- talks
- local radio
- word of mouth
- other methods (please specify)

3 How do you think a counselling service should make it known to its potential clientele that trainees are seeing clients in the service?

Use of trainees on placement

There are special considerations for counselling services that arrange for trainees on placement to see clients. Trainees need to have received adequate skills training prior to being allowed to see clients. In addition, they need to be integrated into a placement agency and know how it operates. For ethical reasons, clients should be informed if they are going to see a trainee and given the chance to decline to do this. Potential clients should be informed that the trainee is under supervision and, where this is the case, that a video or audio recording will be made of the session, played as part of supervision and then scrubbed so there is no permanent audiovisual record.

Clients making initial contact

The nature of clients' first contact with counselling services is extremely important. Clients may already be anxious about needing counselling, so reception staff should be friendly, polite and efficient. Clients may contact the service either in person, by phone or by email. In whatever event, counselling service staff should ensure that a convenient appointment time has been set and, preferably, that the client has a clear record of it. In counsellor training, the issue arises of how to let potential clients know that they may be seeing trainees. There are two main options. One option is to have the client see a regular counsellor for a screening interview to establish whether the client is suitable for and prepared to see a trainee. The other option is to allow trainees to see clients from the start. A compromise involves both options, but at different times. To start with, counsellors refer suitable clients to trainees. Then, when trainees have gained in experience and confidence, clients get referred to them directly. In some placement services, trainee counsellors start by spending time on the front desk arranging appointments before they are assigned clients of their own.

Counselling services may run drop-in and crisis services. Trainees should not work in such capacities until both the counselling service and they themselves think they have sufficient skills to handle the roles adequately.

Arranging suitable support for trainees

Counselling trainees seeing clients on placement require suitable support. Such support can come from numerous people and trainees should know in advance to whom they can go. This should help reduce their anxiety. The counselling course staff may not be running the placement, but can nevertheless be available to answer queries, both administrative and to do with handling clients. The counselling placement staff are under a professional obligation to see that trainees are adequately supported. For example, if a service starts by screening clients, the counsellors who refer clients to trainees must be available for discussion with them.

Trainees on placement are always under supervision by members of the counselling service staff, members of the counselling course staff, or other people brought in to fulfil this function. Trainees should be clear as to who is supervising them prior to seeing clients. (The issue of supervision is elaborated in Chapter 27.) In addition, trainees know that they can receive support in their counselling skills training classes and from peers, though they must always respect confidentiality.

Record-keeping

Bond (2000) writes that there is no consensus among counsellors in Britain regarding whether there is an obligation to keep records. The position taken here is that counselling trainees should know how to keep records before they see real clients. In the lifeskills counselling approach, the issue of keeping written records differs somewhat from other approaches: its view is that clients should keep records too, if in a rather different way to counsellors. The trainee's records help remind her or him of what went on in sessions, including specific attempts to identify and change skills. Clients are asked to keep written records where mind skills and communication/action skills have been identified for changing and to monitor their attempts to do so. For clients the main purpose shifts to providing guidelines for future desired behaviours and checks on attempts to attain them.

In addition to counsellors, trainees and clients, records may be collected to serve others' interests. Records may be required by the agency in which counselling is conducted so that those responsible can monitor the overall work of the service. Trainees' supervisors may also want records to be kept so that they can check both student and client progress and, where necessary, contribute suggestions for change. Written records may also be collected for research purposes.

Content of records

Counselling trainees need to keep the name and contact details of clients, though this information should be separate from the case notes, which may be identified by a code name. The case records will follow the format of the lifeskills counselling model as far as possible. The dates of all appointments are recorded, including missed appointments and reasons for this. Probably, the record of the first session will start with the client's reason or reasons for coming for counselling. In the facilitating client disclosure phase of stage 1, the relating stage, and the reconnaissance and detecting and deciding phases of stage 2, the understanding stage, trainees are encouraged to take notes of anything they think may be relevant to arriving at a shared analysis of the client's problem(s). Sometimes these notes may appear rough as both trainee and client seek to understand the problem(s) better. Agreement on an analysis of a problem in skills terms is likely to come around the end of the first session and may first be written on a whiteboard. Once they have agreed on the mind skills and communication/action skills on which the client needs to work, trainee and client can record this as the basis of their future work.

In the intervention phase of stage 3, the changing stage, trainees may make notes as follows. Say, at the start of the second session, the client elects to work on a mind skill. At some stage during the session both trainee and client should be able to write down – probably from the whiteboard – how the client is going to improve in that skills area. Again, both trainee and client are keeping records. Then the client can practise the skill between sessions, possibly recording progress, and report back at the start of the next session how they have progressed. The trainee will keep a record of progress of the client's out of session work in the skills area and of any further work conducted in subsequent sessions. The same procedure will be followed when working on other skills. Trainees can also record anything else that they think relevant to client progress and to understanding the problem better. If and when new problems occur, the trainee and the client can make appropriate notes, as indicated above. When the time comes for ending, both trainee and client can write down any plan agreed for consolidating skills afterwards. Once formal counselling ends, some former clients may find it useful on their own to record progress while continuing to improve their skills.

Confidentiality

In counsellor training, trainees' records of their interviews are not completely confidential in that, at the very least, the written records – and very likely videotapes or audio cassettes of sessions – will be discussed with supervisors. If others are to have access to information about a trainee's counselling interviews, it is important that the trainee has clients' permission to share it. Those who refer clients to counselling trainees may have told them already about taping and written records. Even so, it is a courtesy for trainees to let clients know about their requirement to keep written records of sessions and to videotape or audiotape them. Trainees should be prepared to explain briefly to clients why records are being collected and who will have access to them.

The purpose of making written records differs from that of making videotapes or audio cassettes. Videos or audios are made mainly to help the trainee to learn skills. They are likely to be seen by the trainee's supervisor and possibly by other trainees in a supervision group and then should be erased, with another videotape or audio cassette being recorded for the next session. Written records are likely to be more permanent. At the very least, trainees will need them for supervision. In addition, the counselling service where the trainee interviews may, as part of fulfilling their professional responsibility, want to keep copies of records for a stipulated period, which might be for as long as six years.

Trainees should be clear as to their responsibility to protect clients' privacy. They should always make sure that case notes and videotapes are securely stored in a locked drawer or file cabinet. The issue of access to records by clients is less likely to be a matter for concern for those undergoing lifeskills counselling than in some other approaches. The whole approach is based on the understanding that clients need to know what is going on if they are to identify and improve their mind skills and communication/action skills. In fact, clients are encouraged to keep records of skills they need to work on and their progress in so doing. I have never had a client who has objected to my taking notes or asked to see them.

Activity 5.2 Record-keeping

1. What information do you think it is important to collect about clients, and why?
2. Are there any special considerations about the kind of information to be collected for the kinds of clients with whom you work or may work in future?
3. Where and how should records about clients be stored?
4. Who should have access to records about clients, and why?
5. To what extent and in what ways should clients be encouraged to keep records?
6. Are there any limitations on confidentiality in the setting in which you see or will see clients? If so, how do you intend informing clients about these limitations?

listening skills 6

Chapter outcomes

By studying and doing the activities in this chapter you should:

- understand more about the counselling relationship;
- know about the importance of active listening;
- know about the importance of possessing an attitude of respect and acceptance;
- understand the client's internal frame of reference;
- know about receiving voice messages accurately;
- know about receiving body messages accurately; and
- be able to give small rewards and ask open-ended questions.

The counselling relationship

Clients come to counselling in pain, with problems, with decisions, in crisis and in need of support. They need to relate to or become connected to counsellors as a means of working on their concerns. The counselling relationship is defined here as the quality and strength of the human connection that counsellors and clients share.

Lazarus (1993) asserts that the counselling relationship should not be the same for all clients. On the assumption of 'different strokes for different folks', he argues for interpersonal and inter-session diversity. 'Relationships of choice' are as important as 'techniques of choice' for effective counselling. The counsellor should be an authentic chameleon who selects different relationship stances or styles with different clients at different stages of counselling. The counsellor–client relationship is on a continuum extending from a rather formal, businesslike investment at the one end to a close-knit, dependent bonding at the other (Lazarus, 2005a). Counsellors need to decide 'when and how to be directive, supportive, reflective, cold, warm, tepid, formal, or informal' (Lazarus, 1993: 404). Counsellors should also take clients' expectations into account. Too great a discrepancy between counsellor style and client expectation makes positive outcomes unlikely.

Listening and showing understanding skills are central to building quality relationships with clients. In reality, all counselling relationships can be seen in two ways: as the counsellor's relationship with the client and the client's relationship with the counsellor. Each of these consists of how the counsellor or client actually behaves, how the counsellor or client perceives and feels about their own behaviour, and the perceptions and feelings that the counsellor or client has about the other.

Throughout all three stages, the lifeskills counselling model heavily emphasizes the importance of the counsellor–client relationship. However, unlike in the person-centred approach where the presence of the counselling relationship is considered both necessary and sufficient for client change to occur (Rogers, 1957), here it is considered necessary, but for the most part insufficient or, in many cases, just too slow. Furthermore, Lazarus's view that skilled counsellors adapt their counselling relationships to their clients is endorsed. Within limits, counselling trainees can join with clients in modes of conversation that lessen discomfort and discrepancy: for example, not focusing extensively on feelings either with emotionally inexpressive clients or with those expecting practical solutions.

A simplified but useful distinction exists between counsellors with relationship orientations and those with task orientations. Effective counsellors focus both on relationships and on the tasks of helping clients to develop lifeskills. They go beyond establishing *talking* relationships, where the relationship overshadows the task, to forming supportive *working* relationships, where the relationship facilitates the task. Though overstating the point, an analogy may be made with school teaching, where good teacher–student relationships are insufficient substitutes for rigorous teaching and learning. In each of the lifeskills counselling model's three stages, counsellors use relationship skills both for supporting counsellor–client rapport and also for supporting the tasks of that stage. Good counselling relationships strengthen clients as they learn self-support and, in a sense, contain from the outset intimations of their own ending.

Active listening

Defining active listening

A distinction may be made between hearing and listening. *Hearing* involves the capacity to be aware of and to receive sound. Listening involves not only receiving sounds but, as much as possible, accurately understanding their meaning. It entails hearing and memorizing words, being sensitive to vocal cues, observing body language, and taking into account the personal and social context of communications. However, it is possible to listen accurately without being a rewarding listener. *Active listening,* a term popularized by Thomas Gordon in his 1970 book *Parent Effectiveness Training,* entails not only accurately understanding speakers' communications, but also showing that understanding. As such, active listening involves receiver and sender skills.

Readers may wonder why active listening is so important when there are so many opportunities for people to be listened to in everyday life. Here, it is possible to distinguish between social and counselling conversations. Social conversations are geared toward meeting the needs of both participants and have facetiously been described as 'two people, both of whom are taking turns to exercise their ego'. Often listening, let alone rewarding listening, becomes lost along the way. Counselling conversations primarily emphasize meeting clients' needs: they place a high premium on rewarding clients by listening and showing understanding to them.

Four kinds of listening take place in any one-to-one counselling conversation. Listening takes place between counsellor and client and within each of them. The quality of inner listening, or being appropriately sensitive to one's own thoughts and feelings, may be vital to the quality of outer listening: listening to others. If the counselling trainee or the client listens either poorly or too much to themselves, they also listen less well to one another. Conversely, if they listen well to one another, this may help the quality of their inner listening. The following saying of Lao-Tse beautifully illustrates the unfolding and healing effect of outer listening on inner listening.

> It is as though he listened
> and such listening as his enfolds us in a silence
> in which at last we begin to hear
> what we are meant to be.

Importance of active listening

Active listening is probably the central skill in developing and maintaining counselling relationships. For clients who come to counselling, occasionally not being listened to may have created mild psychological pain; often not being listened to, moderate pain; and mostly not being listened to, severe pain. Never being listened to is equivalent to a psychological death penalty.

Active listening by counsellors and trainees has a number of important consequences.

Establishing rapport

Trainees are more likely to develop rapport with clients if they feel that the trainees understand them. One study of helpful and non-helpful events in brief counselling identified eight kinds of event perceived as helpful by clients (Elliott, 1985). These helpful events were grouped into two super-clusters corresponding to interpersonal and task aspects of counselling. Understanding was the predominant cluster in the interpersonal grouping.

Establishing trust

Trust is a major issue throughout any relationship. Dictionary definitions of trust focus on a firm belief in the honesty, integrity and reliability of another. Many clients come to counselling perceiving that significant others in their past or present lives have been untrustworthy. Life teaches most people to be wary of being taken advantage of. In face of clients' inevitable mistrust, trainees need to establish their credentials of honesty, integrity and reliability.

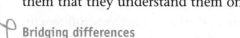

An important way of looking at trust in counselling relationships centres round clients' fears of rejection. The question becomes: 'Deep down can I trust this counsellor to accept me and not to hurt me intentionally?' Here the underlying issue is that of acceptance. A second way of looking at trust is in terms of respect. Here relevant questions are: 'Can I trust this counsellor to continue seeing me as a separate individual and not to distort their perception of me to meet her/his own needs?' and 'Can I trust this counsellor to encourage my growth as a separate person within the interdependence of our relationship?' A third way of looking at trust is in terms of the duty of care and competence: 'Can I trust this counsellor to act in my best interests?' Trust in a counselling relationship is an interactive process. The degree to which counsellor and client trust themselves, one another and the relationship influences the other person's trust. Trainees can expedite the process of establishing trust and dissolving mistrust by listening carefully to clients and showing them that they understand them on their own terms.

Bridging differences

Every counselling trainee has a set of blinkers, depending upon their circumstances. How can they know what it is like to be old, dying, female, male, gay, physically disabled, an immigrant, White, Black, Asian, Aboriginal or Maori … if the description does not fit them? However, if they counsel someone with a different set of life's circumstances, the trainee can greatly assist their understanding if they use good listening skills. By showing understanding trainees can build bridges, not walls.

Helping clients to disclose

Clients are often shy and anxious. They may be divulging highly sensitive information. Even if they are not, clients may perceive disclosure as risky. Many clients are like boxers who have learned to keep their guards up for fear of getting hit if they reveal themselves. Previously they may have received much overt and subtle rejection for disclosing. Good listening helps clients to feel accepted, safe and understood, which in turn helps them to choose to tell their stories and share their inner worlds.

Helping clients to experience feelings

Many clients have been inadequately listened to in the past. Consequently, they may have relinquished, temporarily at least, some of their capacity for emotional responsiveness (Raskin and Rogers, 2005). Active listening can help clients tune into and acknowledge the inner flow of their emotions. The message some clients may require is that it is OK to experience and express feelings. They can become stronger and more centred if they can face and learn to deal with feelings than if they either block them out or only partially acknowledge them.

Gathering information

A facetious remark about a former psychologist colleague of mine was that he had to ask everyone whether they were male or female since he was incapable of gathering information without asking questions. If trainees listen well, most clients collaborate in providing relevant information about themselves. Trainees do not have to interrogate clients. Together they can build a working model of problems and problematic skills patterns. Furthermore, at later stages of counselling, clients provide additional knowledge about how they use their skills in their daily lives. Many beginning trainees question too much and listen too little. However, some ask too few or the wrong sorts of questions.

Creating an influence base

The lifeskills counsellor is a developmental educator actively influencing clients to develop self-helping skills. Active listening is one way trainees can build their influence base so that clients are more likely to listen to them. Furthermore, showing understanding to clients from different cultural groups contributes to perceptions of counsellors as having status and credibility (Sue and Zane, 1987).

Social influence research shows that active listening contributes to clients perceiving counsellors as competent, trustworthy and attractive (Strong, 1978). Some studies indicate that successful counselling relationships start with high agreement, pass through a period of disagreement, and end with high agreement. The middle or disagreement stage results from counsellor efforts to generate change, and client resistance to such efforts (Strong et al., 1992). Building social influence early on increases clients' willingness to accommodate counselling trainees' efforts to generate change.

Helping clients to assume responsibility

Clients who are listened to accurately and supportively are more likely to assume responsibility for working on their problems and problematic skills than those who are not. Active listening may reduce defensiveness and it provides a base for offering well-timed challenges that encourage clients to assume rather than avoid responsibility. Active listening provides a climate in which clients can assume greater personal agency for constructing their actions and meanings (Strong et al., 1995).

This and the next chapter describe 10 basic skills of active listening when counselling. Some of the skills overlap. Each of them requires trainees to make choices. As practitioner-researchers, they can become aware of their choices and evaluate their consequences. The skills are as follows:

Skill 1: Possess an attitude of respect and acceptance.
Skill 2: Understand the client's internal frame of reference.
Skill 3: Receive voice messages accurately.
Skill 4: Receive body messages accurately.
Skill 5: Give small rewards and ask open-ended questions.
Skill 6: Paraphrase.
Skill 7: Reflect feelings.
Skill 8: Use mind skills.
Skill 9: Manage initial resistances.
Skill 10: Show understanding of context and difference.

Skill 1: Possess an attitude of respect and acceptance

An accepting attitude involves respecting clients as separate human beings with rights to their own thoughts and feelings. Such an attitude entails suspending judgement on clients' goodness or badness. All humans should be perceived as fallible, and possess lifeskills strengths and weaknesses that may result in good or bad consequences for themselves and others. Fromm (1956) notes that respect comes from the Latin word *respicere,* meaning to look at. Respect means the ability to look at others as they are and to prize their unique individuality. Respect also means allowing other people to grow and develop on their own terms without exploitation and control. Rogers, the founder of person-centred therapy, which heavily emphasizes counsellor acceptance, grew up afraid that if he said anything significant to his mother she would judge it negatively (Heppner et al., 1984).

This does not mean that trainees must agree with everything that clients say. However, they are secure enough in themselves to respect what clients say as their versions of reality. They do not need to use barriers and filters to protect them from listening to the full range of clients' messages. These barriers can be internal and external. Internal barriers operate on, distort and filter out certain elements of the messages that are being received. At worst, just about the whole message may be denied or blocked out. External barriers manifest themselves in subtle and not so subtle voice and body cues to others that they should edit what they say.

Barriers to an accepting attitude

Counselling trainees need to be psychologically present to clients. This entails absence of defensiveness and a willingness to allow clients' expressions and experiencing to affect them. Ideally, they should be 'all there' – with their body, thoughts, senses and emotions. Psychological accessibility entails an accepting attitude not only to clients, but to oneself. Put simply, a confident person's acceptance of self translates into acceptance of others; the reverse is also true.

What are some of the main barriers and filters that prevent trainees from receiving clients loud and clear? All of them are related to their sense of worth and to how much debilitating anxiety they possess. The stronger trainees are emotionally, the less need there is for them to use barriers and filters and the more open they are to others. The following are some of the barriers likely to influence how a person listens.

Anxiety-evoking feelings

Clients can express feelings that trainees find hard to handle: for instance apathy, depression, happiness, or sexual responses. Trainees may feel threatened by feelings directed toward them, such as hostility or liking. Alternatively, trainee anxiety may be evoked by the intensity of clients' feelings about others, for instance envy of a sibling or grief over someone's death.

> Robyn, 25, who was on a counselling course placement, listened to Anita, 32, pour out her resentment over her girlfriend Ellie's behaviour. Robyn was uncomfortable when people became angry with her outside of the counselling context. Even though none of Anita's anger was directed toward her, Robyn started feeling very anxious and wondered whether the session would get out of control.

Anxiety-evoking clients

Counselling trainees may feel threatened by certain categories of clients: for example, clients of the opposite sex, seriously disturbed clients, highly successful clients, very intelligent clients, and clients who hold strong feelings with which they disagree.

> Henry, 29, a trainee counsellor, became uncomfortable when faced with Lucy, 24, a sexually active lesbian client. His discomfort arose not from prejudice about lesbians, but because he felt out of his depth in being able to relate to her life experiences. He was aware that his anxiety about coping made it even harder to empathize with Lucy.

Anxiety-evoking situations

Anxiety and threat are present in all counselling situations. The following are some common situations where trainees may feel vulnerable: as a consequence, their own agendas may preclude their fully listening to clients:

- the first few minutes of an initial session;
- when concentrating on developing new counselling skills as well as on the needs of clients;
- when trying to agree on a shared definition of a client's problem;
- when feeling and thinking that progress is too slow;
- when a client comes late for an appointment; and
- when recording an interview for supervision.

Trigger words, phrases and attitudes

Certain trigger words and phrases raise a 'red flag' for a trainee. Each trainee has her or his own emotionally charged triggers. For example, trainees can allow themselves to be triggered by sexist comments, prejudice against gays, cross-cultural put-downs, and racist comments. Trigger phrases can also be 'You' messages from clients to trainees – for example, 'You screwed up', 'You don't understand', or 'You're not helping me enough.' Positive words and phrases can also trigger feelings that interfere with listening: for example, flattery like 'Gee, you're wonderful, Mr Murgatroyd.'

Prejudices

Counselling trainees are not immune to prejudice. For reasons connected with their upbringing, they may tune out when dealing with people who differ from them in age, sex, sexual orientation, culture, race, social class, physical disability or intelligence level, among other possible differences.

Current unfinished business

Unfinished business can interfere with trainees being open to clients. For instance, if they have just come from a heated staff meeting, they may be less ready to listen and accept their next client. When they have just rushed to get to a counselling session, they may not listen adequately until they have calmed down. Furthermore, they may be thinking about something said earlier in this or a previous session and fail to attend to the present. Not uncommonly, trainees may also have intrusive personal worries that interfere with their listening, for instance marital difficulties.

Presenting a professional façade

Genuineness is an important characteristic for counsellors (Raskin and Rogers, 2005; Rogers, 1957). A difference exists between being genuine and seeming genuine. Some trainees are too concerned with maintaining a smooth professional façade. Their concern with how clients perceive them may prevent them from perceiving their clients accurately. Such trainees are too busy listening to their own needs to accept clients fully. Maintaining a professional façade is especially difficult for trainees when clients directly challenge their professional adequacy.

Pete, 26, a counselling psychology student on placement at his university's student counselling service, worries that clients will see that he is not yet fully competent. He puts on an act, being too friendly and trying to appear too expert. He takes control rather than forming cooperative working relationships with clients.

Emotional exhaustion and burnout

Frequently, counselling trainees possess a combination of a heavy workload, personal commitments, demanding clients, and poor skills at setting limits on their involvement. Freudenberger defines burnout: 'To deplete oneself. To exhaust one's physical and mental resources. To wear oneself out by excessively striving to reach some unrealistic expectation imposed by one's self or by the values of society' (Freudenberger, 1980: 17). Emotionally exhausted trainees may be less accepting of clients than when they feel well. Their energy level and sense of personal accomplishment are low. Counselling relationships, instead of being positive challenges, can become endurance tests.

Physical barriers

Physical barriers may contribute to trainees being less accepting of clients than desirable. For example, they may be too hot or too cold, they may lack privacy, their room may be dreary, their chair may be uncomfortable, the lighting may be poor, or there may be too much noise.

Patricia, 32, is a nursing student who is required to interview patients assigned to her. There is a shortage of suitable interview rooms. On some occasions the only room available is one that has glass windows facing the corridor. On other occasions Patricia has to interview patients in open wards. Patricia feels distracted by the lack of genuine privacy for herself and her patients.

The above are just some barriers that may prevent counselling trainees from adopting an attitude of respect and acceptance. Undoubtedly, there are others and readers may wish to add to this list.

Activity 6.1 Assessing barriers to an accepting attitude

Complete this exercise on your own, with a partner or in a group.

1 Assess how much each of the following barriers either interferes or might interfere with your possessing an accepting attitude when counselling:

- anxiety-evoking feelings;
- anxiety-evoking clients;
- anxiety-evoking situations;
- trigger words, phrases and attitudes;
- prejudices;
- current unfinished business;
- presenting a professional façade;
- emotional exhaustion and burnout;
- physical barriers;
- others (please specify).

2 Summarize the main barriers to your adopting an attitude of respect and acceptance for your clients.

Skill 2: Understand the client's internal frame of reference

'Taking the client's perspective' is another way of stating the ability to understand the internal frame of reference. There is an American Indian proverb that states: 'Don't judge any person until you have walked two moons in their moccasins.' If trainees are to be perceived by clients as receiving them loud and clear, they need to develop the ability to 'walk in their moccasins', 'get inside their skins' and 'see the world through their eyes'. At the heart of active listening is a basic distinction between 'you' and 'me', between 'your view of you' and 'my view of you', and between 'your view of me' and 'my view of me'. 'Your view of you' and 'my view of me' are inside or internal perspectives, whereas 'your view of me' and 'my view of you' are outside or external perspectives.

The skill of listening to and understanding clients is based on choosing to acknowledge the separateness of 'me' and 'you' by getting inside the frame of reference of the other rather than remaining in one's own external frame of reference. If counsellors show accurate understanding of the client's perspective, they respond as if inside the client's internal frame of reference. However, if counsellors choose not to show understanding of their clients' perspectives or lack the skills to understand them, they respond from the external frame of reference. Box 6.1 provides examples of counsellor responses from external and internal frames of reference.

Box 6.1 Counsellor responses from internal and external frames of reference

External frame of reference responses

- 'Well there were other ways you could have responded to your boss.'
- 'Let me tell you about a similar experience I had to yours.'
- 'Everyone economizes on the truth sometimes.'
- 'You should show you're in control more.'
- 'You're a very angry person.'

Internal frame of reference responses

- 'You're frightened at the news that you have breast cancer.'
- 'You have very mixed feelings about staying in the relationship.'
- 'You're fed up with your mates.'
- 'You really love having him staying with you.'
- 'You're feeling scared about getting your exam results.'

Often trainees can show that they are working from within their client's internal frame of reference by starting their response with 'You'. However, as the statement 'You should show you're in control more' indicates, trainees can make responses starting with the word 'You' which are clearly coming from the external frame of reference and are manifestly directive.

Trainees should always consciously choose whether or not to respond as if inside their clients' internal frame of reference. Think of a three-link chain: client statement/counsellor response/client statement. Trainees who respond from clients' internal frames of reference allow them to choose either to continue on the same path or to change direction. However, if trainees respond from their external frames of reference, they can influence clients in such a way as to divert or block trains of thoughts, feelings and experiences that they might otherwise have chosen.

Activity 6.2 Tuning into the client's internal frame of reference

As appropriate, complete parts of this exercise on your own, with a partner or in a group.

Part A: Assess how counsellors respond

Below are some statement–response excerpts from formal and informal counselling situations. Three counsellor responses have been provided for each statement. Write 'IN' or 'EX' by each response according to whether it reflects the client's internal frame of reference or comes from the counsellor's external frame of reference. Some of the responses may seem artificial, but they have been chosen to highlight the point of the exercise. Answers are provided at the end of this chapter.

Example: Client to school counsellor

Client: I get really upset that Mum and Dad are going to part and probably get divorced.

School counsellor:

EX (a) What do you think they will do about you?
EX (b) Yes, it's very common for parents to get divorced these days.
IN (c) You feel very sad that your parents are splitting up, probably for good.

1 Client to social worker

Client: I'm worried sick that I won't have enough dough to look after the three kids properly.

Social worker:

(a) You're extremely worried about not having enough money to take care of your kids adequately.
(b) How much money do you think you will need?
(c) You will be all right so long as you do not let it get to you.

2 Client to nurse

Client: I'm delighted that I'm starting to feel well for the first time in a long time.

Nurse:

(a) It can take some time to recover from the illness you've had.
(b) The hospital does its best for people like you.
(c) You're really pleased to start feeling better at last.

3 Client to career counsellor

Client: I'm torn between wanting to help other people and making a lot of money.

Career counsellor:

(a) Well, that's a fairly common situation.
(b) You feel pulled between looking after others and getting rich.
(c) Well let's think what you might do to achieve both objectives.

Part B: Summarize another's internal frame of reference

Work with a partner.

1. Person A talks for at least two minutes about what she/he considers important in a counselling relationship (person A's internal frame of reference). Person B does not interrupt.
2. When person A finishes, person B summarizes the main points of what person A was saying. Person A does not interrupt.
3. When person B finishes summarizing, person A comments on how accurate person B was in understanding her/his internal frame of reference. Person B can respond to this feedback.
4. Then reverse roles and repeat 2, 3 and 4 above.

Skill 3: Receive voice messages accurately

As the old saying goes: 'It ain't what you say, but how you say it.' When talking, a person's overall communication consists of voice and body framing messages that in varying degrees match their verbal communication, the literal content of what they say. These framing messages are extremely important. Vocal and bodily communication can either correspond to, heighten, lessen or contradict the intention of clients' verbal communication. For instance, if a client, Maria, were to say about her boyfriend 'I'm really angry with Luke', in a monotonous voice and at the same time as looking away, one could not blame a trainee for being confused about how the client really feels.

I mentioned the following five dimensions of voice messages forming the acronym VAPER – volume, articulation, pitch, emphasis and rate – in Chapter 2 in the context of counselling trainees rather than clients. Here the position is reversed and I explore the dimensions as they apply to clients.

Volume

Clients may speak loudly, softly or somewhere in between. They may not speak at a decibel level that is comfortable and easy to hear. Furthermore, they may have the bad habit of fading, letting their voices trail away at the end of sentences. Sometimes they appear weak and unconvincing because they speak too softly. In counselling sessions, it is probably more common to find clients talking too softly rather than too loudly, though this may not represent how they behave all of the time outside the sessions.

Articulation

Articulation refers to the distinctness and clarity of speech. Clients may speak with adequate loudness, but still be difficult to understand. Such clients need to be helped to enunciate words clearly. Heavy accents can be very difficult to listen to, especially if accompanied by poor use of grammar and language. To be better understood socially, some clients may need to consider modifying strong regional or overseas accents. Those with excessively nasal, guttural or throaty voices might consider speech therapy.

Pitch

Some clients speak with voices that are pitched either too high or too low. High-pitched and shrill voices can disconcert. A harsh tone can threaten. Clients' voices may be higher pitched when they feel anxious.

Emphasis

When communicating major feelings and feeling nuances, clients may become more difficult to understand accurately if they use emphasis in the wrong places. Furthermore, some clients speak with too much emphasis and become difficult to listen to. It is perhaps more common for clients to speak flatly and with too little emphasis, which can contribute to their appearing weak or unmotivated.

Rate

Speech rate is often measured in words per minute and depends both on how quickly words are spoken and on the frequency and duration of pauses between them. Some clients who come to counselling speak very quickly because they are anxious. Their speech rate may become more normal with the passage of time. With highly anxious clients who persist in talking very swiftly it may be a good idea for trainees to speak more slowly in the hope that this will calm them down. If these clients can also speak a little more slowly it may help them to become less nervous and provide them with more time to think of what to say.

How clients use pauses and silences can enhance their capacity to be rewarding talkers. Sometimes clients start counselling by speaking very rapidly and quickly, but then of their own accord use more pauses and silences, which makes them easier to listen to. Other clients speak very little and, even if trainees use good listening skills, they may continue to do so. If clients are silent for a time it may also indicate that they require psychological space both to think things through before speaking and to get more in touch with their feelings. Some trainees find clients' silences threatening – if so, they may have to work on tendencies to interrupt too soon.

Activity 6.3 Assessing voice messages

1 Act as a counsellor with a partner who acts as a client. Assess her/his voice messages on each of the following dimensions:

- volume
- articulation
- pitch
- emphasis
- rate
- others (please specify)

2 Work with your client to identify specific poor voice message skills when she/he speaks, and set goals for change.

Skill 4: Receive body messages accurately

Clients are always sending important body messages to counselling trainees, both when they speak and when they listen. Here, if anything, the emphasis is on the former. Trainees need to become skilled at picking up and understanding what clients' are saying through their bodies, which may vary from what they are saying verbally. Many clients have grown up in circumstances where they did not feel safe revealing material directly through words. Consequently, many of their main messages may come from how they say something rather than from what they say. To some degree they are concealing material rather than deliberately lying and the messages may leak out through their bodies. Like voice message skills, body message skills were mentioned in Chapter 2, again more in relation to how counsellors communicated. The emphasis in the following discussion is on picking up clients' body messages accurately (Argyle, 1999).

Availability

Clients are at different levels of availability for counsellors and for trainees. One reason is that services may be either well or poorly advertised. Punctual clients are the ideal, but clients either miss sessions or are late for a variety of reasons. These include misunderstandings over the time of appointment, leaving insufficient time for getting there, traffic difficulties, and psychological reasons, including real ambivalence over whether or not to come at all.

Reasons for not coming may be innocent, for instance a genuine misunderstanding or a domestic emergency, but in the latter instance it is good if clients can let trainees know in advance. Other reasons for not coming may indicate that clients feel that, for some reason, they will lose more than they gain. For instance, clients may be sent against their wishes, for instance by headmasters or other authority figures. Alternatively, they may have, rightly or wrongly, heard that the counselling service has a poor reputation. Where possible, it is a professional responsibility to try and find out why clients are not coming to a service. Clients may sometimes perceive counsellors as being insufficiently available to help. Counsellors may be overworked. They may be bad at letting their availability or limits on it be known. Whatever the reason, clients may receive messages that create distance.

Facial expressions

Ekman writes: 'The face is a dual system, including expressions that are deliberately chosen and those that occur spontaneously, sometimes without the person even aware of what emerges on his own face' (1995: 123). Ideally, facial expressions represent what people really feel. But since one of the reasons that clients come to counselling is to become more in touch with their feelings, their facial expressions may only partially – sometimes scarcely at all – represent what they truly feel. Clients may choose to inhibit, conceal or falsify what they feel and think. For example, they may smile a lot when meeting trainees and it may take some of them time to get in touch with and reveal what they really feel. While clients rarely directly lie, they almost invariably economize on the truth, especially early on in the counselling process. Some clues that this is going on may come from the face and then a decision must be made on whether or not to bring this to the client's attention and, if so, when and how explicitly to do so. Culture can also influence the showing of emotions through facial expressions; for instance Japanese people are more likely than Westerners to mask any expression of negative emotions with a polite smile.

Gaze

One way in which clients may try to conceal or to control their emotions is through their level of gaze and, also, eye contact. The counselling interview is somewhat threatening for all clients and may be extremely threatening for some. I once had a client who sat at 90 degrees from me and placed a hand by his eyes, taking about nine sessions to come around to looking at me in a normal way. Though this is an extreme instance, other clients have problems both inside and outside of counselling with using an appropriate level of gaze and, hopefully, this will improve as a result of the counselling process. A main reason for clients and counsellors not sitting directly across from one another is to enable the client to control the amount of gaze and eye contact more easily. It is preferable for counsellor and client chairs to be facing each other, but at a slight angle so that vulnerable clients are not forced into what they perceive to be an intense situation too soon.

Eye contact

Eye contact is a more direct form of communication than gaze and for some clients poses extra difficulties. If their underlying self-concept is very negative they may feel safer if they strictly control the amount of eye contact that they make. They may think and feel that they are being seen through and that something negative is being viewed. Then, as they grow more comfortable with themselves and the trainee, they will make better eye contact. Many clients present no observable problems with gaze and eye contact, but this does not mean that there are not other ways in which they are blocking full communication.

Gestures

Though some clients may make gestures that are too large and sweeping, probably many more make gestures that are too small and inhibited. In social interaction, such gestures can have a negative effect on others and be viewed as a sign of uninterest. In addition, clients may make inappropriate gestures that do not really illustrate what they feel: for instance, nodding to indicate 'yes' because they do not have sufficient confidence to allow neutral or negative feelings to be known. Clients may indicate anxiety by numerous gestures and remain unaware of some of them. Such gestures include finger-drumming, hands clenched together, fiddling with pens and pencils, playing with one's hair, putting a hand over one's mouth, ear-tugging, scratching oneself and shaking one's foot or leg.

Posture

Clients may signal insufficient confidence through their posture. Ideally, both trainee and client should have relaxed and open body postures that contribute to the message that they are receptive to one another. Some clients illustrate anxiety by having a rigid or tight body posture: for instance, crossed arms may indicate that the client does not feel fully comfortable. Other clients may slouch or in other ways appear sloppy. Either sitting rigidly or slouching can give the impression that the client is not fully accessible in the counselling process. However, such postures may be the best that clients can offer at the time and may later improve if they persist with counselling.

Whether client and counselling trainee lean forwards, backwards or sideways is another aspect of body posture. If either leans too far back, the other may find this emotionally distancing. It is also possible to lean forward and become too close. However, in moments of intimate disclosure by a client, a marked forward lean by a counsellor may build rapport rather than be perceived as 'imposing' (Sharpley and Sagris, 1995). Especially at the start of the counselling process, clients may be encouraged rather than threatened by trainees with a slight forward lean.

Physical closeness

The degree of physical closeness during most counselling interviews is with client and counsellor heads about four feet apart. Few clients will want to get closer than that. Being much further away may also be unsafe in that clients may interpret this distance as indicating the counsellor's insufficient interest in them. On occasion, clients may appreciate it if trainees do get closer to them, for instance by placing their arm on the back of their chair if they are distressed. However, it is probably better if trainees can show their concern in other ways both for ethical reasons and because they may be invading clients' personal space.

Though some clients might want a personal relationship, trainees should part from clients at the end of practice sessions in a friendly, yet formal way. Occasionally, trainees may be tempted into having secret personal relationships with clients, but this is definitely unethical. Similarly, trainees should refrain both from accepting counselling course staff invitations for personal relationships, including sexual ones, and from initiating them with course staff. If trainees want a close personal relationship with staff after the course, both parties involved should follow the appropriate ethical guidelines of their professional associations as to the advisability and timing for doing this.

Clothes

Clients provide much information about themselves through their clothing. As with counselling trainees' clothes, these messages relate to social and occupational standing, sex-role identity, ethnicity, conformity to peer group norms, rebelliousness and how outgoing they are. In addition, clothes can indicate clients' moods, but trainees need to take care that they are interpreting such matters accurately. Clients can also react positively or negatively to how trainees dress. When on counselling skills placements, within limits trainees need to dress appropriately for their clienteles.

Grooming

Counselling trainees should also pay attention to clients' grooming, though care needs to be taken not to draw the wrong conclusions. For example, depending on the nature of their depression, upbringing and current circumstances, depressed clients may look as though they do not take proper care of themselves, but this is frequently not the case. As trainees get to know clients better, they gain more information about how appropriately clients are groomed and also the reasons for any marked variations from what might be expected. Trainees may need to examine the reality of their own expectations regarding clients' clothing and grooming.

The concept of rules is very important for understanding the appropriateness of body messages. Mention was made in Chapter 2 of differing physical proximity rules depending on whether a person is in a personal or counselling relationship. Relationship rules also differ across cultures: for instance, Arabs and Latin Americans stand very close by Western standards. Counselling trainees require sensitivity to the body message rules of the social and cultural contexts in which they work as well as to their own and clients' individual needs.

Trainees require flexibility in making active listening choices. As their counselling relationships develop, clients get to know whether and when their counsellors are receptive to them. For instance, clients may know from past experience that when a trainee leans back they are still attentive. Trainees should use attending body messages selectively. When appropriate, they can choose to make their body messages less responsive, for instance when they want to check their understanding of what clients say, stop them from rambling, or make their own points.

Both *within* counselling trainees' body messages and also *between* their body messages and their voice and verbal messages, consistency increases the chances of clients perceiving them as rewarding listeners. For instance, they may be smiling and at the same time tapping their feet. Their smile may indicate interest, their foot tapping impatience, and the overall message may be insincerity or, at best, confusion.

Activity 6.4 Assessing body messages

1 Act as a counsellor with a partner who acts as a client. Assess her/his body messages on each of the following dimensions:

- facial expressions
- gaze
- eye contact
- gestures
- posture
- physical closeness
- clothes
- grooming
- others (please specify)

2 Work with your client to identify specific poor body message skills when she/he speaks, and set goals for change.

Skill 5: Give small rewards and ask open-ended questions

Giving small rewards and asking open-ended questions require good voice and body messages. They make it easier for clients to talk.

Small rewards

Small rewards are brief verbal and non-verbal expressions of interest designed to encourage clients to continue speaking. The message they convey is 'I'm with you. Please go on.' Wrongly used, small rewards can encourage clients to respond to counsellor agendas rather than to their own. For instance, trainees may say 'Tell me more' whenever clients talk about topics of interest to them. Many small rewards are body rather than verbal messages: for example facial expressions, nods, and good eye contact. Box 6.2 provides examples verbal small rewards, though perhaps the most frequently used 'Uh-hmm' is more a voice than a verbal message.

Box 6.2 Examples of small rewards

Uh-hmm	Sure
Please continue	Indeed
Tell me more	And ...
Go on	So ...
I see	Really
Oh?	Right
Then ...	Yes
I hear you	You're not kidding

Another kind of small reward is to repeat the last word a client has said:

Client: I'm feeling anxious.
Counsellor: Anxious.

Open-ended questions

Counsellors and trainees may use questions in ways that either help clients to elaborate their internal frames of reference or lead them out of their viewpoints, possibly into the counsellor's own. Open-ended questions allow clients to share their internal viewpoints without curtailing their options. A good use of open-ended questions is when, in the initial session, trainees wish to assist clients to explore why they have come. In subsequent sessions too, trainees are likely to find such questions useful. Open-ended questions include: 'Tell me about it?'; 'Please elaborate?'; and, slightly less open-ended, 'How do you feel about that?'

These may be contrasted with closed questions, which curtail speakers' options: indeed they often give only two options, 'yes' or 'no'.

Open-ended question: How do you feel about your relationship?
Closed question: Is your relationship good or bad?

Open-ended questions may also be contrasted with leading questions, that put answers into clients' mouths:

Open-ended question: What do you think about her?
Leading question: She's a great person, isn't she?

Closed and leading questions may have various negative outcomes. Trainees may be perceived as controlling the conversation. They may block clients from getting in touch with and listening to themselves and responding from their internal frame of reference. They may set the stage for an interrogation. Since closed and leading questions can be disincentives to talking, they may create silences in which the stage is set for further closed questions.

Counselling trainees can sometimes use closed questions: it depends on the goals of their listening. Closed questions can be useful for collecting information. However, they should be used sparingly if trainees wish to help others share their worlds. Trainees may need to use even open-ended questions with some discretion.

Activity 6.5 Using small rewards and open-ended questions

Work with a partner.

1 Each partner spends a few minutes in inner listening to identify a concern on which she or he is willing to work in counselling. During this inner listening or focusing period, attend to emerging feelings as well as emerging thoughts.
2 As a counsellor, start interviewing your partner by using mainly small rewards and open-ended questions to help her/him to share her/his internal frame of reference about her/his concern. Allow your partner responsibility and control over what material she or he presents. Under no circumstances try to lead your partner out of her/his internal frame of reference. For the sake of focusing the activity, try to avoid giving verbal responses beyond small rewards and open-ended questions. It may help you to audio or video record the session and play it back.
3 At the end of the session discuss and evaluate what skills the counsellor used and what were the consequences for the client.
4 Reverse roles and go through steps 2 and 3.
5 Repeat this exercise to the point where you have some proficiency in basic skills of giving small rewards and using open-ended questions.

Answers to Activity 6.2

1 (a) IN; (b) EX; (c) EX.
2 (a) EX; (b) EX; (c) IN.
3 (a) EX; (b) IN; (c) EX.

7 show understanding skills

Chapter outcomes

By studying and doing the activities in this chapter you should:

- know about paraphrasing skills;
- know about reflecting feelings skills;
- know about how mind skills are important for showing understanding;
- know about managing initial resistances; and
- show understanding of context and difference.

Showing understanding

Active listening entails counsellors and trainees showing understanding by tuning in to and reflecting with their verbal, voice and body messages the crux of the meaning contained in the verbal, voice and body messages of clients. Counsellors provide the gift of their listening so that clients genuinely feel understood.

Responding as if from clients' internal viewpoints is sometimes called empathy (Raskin and Rogers, 2005). Rogers described empathy in these terms: 'To sense the client's inner world of private personal meanings as if it were your own, but without ever losing the "as if" quality, this is empathy' (Rogers, 1962: 419). Rogers emphasized the importance of counsellors 'communicating your sensings of his/her world as you look with fresh and unfrightened eyes at elements of which the individual is fearful' (1975: 4). Furthermore, clients need to perceive that counsellors empathically understand them or at the very least communicate the intent to understand (Barrett-Lennard, 1962, 1998; Rogers, 1962). Rogers preferred to think of empathy not as a skill, but as an attitude (Rogers, 1951) or as a way of being (Rogers, 1975).

Rogers's counselling goal was to help people become more in touch with their inner valuing process rather than to develop specific lifeskills. His use of empathy particularly focused on the construct of experiencing. Rogers attempted to improve the quantity and quality of his clients' inner listening to the ongoing flow of experiencing within them. In

Rogers's person-centred counselling empathic reflections are perhaps the counsellor's major tool. In lifeskills counselling, the proportion of such empathic reflections changes according to the stage of the model and to the agendas within specific sessions.

When learning any new skill, from driving a car to driving a golf ball, there is a period when the learner is likely to have to concentrate extra hard on making the correct sequence of choices that constitute the skill. Active listening is no exception. If counselling trainees work at and practise this skill, they are ultimately likely to own it as a 'natural' part of themselves. It is only natural to the extent that it feels natural.

Skill 6: Paraphrase

Along with reflecting feelings, paraphrasing is one of the component skills in how a counselling trainee can show understanding in active listening. It is important to paraphrase, because otherwise trainees would drive clients crazy. As a frustrated husband once said to his wife: 'If I had wanted someone to repeat everything I said after me, I would have married a parrot.' Another example of the importance of not mechanically parroting is the joke (certainly apocryphal) about a prominent American therapist who was counselling a suicidal client in his office near the top of a tall building.

Client: I feel terrible.
Counsellor: You feel terrible.
Client: I feel really terrible.
Counsellor: You feel really terrible.
Client: For two cents I would jump out of that window there.
Counsellor: For two cents you would jump out of that window there.
Client: Here I go.
Counsellor: There you go.
Client: [*Lands on the pavement below with a thud.*]
Counsellor: Thud!

Paraphrasing means rewording speakers' verbal utterances. However, it excludes intentionally showing understanding of their vocal and body messages. Focusing only on the verbal content of clients' messages is a first step in learning to respond to their combined vocal, body and verbal messages. When trainees paraphrase, they may sometimes use the client's words, but sparingly. However, they try to stay close to the kind of language they use. Box 7.1 provides examples of paraphrasing.

Box 7.1 Examples of paraphrasing

Client to counsellor

Client:	I'm delighted that you could see me so quickly.
Counsellor:	You're pleased that I could meet you so soon.

Partner to relationship counsellor

Partner:	I told her to go to hell.
Relationship counsellor:	You instructed her to get lost.

Client to employment counsellor

Client:	Last night I bumped into some of my old mates who wanted to complain about the old firm to me.
Employment counsellor:	Yesterday evening you saw some of your former colleagues who wished to bitch about your previous employer to you.

A good paraphrase can provide mirror comments that may be even clearer and more succinct than the original statements. If so, clients may show appreciation with comments such as 'That's right' or 'You've got me.' A simple tip for paraphrasing is to start responses with the personal pronoun 'you' to indicate that the intention is to mirror the client's internal frame of reference. Another tip for those trainees who struggle with paraphrasing is to slow their speech rate down, thus providing more time to think. Trainees need a good memory and a good command of vocabulary to paraphrase well. To gain confidence and fluency, they should practise paraphrasing both in and out of class.

Activity 7.1 Paraphrasing skills

Paraphrase the content of each of the following client statements in clear and simple language. Use 'you' or 'your' where the speaker uses 'I', 'me' or 'my'. There is no single correct answer, so, if you wish, you can give more than one answer.

Example

Client: I think that she is better than me.
Counsellor: You believe that she is superior to you.

Client statements

1 I'm really happy to have got the job done at last.
2 I hate going to work there.
3 I'd like to stop smoking so much.
4 I think she is really cute.

Suggested answers to this activity are provided at the end of the chapter.

Skill 7: Reflect feelings

Skilled counsellors are very sharp at picking up clients' feelings. Reflecting clients' feelings at the start of initial sessions shows that one is tuned into them as persons. Furthermore, reflecting feelings, rather than reflecting thoughts alone, can establish a climate for initial and subsequent sessions where clients share rather than bury feelings.

Reflecting feelings is both similar to and different from paraphrasing. Both involve mirroring, and reflecting feelings usually involves paraphrasing. However, the language of feelings is not words. Feelings are bodily sensations to which word labels can be attached: for example, clients may send voice and body messages that qualify or negate verbal messages. Rachel says 'I'm OK', yet speaks softly and has tearful eyes. A good reflection of feelings picks up these other messages as well. Reflecting feelings means responding to clients' music and not just to their words. To do this, counselling trainee responses need to incorporate appropriate vocal and body messages.

Reflecting feelings involves empathizing with a client's flow of emotions and experiencing and communicating this back. Often trainees have trouble with this. They may just talk about feelings rather than offer an expressive emotional companionship. Inadequately distinguishing between thoughts and feelings can be another problem for both clients and counsellors. For example, 'I feel that equality between the sexes is essential' describes a thought rather than a feeling. On the other hand, 'I feel angry when I see sex discrimination' labels a feeling. This distinction between thoughts and feelings is important both in reflecting feelings and also when helping clients to influence how they feel by altering how they think. Constant reflections of feelings run the risk of encouraging clients to wallow in feelings rather than to move on to how best to deal with them.

Reflecting feelings involves both receiver and sender skills.

Receiver skills

Understanding clients' face and body messages
Understanding clients' vocal messages
Understanding clients' verbal messages
Tuning into the flow of one's own emotional reactions
Taking into account the context of clients' messages
Sensing the surface and underlying meanings of clients' messages

Sender skills

Responding in ways that pick up clients' feelings words and phrases
Rewording feelings appropriately, using expressive rather than wooden language

Using vocal and body messages that neither significantly add to nor subtract from the emotions conveyed
Checking the accuracy of one's understanding

Pick up feelings words and phrases

Let's start with the obvious. A good but not infallible way to understand what clients feel is to listen to their feelings words and phrases. Feelings phrases are colloquial expressions used instead of feelings words: for example 'I've got the blues' is a feelings phrase describing the word 'depressed'. Picking up feelings words and phrases is similar to paraphrasing, but with a heightened focus on feelings rather than informational content. Sometimes counselling trainees ask, 'Well, what did you feel?' after clients have just told them. They need to discipline their listening more. On occasion feelings words are not the central message. For instance, Emma may say 'It's just great' that, after the break-up of a relationship, she is living on her own again, at the same time as her voice chokes, her face looks sad and the corners of her mouth are turned down.

Box 7.2 provides a list of feelings words. Incidentally, it is cumbersome, when reflecting feelings, always to put 'You feel' before feelings words: sometimes 'You're' is sufficient': for example, 'You're sad' instead of 'You feel sad.'

Box 7.2 Feelings words

accepted	dependent	involved	supported
adventurous	depressed	irresponsible	suspicious
affectionate	discontented	jealous	tense
aggressive	embarrassed	joyful	tired
ambitious	energetic	lonely	trusting
angry	envious	loved	unambitious
anxious	excited	loving	unappreciated
apathetic	fit	optimistic	unassertive
appreciated	free	outgoing	unattractive
assertive	friendly	pessimistic	underconfident
attractive	frightened	powerful	uneasy
bored	grieving	powerless	unfit
carefree	guilt-free	rejected	unfree
cautious	guilty	relaxed	unfriendly
cheerful	happy	resentful	unloved
competitive	humiliated	responsible	unsupported
confident	hurt	sad	unwanted

confused	indecisive	secure	uptight
contented	independent	shy	vulnerable
cooperative	inferior	stressed	wanted
daring	insecure	strong	weak
decisive	interested	superior	worried

The following are some dimensions of reflecting feelings words and phrases.

Strength of feelings

Mirror the strength of clients' feelings words in reflections. For example, Jack has just had a negative experience about which he might feel either 'devastated' (strong intensity), 'upset' (moderate intensity) or 'slightly upset' (weak intensity). Corresponding mirroring words might be either 'sent reeling' (strong intensity), or 'distressed' (moderate intensity), or 'a little distressed' (weak intensity). Trainees may err on the side of either adding or subtracting intensity.

Multiple and mixed feelings

Sometimes clients use many words to describe their feelings. The words may form a cluster around the same theme, in which case a trainee may choose only to reword the crux of the feeling. Alternatively, clients may have mixed feelings ranging from simple opposites, for instance happy/sad, to more complex combinations, for instance hurt/angry. Good reflections pick up all key elements of feelings messages. For example:

Client: I'm happy, but scared at what is involved in getting promoted.
Counselling trainee: You're glad, but frightened about the extra responsibility in the promotion.

Assist labelling of feelings

Sometimes counsellors and trainees assist clients in finding the right feelings words. Here reflecting feelings extends to helping choose feelings words that resonate for them.

Client: I don't quite know how to express my reaction to finding a job at last ... possibly pleased ... a weight off my mind ... unsure of myself ...
Counsellor: Glad, relieved, uncertain ...
Client: Relieved, that's what I really feel above all.

Pick up vocal and body messages

Much information about clients' feelings does not come from what they say, but from how they say it. Sometimes their verbal, vocal and body messages are consistent, and it is relatively easy to label feelings and their intensity accurately. However, frequently clients' messages are heavily encoded. Clients may struggle to express what they *truly* feel in face of their conditioning about what they *should* feel. As it takes time for clients to trust counsellors and counselling trainees, many emotional messages 'come out sideways' rather than loud and clear. Effective counsellors are skilled at listening with the 'third ear' to clients' vocal and body messages and to what is left unsaid or camouflaged. They realize that certain clients take time to develop skills of clearly identifying and articulating feelings. Trainees need to be sensitive to the pace at which clients can work: clients may require patience rather than pressure.

Trainees uncertain about clients' real or underlying feelings can check with them. For instance, they can make comments like 'I think I hear you saying [*state feelings tentatively*] ... Am I right?' or 'I would like to understand what you're feeling, but I'm still not altogether clear. Can you help me?' Another option is to say: 'I'm getting a mixed message from you. On the one hand you are saying you do not mind. On the other hand you seem tearful.' After a pause, they might add: 'I'm wondering if you are putting on a brave face.'

A further consideration is to understand whether and to what extent clients possess insight into their feelings. For instance, a trainee may infer that a parent is absolutely furious with a child. However, the parent may not be able to handle such an observation since it clashes with her or his self-image as a loving parent. Consequently, three feelings may need to be picked up: the parent's stated feeling of unconditional love for the child; the underlying anger with the child; and the feeling of threat were the parent's self-picture to be challenged by a reflection of how intensely angry she or he was.

Sender skills of reflecting feelings

When reflecting feelings, a trainee may wonder how best to respond to the numerous verbal, vocal and body messages that they have received. There are no simple answers. What they should try to do is to (1) decode the overall message accurately, and (2) formulate an emotionally expressive response. Here are a few guidelines.

Send back the crux of the client's message

Where possible, trainees should show that they have understood the client's main message or messages. Whatever else they do, they should try to communicate back the core feeling.

Client:	We just argue and argue and don't seem to get anywhere. I don't know what to do. It's so frustrating. I wish I knew the answer. I don't seem to be able to handle our relationship.
Counselling trainee:	You're extremely frustrated with constant unproductive arguments and not knowing how to improve matters.

When responding, state the client's main feeling first

Even though the clients may not start with their main feeling, they may feel better understood by trainees who reflect their main feeling at the front of their response than if they reflect information first.

Client:	My offer on the flat has been rejected and someone else has it. I'm so disappointed.
Counselling trainee:	You're extremely upset at not getting the flat that you wanted so badly.

In the above example, the trainee has tuned into feelings immediately. However, imagine the trainee had replied: 'You did not get the flat that you wanted so badly and are extremely upset.' The trainee has started by responding from the head to the client's head. By the time the trainee reflects the feeling of disappointment, it may be too late for the client to experience being fully emotionally understood.

Be sensitive to clients' underlying feelings and agendas

Sometimes there are no hidden agendas in what clients communicate. On other occasions, they may require help to articulate underlying feelings. However, sometimes it may be best intentionally not to respond to underlying feelings and agendas. Clients may require more space to acknowledge the feelings on their own, or they may not be ready for a deeper reflection. Furthermore, when making deeper reflections, a counsellor runs a greater risk of being wrong than when making surface reflections.

Keep your response appropriately simple

Use simple and clear language. Avoid unnecessary words and qualifications. However, be prepared to state different parts of multiple and mixed messages.

Use voice and body messages to add expressiveness to verbal message(s)

Counselling trainees are not just talking about feelings, they are reflecting feelings. For instance, if a hypothetical suicide-prone client says 'I feel terrible', they can adjust their voice and facial expression to mirror, to some extent, a sense of desperation. Consistency in verbal, voice and body messages is important. If they send mixed messages, clients may perceive them as insincere.

Check understanding

Trainees respond to client statements with different degrees of tentativeness, depending on how clearly the messages were communicated and how confident they are that they have received them accurately. All reflections should contain an element of checking whether they have accurately understood clients' internal viewpoints. Sometimes they can check by slight voice inflections. On other occasions they can check more explicitly.

Reflect feelings and reasons

A useful variation in active listening is to reflect both feelings and the reasons for them. Reflecting back reasons does not mean that a counselling trainee makes an interpretation or offers an explanation from their external viewpoint. Instead, where clients have already provided reasons for a feeling, they reflect these feelings back in a 'You feel ... because ...' statement that mirrors the internal viewpoint. Here is an example:

Tricia: Ever since he left, I'm afraid that I will find no one new for a relationship.

Counselling trainee: You're scared because you fear you won't meet another boyfriend.

Tricia: Yes. I get anxious just thinking of how difficult it is.

Here the trainee's 'You feel ... because ...' response showed more understanding of Tricia's predicament than if the response had stopped after 'You're scared'. Put another way, the 'because' part of the trainee's response identified the thinking contributing to Tricia's feeling. This type of reflection is useful not only for helping clients tell their stories, but also for assessing how clients' thinking contributes to unwanted feelings.

Activity 7.2 Reflecting feelings skills

Part A: Identify and reflect feelings words and phrases

For each of the following statements: (a) identify the words and phrases that the client has used to describe how she or he feels; and (b) reflect the client's feelings, starting your responses with either 'You feel' or 'You're'.

Example

Linda to counsellor: I'm so glad and have a weight off my shoulders now that I've passed the mid-term.

(a) Linda's feeling words and phrases: so glad, weight off my shoulders.

(b) Reflection of feeling: You feel happy and really relieved to have got through the mid-term OK.

1 *Lindsay to counsellor*: I love it when she phones me every night.

 (a) Lindsay's feelings words and phrases
 (b) Your reflection of feeling

2 *Yasmin to counsellor*: I'm really happy and pleased that Toby and I are not quarrelling so much.

 (a) Yasmin's feeling words and phrases
 (b) Your reflection of feeling

3 *Glen to social worker*: I don't want to take heroin no more and want to look after my health more.

 (a) Glen's feelings words and phrases
 (b) Your reflection of feeling

Part B: Pick up feelings from voice and body messages

1 Indicate what voice and body messages might serve as cues for you to pick up each of the following emotions:

 (a) anger
 (b) anxiety
 (c) depression

Part C: Reflect feelings and reasons

For each of the following client statements formulate a reflective response that strictly uses the 'You feel … because …' format.

Example

Tom: I've struggled so hard to get to the end of the course and now I'm afraid I'm going to fail the last semester.

Counsellor: **You feel** worried **because** after all that effort you might fall at the final hurdle.

1	*Heidi to nurse*:	I hate being teased. I just hate it. I'm really no different from the other girls and yet they seem to enjoy ganging up on me.
2	*Kathy to social worker*:	I've got this neighbour who wants her little girl to play with my son. I would like to please her, yet her girl is very naughty. I'm confused about what to do.

Suggested answers to this activity are provided at the end of the chapter.

Skill 8: Use mind skills

Many if not all counselling trainees' minds interfere with their listening. However, they can use their minds to guide them in listening well. Here it is briefly illustrated how each of the mind skills mentioned in Chapter 2 can be used either to support or to sabotage good listening skills.

Creating rules

Two major listening mistakes are being too judgemental and giving gratuitous advice. Here trainees' rules and personal agendas may intrude on their capacity to care for and nurture the growth and happiness of clients. For instance, if trainees are inwardly or outwardly critical of aspects of clients' thoughts, feelings and experiences, there is a good chance that they possess one or more unrealistic rules that 'drive' unhelpful communication. If this is the case, they can detect, challenge and restate the unrealistic rules so that they become realistic rules that enhance rather than erode their ability to listen.

Creating perceptions

Humility is always in order when contemplating how good a listener one is. Without knowing it, trainees can easily distort clients' experiences by passing them through a filter of their own experiencing and life histories. In relation to certain topics and situations anxiety may interfere with their ability to perceive clients' communications accurately. For instance, some trainees become anxious when the topic turns to sexuality or suicide. Trainees, and experienced counsellors too, can feel threatened by certain categories of client: for example, as noted previously, clients of the opposite sex, highly successful clients, very intelligent clients, and clients who hold strong views with which they disagree. When anxious, trainees' mind tricks and self-protective habits can interfere with the accuracy of their perceptions. They may become defensive when clients provide feedback that differs from their picture of themselves: for instance, suggesting that they do not always listen well.

Trainees can test the reality of their perceptions so that their own experiencing, defensiveness and agendas do not distort how they perceive clients. They can also strive to create compassionate rather than judgemental perceptions of clients and of their human frailties.

Creating self-talk

Counselling trainees can create *goal-setting self-talk* that disciplines them to focus on listening: for example 'STOP ... THINK ... I can show my respect for my client by listening well to her/him.' When they feel themselves getting emotionally aroused, for instance anxious or angry, they can use *cooling and calming self-talk* statements such as: 'Calm down ... my anxiety is a signal that I need to listen carefully.' Trainees can also create *coaching self-talk* statements for the skills of listening well: for instance, 'Let's make the effort to understand her/his perspective.' And as shown in Box 7.3, they can create *corrective self-talk* once they realize that they are prone to making mistakes that interfere with listening.

Box 7.3 Examples of corrective self-talk

For interrupting:	Remember to hear her/him out.
For being too controlling:	Counselling involves respecting clients as separate individuals and freeing them to develop their unique potentials.
For being too judgemental:	Clients are more likely to disclose if they are feeling safe.
For giving too much advice:	I am more helpful if I let clients own their problems.

Creating visual images

Counselling trainees can use visual images to enter into their clients' internal frames of reference. When clients describe past or current experiences, trainees can create imaginary pictures that may help them understand these experiences; when clients describe visual images or fantasies, they can try to picture them visually too. However, trainees should remember that their visual images can contain errors. Their imagination may be heavily coloured by their own personal experiences, developmental history and current social and cultural environment. Asking clients to describe their experiences and visual images more graphically is one skill trainees can use to guard against this potential to distort images.

Creating explanations

Counselling trainees must assume responsibility for how well they listen. Even if they consider that clients behave unreasonably in their private lives, they still need to assume responsibility for listening to their pain, so that they can help them as much as possible. Being critical/defensive, dominant/controlling, and withdrawn/submissive are three styles of interacting that may interfere with listening. If trainees possess any of these three styles, they need to assume more responsibility for disciplining their listening. If trainees are critical/defensive or dominant/controlling, their outward communication shows that they do not listen properly. The effects of being withdrawn/submissive on listening may be less obvious. If trainees allow clients to be rude and inconsiderate, their irritation with them may cause them inwardly to tune out. If they are to tune in again, they need to create explanations that allow them to be more assertive and set limits on clients' behaviour.

Creating expectations

An important skill for counselling trainees is to avoid mind reading or responding on the basis of unnecessary expectations concerning what clients think or are about to say. If trainees rush in to finish off sentences, their responses can get clients' trains of thought wrong. Even when clients correct them, trainees may still erroneously think that their version is best. One skill for creating accurate expectations about what clients may say next is to listen carefully to what has already been said. Ways of testing the reality of expectations include holding back and waiting for them to speak again, and using active listening skills so that they can disclose further. It is even possible to ask them tactfully what they are thinking.

Activity 7.3 Using mind skills

As a counselling trainee, assess your strengths and weaknesses in using each of the following mind skills early on in counselling:

- creating rules
- creating perceptions
- creating self-talk
- creating visual images
- creating explanations
- creating expectations

Summarize your ability to use mind skills early on in counselling.

Skill 9: Manage initial resistances

Resistance may be broadly defined as anything that gets in the way of counselling. Resistances can be present at any stage of counselling. Clients can both bring resistances to counselling and also have them activated during it. At best most clients are ambivalent when they come to counselling. At the same time as wanting change, many have anxiety about changing from their safe and known ways and also about participating fully in the counselling process – by, for instance, revealing personal information. Clients may resist counsellors and counselling trainees whose behaviour is too discrepant from their expectations and from what they think they need.

Reluctance on the part of potential or actual clients to enter into the counselling process is an aspect of being resistant to counselling. Some clients do not see the need for help and come to counsellors only to meet others' wishes. Children sent by teachers or parents, or substance abusers and perpetrators of domestic violence sent by the courts, may experience such reluctance.

Trainees may wrongly attribute the source of clients' resistances and, as a result, are too quick to blame them for lack of cooperation and progress. Clients' resistances may be the consequence of or exacerbated by poor counselling skills: for instance, unrewarding listening. Some counselling approaches, especially if incompetently applied, may themselves engender resistances: for example, the apparent lack of structure of person-centred counselling or the seemingly over-didactic nature of rational emotive behaviour counselling.

Counsellors and trainees may also bring resistances to their work: for example fatigue, burnout and prejudices. Yalom (1989) mentions his difficulty, when faced with a huge female client, in overcoming his resistance to fat ladies. Once I counselled a 59-year-old female client whose manipulative manner triggered anxieties in me because she reminded me of how my mother sometimes controlled how I should feel and think when an adolescent. Counsellor and client resistances may interact to impede the counselling relationship and slow down or stop progress.

Deal with initial resistances

Resistance is a normal feature of initial sessions. The following are skills for understanding and dealing with this. Since there are so many variations and reasons for resistances, it is impossible to cover all contingencies.

Use active listening skills

Beginning, and even more experienced counsellors and counselling trainees may both create and sustain clients' resistances through poor listening skills. By using good active listening skills, trainees do much to build the trust needed to lower resistances. Some clients' resistances manifest themselves in aggression. Rather than justify oneself or allow oneself to be sucked into a competitive contest, one approach to handling such aggression is to reflect it back, locating the feelings clearly in the client but indicating that they have been picked up loud and clear. Where clients provide reasons for their hostility, these can be reflected too. Just showing clients that their internal frame of reference is understood, especially if done consistently, may diminish resistance.

Join with clients

Sometimes counselling trainees can lower clients' resistances by helping them feel that they have a friend at court. For instance, trainees can initially listen and offer support to children expressing resentment about parents.

Client:	I think coming here is a waste of time. My parents keep picking on me and they are the ones who need help.
Counselling trainee:	You feel angry about coming here because your parents are the people with problems.
Client:	Yeah [*proceeds to share her/his side of the story*].

Here parental deficiencies can be focused on prior, possibly, to then focusing the client back on herself or himself. The client's need to talk about parental injustices can be used to build the counselling relationship.

Another example is that of a pupil referred to the school counsellor by a teacher. Here the counsellor responds more to voice and body than to verbal messages.

Pupil:	[*looks down and sighs*]
School counsellor:	I sense that you are uncomfortable about being here ... [*If no response after a pause*]: Would you care to tell me how you view the situation? I'd really like to understand your viewpoint.

Give permission to discuss reluctance and fears

If trainees receive overt or subtle messages from clients that they have reservations about being in counselling, they can bring the agenda out into the open and give clients permission to elaborate. In the following example, a parole officer responds to a juvenile delinquent's seeming reluctance to disclose anything significant.

> *Parole officer*: I detect an unwillingness to open up to me because I'm your parole officer. If I'm right, I'm wondering – what specifically worries you about that?

Counselling trainees may also give permission for differences in counsellor–client characteristics to be discussed – for instance culture and race – that may have created reluctance to participate in counselling.

Invite cooperation

The cooperative nature of the relationship in lifeskills counselling both prevents and overcomes many client resistances. Initial statements by counselling trainees aim to create the idea of a partnership, a shared endeavour in which clients and counsellors can together perform the detective work of finding out how clients can better attain goals.

Enlist client self-interest

Clients can be helped to identify reasons for participating in counselling. For instance, children who perceive their parents as picking on them and as the ones with problems can be helped to see that they themselves might be happier if they had better skills to cope with their parents. Questions that challenge clients with the adequacy of their own behaviour may enlist self-interest. Such questions include: 'Where is your current behaviour getting you?' and 'How is that behaviour helping you?' (Glasser, 1984; Glasser and Wubbolding, 1995). Questions that encourage clients to think about goals are also useful: for example, 'What are your goals in the situation?' and 'Wouldn't you like to be more in control of your life?'

Reward silent clients for talking

Some clients find it difficult to talk, whether in or out of counselling. Others may find it particularly difficult to talk to counsellors and counselling trainees. Without coming on too strong, with such clients trainees can respond more frequently and more obviously, for example, using more small rewards when clients talk. In addition, they can offer encouragement by reflecting and making the most of what clients say. They can also reflect the difficulty certain clients have in talking, even though they may not have verbalized this themselves.

The above are just some ways of working with resistance and reluctance. Trainees need to be sensitive to the pace at which different clients work.

Clients who feel pressured may become even more resistant and, if attacked prematurely and clumsily, may reinforce their defences. When dealing with client resistance, trainees require sensitivity, realism, flexibility and, often, a great deal of tact.

Activity 7.4 Managing resistances skills

Part A: Identifying and responding to resistances

1 For a counselling setting in which you work, or might work, list the main ways clients might show resistances in initial counselling sessions.
2 Formulate the following kinds of responses:

   (a) joining response
   (b) permission to discuss reluctance and fears response
   (c) enlisting client self-interest response

Part B: Practise with a partner

Conduct mini interviews in which the partner acting as client engages in resistant behaviour at or near the start of counselling and the counsellor uses active listening plus one or more of the following managing resistances skills:

- joining with clients
- giving permission to discuss reluctance and fears
- inviting collaboration
- enlisting client self-interest, and
- rewarding silent clients for talking

At the end of each interview have a feedback and discussion session prior to reversing roles. If helpful, record and play back your mini interviews.

Skill 10: Show understanding of context and difference

Understand clients in context

Counsellors and trainees need to understand the contexts of clients and their problems. Issues of context and of clients' differences from counsellors pervade counselling. Clients with problems do not exist in a vacuum. Rather, they exist in networks of contextual variables whose relevance differs in each instance. Figure 7.1 shows just some possible contexts. These are also relevant to negotiating areas of difference between counselling trainees and clients.

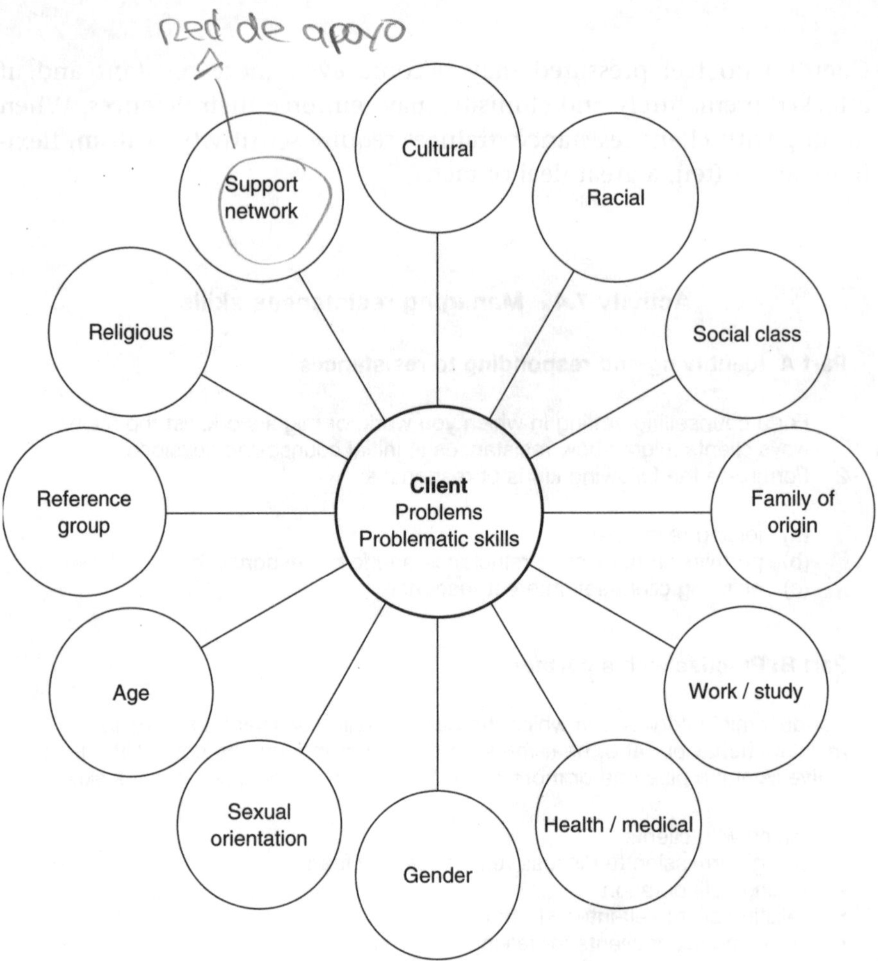

Figure 7.1 *Areas for understanding context and difference*

Cultural context

The values and communication patterns of clients' cultures. This includes the degree of exposure of clients to mainstream cultures, and their wishes for assimilation. Cultural context also includes culture shock, alienation, mistrust and loneliness. Cross-cultural issues can be relevant to both native-born and migrant clients. Both types of client can have issues of internalized culture, which Ho defines 'as the cultural influences operating within the individual that shape (not determine) personality formation and various aspects of psychological functioning' (1995: 5). For example, native-born children of migrants to Australia and Britain frequently feel torn between two cultures. Clients differ in cultural autonomy and in their ability to choose those aspects of different cultures that work for them rather than being entrapped by mainstream culture.

Racial context

The extent of clients' racial identity and pride. An important aspect of racial context is exposure to racial discrimination, and skill in handling it. Racial context also includes values, communication patterns and family structures that differ from the culture of the racial majority.

Social class context

Rules for behaviour differ widely among social classes. Trainees need to understand many client behaviours – for instance manners, dress and language – in the context of their social classes.

Family of origin context

Here family of origin refers to parents and step-parents. The family of origin context may be direct or indirect. Take the example of Jock and Sally, a couple in their twenties who have a troubled marriage. Up to four natural parents, and possibly some step-parents too, may directly tell them how to behave. They may also receive advice from other relatives. In addition, families of origin indirectly influence Jock's and Sally's relationship through parental 'voices in the head', many of which go unrecognized. In multicultural societies, such as Australia, cultural and family of origin contexts intermingle. In extreme cases it could be that all four of a couple's natural parents are culturally different.

Work/study context

The work/study context can be relevant both to work-related problems and non-work problems. For instance, workers whose companies are being rationalized after takeovers may experience additional work stress and psychological bullying (Rennie-Peyton, 1995). This may manifest itself in increased irritability at home, creating problems there too.

Health/medical context

Clients' states of physical health can contribute to psychological problems. Glandular problems, for example, often cause apathy. Clients may behave differently when on medication. Frequently, trainees need to explore the past and current medical contexts of clients' problems. Often opinions from medical practitioners are essential. Clients' prior experiences of seeking and receiving psychiatric and psychological help can also merit exploration.

Gender context

Feminist counsellors and gender-aware counsellors consider that most, if not all, problems need be understood within gender perspectives.

Counselling trainees require sensitivity to differences in biological functioning and experiencing, for instance in regard to menstruation and the menopause. However, the main area of gender sensitivity relates to learned sex-role behaviour and expectations, more particularly perhaps in relationships and career choice. Gender-aware counsellors emphasize the need to understand the historical, social and political contexts of gender learning and discrimination.

Sexual orientation context

Homosexual clients may or may not live within the context of the rules and values of the gay and lesbian communities. The attitude of mainstream or straight culture to homosexual or bisexual orientation provides a further context for understanding certain clients' problems. Changing attitudes to homosexuality within the helping professions, whereby the stigma of mental illness is no longer attached to it, provide still another context.

Age context

The physical process of ageing may contribute to some clients' problems. Others may face deprivation – for instance of companionship and employment – on account of age. The respect accorded to age differs greatly across cultures. Ageism (discrimination on the basis of age) may be more a feature of Western than of Asian cultures.

Reference group context

Humans are social animals. Valuable understanding of clients' behaviours may be gained by placing them in the context of reference group norms. For example, a different understanding of a problem may stem from a trainee discovering that a teenager stole a car in response to a delinquent peer group dare rather than on his own.

Religious context

Clients' religious faith can be a source of strength and, when it occurs, sharing the same religious beliefs and ethics may strengthen the counselling relationship. However, religious faith, albeit sometimes misunderstood, can also be a source of self-oppression. In addition, some poor skills may be sustained on religious grounds: for instance, confusing lack of assertion with humility. Since religion forms such a central part of many clients' lives, trainees need to be sensitive to the religious context and its influence. Some trainees may well require help to become aware of their limitations in understanding religiously motivated people.

Support network context

A valuable insight for understanding clients and their problems may be gained by exploring their support networks. When people seek help from strangers it is often a sign that their own support networks are inadequate. Such networks may consist of spouse, family, friends, work colleagues, church ministers and helping professionals, to mention a few. How isolated are clients? Who is available to offer support and how useful is or might their support be? What are the clients' skills of accessing and using a support network?

Possess understanding context and difference skills

Clients vary in the number of contextual considerations relevant to identifying and clarifying their problems. Counsellors also vary in the range of clients they see. Counselling trainees may need a range of understanding context and difference skills, some of which are presented below.

Develop a knowledge base

If trainees work with specific groups, for instance migrants from a certain country or gay and lesbian clients, they should be familiar with the assumptions, values and shared experiences of these groups. In addition, they should understand what are the major counselling problems for any minority group with whom they work. They should also know about the ways in which stereotyping and feelings of powerlessness may leave major scars. If they lack such knowledge, they can find it out. Even trainees who have a good understanding of specific cultures and minority groups always need to update their knowledge. For example, those working with homosexual groups require the most up-to-date information about legislation concerning homosexual behaviour and about the transmission and treatment of AIDS.

Trainees should be conscious of the assumptions underlying the sources from which they gain information. For instance, information and investigations relating to minority cultural groups may primarily reflect the perspective of members from the majority culture. The same may hold true for at least some of the literature in other areas. Trainees can gain knowledge by speaking to leaders and members of the minority cultures or groups that they wish to target. Here, the risk is of course that the information they gain may overly reflect the perspective of the minority culture. However, knowing what a predominant minority group perspective is, including its main variations, is in itself valuable in understanding clients who come from that group.

Demonstrate contextual empathy

Counselling trainees can show contextual empathy with their voice, body, verbal and action messages. Take demonstrating cultural empathy as an example. British people tend to speak more softly than many Australians. Japanese do not use eye contact so much as people from Western cultures (Pease, 1981). In the Arctic, 'it may be best to sit side by side rather than opposing with a forward trunk lean' (Ivey, 1987: 169). Trainees dealing with people from different cultures need the ability to send and receive both verbal and non-verbal messages accurately and appropriately. They should not assume that good intentions are sufficient.

When responding to verbal messages, trainees need to be sensitive to topics that may have particular meaning to people from different cultures. For instance, a desire for harmonious family relationships may send a much stronger cultural message when expressed by Asians than Anglo-Saxons. Sometimes a high level of empathy can only be offered by a counsellor speaking the client's primary language. If necessary, trainees can seek the services of translators with cultural knowledge or refer to bilingual counsellors, if appropriate people are available. Often cross-cultural sensitivity is far more important than the cultural matching of clients and counsellors. On occasions, migrant clients may prefer counselling trainees from the majority culture since they can assist their integration into it.

Another important skill is that of assessing whether these clients' 'problems' stem from either others' personal biases or from discriminatory bias in institutional structures. If so, trainees can assist clients not to personalize problems inappropriately and then blame themselves. They may also consider using institutional intervention skills on behalf of clients.

A related skill is the ability to assess when clients are using the context as a way of avoiding critically looking at their own behaviour. For instance migrants who make little or no attempt to understand the language of their host country contribute to their feelings of cultural alienation. In showing understanding a delicate balance may need to be struck between acknowledging clients' internal frames of reference, yet not colluding in the erroneous efforts of clients to characterize themselves as simply victims of oppressive majority cultures. Even when majority cultures are oppressive, trainees can empower clients with skills to manage their lives better in them. Trainees can also teach clients skills to counteract institutional oppression.

Each client has a unique life history and way of interpreting the cultural and minority group influences that have affected her or him. Trainees should be careful to avoid pigeonholing clients into their versions of cultural and minority group contexts rather than understanding them as individuals.

Give permission to discuss counsellor–client differences

Often counselling trainees and clients come from different contexts. Trainees may quickly become aware that they differ in significant ways from clients. One possibility is to acknowledge the difference – for instance racial or cultural – and ask what clients think and feel about this. Being direct may provide clients with opportunities to air and work through mistrust. A risk is that such questions may reflect trainees' rather than clients' concerns, and unnecessarily side-track clients. Possibly a more neutral way to unearth clients' concerns about obvious differences is to say: 'Are there any questions you would like to ask me?'

Give permission to discuss problems in terms of their broader contexts

Even without counsellor–client matching, trainees can show sensitivity to contextual issues in clients' problems. One way to do this is to acknowledge a possible deficiency in understanding the context of clients' problems and ask them to fill in gaps (Poon et al., 1993). The following is a simplified illustration.

Asian student: My father wants me to go into the family building business and I feel under a lot of pressure to continue on my building course to please him.

Counsellor: It sounds as though you have mixed feelings. You have reservations about continuing your building course, yet don't want to go against your father's wishes. Cultural considerations are often important in understanding such problems and if you feel they are relevant to your case, please feel free to share them.

Activity 7.5 Understanding context and difference skills

Part A: Analyse a counselling setting

Analyse the importance of the following considerations in relation to the client population of a counselling setting in which either you work or might like to work:

- culture
- race
- social class
- family of origin
- work/study
- health/medical
- gender
- sexual orientation
- reference group

- religion
- support network
- other important contexts (please specify)

You may carry out the above analysis for the contexts of individual clients' problems. In addition, you may use the categories to identify counsellor–client differences and assess their implications for counselling.

Part B: Use understanding context and difference skills

Try to find partners who differ from you on one or more significant context variables. Conduct at least one mini session with each partner in which the counsellor uses one or more of the following skills:

- demonstrate contextual empathy
- give permission to discuss counsellor–client differences
- give permission to discuss problems in terms of their broader contexts; and
- focus questions on broader contexts.

Have a feedback and discussion session after each mini session, then reverse roles. Use audio or video feedback if helpful.

Concluding comment

Active listening is the fundamental skill in developing supportive counselling relationships. Without getting inside clients' internal frames of reference and showing that counsellors and trainees understand and care about what clients communicate, they severely, if not fatally, limit their capacity to help. Furthermore, they may just add to clients' pain and distress by sending negative messages. In lifeskills counselling, active listening is central to assisting clients in managing problems and overcoming problematic skills patterns. Trainees need to work and practise to develop fluency as skilled counsellors. Even experienced counsellors should pay close attention to whether they maintain high listening standards at all times or let bad habits interfere. In most instances, active listening needs be accompanied by other skills for managing problems and developing lifeskills.

Answers to activities

Activity 7.1
Paraphrases other than those suggested may be appropriate as well.
'You are very glad to have finished the task finally.'
'You intensely dislike your job at that place.'
'You want to give up cigarettes very badly.'
'You believe she is very attractive.'

Activity 7.2

Part A

1 Lindsay's feelings words and phrases: love it
Reflection of feeling: You feel great when she calls you each evening.
2 Yasmin's feelings words and phrases: really happy and pleased
Reflection of feeling: You're delighted that you and Toby are not arguing so much.
3 Glen's feelings words and phrases: don't want to, want to
Reflection of feeling: You feel that you wish to stop your heroin habit and take better care of yourself.

Part B

Anger

Illustrative voice messages: loud volume – even shouting and screaming, harsh pitch, fast speech rate.

Illustrative body messages: clenched teeth, raised posture, glaring eyes, clenched fists, finger pointing, chopping arm and hand gesture.

Anxiety

Illustrative voice messages: quiet and timid volume, either quickened or faltering speech rate, sometimes poor articulation – mumbling or lack of emphasis.

Illustrative body messages: poor gaze and eye contact, strained facial expression, tense body posture, drumming fingers, biting fingernails, tugging hair, bouncing leg.

Depression

Illustrative voice messages: sighing, soft voice, lack of emphasis, slow speech rate.

Illustrative body messages: averted gaze, poor eye contact, tearfulness, corners of mouth turned down, slouched posture, holding head in hands.

Part C

1 **You feel** you loathe being played about with and picked on **because** you see yourself as the same as your peers.
2 **You feel** torn both ways about your son playing with your neighbour's little girl **because** you want to get on with her, yet fear that her daughter may be a bad influence.

start the counselling and helping process

8

Chapter outcomes

By studying and doing the activities in this chapter you should:

- know about some purposes of initial sessions;
- have basic skills at meeting, greeting and seating clients;
- be able to make opening statements;
- possess some introductory structuring skills;
- possess basic summarizing skills;
- be able to help clients to talk about why they have come for counselling;
- understand some issues to do with making contracts;
- know about making referrals; and
- know about crisis counselling.

Goals for the initial counselling session

Prior to reviewing specific skills, five goals of the first two stages of the lifeskills counselling model are outlined. Where clients' problems have a limited focus, these goals can be attained in the initial session. More than one session may be required where clients' problems are complex or there are other factors – for example, ventilating strong feelings or verbosity – that slow the process down. These goals apply to clients as well as to counsellors and counselling trainees.

Develop a relationship

From the beginning of counselling, trainees convey support and understanding as a base for developing clients' skills. In lifeskills counselling the relationship is a vehicle for assisting clients to work on problems and problematic skills. Thus, relationships in lifeskills counselling usually have both talking and working goals.

Develop a working model

Clients tend to be stuck at their present levels of understanding problems. Trainees and clients can collaborate to develop working models. A working model consists of a set of hypotheses about how clients function in problem areas and is a statement of how they feel, think and act.

Many advantages stem from this detective work of developing working models. First, clients can provide valuable insights if allowed to do much of the work themselves; their contributions are greater when they are treated as active partners. Second, clients as well as trainees are hypothesis makers and testers. Collaboration improves both parties' skills as practitioner-researchers. Third, clients are more likely to own responsibility for possessing and altering poor skills when they have played some part in discovering them. Fourth, collaborating can develop the counselling relationship more than active listening alone. Clients may perceive trainees as more empathic when they are active.

Develop a shared analysis of problems in skills terms

Counselling trainees assist clients to identify not only problems, but also the component parts of problems. However, it is insufficient to leave clients stranded at the identification stage. Trainees need to help clients to restate their problems in skills terms so that they then have 'handles' for working on them. Here the distinction between *descriptive* summaries and *skills* definitions of problems becomes important. Descriptive summaries can certainly clarify problems, but do not move much beyond clients' existing concepts and internal frames of reference. Skills analyses identify the specific mind skills and communication/action skills weaknesses which perpetuate problems. Where possible, trainees should reach agreement with clients on how to restate their problems in skills terms.

Develop working goals and interventions

By the end of the initial session, or if necessary initial sessions, trainees and clients should agree on preliminary statements of working goals in skills terms to guide future work. All the better if trainees can indicate how the goals might be attained. As part of this process, they may discuss the appropriateness of different interventions. Bordin (1979) has suggested that there are three main elements that determine the quality and strength of the counsellor–client working alliance. In addition to the development of a personal bond (relationship), counsellors and clients require agreement on treatment goals (goals) and on the tasks to achieve these goals (tasks). Those who achieve each of these three elements in the initial session or sessions have a strong foundation for continuing to develop the working relationship. Sometimes trainees can start implementing interventions during as well as at the end of initial sessions.

Develop a framework for future work

Counselling trainee and client need to decide on practical considerations: for example, when and where to meet and the matter of fees.

Starting initial sessions

Meeting, greeting and seating

The initial session starts at the moment of first contact with clients. Skilled counsellors and trainees possess good meeting, greeting and seating skills. Box 8.1 illustrates the difference between good and poor skills.

Box 8.1 Meeting, greeting and seating skills

Imagine two counselling trainees, each of whom is using an office near the waiting area, meeting, greeting and seating a client for the first time.

Poor skills
Counselling trainee A, who has just had an emotionally draining session with a client, decides to see the next client without any break. Still feeling distracted by unfinished business from the last client, she/he opens her/his office door, peers out, takes a few steps in the direction of the waiting area and calls the next client's surname correctly but without any warmth. When the client looks up, the trainee offers no further introduction and in a neutral voice says: 'Come this way please.' Trainee A then goes into the office first and, when the client enters, shuts the door, points a finger in the direction of a chair and says 'That's for you.'

Good skills
Counselling trainee B takes a moment to calm down after an emotionally draining session with the previous client. Then she/he calmly comes out of the office, goes over to the waiting area, smiles and calls out either the client's first name and surname or the client's first name alone, depending on the nature of the setting. The client gets up and the trainee introduces herself/himself along the lines of 'Hello, I'm ——. Please come this way' and then escorts the client to the office, smiles again as the client enters and then, with an open palm gesture, indicates where the client should sit and says 'Please sit down.'

Many trainees require practice at becoming comfortable people for clients to meet from the moment of first contact. An issue that some trainees raise is whether or not to engage in small talk when first meeting clients. This is partly a matter of individual style. As long as the small talk is minimal and does not give the impression of a social relationship, it may humanize the meeting and greeting process. However, it is wise to be sensitive to clients who are nervous about their conversational ability, to those who want to get straight into counselling, and to clients in crisis. Trainees can convey many of the main messages of warmth, welcome and interest through good bodily communication without the need for inappropriate small talk.

Opening statements

Opening statements can have various functions: greeting the client again, indicating the length of the counselling session, checking 'where the client is at', and, where necessary, obtaining permission to record the session. Counselling trainees need to convey that they are not all-knowing. Opening statements, openers or permissions to talk, are brief remarks indicating that they are prepared to listen and be informed. Trainees start initial sessions with statements that build rapport and encourage clients to say why they have come. Trainees can leave until later explanations of how they work. Opening statements are 'door openers' that give clients the message 'I'm interested and prepared to listen. Please share with me your internal frame of reference.'

The common opening statement 'Please tell me how I can be of help' and similar remarks are probably best avoided. Such statements can get initial sessions off to an unfortunate start by implying that clients are dependent on counsellors or trainees rather than on their capacity to help themselves.

Trainees should remember that when making opening statements, their vocal and bodily communication is very important in indicating that they are comfortable and trustworthy persons with whom to talk. They should speak clearly and relatively slowly, be comfortably seated and look at the client. They should avoid crossing their knees or arms. However, they can still sit with an open posture if they are crossing their ankles.

Good vocal and bodily communication can also make it easier to record sessions. Trainees who ask permission in a nervous or hesitant way are more likely to trigger doubts and resistance in clients than students who ask calmly and confidently. Box 8.2 provides examples of opening remarks that might be used for initial lifeskills counselling sessions.

Box 8.2 Examples of opening statements

When meeting the client outside the office
'Hello [*state client's name*], I'm [*state your name*]. Please come in.'

Acknowledging time boundaries
When the client is seated, a counselling trainee can first indicate the time boundaries of the session by saying something like 'We have about 45 minutes together', and then give permission to talk.

Permissions to talk
'Please tell me why you've come.'
'Please tell me why you're here.'
'Please tell me what's concerning you.'
'Please tell me what's the problem.'
'Please put me in the picture.'

Permission to talk acknowledging a referral
'You've been referred by ——. Now how do you see your situation?'

Permission to talk responding to a client's bodily communication
'You seem upset. Would you care to say what's bothering you?'
'You seem very nervous.'

Permission to record a session
Before giving a 'permission to talk' statement, a counselling trainee may need to get permission to record the session:
'Would you mind if I videotaped this session for supervision purposes? Only my lecturer' [*if relevant add 'and counselling skills training group'*] will see the tape, which will be scrubbed clean once it has been reviewed. If you wish we can turn the recorder off at any time.'

The opening remark 'You seem very nervous' gives clients the opportunity to talk either about a problem they bring to counselling or about how they feel here-and-now in the interview. Trainees can sometimes give permission to talk by body messages alone: for instance a look, possibly accompanied by an arm gesture. On occasion they may sense that clients want to talk but have difficulty doing so. In such instances, if they follow up their opening remark with another, this may make it easier for clients to talk. Examples of 'lubricating' comments include:

'It's pretty hard to get started.'
'Take your time.'
'When you're ready.'

Some counselling trainees have contact with clients outside formal interviews: for instance: correctional officers in facilities for delinquents, residential staff in half-way houses for former drug addicts, or nurses in hospitals. Here they may use permissions to talk when they sense that someone has a personal agenda that bothers them, but requires that extra bit of encouragement to share it. Opening statements for use in informal counselling include:

'Is there something on your mind?'
'You seem tense today.'
'I'm available if you want to talk.'

Sometimes trainees may need to complete organizational requirements for gathering basic information before giving clients permission to talk. However, they require flexibility: for instance, clients in crisis require psychological comfort before bureaucratic form filling, which can come later. On occasion, limitations of confidentiality surrounding a session may need to be explained: for example the need to report to a third party, or any legal limitations. Where necessary, trainees who take notes may offer brief initial explanations for so doing and even ask clients' permission.

Activity 8.1 Starting counselling sessions

If appropriate, readers who work in informal settings can adapt this activity to suit their circumstances. In addition, those training to use counselling skills for roles other than that of counsellor can adapt the activity for maximum relevance.

Part A: Meeting, greeting and seating

Role-play with a partner meeting a client in a waiting area, showing them to your office, and getting them seated – see Box 8.1 for suggestions. Then hold a feedback and discussion session and, if necessary, do more role-plays until you feel confident about your performance.
Afterwards, reverse roles.

Part B: Making an opening statement

Role-play with a partner making an opening statement – see Box 8.2 for suggestions. Then hold a feedback and discussion session and, if necessary, do more role-plays until you feel confident about your performance.
Afterwards, reverse roles.

Part C: Combining meeting, greeting and seating and making an opening statement

Role-play with a partner meeting a client in a waiting area, showing them to your office, getting them seated and making an opening statement. Then hold a feedback and discussion session and, if necessary, do more role-plays until you feel confident about your performance.
Afterwards, reverse roles.

Structuring skills

Objectives of structuring

Clients come to counselling in various states of knowing what to expect. Even those who think they know, may be misinformed. 'Structuring' is a term used to describe how counsellors and trainees let clients know their respective roles at different stages of counselling. Cormier and Nurius (2002) observe that structuring refers to an interactional process between counsellors and clients in which they arrive at similar perceptions of the role of the counsellor, an understanding of what occurs in counselling, and an agreement on which outcome goals will be achieved. Structuring occurs throughout counselling and even prior to counselling: for example through the publicity, image and reputation of counsellors and counselling agencies. Here the focus is on structuring skills in the early part of counselling, which may occupy only the first 10 to 15 minutes of initial sessions.

Effective structuring leads to positive outcomes as well as preventing or minimizing the chances of negative outcomes. The functions of structuring in initial sessions include: reducing anxiety by clarifying roles, explaining the purpose of the initial session, establishing the expectancy that clients will work on rather than just talk about problems, providing an introductory rationale for working within the lifeskills counselling model, establishing the possibility of change, and, if necessary, communicating limitations concerning the counselling relationship such as any restrictions on confidentiality.

When structuring in initial sessions, counselling trainees are, in fact, beginning the process of assisting clients to assume responsibility for developing their skills. Trainees can establish cooperative alliances with clients as partners in developing their skills rather than doing things either to or for them. In the medical model of counselling, physicians might think: 'What can I do to cure my patients?' In the lifeskills counselling model, counsellors think: 'How can I best cooperate with clients to develop their self-helping skills?'

Too much and too little structure

Counsellors and trainees can provide both too much and also too little structure. If they provide too much structuring, clients may feel stifled by their agendas and reluctant or unable to reveal their own. Trainees may establish a 'teacher knows best' emotional climate that is conducive to dependency and resistance. Clients may perceive trainees as too set on fitting them into their way of working whether it suits them or not. Furthermore, if trainees talk too much at the beginning of sessions, not only do they make it difficult for clients to talk, but they may structure the counselling process in too intellectual a way. Too little structuring also has dangers. Clients may feel anxious and confused. Trainees too may be anxious and confused. In addition, clients may perceive that trainees have nothing of value to offer.

Counselling trainees' voice and body messages may enhance or impede structuring. Again, negative outcomes may arise if trainees come on either too strong or too weak. For instance, clients may feel overwhelmed and put off by trainees who structure in loud voices and gesticulate too much. On the other hand, trainees who structure in diffident voices, with minimal use of gesture and eye contact, may convey insufficient commitment.

Some structuring skills

A choice that counselling trainees face is how much to structure at the start of initial sessions. Lifeskills counselling always starts with checking out 'where the client is at'. It is probably best to do initial structuring in two statements, an opening statement and a follow-up statement. If trainees offer the whole explanation at once, they may fail to respond to clients who want emotional release or are desperate to share information.

In two-part structuring, the opening statement provides the first occasion for structuring. Here trainees can establish time boundaries and give clients permission to talk. After trainees have used their active listening skills to enable clients to say why they have come, they may summarize the main points for clients and check the accuracy of their summaries. Then trainees can briefly and simply explain the remainder of the helping process to clients. Box 8.3 presents two possible second structuring statements providing a framework for the lifeskills counselling model presented in Chapter 4. The first statement applies where the client clearly has only one main problem, and the second statement where the client has presented with more than one problem. If a specific situation has not already emerged, then a trainee's follow-up statement may request the client to identify a situation within a main problem area for their work together.

Box 8.3 Examples of structuring statements

Opening or first structuring statement
'We have about 45 minutes together. Please tell me why you've come.'

Possible second structuring statements
Single problem
'You've given me some idea why you've come. Now what I'd like to do is to ask some more questions to help us understand more fully your problem [*specify*]. Then depending on what we find, I will review with you some skills to help you cope better. Once we agree on what skills might be useful, then we can look at ways to develop them. Does this way of proceeding sound all right?'

More than one problem
After summarizing the different problem areas, the counselling trainee says: 'Which of these would you like to focus on? [*The client states her or his choice.*] Good. Now I wonder if we can identify a particular situation within this problem that it is important for you to manage better. Then we can explore this situation more fully and perhaps come up with some useful skills for dealing with it. Is that all right with you?'

Structuring can strengthen collaborative working relationships by establishing agendas or goals for the counselling process as well as obtaining agreement on how to proceed. Trainees may need to help clients choose a particular situation to work on that is important for them. Trainees may also need to respond to questions. However, they should not allow themselves to be lured into an intellectual discussion of the counselling process. If they make structuring statements in a comfortable and confident way, most clients will be happy to work within the suggested framework.

How counselling trainees send voice and body messages matters. Their voice messages should indicate their commitment to what they do. Good voice message skills include easy audibility, comfortable speech rate, firm voice, clear articulation, and appropriate variations in emphasis. Trainees' body messages should support their verbal and voice messages: for example by appropriate gaze, eye contact and use of gestures. A theme throughout this book is the need for counsellors and trainees to pay great attention to voice and body messages. Structuring is a clear instance where ineffective voice and body messages can countermand verbal messages.

Basic summarizing skills

Summaries are brief statements of longer excerpts from counselling sessions. Summaries can pull together, clarify and reflect back different parts of a series of client statements either during a discussion unit, at the end of a discussion unit or at the beginning and end of counselling sessions. Clients also use summaries: sometimes of their own accord and sometimes at the request of those counselling them.

Here the focus is on counselling trainees' summaries in the facilitating client disclosure phase of initial sessions. Such summaries can clarify what clients have communicated and, if they have had a lengthy period of talking, trainees can summarize to establish their presence and make the interaction more two-way. If clients are telling their stories very rapidly, it can help them to calm down if trainees deliver summaries in a measured and unhurried way.

When clients explain why they have come for counselling, trainees may use summaries that reflect whole units of communication. Such summaries tie together the main feelings and content of what clients say. Basic reflection summaries serve a bridging function for clients, enabling them to continue with the same topic or move on to another. Other functions include ensuring accurate listening, rewarding clients and clarifying both parties' understanding. A variation of the basic reflection summary is the reflecting feelings and reasons summary that links emotions with their perceived causes.

Starting the counselling and helping process

In this and previous chapters skills for beginning the initial session have been reviewed. Box 8.4 puts many of these skills together in an abbreviated example of the starting the initial session and the facilitating client disclosure phases of the relating stage of the lifeskills counselling process model. In actual fact, there is often no clear dividing line

Box 8.4 Example of basic reflection summary

Marital counsellor to wife: Just to summarize so far. You've known Jack for 10 years and been married for five. You now have two children, Denise aged 3 and Jonathan, aged 2. Your relationship with Jack has always had some problems, but in the last year they have become greater. One of the problems has to do with money. At the moment, you do not go out to work and you feel that Jack could be making a fairer division of his salary to look after you and the kids better. Another issue has to do with Jack's spending a lot of time with his mates rather than with you and the kids. At the moment you do not feel Jack is really committed to the marriage and wonder what you can do about this. Is that about right?

between the facilitating client disclosure phase of the relating stage and the reconnaissance phase of the understanding stage – it is more a matter of degree.

In the next example (Box 8.5) a male counsellor assists a male client to start telling his story, though the sexes could just as well be different. The setting is that of a college counselling centre. Readers should note that during the facilitating client disclosure phase, the counsellor is just 'tracking' the client by staying in his frame of reference. Remember, the most important thing for the counsellor to do at this stage is to start creating a relationship with the client that enables him to feel understood. Those trainees learning to use their skills as part of other roles or in informal helping settings are asked to modify the way the relating stage is presented to suit their future work.

Box 8.5 Example of the relating stage

Counsellor: We have about 45 minutes. Would you please tell me why you've come.
Client: Well, it's my exams coming up.
Counsellor: Uhm. When?
Client: In three weeks. These are the final exams on my accounting course and I'm scared that I will fail.
Counsellor: You feel extremely worried about passing your final accounting course exams.
Client: I'm never really good in exams, but this time I feel that I'll really make a mess of them.
Counsellor: So you really fear the worst.
Client: My parents tell me it's all right and to just do as well as I can, but I just don't feel that way.
Counsellor: So your parents are trying to support you, but it's hard to support yourself.
Client: I'm not revising well. I'm going much too slowly because I'm worrying.
Counsellor: Your anxiety is causing you to get behind ...
Client: And that makes me worry even more.
Counsellor: So you're in a vicious circle.
Client: I'm also concerned about how I am going to do in the exam room.
Counsellor: What do you think may happen?
Client: I'll be very nervous and that will make matters even worse.
Counsellor: Your nervousness will add to your revision difficulties.
Client: I tend to get uptight before and in exams.
Counsellor: Can you tell me more?

Client:	Yes. I don't sleep properly and feel tired most of the time.
Counsellor:	You feel worn down because you do not sleep well.
Client:	And, in the exam room, my mind blocks until I am able to calm myself down.
Counsellor:	So you have difficulty attending too, and have to make a real effort to concentrate. Can I summarize the ground we have covered so far?
Client:	OK.
Counsellor:	Right now you are really worried about your final accounting exams in three weeks' time. You think that you are revising too slowly and inefficiently. You are also concerned that you will get very nervous both before and in your exams. You feel very tired because you're not sleeping properly and in the exam room fear that your mind will block for a time. Is that about it so far?
Client:	Yes, it is.

Activity 8.2 Practising relating stage skills

Work with a partner. Each of you thinks of an area in your personal or work life that you are prepared to share in role-playing the relating stage of an initial session. Alternatively, you can role-play a client with a genuine concern. One of you acts as client. The counsellor/helper conducts an interview of up to 15 minutes using the following skills:

- preparation skills, for instance setting up the room and any recording equipment
- meeting, greeting and seating skills
- making an opening statement skills
- active listening skills
- structuring skills
- summarizing skills

See Box 8.5 for an example of this activity. After the relating stage session, hold a feedback and discussion period, possibly illustrated by going through a videotape or audiotape of the session.

After a suitable interval, reverse roles.

Contracting

Contracting refers to making agreements about the process of counselling and establishing the respective roles of counsellor and client. Contracts can be of varying degrees of formality. Each counselling approach has an implied or explicit contract built into it: for instance, a person-centred contract for person-centred counsellors and a cognitive therapy contract for cognitive counsellors. Likewise, lifeskills counselling has an assumed contract. The matter then becomes that of how formal and explicit to make the contract and when to do this. Related to this is the matter of whether contracts are more suitable for some kinds of counselling, for instance where there is a specific and limited goal to be attained, than where the goals are broader, for instance personal growth.

In reality, contracting is often assumed rather than explicit. For example, a client undergoing rational emotive behaviour therapy will have the approach explained up to a point as part of the process and by continuing in REBT might be perceived as participating in a contract, even though the word 'contract' may never be mentioned. Similarly in lifeskills counselling, the counsellor does not provide a full explanation of the approach, but describes enough of it to motivate clients, let them know how to participate, and answer any queries. This does not mean that both rational emotive behaviour counsellors and lifeskills counsellors might not draw up formal contracts if they considered that to be of most benefit to clients. However, most counsellors do not consider this necessary. Instead they choose to explain the process a little at or near the beginning and explain it further as it unfolds.

The lifeskills counselling process model may be viewed as having a contract built into it. The stages and phases are an outline of how counsellors intend to work with clients, though there is allowance for variation depending on specific client needs and wishes. For instance, phase 3 of the understanding stage, where counsellor and client agree on a shared analysis of the client's problem, means that a contract defining what is wrong is part of lifeskills counselling. Similarly, the first or intervening phase of the changing stage follows on from the understanding stage to outline a plan of action and could be viewed as a contract between counsellor and client regarding remedying what is wrong. When counsellor and client agree on homework assignments, this might equally be viewed as making an informal contract.

An implicit feature of contracts is that of commitment to keeping them. Contracts that are signed and sealed can, of course, be broken and more informal contracts may be scrupulously kept. In lifeskills counselling, contracts tend to be verbal and their usefulness depends on the shared perception of counsellor and client that they have value.

Another aspect of contracting in counselling has less to do with the treatment approach and more to do with practical and business arrangements. An important issue is that of time-keeping. Here part of the lifeskills counselling's informal and, if necessary, explicit contract is that both counsellor and client will turn up on time and, if not, provide notice if possible and have a good reason for lateness or absence. Confidentiality is another key issue and, where possible, any limitations on it should be shared in advance. However, both time-keeping and confidentiality can be matters of agreement between counsellors and clients rather than part of formal written contracts unless, of course, a counselling agency has its own strict rules which both counsellor and client are expected to observe.

Referral skills

In any session, counselling trainees may face decisions about referring clients elsewhere. Even experienced counsellors have types of client with whom they feel competent and comfortable and others where they feel less so. Lazarus states that an important counselling principle is to 'Know your limitations and other clinicians' strengths' (Dryden, 1991: 30). He considers that referrals should be made where other counsellors have skills that the counsellor does not possess or more appropriate personal styles for particular clients. Important ethical issues surround referral, for instance ensuring the best treatment for clients where other counsellors are more expert with specific problems, for instance schizophrenia or traumatic stress disorders.

Referral may not be an either/or matter. Sometimes counsellors continue working with clients but also refer to other counsellors and helping professionals. Alternatively, counsellors may be the recipients of referrals from other helping professionals who continue to work with the clients concerned. I worked as a sessional counsellor in a leading career outplacement company where all my clients were referred by other professionals who continued seeing them for job search counselling. I acted as a 'back-stop' for clients whose problems were more severe or different from the normal clientele presenting for job search assistance.

Sometimes clients are referred to gain additional knowledge about their problems. For example, clients with thought-blocking problems or sexual dysfunctions might be referred for medical checks. Depending on the outcome of these checks, the counsellor may gain relevant information to help determine whether or not to continue seeing them.

On other occasions counsellors and trainees can refer the clients' problem rather than the clients themselves to other counsellors and helping professionals. For example, they can discuss with colleagues or supervisors how best to assist certain clients. Occasions when one may refer the client's problem rather than the client include being the only counsellor available in an area, or when clients state a clear preference for continuing working with their current counsellor, or when clients are unlikely to follow through on referrals in any case.

The following are some skills for making referrals.

- **Know one's strengths and limitations**. Be realistic about the kinds of client with whom one works well and those with whom one is less skilled. Be realistic about one's workload and set appropriate limits on it.
- **Build a referral network**. Get to know the resources available in the area so that good referrals are made. Where possible, avoid referring 'blind' to someone whose competence is unknown. Furthermore, check whether another counsellor or helping professional has the time available to see the client.
- **Provide appropriate information**. Provide the client with relevant information about an agency or individual to whom they are referred: for instance a contact person, their telephone number and professional address, their theoretical orientation, and the scale of fees charged, if any.
- **If possible, refer early on**. When counsellors and trainees defer referrals longer than necessary, they waste clients' and their own time. In addition, it is preferable to refer clients before emotional bonding takes place.
- **Avoid unnecessary referrals**. Sometimes it is better for clients to continue working with the counsellors that they have. Tune into anxieties and fears about seeing certain clients. Counselling trainees build confidence and skills by expanding the range of clients with whom they can work. However, wherever possible, they should ensure that they have adequate supervision and support.
- **Build a support network**. A support network provides professional support for a counsellor or trainee when they want to refer clients' problems rather than the clients themselves. Their support networks are likely to overlap with their referral networks.

Activity 8.3 Referral skills

Answer the following questions on your own, in pairs or in a group.

1 When might you refer clients to other counsellors or helping professionals?
2 What categories of counsellors and helping professionals do you require in your referral network?
3 What categories of counsellors and helping professionals do you require in your support network – when you refer problems but not clients?
4 What are some considerations in making good referrals?
5 When might you be at risk of making unnecessary referrals?

Crisis counselling

Though counselling trainees should at first not be faced with clients in crisis, this cannot be guaranteed. Since the fact that clients are in crisis often becomes apparent at the start of initial sessions, the topic is dealt with here. In crisis counselling, trainees are faced with making immediate choices to help clients get through their sense of being overwhelmed. Some of these choices may also help clients to manage better any underlying problems contributing to the crisis.

Defining crises

Crises may be defined as situations of excessive stress. Stress tends to have a negative connotation in our culture. This is unjustified if one thinks of stress in terms of challenges in life. Each person has an optimum stress level or a particular level of stimulation at which they feel comfortable. At this level they may experiece what Selye terms 'stress without distress' (Selye, 1974). Beneath this level they may feel insufficiently stimulated and bored. Above this level they are likely to experience physiological and psychological distress. If the heightened stress is prolonged or perceived as extremely severe, clients may feel that their coping resources are inadequate to meet the demands being made upon them. In such circumstances they are in situations of excessive stress or are in states of crisis.

This section relates mainly to clients who are in fairly acute states of distress. They may be experiencing heightened or maladaptive reactions in a number of different, though interrelated, areas.

Physical reactions

Physical reactions may include hypertension and proneness to such things as heart attacks and gastric ulcers. The weakest parts of different clients' bodies tend to be most adversely affected by stress.

Feelings

The feelings associated with excessive stress include shock, depression, frustration, anger, anxiety, disorientation and fears of nervous breakdown or insanity.

Thoughts

Some of clients' main thoughts associated with excessive stress are that they are powerless to make a positive impact on their situation, that things are getting out of control; and thoughts associated with despair and lack of hope for the future. The notion of excessive stress can imply that clients' thought processes have become somewhat irrational. They think ineffectively, for example with tunnel vision, focusing on only a few factors in a situation.

Communication/actions

Avoidance and over-activity are two of the main ways in which clients handle excessive stress. Their behaviour may range from giving up and not making an effort to rigid, repetitive and frenetic attempts to deal with their problems. Violence, turned either outwards or self-inflicted, is more likely at times of excessive stress than when clients' stress levels are lower.

It is very important to realize that crises, however large or small they may appear to outsiders, tend to seem overwhelming from insiders' frames of reference. Some crises have been simmering in the background for a long time and suddenly erupt, whereas others are more clearly a reaction to an immediate precipitating event, for instance a bereavement or loss of a job. Perhaps many stressful situations only really turn into psychological crises at the point where clients feel that their efforts to adapt and cope are totally insufficient. Numerous situations may cause clients to feel that they are at the limit of their coping resources, though there are wide differences in people's abilities to tolerate these various stressors. Resilience in the face of stress depends partly on personal resources and skills. However, it may also be heavily influenced by the amount of family, social and community support available.

Guidelines for crisis counselling

Crises for clients can be crises for counsellors and trainees too. They may feel under great pressure to relieve clients' distress at the same time as being threatened by the strength of their emotions. Below are some guidelines for crisis counselling.

Be prepared

Those responsible for clients can relieve much of their stress if they realize that, since these events are likely to be part of any counsellor's life, they should be prepared. One means of preparing is to ensure that they can quickly mobilize a good support system: for example a competent physician or a bed in a psychiatric hospital. They can also prepare for crises by being clear about the limit of their responsibility for clients.

Act calmly

Even though it may seem a limitation on being genuine, it is important to act calmly. Counselling trainees should not add their anxieties to clients' agitation and distress. Responding in a warm yet firm and measured way may both give clients the security of feeling helped by a strong person and also calm their heightened emotions.

Listen and observe

One of the main reasons that stressful situations become crises for many clients is that they feel that they have no one to whom they can turn who will listen to and understand their difficulties. Clients may become calmer and feel less isolated and despairing simply by being able to share their problems and air the related emotions. Catharsis is another word for this process of letting out pent-up feelings. Listening, observing and empathic responding help one to understand clients' worlds as well as contributing to their feelings of being heard and accepted.

Assess severity and risk of damage to self and to others

One area of assessing severity concerns the degree to which clients are in contact with reality. Assessing risk may also mean assessing the damage clients may do to other people. However, it is more likely to involve assessing the damage that clients may do to themselves, including committing suicide. A high proportion of suicidal people talk about the possibility before making any attempt. Trainees need to be sensitive at picking up cries for help and not allowing their anxieties to interfere with their listening skills. Suicidal people are often ambivalent about doing it. A caring question about whether or not they are suicidal may be very appropriate. Avoidance or dealing with the topic indirectly may increase rather than diminish risk.

Assess client strengths and coping skills

Counselling trainees can both assess and help their clients to explore and assess their strengths and coping skills. Often in crises clients are so overwhelmed by negative thinking that they allow themselves to forget their strengths. While not advocating superficial reassurance, the following remarks may be helpful to some clients in some situations: 'Well, we've explored your problems in some detail. I'm now wondering whether you feel that you have any strengths or resources for dealing with them?'; 'You've been telling me a lot about negative aspects of your life. Can you tell me if there are any positive aspects as well?'; and 'As you talk you seem to be facing your problems very much on your own.

I'm wondering whether there are any friends, relatives or other people who might be available to offer you some support.'

Assist exploration and clarification of problem(s)

Clients in crises have often lost perspective on themselves and their problems. One reason for this is that crises involve very intense feelings. Until some progress is made in relieving the intensity of feelings, clients may have insufficient ability to be rational about the factors generating their strong emotions. Skills during the work of exploring and clarifying problems are likely to include empathic responding, use of questions, summarizing and challenging any distortions in clients' thinking that make their lives seem hopeless.

Assist problem management and planning

A primary emphasis in crisis counselling is to help clients regain some sense of control over their lives. For some clients the opportunity to talk with an understanding person may give them enough confidence in their ability to cope with life to move out of the danger zone. With other clients, a counselling trainee's role will include helping them to develop strategies for coping with their immediate distress and, where appropriate, initiating ways and skills for dealing with their longer-term problems. If clients are at any risk, plans for coping with immediate situations should be formulated as specifically as possible. For example: 'We have agreed that you will stay at your sister's tonight and that we will meet at 11 a.m. tomorrow. Do you think there is any reason why you cannot do this?'

Assisting problem management and planning may involve mobilizing additional resources, which may be supplied by either professional helpers, such as doctors and priests, or friends and relatives. In some instances it is best for clients to take responsibility for making contact, but not invariably. Trainees always need to assess what is in clients' best interests and, at highly vulnerable times in their lives, act accordingly.

Be specific about availability

Part of a crisis management plan with certain clients may be to give them the security of another appointment in the near future. In addition, attention needs to be paid to the matter of between-session contact. If such contact seems appropriate, a counselling trainee can say something along the lines of 'If you feel you need me in an emergency, please don't hesitate to get in touch with me either here or on my mobile phone. The numbers are —— .' In most instances clients will not get in touch until the next session. However, willingness to be contacted can reassure distressed clients.

Apparently the Chinese use two symbols for the concept of crisis: one for danger and another for opportunity. Crises can be the impetus for certain clients to work hard on problems that have been simmering in the past, yet which have to date not been properly confronted. At best, crises can give both counsellor and client the opportunity to form an effective relationship. Such relationships can provide the basis for clients to develop confidence and skills either to prevent or to cope better with future crises.

Activity 8.4 Crisis counselling skills

1 Identify, with regard to your present or future counselling work, the kinds of stressors that bring or may in future bring clients in crisis to see you.
2 Counsel a partner, who role-plays a client in crisis. As far as possible, keep in mind the following guidelines:

- Act calmly.
- Listen and observe.
- Assess severity and risk of damage to self and others.
- Assess client strengths and coping skills.
- Assist exploring and clarifying problems.
- Assist problem management and planning.
- Be specific about your availability.

Afterwards discuss and reverse roles.

III the understanding stage

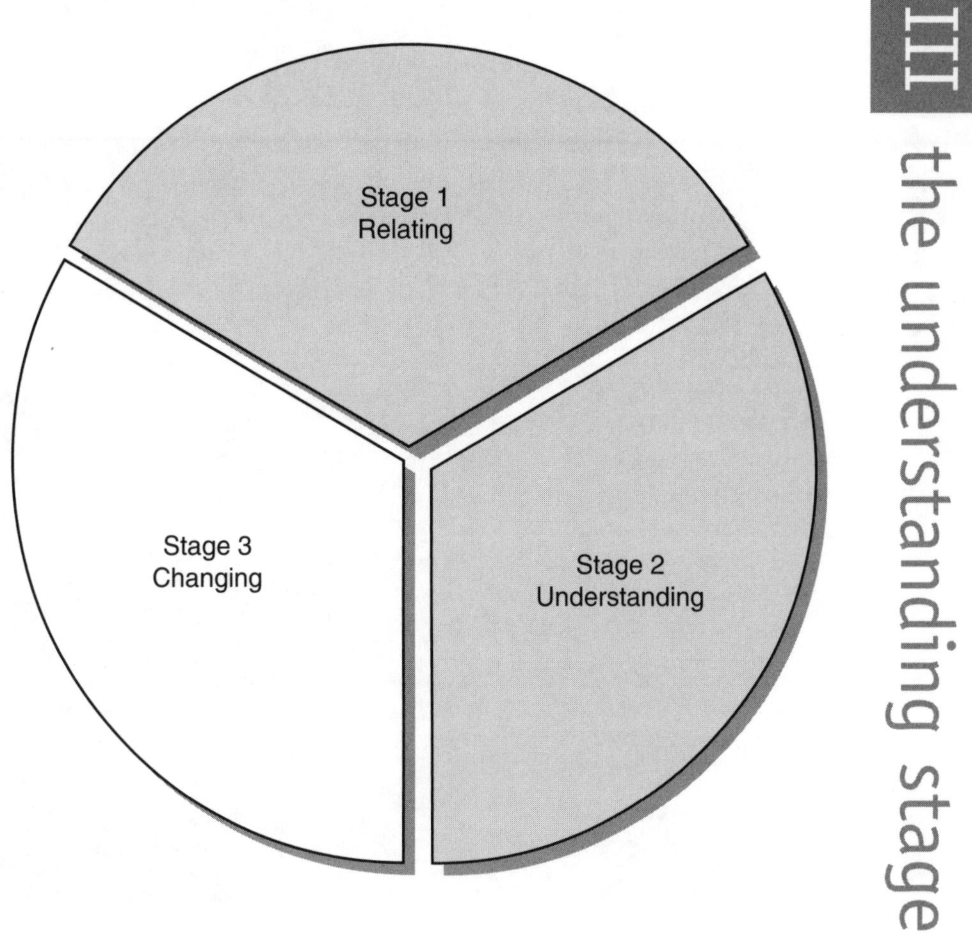

The lifeskills counselling model

The relating stage's main task: to form a collaborative working relationship

The understanding stage's main task: assess and agree on a shared definition of the client's problem(s)

The changing stage's main task: achieve client change and the maintenance of change

clarify problems skills 9

Chapter outcomes

By studying and doing the activities in this chapter you should:

- know something about the understanding stage;
- develop some questioning skills;
- develop some challenging skills;
- develop some feedback skills; and
- develop some self-disclosure skills.

Welcome to the understanding stage of the lifeskills counselling model. In this stage, counsellors and trainees go beyond facilitating clients to trying to understand how they are perpetuating their problems. When facilitating client disclosure during the relating stage, trainees mainly try to assist their clients to say why they have come for counselling. The main emphasis is on helping clients to talk and on building relationships with them. However, for most clients this is unlikely to be either sufficient or sufficiently expeditious to help them to deal with their problems. Facilitating clients in talking is frequently not enough to help them to identify their problems and the poor problematic skills that maintain them.

Whereas the emphasis in the relating stage is on assisting clients to share their frame of reference, the emphasis in the understanding stage is on trying to identify the client's problem or problems. For at least one problem, they also attempt to define the poor mind skills and poor communication/action skills that contribute to maintaining it.

In introducing the understanding stage a number of observations need to be made. The stage has been presented in Box 4.1 (see p. 47) and the diagram at the front of Part Three as though it were for a client with a reasonable time to work on one or more problems. However, this is often not the case. Clients may either want to focus or only have time to focus on just one problem. They and those helping them may consider that little time need be spent on a broad reconnaissance. Even when only one problem is identified, time may be limited for detecting and deciding and agreeing on a shared analysis of the clients' problem phases. In such instances, trainees may be forced to do the best they can. For example, they may only identify one main mind skill and one main communication skill to work on. Even with clients who have more time, it may also be desirable to focus on a limited number of skills when defining a problem.

There is the issue of whether to mention the word 'skills' at all. In very brief counselling, the case for not using skills language is stronger than in longer-term counselling. In counselling for just one or a few sessions, there is often insufficient time to build lasting skills. It can also take clients time to adjust to the notion of skills and to understand some of the specific skills, for instance a mind skill like creating perceptions. As the time available becomes longer, it is more appropriate to focus on poor skills that underlie problems and that leave clients vulnerable to repeating problems if the skills are not clearly identified and addressed. However, even when working with client skills, it is possible to do this without using skills language. Albert Ellis's rational emotive behaviour therapy and Aaron Beck's cognitive therapy are both approaches that target clients' mind skills and, to a lesser extent, communication/action skills, but on the whole they manage to do so without using the word skills. The lifeskills counselling approach considers that many clients gain from working on clearly identified and labelled skills. Nevertheless, the issue of skills needs to be introduced sensitively and, even then, a few clients may prefer not to think explicitly in skills terms.

The example of George was provided in Chapter 4 (pp. 58–62) to show how a counsellor would work with a client in each of the three phases of the understanding stage. The remainder of this chapter explores four sets of skills: questioning, challenging, feedback and self-disclosure skills. Though such skills may be used in the relating stage, since this stage is usually short these skills are more likely to be used in the understanding stage and also again in the changing stage. Part Three continues with the presentation of three chapters on skills for assessing feelings and physical reactions, for assessing thinking and for assessing communication/actions, respectively. It ends with a chapter on how counsellors and trainees can work with clients to agree on a shared analysis of their problems or problem situations by identifying at least one mind skill and one communication/action skill that they can work on together in counselling.

Questioning skills

Goals of questioning

Viktor Frankl tells the following psychiatrist joke:

> 'Are you a psychiatrist?'
> 'Why do you ask?'
> 'You're a psychiatrist.' (Frankl, 1975: 94)

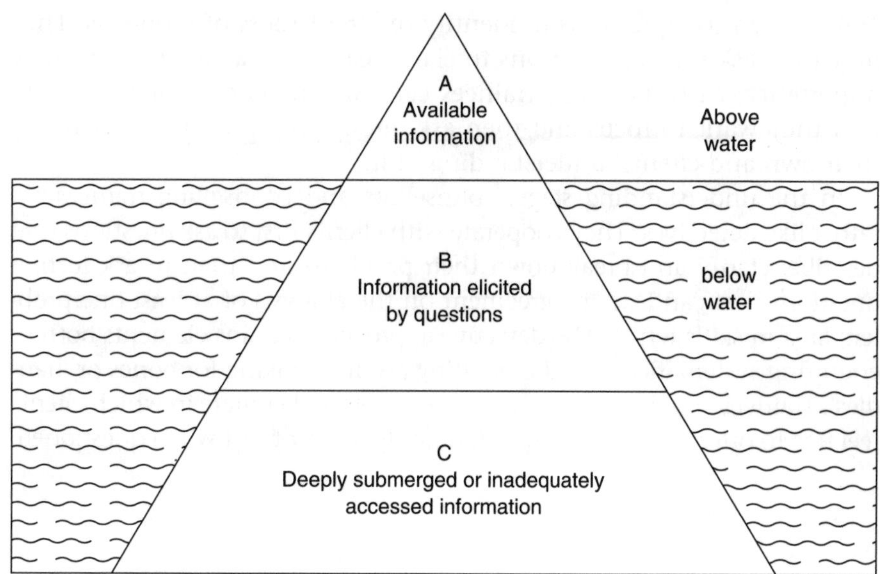

Figure 9.1 *The information about problems iceberg*

Here, instead of unmasking, the psychiatrist has been unmasked. Often, as in this instance, counselling trainees ask questions inappropriately. A major reservation about using questions is that they take clients out of their internal frames of reference. Some questions are asked more to make counsellors feel secure than to help clients. However, judicious questioning can help clients better explore, clarify and understand their internal frames of reference. Questions can also assist trainees to identify clients' problems and, where appropriate, to break them down into component parts. Once this is done both client and trainee possess more information for developing hypotheses about how problems are sustained. In this chapter the primary focus is on the use of questions to identify, clarify, and break problems down into their component parts.

The iceberg provides a good analogy for understanding the role of questioning in stage 2 of lifeskills counselling. Much relevant information lies below the surface. In general, clients responding to permission to tell their stories reveal useful information. Area A in Figure 9.1 depicts this information. However, effective questioning enables clients to provide much additional information for identifying, clarifying and breaking down problems. Area B depicts this further information. There may be further information that clients may be either unaware of or unwilling to disclose. There is no guarantee that counsellor questions will tap this information. Area C depicts this either highly private or unconscious information. Another analogy for the role of questioning in initial sessions of lifeskills counselling is that of plants and their root system.

Trainees can use questions to identify different roots of problems. They may then ask further questions to clarify each root area and its relative importance. At some stage, trainees can ask clients on which problem root they want to focus and then ask questions relevant to expanding their own and clients' understanding of it.

In the understanding stage, counsellors and counselling trainees act rather like detectives. They cooperate with clients first to ask questions that describe, clarify and break down their problems and then to ask further questions that can lead to agreement on the analysis of at least one problem area in skills terms. The detective approach contains elements both of enquiring systematically and of sniffing around looking for bones or 'handles'. Trainees should try to create a safe emotional climate in which clients feel free to offer information spontaneously and not just when questioned.

Choices when questioning

Counselling trainees have numerous choices when questioning, including the following.

Purpose of questions

Effective trainees ask questions that expand their own and their clients' understanding of problems and problematic skills patterns. They do not ask questions just for questioning's sake. They are mindful that too much or the wrong sort of questioning can be very detrimental to clients' participation and progress in counselling.

Present versus past focus

Questioning in lifeskills counselling tends to focus more on understanding clients' present situation than on knowing about their past. However, information about the past can throw light on the present, so the past cannot be totally excluded.

Amount of topics covered

An issue is that of whether just to ask questions in the area of the presenting problem(s) or to conduct a broader reconnaissance (Sullivan, 1954). Practical considerations, for instance what the client wants from counselling and the time and resources available, often influence how many topics get covered.

Amount of detail

How detailed should enquiries into each topic area be? When should trainees move on? Through intuition, experience and reasoning, effective practitioners assess when areas may continue to yield valuable information and when to move on.

Intimacy level

Trainees need to be sensitive to the intimacy and threat level of questions. However, they will still tactfully ask intimate questions, if appropriate.

Timing

Trainees require caution regarding the timing and ordering of questions. They may defer some intimate or probing questions pending the establishment of greater trust. However, if skilled, they may ask relevant intimate questions early on, depending on the client.

Number of questions

When in doubt as to what to say or do, trainees are at risk of asking questions as if amassing information is the goal of the counselling interview. They need to be careful not to conduct interrogations that may lead to either defensiveness or dependence or both.

Confirmatory questions

Trainees should beware of asking questions designed to elicit responses fitting pet theories. Sometimes trainees prematurely decide what are clients' problems and the poor skills that sustain them. Then, they only ask questions to confirm their judgements.

Types of question

Counselling trainees also need to choose among different types of questions, including the following.

Open-ended versus closed questions

As mentioned in Chapter 6, open-ended questions give clients considerable choice in how to respond, whereas closed questions restrict choice. When working with new clients many counsellors use open-ended questions prior to asking more focused questions.

Open-ended question: 'What do you think of your previous experience in counselling?'
Closed question: 'Was your previous counsellor good or bad?'

Clarification questions

Clarification questions seek information about and clarify the counsellor's perception of clients' words and phrases. Examples include:

'When you say ——, what do you mean?'
'Sounds to me like you're saying ——?'

Elaboration questions

Elaboration questions are open questions that give clients the opportunity to expand on what they have already started talking about. Examples include:

'Would you care to elaborate?'
'Is there anything more you wish to add?'

Specific detail questions

Specific detail questions aim to collect concrete information about clients' problems and problematic skills patterns. These questions focus on how, what, when, and where.

- *How questions* include 'How do/did you think, feel or act [or a combination of these]?', 'How did she/he think, feel or act [or a combination of these]?', and 'How often does it happen?' How questions are particularly useful for eliciting details of how clients act.
- *What questions* include 'What happened?', 'What do you perceive as the problem?', and 'What are the likely consequences of doing that?'
- *When questions* include 'When did it start?' and 'When is your next public speech?'
- *Where questions* include 'Where does it happen?' and 'Where in your body do you experience the tension?'

'Show me' questions

'Show me' questions ask clients to show the counselling trainee how they communicated. Sometimes trainees act the other person in a role-play. Examples include:

'Can you show me how you actually spoke to ——?'
'Imagine I am your ——, can you show me how you behaved to me?'

Eliciting personal meaning questions

The information clients provide often has personal or symbolic meaning for them. For example, whenever a husband came home late without having called her, his wife would think he did not care about her (Beck, 1988). Eliciting personal meanings questions should be open and tentative since the client should in principle know the answer better than anyone else but may turn out not to. Illustrative questions include:

'I'm wondering about the meaning of —— for you?'
'What do you make of that?'
'Why is it so important for you?'

Searching for strengths questions

Ivey and Ivey use the term 'positive asset search' to describe searching for clients' strengths. They observe that, since people grow from their strengths, the positive asset search is a useful method to ensure a more optimistic and directed interview (Ivey and Ivey, 2003). Illustrative questions include:

'What do you see as your strengths?'
'What are your assets?'
'Was there anything good in the way you behaved?'
'What skills do you bring to this problem?'

Solution-focused questions

Solution-focused questions ask clients to provide information concerning the extent to which they have tried or are trying to do something about their problems:

'What have you attempted to do about the problem to date?'
'What are your options?'
'What are you planning to do?'
'How can you change your behaviour?'

Areas of information for questions

Once counselling trainees agree with clients on a specific problem to address, they are encouraged to cover the following areas of information in their questioning. In each area, they can start with open-ended questions and then, if appropriate, become more specific. There is no set order, though I prefer to find out information about clients' feelings early on. Let's take the example of Cath, an 18-year-old university student who sees a trainee because she is anxious about taking an upcoming driving test. Sample questions are as follows:

Brief history of problem

'For how long has this been a problem for you?'
'Have you ever sought help for this problem before?'
'How have you attempted to cope in the past?'

Feelings

'When you say you get anxious about taking the driving test, how exactly do you feel?'
'On a scale of 1 to 10, how anxious do you feel about the test?'
'How anxious are you while preparing for the driving test and how anxious will you be when taking the test?'

Physical reactions

'What happens to your body when you feel anxious?'
'Do you have any distressing physical symptoms of anxiety?'
'Where exactly do you feel the tension in your body?'

Thoughts

'What thoughts and images accompany your anxious feelings?'
'What are the consequences for you of not passing the test?'
'Where is the evidence that you do not do well in test situations?'

Communication/actions

'How do you drive when you are anxious?'
'How might the person taking the driving test know that you were very anxious?'
'Apart from your anxiety over the test, what sort of driver do you think you are?'

Miscellaneous

'Are there any other current stresses in your life?'
'Are you on any medication?'
'To whom can you turn for support?'

At the end of a series of questions such as the above, both the trainee and Cath should have a clearer picture of the nature and extent of her driving test problem. The trainee could ask further questions depending on the answers Cath provided. In addition, a trainee working within the lifeskills counselling model would probably have some hypotheses about the poor mind skills and poor communication/action skills that might be sustaining Cath's anxiety about the test. The trainee might ask further questions to confirm or negate hypotheses either as the information suggesting a hypothesis became available or later.

Throughout this process of asking questions, the trainee should take brief notes. Some trainees dislike taking notes since they fear it blocks their relationships with clients. However, discreetly taking notes can enable trainees to be more, not less, psychologically present to clients – it relieves the pressure on them to memorize information. When later they come to redefine clients' problems in skills terms, they can draw evidence for their suggestions from their records of what clients have said, and it is useful to have a record to which they can refer back, if necessary, in subsequent sessions.

Work in partnership with clients

In lifeskills counselling questions aim to provide information as much for clients as for counsellors. Counselling trainees should try to avoid questioning in ways that create dependency, passivity and resistance. Below are some skills for cooperating with clients when asking questions.

Ask establishing agenda and transition questions

These questions have the advantage of getting clients involved in the detective work of identifying and clarifying problems. Clients are invited to participate in working in areas important for them. Illustrative questions include:

'You've mentioned three areas [specify]. Which one would you like to focus on first?'
'Is there anything you would like to add before we move on to ...?'

Intersperse active listening with questions

Clients feel interrogated when trainees ask a series of questions in quick succession. Trainees can greatly soften their questioning if they pause to see if clients wish to continue responding and then reflect each response. Interspersing active listening ensures that trainees check the accuracy of their understanding. The following excerpt shows what you should avoid.

Cath:	I'm getting very anxious over my upcoming driving test.
Counselling trainee:	What makes you so anxious?
Cath:	The fact that I may fail.
Counselling trainee:	Why are you so afraid of failing?
Cath:	Because then it will be harder to get a part-time job.
Counselling trainee:	What sort of job do you want?

Below is a gentler approach to the same initial statement.

Cath: I'm getting very anxious over my upcoming driving test.
Counselling trainee: You're very worried about your driving test. Would you care to say more about this?
Cath: Yes. It is in three weeks' time and I feel overwhelmed.
Counselling trainee: So you experience taking the test as overpowering.
Cath: I feel my whole future depends on it.
Counselling trainee: You think it is make-or-break. Can you explain this further?

Though these are only short excerpts, it is clear that the first trainee controls and dominates the client whereas the second facilitates Cath's description of her internal frame of reference. The emotional climate in the first excerpt is 'in the head'. In the second excerpt, the trainee asks questions in ways that encourage the expression of feelings as well as of thoughts.

Ask follow-on questions

Counselling trainees should avoid jackrabbiting, quickly hopping from one topic to another. They should always listen carefully to and respect what clients have just said. Their next question can often follow on from, and encourage clients to build upon, their last response. Questioning that is logically linked to clients' responses creates a feeling of working together rather than of being directed by the counsellor.

Encourage clients to do their own work

Often clients can both ask and answer their own questions. Interspersing reflections with questions provides clients with the psychological space to do their own work. If trainees establish good relationships, clients will give them much information without being asked. In addition, trainees can use silences to encourage clients to engage in self-exploration and move beyond superficial answers. Furthermore, they can ask questions that encourage clients to think and feel for themselves. Illustrative questions are:

'What information is important for helping understand your problem?'
'Would you like to stay with the problem and try to get in touch with what you truly think and feel about it?'

Carefully observe how questions are answered

Much of the art of questioning lies in decoding clients' answers. A lot of information is conveyed by what is left unsaid or only partially said, and by voice and body messages. Effective counsellors are finely tuned to subtle client messages. They use tact both in asking questions and in responding to clients' answers. Clients with anxieties, confusions and vulnerabilities that counselling trainees sensitively pick up are more likely to answer questions honestly than clients listened to clumsily.

Use good voice and body messages

How counselling trainees question is very important in addition to what they say. For example, clients may feel overwhelmed if trainees' voices are loud and harsh. If trainees use little eye contact and have a stiff body posture, clients may also feel less inclined to answer their questions. When questioning, trainees should use good volume, articulation, pitch, emphasis and speech rate. Their body messages should also clearly show clients their interest in what they say.

Activity 9.1 Questioning skills

Part A: Exploring the role of questions in initial counselling sessions

Answer the following questions.

1 What are some of the main reasons for and against asking questions in initial counselling sessions?
2 What are some of the main considerations for counselling trainees when asking questions in initial sessions?

Part B: Formulating questions

Formulate two examples of each of the following types of question:

- open-ended
- closed
- clarification
- elaboration
- specific detail
  - how question
  - what question
  - when question
  - where question
- 'show me'
- eliciting personal meaning
- searching for strengths
- solution-focused

Part C: Practising in pairs or in a group

1 *In pairs*

(a) Together go through Parts A and B of this exercise.
(b) Counsel each other for sessions consisting of:

- initial structuring;
- facilitating the 'client' who responds to the initial structuring by sharing his or her reasons for coming;
- making a second statement to establish the structure for asking questions to identify and clarify the 'client's' problem or an aspect of it;
- interspersed with active listening, asking appropriate questions for your 'client' and you to gain greater clarification and understanding of the problem.

At the end of each session, the 'client' gives the 'counsellor' feedback on her/his questioning skills. It can help to play back audio recordings or video recordings of your work.

2 *In a group.* One person acts as client and presents a problem to the group who sit in a semicircle facing her/him. Each member takes a turn in responding to the client, first by reflecting what she/he has just said and then by asking a question that helps clarify her/his problem. When the client answers, the next member reflects the answer and then asks a question, and so on. When finished, the client provides feedback on the 'session'. Members take turns as clients.

Challenging skills

Challenging is an alternative, and gentler, word for confronting. Challenges focus on acknowledging and reflecting discrepant, inconsistent and mixed messages. Though clients can challenge counsellors, this section deals more with counsellors challenging clients. The starting point is for counselling trainees to recognize their own feelings and thoughts. Trainees must ask themselves whether the feelings they are experiencing indicate problems they have as persons or are reasonable reactions to clients' disclosures (Brammer and MacDonald, 2002). Trainees must earn the right to challenge by knowing their motivation for doing it. They should only challenge clients if they feel invested in them and have the time and effort to continue building the relationship (Corey and Corey, 2003). If trainees have not established good working relationships with clients, they risk challenges being received defensively.

Challenging clients to speak for themselves

Frequently clients require help in speaking for themselves. By failing to send 'I' messages, clients may distance themselves from their feelings, thoughts and actions (Gordon, 1970). 'I' messages involve the use of the first person singular. Ways in which clients avoid speaking for themselves include making statements starting with words like 'You', 'People', 'We', and 'It'. In addition, sometimes clients avoid sending 'I' messages by asking questions in the hope that they can agree with the answer. Box 9.1 provides examples of 'non-I' messages being altered into 'I' messages.

Box 9.1 Sending 'I' messages

Owning a feeling

Client's 'non-I' message:	'It's hard to feel good about behaviour like that.'
Client's 'I' message:	'I dislike the way she/he behaves.'

Owning a thought

Client's 'non-I' message:	'What do you think my wife should do?'
Client's 'I' message:	'I think that my wife should look for another job.'

Owning a communication/action

Client's 'non-I' message:	'The invitations did not go out on time.'
Client's 'I' message:	'I did not send the invitations out on time.'

Counselling trainees need to challenge clients to speak for themselves. The following are three ways to encourage clients to send 'I' messages.

Respond as though clients send 'I' messages

Trainees can respond to clients in ways that use the word 'You' as though they had sent an 'I' message, even when they have not. For instance, to a client who says 'He is a difficult person to be around', a trainee might respond, 'You feel uncomfortable when you're together.' The trainee's response implicitly challenges the client to express feelings directly.

Request that clients send 'I' messages

If clients fail to send 'I' messages, consider openly drawing this to their attention. An example of a tactful approach to challenging clients to speak for themselves is: 'You're asking me what I think your wife should do, but I get the impression you have your own ideas on this matter.' Even more direct is to ask clients: 'Please use the word "I" when you wish to own a feeling, thought or action.' Where appropriate, clients can also be educated in the distinction between 'I' messages and 'non-I' messages. Doing so may challenge their existing perception that they speak for themselves.

Even after clients are requested to send 'I' messages, they may revert to their old ways. Then both trainees and client require persistence – trainees in challenging clients and clients in challenging their old habits. However, be careful not to threaten clients prematurely.

Model sending 'I' messages

Trainees who are open in their own behaviour and use 'I' messages to own their feelings, thoughts and communications may set examples that helps clients do likewise.

Challenging inconsistent messages

Much of the literature on challenging and confrontation deals with identifying and bringing to clients' attention inconsistencies in the messages that they send. Such challenges can come from counselling trainees' external frames of reference with the aim of helping clients develop new and better perspectives about themselves. As Box 9.2 indicates, there are many areas in which mixed messages may be challenged.

Box 9.2 Challenging inconsistent messages

Inconsistency between verbal, voice and/or body messages:
'You are telling me how angry you feel, but you smile.'

Inconsistency within verbal message:
'You say you are doing poorly, but report being in the top 10 per cent of your class.'

Inconsistency between words and actions:
'You say you love your children from your former marriage, but you are behind on your maintenance.'

Inconsistency between giving and keeping one's word:
'You said that you would make contact with Paul this past week, but so far you have not done so.'

Inconsistency between earlier and present statements:
'You've spent a lot of time saying negative things about your parents, but now you say they did their best.'

Inconsistency between statements and evidence:
'You said your girlfriend never goes out of her way any more to do things for you, but now you say she was really pleased at your promotion.'

Inconsistency between own and others' perspectives:
'I'm getting two messages. You see yourself as doing your share around the flat, but your boyfriend says that you leave most of the housework to him.'

How challenges are given involves verbal, vocal and bodily communication. A common response when challenging mixed or inconsistent messages is: 'On the one hand you say ..., but on the other hand ....' – for example 'On the one hand you say you are fine, but on the other hand I catch a note of pain in your voice.' This way of challenging is often shortened to 'You say ..., but ...' – for example, 'You say that you are fine, but I catch a note of pain in your voice.' Sometimes, counselling trainees may wish to express this: 'I'm getting a mixed message: you say that you are fine, but I catch a note of pain in your voice.'

Challenging possible distortions of reality

When clients talk in counselling, they may make statements like the following.

> 'They are all out to get me.'
> 'I have no friends.'
> 'I'm a terrible mother.'
> 'I'm no good with women (or men).'
> 'She/he doesn't love me any more.'

All of the above may be examples of unrealistic perceptions that can harm rather than help clients. Clients' perceptions are not always accurate. Sometimes counselling trainees need either to challenge such perceptions directly or else help clients test the reality of their own perceptions (Beck, 1976, 1988; Beck and Weishaar, 2005). Clients often jump to conclusions on insufficient evidence ('I have no friends'), and use black-and-white thinking ('Either I'm perfect or no good at all'). They may also fail to own responsibility for their thoughts, feelings and actions ('They made me do it'). Trainees should use their judgement about whether to continue listening within clients' internal frames of reference or challenge their possible distortions of reality.

A useful format for challenging possible distortions of reality is 'You say ——, but where's the evidence?' An example is 'You say that you have no friends, but where's the evidence?' Such a response reflects the client's internal frame of reference and then invites her or him to produce evidence to support it. The client may then make a remark like 'Well Rio never calls me any more.' Then trainees may challenge the client again with a question like 'Is there any other way of looking at that?' With the questions, 'Where's the evidence?' and 'Is there any other way of looking at that?' they invite clients to produce their own evidence or provide different perceptions to confirm or negate their version of reality. On other occasions trainees may suggest some evidence from their external frame of reference.

Challenging insufficiently acknowledging strengths

Though it is good to provide clients with the safety and space to talk about areas of their behaviour with which they are dissatisfied, this can be overdone. Some clients benefit from being helped to acknowledge strengths and thus obtain a more balanced picture of themselves. Questions that trainees can ask clients go beyond 'Where is the evidence?' and 'Is there any other way of looking at that?' to focus on identifying positive behaviour: for example, 'Was there anything positive for you in the situation?' or 'Did you do anything right in the situation?' Clients can be encouraged to search for positive behaviours, even though they may need further work to turn these into real strengths. On occasion, clients may be overly focused on what is negative and be insufficiently in touch with the strengths that they possess for dealing with situations. In addition, they may have tendencies to perceive others excessively negatively. They could be kinder to both others and themselves if they checked and altered such perceptions.

Trainees may challenge clients by mentioning their perceptions of the strengths and assets that they possess. For instance, Kim, 27, has a client Jody, 23, who is very hard on herself and feels at times that she is totally alone. Kim lets Jody share these feelings and then asks Jody to explore whether she has the full picture. When Jody has trouble answering, Kim reminds her that she has mentioned a number of people with whom she is friendly and suggests to Jody that she does have some skills in making friends. Kim also mentions that one of the areas in which Jody may need to work in counselling is that of acknowledging strengths and trying to see her relationships in a more balanced way.

Challenging not acknowledging choice

Lifeskills counselling heavily emphasizes personal responsibility. Trainees can confront clients with their role as choosers in their lives. One way to do this is to highlight their choice processes. For example, clients as parents who say: 'I have no choice but to punish her/him' might be challenged with the fact that they do have some choice in the matter. Another example is that of Wayne, aged 37, who says of his mother: 'I resent having to visit her every weekend.' Here a trainee could respond by both reflecting his resentment and challenging his apparent failure to assume responsibility for being a chooser: 'You feel resentful, but I wonder whether you sufficiently acknowledge that you *choose* to visit her every weekend.' Such a challenge might open the way to exploring both how Wayne thinks – for instance he does not always acknowledge that he has choices – and how he acts, in that he does not perhaps assert himself enough with his mother. Yet another way of challenging clients with their choices is to focus on the verbs that they use. For example, if a client says 'I *can't* do that', the trainee may ask, 'Can you say "I *won't* do that"?'

Challenging by reframing

Counselling trainees may also challenge clients' existing perceptions by offering new perspectives. Sometimes skilful counsellors can change the way clients perceive events or situations by 'reframing' the pictures that they have painted. The facts remain the same, but the picture may look different in a new frame. Beck observes of relationships going downhill that partners begin to see each other through negative frames: for instance 'He's mean and manipulative' or 'She's irresponsible.' He states that reframing consists of seeing these negative qualities in a different light (Beck, 1988).

Beck provides the example of Sharon and Paul, whose image of each other changed for the worse after a few years of marriage. However, there were elements of the original perceptions that could be used to recapture some of the good feelings. For example, Sharon's view of Paul started to improve when she reframed some of her negative views of him: for example, 'He's lazy' to 'He's laid-back, easygoing.' Similarly Paul reframed some of Sharon's behaviour: for example, 'She's critical' became 'She's sharp and incisive; she's very successful; she doesn't intend to hurt me.' Though change did not happen overnight, by viewing each other from different perspectives, Sharon and Paul were able to recapture many of the positive feelings that originally drew them together.

Reframing is integral to the lifeskills counselling model. Most clients do not perceive how they think and act in skills terms. By the end of stage 2 of the model, counsellor and client have reframed the original picture of at least one of the client's problems by describing it in terms of the mind skills and communication/action required to manage the problem more successfully.

How to challenge

The following are some guidelines on how to challenge.

Start with reflecting

Counselling trainees can start to respond by showing that they have heard and understood clients' messages. Then they can build on this understanding with their challenging responses. This way they are more likely to keep clients' ears open to their viewpoint.

Where possible, help clients to challenge themselves

By reflecting mixed messages, trainees can allow clients to come to their own conclusions about them. Similarly, by asking clients to search for evidence to back their statements, they help them to challenge themselves. Assisting clients in self-challenging often results in less resistance than directly challenging them from the counsellor's external frame of reference. Strategies that clients can use to resist challenges include discrediting challengers, persuading challengers to change their views, devaluing the issue, seeking support elsewhere for views being challenged, and cooperating in the counselling session but then doing nothing about it outside (Egan, 2002).

Do not talk down

Give challenges in a democratic way. Remember that challenges are invitations for exploration. Counselling trainees should take care to avoid sending 'You' messages. A major risk is that clients may perceive challenges as put-downs.

Use a minimum amount of 'muscle'

Only challenge as strongly as the goal requires. Strong challenges can create resistances. Although sometimes necessary, such challenges are generally best avoided – especially in initial sessions where rapport and trust are still being established.

Avoid threatening voice and body messages

Try to avoid these – raising one's voice a lot and pointing one's finger are extreme examples.

Leave the ultimate responsibility with clients

Allow clients to decide whether challenges actually help them to move forward in their explorations. Often challenges are only mildly discrepant to clients' existing perceptions. If well timed and tactfully worded, such challenges are unlikely to elicit a high degree of defensiveness.

Do not overdo challenging

Nobody likes being persistently challenged. With constant challenges trainees can create an unsafe emotional climate. If trainees challenge skilfully, they can help clients enlarge their understanding and act more effectively. If trainees challenge too often and too clumsily, they can harm the relationship and block clients' participation.

Do not avoid challenging

Egan (2002) writes that reluctance to challenge is not a bad starting point: it is better than being too eager to challenge. However, counselling trainees need to examine themselves to see whether they are too reluctant to challenge. For example, they may have developed social interpersonal styles that involve much agreeing and little challenging and then transfer these styles to counselling. They may be afraid that they will hurt clients and damage them in some way. In addition, trainees may fear that clients will challenge them in return. All of these are reasons why trainees need to be careful when challenging and work hard at developing their skills at it rather than avoid doing it altogether.

Activity 9.2 Challenging skills

Part A: Formulating challenges

1 *Challenge clients to speak for themselves*
Formulate one or more counsellor direct requests for clients to send 'I' messages.

2 *Challenge mixed messages*
Formulate illustrative counsellor challenges relating to inconsistency in each of the following areas:

(a) between a client's verbal, voice and/or body messages
(b) within a client's verbal message
(c) between a client's words and actions
(d) between a client giving and keeping her/his word
(e) between a client's earlier and present statements
(f) between a client's statements and the evidence
(g) between own and other's perspectives

3 *Challenge possible distortions of reality*
Give two examples of counsellor responses that challenge possible distortions of reality.

4 *Challenge not acknowledging choice*
Give two examples of counsellor responses that challenge clients with insufficiently acknowledging choice.

5 *Challenge insufficiently acknowledging strengths*
Give two examples of counsellor responses that challenge clients with insufficiently acknowledging strengths.

6 *Challenge by reframing*
Give two examples of counsellor responses that challenge clients by reframing or offering new perspectives.

Part B: Practising in pairs or in a group

1 *In pairs.* Suggestions include:

(a) Together work through the items in Part A of this exercise.
(b) Conduct mini interviews with each other. Focus each interview on a particular challenging skill. 'Counsellors' should ensure that they make at least one response of the targeted challenging skill in the interview. Pay attention to voice and body as well to verbal messages. After each mini interview, the 'client' gives feedback on the use of the challenging skill, followed by discussion. Play back recordings, if helpful.
(c) Conduct longer interviews with each other, say for 15 minutes or more, in which the 'counsellor' attempts to incorporate challenges. Again pay attention to voice and body as well as verbal messages. Debrief and give feedback after each session.

2 *In a group.* One person acting as a client presents a problem to the group who sit in a semicircle facing her/him. The client deliberately introduces discrepancies into what she/he says. Each member takes a turn in responding to the client, first by reflecting what she/he has just said and then, when a discrepancy occurs, making a challenging response. When finished, the client provides feedback on the 'session'. Members take turns as clients.

Feedback skills

Feedback skills and challenging skills overlap. However, challenging skills are used in response to clients' inconsistencies, whereas there is no assumption of inconsistency in this section on feedback skills. Here a distinction is made between observational feedback, 'I observe you as ... ', and experiential feedback, 'I experience you as ... '.

Observational feedback

Counselling trainees observing clients' communication may see it differently and possibly more accurately than clients themselves. When working together to try and understand clients' problem situations, there may be occasions where trainees decide to provide feedback to clients based on their observations. Take clients who have just shown how they communicate in a specific situation. After participating in mini role-plays, they may show some insight into their communication. However, as an observer, the trainee wishes to bring something else to their attention.

Many of the same skills used when learing counselling skills are relevant to giving feedback to clients: for example, using 'I' messages; being specific and, where possible, stating feedback in the positive; using confirmatory as well as corrective feedback; considering demonstrating feedback; and providing opportunities for clients to respond to feedback (see Box 9.3).

Box 9.3 Guidelines for offering feedback

Use 'I' messages rather than 'You' messages
'You' message: 'You did...'
'I' message: 'I thought you...'

Be specific and, where possible, state feedback positively
Non-specific and negative: 'You performed poorly.'
Specific and positive: 'I thought you could use more eye contact and speak in a louder voice.'

Use confirmatory as well as corrective feedback
'I thought your use of eye contact was good, but that you could still speak in a louder voice.'

Consider emotional as well as behavioural feedback
'When you made very direct eye contact and spoke in a loud voice, I felt overpowered by you.'

Consider demonstrating feedback
'I would like to show you how your eye contact came over to me [*then demonstrate*].'

Provide opportunities for clients to respond to feedback
'What's your reaction to what I've just said?'

After a mini role-play it can be a good idea to ask clients to evaluate themselves before providing any feedback. Reasons for this include keeping clients as active participants, reducing the need for external feedback since clients may have noticed the points anyway, building clients' skills of self-observation, and sensing that clients are more likely to be receptive to feedback if they have first had the opportunity to assess themselves. For instance, after inviting clients to comment on their performance and listening to their responses, a trainee can summarize them and enquire, 'Would you mind if I added one or two observations...?' and then, if given permission, succinctly provide feedback.

Experiential feedback

Feedback can also involve counselling trainees in using their experiencing of clients as the springboard for making observations about both the client and the counselling process. To an extent counselling sessions are a microcosm of outside life. Clients can bring to the sessions the same patterns of communication that create difficulties for them outside of them. Trainees have to be very careful not to let their own personal unfinished business interfere with how they experience clients.

Counselling trainees may not need to engage in role-plays to experience how clients may come across to others in their problem situations. For example, I once had a very bright and able businesswoman client, Louise, who was repeatedly getting turned down at interviews. I used questioning and active listening to explore what might be going on in these situations. However, the most powerful information came from my feeling of being overpowered by Louise's bombastic and lecturing interpersonal style. My first decision was, 'Should I share this experientially based information or sit on it?' Having decided that I might try to share the information, the second decision was, 'How do I provide this experiential feedback to Louise, who has shown limited insight so far?'

I tentatively suggested to Louise that I experienced her as coming over rather strong as she talked with me and that this might be relevant to panel members' reactions at her interviews. Furthermore, I fed back to her that she had a fairly booming voice. I could have done this more tactfully if I had remembered a comment that she had made about the possibility that she was 'too educational' at interviews. I could then have introduced this feedback about her booming voice as a hypothesis to clarify an aspect of her comment about being 'too educational'. Had I done this, my feedback might have been closer to her perspective and less from my own.

Instances where counselling trainees' experiencing of clients' interpersonal style may throw light on their problems outside relate to clients who do not come on time for interviews, or who speak in distant ways, are aggressive or disparage themselves. Giving positive experiential feedback to clients with low self-esteem can sometimes be helpful: for example 'I experience you as having some strength to deal with the situation' or 'I experience you as having much to offer a friend.' Such comments need to be genuine feedback rather than superficial reassurance.

Trainees can also provide experiential feedback concerning the counselling process. For example, if a client is repetitively going over the same ground, the student might say: 'I experience you as having taken that topic as far as you can go at the moment and it might be profitable to move on. What do you think?' Another example is that of a trainee who shares her or his experiencing of a client who uses humour as a distancing device whenever topics become too personal: for instance, 'I get the sense that this topic is getting too close for comfort and so you're starting to act the clown to avoid dealing with it directly.' Needless to say, tact and good timing are very important if clients are to use such experiential feedback to move forwards rather than backwards.

Activity 9.3 Feedback skills

Part A: Observational feedback

1 Refer to the guidelines for offering feedback in Box 9.4 and formulate statements for illustrating each of the different guidelines.
2 Work in a pair with partner A as 'client' and partner B as 'counsellor'.

- Partner A selects a problem situation involving another person where she/he thinks she/he might communicate better.
- Partners A and B conduct a mini role-play in which partner B plays the other person and Partner A demonstrates how she/he currently communicates in the situation.
- Afterwards, partner B invites partner A to comment on her/his verbal, vocal and body messages in the situation. Then partner B gives observational feedback to partner A.
- Next hold a sharing and discussion session about partner B's observational feedback skills.
- If appropriate, reverse roles.

Part B: Experiential feedback

1 What does the concept of offering experiential feedback mean to you?
2 Formulate one or more statements offering experiential feedback.

Self-disclosure skills

Should counselling trainees talk at all about themselves in counselling sessions? How can they show genuineness and humanity if they stay as a blank screen to clients? Self-disclosure relates to the ways in which people let themselves be known to one another. Usually the term refers to intentional verbal disclosure. However, there are numerous other ways in which people disclose, including their vocal and body messages, their availability, and via phone, written or email communications. A useful distinction exists between disclosures showing involvement and the sharing of personal experiences.

Trainees' self-disclosure, even in brief contact with clients, can be for good or ill. Possible positive consequences of such disclosure include providing new insights and perspectives, demonstrating a useful skill, equalizing and humanizing the helping relationship, normalizing clients' difficulties, giving encouragement, and reassurance (Edwards and Murdoch, 1994; Knox et al., 1997; Simone et al., 1998).

However, there can be grave dangers if trainees inappropriately disclose themselves. Boundaries may get blurred as they burden clients with their problems and shift the focus of the counselling conversation to themselves. They may come across as weak and unstable when clients who feel vulnerable want helpers who have 'got their act together'. In addition, trainees may either intentionally or unintentionally use self-disclosure to manipulate clients to meet their own needs for approval, intimacy and sex.

Showing involvement

Disclosures that show counselling trainees' involvement can humanize counselling so that clients feel they relate to real people. There is a 'here-and-now' quality in showing involvement by sharing reactions to clients. Three areas for disclosing involvement are responding to specific client disclosures, responding to clients as people, and responding to clients' vulnerability. Box 9.4 provides examples of statements for each area.

Box 9.4 Examples of counsellor disclosures

Showing involvement
Responding to specific disclosures:
'I'm delighted. That's great.' 'That's terrible. I'm really sorry to hear that.'
Responding to clients as people:
'I admire your courage.' 'I appreciate your honesty.'
Responding to clients' vulnerability:
'I'm available if you get really low. I'm very concerned about what you're going through.'

Sharing personal experiences
'Diane, at one stage in my life I was unemployed too and found it a very scary and difficult time. Though clearly our experiences differ, I think I do have some idea of what you're going through.'

Trainees who show involvement can help clients feel that they genuinely care. Positive self-involving statements that express positive rather than negative feelings about clients can draw favourable reactions

(Watkins, 1990). However, trainees need to be careful about being too gushing and nice. Clients want detached involvement rather than involvement with psychological hooks attached. Furthermore, some clients may need tough alongside tender love.

Sharing personal experiences

Sharing personal experiences may help clients feel that a counselling trainee understands what they are going through. For instance, unemployed people might feel differently about those who share that they too have been unemployed (see Box 9.4). In some types of counselling, disclosure of shared experiences is an important part of the process: for instance Alcoholics Anonymous and some drug addiction programmes.

Trainees have many choices in sharing personal experiences. Included among these are whether to mention them or not, whether to restrict themselves to past experiences or discuss current experiences, how honest to be, whether to go beyond disclosing facts to disclosing feelings – for instance not only having been unemployed but then having to struggle against feelings of depression and uselessness, how they coped with their experience, and how they feel about it now. In brief counselling, trainees will not have the opportunity to develop the 'relational depth' that some counsellors achieve with some clients later in a series of sessions (Mearns, 1997; Mearns and Thorne, 1999).

Below are some guidelines for appropriate sharing of personal experiences.

- *Talk about oneself.* Do not disclose the experience of third parties whom one knows.
- *Talk about past experiences.* Counselling trainees may not have sufficient emotional distance from current experiences, for instance if they are going through a messy divorce.
- *Be to the point.* Personal disclosures should follow similar client disclosures. Avoid slowing down or defocusing the counselling session through lack of relevance or talking too much.
- *Be sensitive to clients' reactions.* Have sufficient awareness to realize when disclosures might be helpful to the client and when they might be unwelcome or a burden.
- *Share personal experiences sparingly.* Be careful not to switch the focus of counselling from clients to oneself.
- *Be sensitive to counsellor–client differences.* Expectations of counselling differ across cultures, social class, race and gender and so do expectations regarding appropriateness of trainee self-disclosure.

- *Beware of counter-transference.* Counter-transference refers to negative and positive feelings towards clients based on unresolved areas in counsellors' or counselling trainees' lives. Intentionally or unintentionally some trainees use both showing involvement and sharing information self-disclosures to manipulate clients to meet their own needs for approval, intimacy and sex. This highlights the importance of being aware of one's motivation and of behaving ethically.

Activity 9.4 Self-disclosure skills

Part A: Showing involvement

1 With respect to your present or future counselling work, write down the sorts of situations in which it might be appropriate for you to show involvement to clients early on in counselling.
2 Using Box 9.4 as a guide, formulate one or more showing involvement disclosures in each of the following areas:

- responding to specific client disclosures
- responding to clients as people
- responding to clients' vulnerability

3 Work with a partner and use basic counselling skills to help her/him to discuss a personal concern or to role-play a client. During the course of a mini session, try on a few occasions to make disclosures showing involvement.
4 Afterwards discuss with your partner the impact of your showing involvement disclosures. Then reverse roles.

Part B: Sharing personal experiences

1 With regard to your present or future counselling work, write down the sorts of situations in which it might be appropriate for you to share personal experiences with clients early on in counselling.
2 For each situation formulate one or more sharing personal experiences responses.
3 Work with a partner and use basic counselling skills to help her/him to discuss a personal concern or to role-play a client. During the course of a mini session, try on one or more appropriate occasions to share personal experiences.
4 Afterwards discuss with your partner the impact of your sharing personal experiences disclosures. Then reverse roles.

assess feelings and physical reactions 10

Chapter outcomes

By studying and doing the activities in this chapter you should:

- understand more about the role of assessment in lifeskills counselling;
- understand the importance of assessing feelings and physical reactions;
- know some of the main physical reactions accompanying feelings;
- understand some of the main dimensions of feelings; and
- know about a number of skills for eliciting and assessing feelings and physical reactions.

Role of assessment

Assessment in lifeskills counselling is performed both with clients and for clients. Its purposes include helping both counsellor and client understand the nature of the client's presenting concerns and facilitating the client's learning and motivation by sharing the counsellor's or trainee's view of the problem (Bayne et al., 1999). During the relating stage counsellors and trainees start to develop working models of clients' problems and problematic skills. Clients come to counselling with hypotheses, most often inadequate, of what their problems are and how they are sustained. Right from the beginning of counselling, clients may start revising their ideas.

During the understanding stage, often the process of systematically eliciting descriptive information about clients' problems loosens their existing ways of viewing them. However, the process does not stop there. The desired outcome of this stage is to reconceptualize problems so that clients now have 'handles' for change – similar to what Egan (2002) calls 'leverage' for helping clients to work on the right things. Counselling trainees can use skills both to elicit basic descriptive information and to explore hypotheses about the problematic skills that may be sustaining problems. Trainees can assess information that is both volunteered and elicited. Together with clients, they can reform descriptive summaries of problems into shared analyses of them in skills terms.

The counsellor's role

Counsellors and trainees should always offer supportive relationships when assessing and restating clients' problems in skills terms. Active listening skills are fundamental. Furthermore, many skills used for clarifying problems – for instance focusing and summarizing – are relevant for assessing and agreeing on shared analyses of problems.

Counselling trainees are practitioner-researchers who formulate hypotheses about how clients sustain problems. Sources of such hypotheses are descriptive information provided by clients, information elicited as trainees 'try on' initial hypotheses, counselling theory, knowledge of relevant research, and previous experiences with clients. Where possible, trainees should work openly with clients and treat them as intelligent people who, despite defences and anxieties, wish to help themselves by gaining greater self-understanding. They can assist clients to do much of their own assessing rather than do all of it for them. Especially where client contact extends over a number of sessions, trainees can also teach clients how to think of their problems in skills terms.

Can assessment be overdone? The answer is a resounding 'yes'. Trainees need to be sensitive to the amount of information required for assessing problems and also take into account clients' perceptions of when 'enough is enough'. Where possible, they should collect information and also agree on shared analyses of problems in skills terms with a lightness of touch that avoids a sense of imposition, let alone of diagnostic inquisition.

The client's role

Like counsellors and trainees, clients are also hypothesis makers and testers. To date, their hypotheses about how to solve their problems have been inadequate. Frequently, they are stuck in faulty definitions of problems. Clients can actively collaborate with those helping them in generating hypotheses, providing information for assessing hypotheses, and evaluating conceptualizations of problems. They can participate in attempts to assess their feelings, thoughts and actions. For example, they can strive for honesty in experiencing and expressing feelings. They can be open about how they think, even if in socially undesirable ways. They can assist in exploring and evaluating hypotheses about how they think. Most usefully, they can share specific details of how they have acted in the past. They can then monitor their current actions, and agree to participate in role-plays in order to explore new ways of behaving.

Assessment is for clients' even more than for counsellors' benefits. Clients can engage in testing the adequacy of initial understandings of problems and make corrections, if appropriate. They can provide confirmatory, corrective or negative feedback about counselling trainees' hypotheses. Clients can cooperate with trainees to develop more accurate and parsimonious skills analyses of problems. If they are active in assessing and agreeing on shared analyses, clients are likely to become more motivated to change. Furthermore, active participation in assessing and redefining problems assists clients to develop these skills for later self-helping.

Why assess feelings and physical reactions?

The following are examples of feelings and physical reactions statements made by clients:

'I get very nervous.'
'I have suicidal thoughts.'
'I feel tense much of the time.'
'I shake with fury.'
'I'm at sixes and sevens.'
'I lack motivation.'
'I'm slow to turn on sexually.'

Counsellors and trainees assess feelings and physical reactions (the physical manifestations of feelings) for numerous reasons. Some of these are given below.

Protect clients

Counselling trainees have an ethical duty to protect clients. At the back of most counsellors' minds when meeting new clients is the question: 'Is this client a suicide risk?' Trainees also seek to understand the intensity and nature of clients' pain: partly to protect clients, but also to make appropriate shared analyses of clients' problems in skills terms.

Evaluate emotional responsiveness

Trainees always need to be mindful of clients' ability to experience feelings. Feelings may be viewed as the core of human personhood and identity. Trainees seek to assess how responsive clients are both to themselves and others. To what extent are clients in touch with their valuing process? Are they in touch with significant feelings or do they deny and distort such feelings? To what extent are clients in touch with their desires?

Clarify real agendas

Attending closely to feelings and physical reactions may assist trainees to clarify clients' real agendas. Sometimes clients give feelings clues that more substantial problems underlie their 'calling card' explanations for coming. For example, by voice and body messages a woman who presents wanting to discuss a 'problem' child may indicate that her real agenda is marital dissatisfaction. Sometimes trainees need to allow clients sufficient space to clarify feelings before they can know which problem to work on in skills terms.

> Alan, 48, had been divorced for four years and had custody of three children – Marcia, 16, Angela 15 and Duncan 13. For the last year, Alan had been seeing Amy, 45, a divorcee who also had three children with ages ranging from 8 to 15. Alan came to counselling confused about whether or not he wanted to develop his relationship with Amy further or get out of it. Alan's counsellor, Glen, spent much of the initial session assisting Alan to get in touch with and explore his feelings concerning his past, present and possible future with Amy; his fears of commitment after the pain of his divorce; his anxieties about how good he was at communicating in close relationships; his needs for companionship; and his fears of being lonely for the remainder of his life. As the session progressed Alan became clearer regarding his wish to work on his skills at relating to Amy.

Obtain leads about poor mind skills and communication/action skills

Another reason for assessing feelings and physical reactions is to help clients regulate unwanted feelings and express appropriate feelings. Since feelings and physical reactions tend to be, or to become as if, instinctive they are not in themselves skills. Nevertheless, assessing feelings accurately can be a major route to identifying mind skills and communication/action skills weaknesses. For example, clients admitting their anger, hurt and guilt – and what these do to their bodies – have a better starting point for developing the mind skills and communication skills to manage these feelings than clients who deny or distort them. It is usually also important to pay attention to clients' skills at expressing feelings. For example, Helen knows what she feels about her boyfriend, Ricky, but is too inhibited to reveal it.

Screen for medical and psychiatric considerations

A simple mind–body split is erroneous. Nevertheless, counselling trainees need to be aware that medical considerations can influence how clients feel. Non-medically trained helpers should acknowledge their limitations and seek appropriate medical or psychiatric advice, for example: when clients are on medication; have a physical illness, for instance cancer, that affects how they feel; show psycho-physiological symptoms, such as peptic ulcers and migraine headaches; exhibit the effects of substance abuse; and suffer from mental disorders (American Psychiatric Association, 2000).

Develop clients' self-assessment skills

Counselling trainees can work together with clients to assess feelings and physical reactions. In their past many clients have had their feelings and physical reactions invalidated. Skilled assessment can both affirm the need for awareness of feelings as well as help clients to experience, identify and explore significant feelings. Clients' feelings may take time to emerge and be shared. Revealing and assessing feelings occurs throughout counselling and, where possible, students can also assist clients to develop skill in assessing feelings after counselling.

Physical reactions

Physical reactions, or bodily sensations, both represent and accompany feelings and, in a sense, the two are indistinguishable. Assessing physical reactions is discussed prior to assessing feelings, since this ordering emphasizes that feelings are located in the body. Box 10.1 shows some bodily changes or physical reactions associated with feelings.

Box 10.1 Bodily changes and feelings

Galvanic skin response
Detectable electrical changes take place in the skin.

Blood pressure, distribution and composition
Blood pressure can rise. The distribution of blood may alter: for instance, in blushing (going red) or blanching (going white) the blood vessels near the skin's surface dilate or constrict, respectively. In addition, there can be changes in blood composition – for instance in blood sugar, acid-base balance, and adrenalin content.

Heart rate and pulse rate
A pounding heart and a rapid pulse characterize intense emotion.

Breathing
Shallow, rapid breathing can characterize anxiety.

Muscular tension
Muscular tension is associated with intensity of feeling. Clients can feel tension in different parts of their bodies. Sometimes trembling accompanies muscular tension.

Slower and quicker body movements
Body movements can slow down, for instance when depressed, or speed up, for instance when excited or anxious.

Dry mouth
Emotional excitation can produce a decrease in saliva.

Dilation of eye pupils
In moments of heightened feeling, for instance anger or sexual attraction, the eye pupils tend to dilate.

Stomach problems
Emotional excitement may contribute to nausea or diarrhoea. Persistent emotional excitement may lead to ulcers. Appetite may become poor.

Goose pimples
A response in which the hairs of the skin stand on end, often because of fear.

Thought blocking
Tension may contribute to clients' minds going totally or partially blank.

Speech difficulties
Heightened excitation can lead to stammering, speaking rapidly and the slurring of words. In extreme instances, the ability to speak may be temporarily lost.

Sleep difficulties
Sleep difficulties include time taken to get to sleep, disturbed sleep and early morning waking.

Sex difficulties
Complete or partial loss of desire is a common sex difficulty associated with tension.

Physical reactions and feelings

Word labels or linguistic symbols describing feelings are attached to different clusters of physical reactions. For example, physical reactions associated with the word 'shyness' include dry mouth, blushing, nausea, feeling faint, perspiring, knotted stomach, pounding heart, shaking, mind going blank and shallow, rapid breathing. Most, if not all, of these physical reactions also characterize anxiety. Often in the psychological literature, shyness is called social anxiety. Sometimes clients react further to their physical reactions. For example, in anxiety and panic attacks, clients may first feel tense and anxious and then become even more tense and anxious because of this initial feeling. Counselling trainees need to develop skill in empathically describing with appropriate words clients' physical reactions.

Energy level

Related to clients' ability to experience feelings is their energy level. Changes in energy level may precede, be concurrent with or follow from changes in how clients feel and think. For example, energetic clients may feel more confident. On the other hand, once clients lose their confidence, they may feel less energetic. Trainees can assess how much mental and physical energy clients have and how vital or apathetic they are. If clients' energy levels are very low trainees can ask them to check with their doctors for medical explanations.

Psycho-physiological disorders

Psycho-physiological or psychosomatic disorders are physical reactions caused and maintained primarily by psychological and emotional rather than by physical or organic factors. Psycho-physiological disorders can affect the skin, for instance causing acne, and the body's musculoskeletal, respiratory, cardiovascular, blood and lymphatic, gastrointestinal, and endocrine systems. The more common of these disorders are peptic ulcers, migraine headaches, asthma, and high blood pressure. Psycho-physiological disorders may be distinguished from somatoform disorders, the latter being phoney or imitative rather than actual physical disorders.

Dimensions of feelings

Feelings are private internal states of affect that may not be immediately observed externally (Heesacker and Bradley, 1997) and, even when observable, they may be either disguised or interpreted wrongly. Dimensions of feelings overlap with physical reactions. When discussing reflecting feelings (see Chapter 7), some ways were discussed of identifying feelings by picking up feelings words and by attending to voice and body messages. Here dimensions of feelings are explored more from the viewpoint of assessing problems than of making active listening responses.

Mood

A mood is a state of mind or feeling associated with physical reactions. Moods may last for two weeks or more. For instance, the essential feature of a major depressive disorder is a period of at least two weeks during which there is either depressed mood or the loss of pleasure or interest in nearly all activities (American Psychiatric Association, 2000). However, often moods can be relatively transient in duration: for instance a few moments, a day, or a week. McNair, Lorr and Droppleman's (1981) *Profile of Mood States* (POMS) provides scores on six identifiable mood states: tension-anxiety, depression-dejection, anger-hostility; vigour-activity; fatigue-inertia and confusion-bewilderment. Counselling trainees can assess severity, direction, duration and fluctuations in clients' moods.

Capacity to feel

Trainees need to be aware of clients' abilities to experience feelings (Rogers, 1951, 1959, 1961, 1975). Some clients lack emotional responsiveness across a wide range of feelings. Other clients may have difficulty experiencing specific feelings: for example those concerned with sexuality or anger. Clients' difficulties in experiencing feelings can be at different levels. An extensive and long-standing incapacity to experience feelings may have different implications for a counselling process than a more focused and less severe problem in this area. One of the outcomes of any extended counselling contact is that clients should become better at experiencing and expressing feelings.

Self-esteem

Counselling trainees need to be aware of clients' confidence levels. Clients with very low self-esteem may be potential suicide risks. Clients with reasonable self-esteem possess a useful asset for working on problems and problematic skills. Words to describe low self-esteem include worthlessness, hopelessness, helplessness, pessimism and despair. Self-statements indicating lack of self-esteem include; 'I'm no good', 'I never do anything right' and 'I can't cope.' Adjectives to describe high self-esteem include confident, strong, self-accepting, worthwhile, optimistic and emotionally resilient.

Anxiety and defensiveness

Counselling trainees need to assess how anxious clients are and in what areas of their life anxiety occurs. Is their anxiety a pervasive trait or is it a state attached to specific situations? They also need to assess how clients show anxiety, both in obvious ways and also in terms of their less overt defensive processes or security operations (Clark, 1991;

Sullivan, 1953, 1954). The American Psychiatric Association's *Diagnostic and Statistical Manual of Mental Disorders* (2000) views defence mechanisms (or coping styles) as automatic psychological processes that protect the individual against anxiety and from the awareness of internal or external dangers or stressors. It states that individuals are often unaware of these processes as they operate. Trainees should pay attention to ways in which clients' anxieties – and theirs too – can distort the counselling process.

Psychological pain

Effective counsellors are skilled at locating clients' areas of psychological pain and assessing their severity. Sometimes during counselling clients acknowledge major areas of psychological pain that they have hitherto either repressed or suppressed. Counselling trainees also need to be conscious of the pain and distress that clients may experience when discussing certain material: for instance a bereavement, rape or sexual abuse.

Predominant feelings

Sometimes clients present with a specific feeling that they wish to handle better, for example anxiety in exam or public speaking situations. In other instances, a predominant feeling may emerge as counselling progresses: for instance self-pity, resentment, anger or wariness. Teyber (2000) uses the term 'characterological feeling' to describe these central feelings that clients experience as their inevitable fate because they have always been there and it seems that they always will be. Trainees need to keep an eye and ear out for repetitive and central feelings that clients handle with difficulty. Prior to and even during counselling clients may find it hard to acknowledge such feelings.

Strength and persistence of feelings

Often feeling intensity is described by words like 'mild', 'moderate' or severe'. For example, clients may be mildly depressed, moderately depressed or severely depressed. There are different perceptions of what is mild, moderate or severe both among those who counsel and between counsellors and clients. Persistence of feelings may be described by words like chronic and acute. Chronic implies persistent whereas acute implies sharp and short. In addition, disorders like schizophrenia may be in partial remission or full remission (American Psychiatric Association, 2000).

Complex and conflicted feelings

Clients' feelings are frequently complex. Counselling trainees require skills at eliciting, clarifying and articulating the different elements of what may be multiple and mixed feelings. Clients may need to learn to avoid thinking about their feelings in static, rigid and simplistic terms. Feelings often come in twos and threes. For example, anger may be accompanied by hurt and guilt, or depression by anxiety and sadness. What is more, feelings are often accompanied – even if at a less intense level – by their opposites. Ambivalent feelings include: happy–sad, love–hate, pleased–displeased, and approach–avoidance. Clients may experience contrasting feelings simultaneously or sequentially.

Unclear feelings

Clients may be either unclear about feelings or communicate feelings unclearly, or both. Sometimes feelings are masked: for instance depression may mask anger. On other occasions feelings are displaced: anger at failing an exam may be 'taken out' on a room-mate, spouse or parent. Sometimes the real agenda is unclear. For instance, married couples may argue over little things and avoid confronting more serious differences and relationship fears. Frequently, expression of feelings is inhibited or diluted.

Some clients obscure feelings by portraying the opposite of what they feel. They can also dramatize and magnify feelings. Social desirability considerations may pervade the early stages of counselling and, as a result, clients may play out social roles to please those counselling them. Clients may also have acquired poor skills at using feelings words and framing their verbal feelings messages with appropriate voice and body messages. Many feelings take time to emerge. As mentioned earlier, sensitivity is required about the pace at which clients both can and wish to reveal their emotional selves.

Antecedents and consequences of feelings

When assessing feelings, counselling trainees may assess their antecedents and consequences. The antecedents of feelings can stretch back into clients' childhoods. For example, the pain of a present loss may reactivate the pain of an earlier loss. Anger may be hard to express now because such feelings were suppressed in clients' families of origin. Frequently, counsellors explore current antecedents and consequences of feelings: for example, clients' thoughts prior to experiencing feelings and the positive and negative consequences that follow from expressing certain feelings.

Appropriateness of feelings

Often counselling trainees and clients can attempt to assess appropriateness of feelings. Did the client experience an appropriate feeling at an appropriate level and was this appropriately expressed? Clients' unique styles of expressing feelings and numerous situational, contextual and cultural considerations must be taken into account. One way of assessing appropriateness of feelings is to judge their consequences for clients and others. To what extent and in what ways were there positive or negative emotional and behavioural consequences?

Feelings about counselling and counsellors

Clients invariably have feelings both about counselling and about those counselling them. They may either resist or cooperate in the counselling process. They may feel pleased or frustrated with their progress. Clients' feelings about those counselling them may have a range of dimensions, such as like/dislike, trust/mistrust, competent/incompetent and dependent/independent. Sometimes clients express feelings that counselling trainees find difficult to handle: for example liking, sexual attraction, anger and sadness. Often there is reciprocity of feeling between clients and their counsellors, for example mutual like or dislike.

Skills for eliciting and assessing feelings and physical reactions

Feelings are central to clients' abilities to function effectively and to grow and develop as unique individuals. Counselling trainees need to learn to work closely with clients who are ultimately the experts on their feelings and physical reactions. Forming good collaborative working relationships with clients can help them to get in touch with, experience, express and explore their feelings. Assessing feelings and physical reactions can be a sensitive process in that clients' feelings, especially the more threatening and delicate ones, require particularly favourable counsellor-offered conditions if they are to emerge and be shared. Clients' feelings may fluctuate and, hopefully, change for the better as counselling proceeds. Rather than being able to identify clients' feelings clearly, counsellors are forming hypotheses much of the time and either waiting for or eliciting further evidence to confirm or negate their hunches. Below are some skills useful for eliciting and assessing feelings.

Active listening

In supportive and trusting relationships, clients can assist counselling trainees to understand how they feel. Active listening provides a safe emotional climate for clients to experience and share feelings. Trainees sensitive to clients' feelings and feeling nuances legitimize the importance of experiencing and discussing feelings. They require good skills at picking up and reflecting back the messages conveyed by feelings.

Receiver skills include paying attention to feelings words, observing voice and body messages, and being keenly attuned to any mismatch between voice, body and verbal messages. Sometimes feelings can be inferred from what is left unsaid or partially said. Sender skills that trainees can use to help clients share feelings include showing attention with voice and body messages, reflecting feelings and offering companionship to clients as they explore new and sometimes unexpected feelings.

Counselling trainees need to use tact and sensitivity when clients encounter feelings that are difficult either to experience or share and it is important at all times to remain aware of the pace at which clients wish to reveal feelings. Often a box of Kleenex helps to facilitate the process! Trainees can make the following kind of remark to encourage clients to share feelings without pressurizing them.

'I realize that this may be a painful area for you to discuss.'
'You seem upset. Just take your time in sharing what you feel.'

Clients' voice and body messages probably provide the most valid source of information about how they feel. From the moment of first contact, skilled counsellors observe body messages closely and listen attentively for voice messages. Clients differ in how clearly they send messages. To be really effective trainees need to listen both consciously and intuitively 'with the third ear' and observe 'with the third eye' for deviations, omissions and discrepancies in communications. They look out for feeling fragments or occasional glimpses that are clues to more substantial and as yet unshared feelings. Skilled counsellors have a highly developed capacity for sensing where clients' real emotional agendas are and also what seems false. Their ability to tune into their own feelings as well as their experience of numerous previous clients provides a base for formulating hypotheses about feelings that clients are experiencing.

Advanced reflection of feelings

As a result of observing and listening, counselling trainees may sense clients' underlying messages. Frequently clients repress, suppress or otherwise inhibit feelings. Advanced reflection of feelings, what Egan calls advanced empathy, entails making exploratory responses that help clients articulate more personally relevant, emotionally tinged and potentially threatening areas of their experiencing. Relevant questions that students can ask themselves include:

- What is this person only half saying?
- What is this person hinting at?
- What is this person saying in a confused way?
- What messages do I hear behind the explicit messages? (Egan, 2002: 200)

Counselling trainees require sensitivity to reflect partially hidden agendas. Sometimes they may choose not to mention such agendas for fear of upsetting clients. Advanced reflections of feelings check out counsellor 'hunches' or hypotheses. Such responses generally require humility and tentativeness. Inaccurate, clumsily worded, and badly timed responses can do more harm than good. Box 10.2 provides two examples of advanced empathy.

Box 10.2 Advanced empathy

Example 1

The counsellor gets the impression that the client, Linda, may be talking around the area of her lesbian feelings:

Counsellor: You've talked about a couple of people you know who do not find lesbian life easy. I'm wondering whether lesbianism might be a sensitive issue for you too?

Example 2

The counselling trainee has a hunch that a client, Scott, who recently had a blazing row with his father, either feels or soon will feel guilty about how he behaved:

Counselling trainee: On the one hand you have a sense of triumph at giving Dad a piece of your mind, but I catch an undercurrent of guilt and sorrow at how you behaved and a concern about your dad's loneliness and vulnerability. Am I on the right track?

Ask questions about feelings and physical reactions

Questions can assist clients in being specific about feelings and physical reactions. Frequently, since counselling trainees cannot assume a common meaning, they need to clarify labels clients attach to feelings. For instance, follow-up questions to a client who says 'I am very depressed' might be: 'When you say you are very depressed, what exactly do you mean?' or 'When you say you are very depressed what are your specific feelings and physical reactions?' or 'You feel very depressed. Can you tell me more about that feeling?' Then the trainee can collaborate with the client to identify the relevant feelings and physical reactions. Sometimes trainees can directly check out specific feelings or physical reactions, for instance 'Do you feel suicidal sometimes?' or 'How is your appetite?'

Counselling trainees can assist clients to distinguish between feelings and thoughts. If clients respond to questions focusing on feelings with how they think, students may choose to bring them back to feelings.

Client: I feel very anxious.
Counselling trainee: When you say you feel very anxious what exactly do you mean?
Client: I am having problems in my job and in my marriage.
Counselling trainee: You're having problems at work and at home. These are thoughts or reasons why you may be very anxious. However, could you tell me more about the actual anxious feelings you experience?

Trainees often need to help clients to expand and elaborate their feelings and physical reactions. Box 10.3 provides some illustrative questions that focus on feelings.

Box 10.3 Focusing on feelings and physical reactions

'When did you start feeling this way?'
'Tell me more about the feeling.'
'Describe how your body experiences the feeling.'
'In which part of your body do you experience the feeling?'
'Do you have any visual images that capture the feeling?'
'Are there any metaphors that illustrate the feeling?'
'How has your mood been and how is it today?'
'Are there any other feelings that accompany or underlie that feeling?'
'How do you feel here and now?'
'On a scale of 0 to 10 (or 0 to 100) how strong is the feeling?'
'How persistent is the feeling?'

Emotion-eliciting strategies

Sometimes counselling trainees deliberately attempt to induce feelings so that they and clients can observe and assess them.

- *Visualizing.* Clients can be asked to shut their eyes, visualize a scene and re-experience the emotions attached to it. For example, socially phobic clients can be asked to conjure up the images immediately before and during anxiety-provoking social situations (Hackman et al., 1998).
- *Role-playing.* Trainees may conduct mini role-plays of scenes with clients, for example a parent arguing with a teenaged daughter or son who has come home much later than agreed. Then trainees can assist clients to identify and clarify the emotions elicited in these role-plays.
- *Self-disclosure.* To promote client insight into their feelings and to make it easier to talk about them, trainees may share personal information about experiences similar to those of clients. Such disclosure always needs to have the clients' best interests in mind (Simone et al., 1998). Usually, it is preferable to talk about past experiences, where trainees have obtained some emotional distance, than about current experiences. In certain kinds of counselling, such as in some alcohol and drug treatment programmes, peer self-disclosure is built into the process.
- *Live observation.* Where appropriate, counselling trainees can take clients into difficult situations, observe their reactions and listen to what they say about how they feel. For example, a trainee might go with an agoraphobic client into a supermarket, offer support, and observe her or his reactions.
- *Task assignment.* Trainees and clients may agree on between-session tasks for clients: for instance, a recently divorced man asking someone for a date. Clients can record their feelings and physical reactions before, during and after these tasks.

Encourage clients to monitor feelings

Counselling trainees can encourage clients to monitor their feelings and physical reactions on a regular basis. Such monitoring can raise self-awareness as well as help clients to learn a valuable skill: namely listening closely to their feelings.

One approach to doing this is to use daily rating forms on which clients can rate themselves on feelings such as mood (very happy to very depressed), anxiety level (not anxious at all to very anxious), feelings of stress (very relaxed to very stressed) and so on. Ratings may be on scales ranging from 0 to 3, 5, 7, 9,10 or 100. In the example below, clients are asked to give themselves a daily mood score using the following scale.

Very depressed 0 1 2 3 4 5 6 7 **Very happy**

Counselling trainees can train clients in the skills of identifying and rating the key or important feelings and physical reactions they experience in specific situations. In cognitive therapy, going from situation to feelings is a useful entry point for then examining the thoughts that contribute to the feelings (Beck and Weishaar, 2005; Greenberger and Padesky, 1995). Clients can also be asked to rate their feelings and physical reactions on either a 0–10 or 0–100 scale.

Box 10.4 provides an example of a worksheet filled out by a client identifying and rating their key feelings and physical reactions during or immediately after being in a situation. This worksheet can be expanded in two ways. The same questions can be repeated for situation 1, situation 2 and so on. Alternatively, it can concentrate on a single situation and then examine the thoughts that were going through clients' minds just before they started to feel and physically react this way.

Box 10.4 Worksheet for identifying and rating key feelings and physical reactions regarding a situation

Situation
(*Who? What? When? Where?*)
Wednesday, 8.30 p.m.
I come home late from work and my partner says 'Where on earth have you been?'

Key feeling(s) and physical reaction(s)
(What did I feel? How did I physically react? Rating for each key feeling and physical reaction (0–100%))

Angry	70%
Hurt	80%
Tense	65%

Another way to monitor feelings is to use brief questionnaires that clients can fill out daily. Greenberger and Padesky (1995) provide examples of a 19-item 'Mind Over Mood Depression Inventory' and a 24-item 'Mind Over Mood Anxiety Inventory' that can be used for monitoring these feelings.

Be sensitive to cultural and other differences

Cultures differ greatly in the ways in which they express feelings. In addition, somatic symptoms (physical reactions) associated with distress differ across cultures. In some cultures depression is experienced largely in somatic terms rather than with sadness or guilt. For example, in Chinese and Asian cultures, depressed people may complain of weakness, tiredness or 'imbalance'. Western counselling trainees should be particularly careful in assessing feelings of people from non-Western cultures. Clients' perceptions of counsellors as dissimilar on cultural, racial, gender and social class characteristics may influence the degree to which they disclose feelings and physical reactions to them.

Wait and see

A big risk in assessing feelings is to jump to premature conclusions on insufficient evidence. For example, trainees may be too ready to label inaccurately women as hyper-emotional and men as hypo-emotional or lacking in emotion (Heesacker et al., 1999). Even with skilled counsellors and therapists, clients' feelings can take time to unfold. For example, clients either brought up to deny feelings or for whom expressing feelings was dangerous in their family of origin may change slowly. It is important to allow clients to share feelings and physical reactions at a pace comfortable for them. Invariably, initial session assessments of feelings require updating. Sometimes such assessments require substantial modification as counselling trainees get to know clients better and as clients learn more about themselves.

Activity 10.1 Eliciting and assessing feelings and physical reactions

Part A: Formulating responses

Think of a problem, in either your or a client's life, involving strong feelings. Regarding this problem, give examples of the following skills:

- active listening;
- advanced reflection of feelings;
- questions about feelings and physical reactions;
- emotion-eliciting techniques (e.g. live observation, visualizing, role-play, and/or task assignment);

- use of monitoring feelings measures (e.g. daily rating forms and/or critical incident logs);
- use of questionnaires;
- sensitivity to cultural and other differences;
- waiting and seeing.

Part B: Practising eliciting and assessing feelings

1 *In pairs* Ways in which you can practise with a partner include the following:

(a) Work through the items in Part A of this activity together.
(b) Conduct counselling sessions with one another in which the counsellor focuses mainly on helping the client experience, disclose, explore and assess her/his feelings about a problem. The counsellor uses skills such as active listening, advanced reflection of feelings, and questions focusing on feelings and physical reactions. At the end of each counselling session, the counsellor shares and discusses her/his feelings and physical reactions hypotheses about the client on each of the dimensions listed in Part A of this activity.
(c) Counsel a partner using two experimental modes. Practise each mode prior to conducting the experiment.

- *The focusing on information mode*: Here the counsellor mainly reflects and asks questions about information or content. You consciously try not to help the client experience, disclose and explore feelings. You attempt both to interview 'from the head' and to get the client responding 'from the head'.
- *The focusing on feelings and physical reactions mode*: Here the counsellor demonstrates great sensitivity to helping the client experience, disclose and explore feelings and physical reactions. You and your client work together to understand and assess the client's feelings. You use interventions such as reflection of feelings and physical reactions, advanced reflection of feelings, and questions focusing on feelings and physical reactions. You aim to help the client respond 'from the heart' rather than 'from the head'.

Spend at least three to five minutes counselling in each experimental mode. Then, together with your partner evaluate the consequences of the differences in your behaviour. Playing back a video recording of the session may help you assess the consequences of the experimental modes. Afterwards, reverse roles. Has this experiment taught you something about how you can be a more effective counsellor? If so, what?

2 *In a group* One person acts as client. The remainder of the group sit in a semicircle round the client and counsel the client in such a way as to assess her/his feelings about a problem. Every now and then stop and discuss both what's happened and where to go next. Repeat this activity with other 'clients'.

assess thinking 11

Chapter outcomes

By studying and doing the activities in this chapter you should:

- understand the importance of assessing and helping clients to assess their thinking;
- know some important things to look out for when assessing thinking; and
- learn some important skills of eliciting and assessing thinking.

In Chapter 3, the area of mind skills was introduced by encouraging readers to explore their own thinking. Some readers may find it valuable to review this before proceeding with the present chapter, since the six central mind skills are reviewed there, albeit from the viewpoint of counselling trainees. These mind skills are: creating rules, perceptions, self-talk, visual images, explanations and expectations. Though trainee and client mind skills are the same, the focus in this chapter is on assessing clients.

Counsellors and trainees who discover much about clients' feelings and physical reactions still face the problem of what to do next. Knowledge of inhibited, troublesome and unwanted feelings is insufficient in itself. Such knowledge raises questions about what thoughts, communications and actions contribute to sustaining these negative feelings and physical reactions. This chapter focuses on thinking; assessing communication and actions is the topic of the next chapter.

Many feelings and physical reactions can be influenced by how clients think. For this reason, if for no other, counselling trainees need to ask: 'What thoughts and mind skills engender or fail to engender feelings and physical reactions conducive to this client's well-being rather than causing her/him distress?' They also need to ask 'What thoughts and mind skills influence how clients communicate and act?' Trainees must develop hypotheses about poor mind skills that may be maintaining problems. Assessing how clients think is a vital step in formulating shared definitions of problems acceptable to both parties.

Clients' problems take place in a variety of influencing and sometimes very influential contexts. A number of social and cultural characteristics may affect the nature of their problems. In addition, a series of other past or current events in their lives impact on how well they cope with their problems.

Trainees can attend not just to clients' thoughts but to *how* they think. Skilled counsellors assist clients to think about how they think, improve their mind skills and develop self-helping skills so that they can monitor and, if necessary, change their thinking after counselling. If counselling trainees think about how they think in skills terms they will acquire a new way of thinking about themselves as well as about their clients. Assessing and working with one's own thoughts and mind skills is one of the best ways to learn to work effectively with clients' thoughts and mind skills. In some ways counsellors always remain their primary and most influential clients!

Skills for eliciting and assessing thinking

When eliciting and assessing thinking, counselling trainees need to develop and maintain good collaborative relationships with clients. Both should actively participate in the detective work of discovering clients' self-defeating thoughts, including visual images, and poor mind skills. Since clients are unlikely to be skilled at thinking about their thinking, they will often not realize the significance of what they are reporting about their thoughts as they seek to identify how they are sabotaging their happiness.

Counselling trainees require skills in recognizing clues to the various poor mind skills. Then, if necessary, they can investigate or 'sniff around' further to develop more accurate hypotheses about clients' self-defeating thoughts. Assessing thinking is a continuing process. At best, all trainees and clients can do in a first session is to form some initial ideas about where clients may need to focus in future. Thoughts interweave with feelings and, as counselling proceeds, clients often become clearer about what they feel and think. In successful counselling, clients will become better at developing the self-helping skills of monitoring and changing how they think. The following are some skills for eliciting and assessing thinking.

Build a knowledge base

It is essential that counselling trainees wishing to work with clients' mind skills develop their knowledge of how people think. They cannot help clients if they do not know what to look for. In addition, they may limit their effectiveness if they only focus on one or two mind skills. However, focusing on just a few mind skills can be a good way to start.

How can counselling skills students develop their knowledge base? First, they can read the works of cognitive therapists such as Ellis (2001, 2003, 2005; Ellis and Dryden, 1997; Ellis and MacLaren, 1998), Beck (1976, 1988; Beck and Weishaar, 2005) and of other therapists such as Frankl (1963, 1967, 1988), Glasser (1998; Glasser and Wubbolding, 1995), Lazarus (1984, 1997, 2005a), Meichenbaum (1977, 1983, 1985, 1986) and Yalom (Yalom, 1980, 2001; May and Yalom, 2005). They may go on to read secondary sources: for instance self-help books, like Greenberger and Padesky's excellent client manual for cognitive therapy, *Mind Over Mood* (1995), and textbooks, like the author's *Theory and Practice of Counselling & Therapy* (Nelson-Jones, 2001) or Corsini and Wedding's *Current Psychotherapies* (2005). They can then work on their own mind skills either independently or in personal therapy or in training groups. Finally, they can work with clients, definitely at first under supervision.

Important cognitive theorists such as Beck, Ellis and Meichenbaum rarely use the word 'skills' when writing about how clients think, though some of their followers are much more explicit about teaching skills. For example, Greenberger and Padesky write: '*Mind Over Mood* teaches you skills that are necessary to make fundamental changes in your moods, behaviors, and relationships' (1995: 2). The lifeskills counselling model advocated in this book adopts a similar emphasis on teaching skills to clients. This does not alter the fact that trainees require caution and tact in how they introduce the concept of skills to any client.

Ask questions about thoughts

Counselling trainees can help clients to reveal their thoughts by asking appropriate questions. One approach to asking questions about thinking is called 'Think aloud'. Think aloud involves encouraging clients to speak aloud their thought processes in relation to specific situations. For instance, clients can be asked to take trainees in slow motion through their thoughts and feelings in relation to specific anxiety-evoking experiences.

When asking questions, it is important that counselling trainees use active listening skills. Clients feel interrogated when trainees ask a series of questions in quick succession. Though they should not follow this guideline slavishly, trainees can greatly soften their questioning if they pause to see if clients wish to continue responding and then check that they reflect each response. Interspersing active listening has the added advantage of ensuring the accuracy of their understanding.

Sometimes trainees can access thinking from feelings, for instance 'What thoughts preceded or accompanied those feelings?' On other occasions they may choose to access thinking from a client's or another person's behaviour, for example: 'When you did that, what were you thinking?' or 'When she/he said that, what went through your mind?' Trainees can also ask follow-up questions, such as 'Were there any other thoughts or images?'

Thoughts can be considered in terms of their strength. One way to do this is to label thoughts as cool, warm and hot. In particular, trainees can help clients to look out for hot thoughts that may trigger unwanted feelings and self-defeating communications. Often, clients' thoughts about what other people are thinking are the hot thoughts that drive their poor communication. For example the thought 'She/he is out to get me' may produce an angry and unwarranted outburst against that person.

Box 11.1 provides some illustrative questions focusing on clients' thinking. Clients can ask themselves many of the same questions when on their own.

Box 11.1 Examples of questions focusing on thinking

'What thoughts did you have before/during/after the situation?'
'What was going through your mind just before you started to feel this way?'
'What images do you get in the situation?'
'Can you go in slow motion through your thoughts in the situation?'
'How frequently do you get those thoughts?'
'When she/he acted like that, what did you think?'
'Which of those thoughts is the hot thought?'
'What do you think she/he was thinking?'
'What are you afraid of?'
'What resources or strengths do you have in the situation?'
'Where is the evidence for this thought?'
'Are there other ways of looking at the situation?'
'What is the worst thing that could happen?'
'What memories is this situation stirring up?'
'Were there any other thoughts or images?'

Thought-eliciting strategies

The same strategies may be used to elicit thoughts and images as are used to elicit feelings and physical reactions.

- *Visualizing.* Clients can be asked to conjure up images that elicit feelings and asked to identify the accompanying thoughts. Clients can visualize past, present or future scenes and get in touch with harmful and helpful thoughts.

- *Role-playing*. Counselling trainees can conduct role-plays with clients, for instance telephoning someone for a date, and then explore their thoughts and feelings.
- *Live observation*. Where appropriate and taking care to maintain correct boundaries, trainees can accompany clients into situations that cause them difficulty, for instance returning something to a store or driving a car after an accident, and ask them to recount their thoughts.
- *Task assignment*. Trainees can encourage clients to perform feared tasks in between sessions and afterwards record their thoughts and feelings. Clients can view such tasks as personal experiments to collect evidence about themselves.

Encourage clients to monitor their thoughts and perceptions

Sometimes thoughts, perceptions and images are monitored in conjunction with the monitoring of feelings and physical reactions. One approach is to ask clients to count every time they get a specific self-defeating perception, for instance 'I'm no good.' Clients can use wrist counters for this purpose, as counting can help clients to become aware of the repetitive nature of their thinking. Clients may then record over a period of time the daily frequency of targeted thoughts and perceptions.

Another approach to monitoring thoughts is to expand the worksheet for identifying key feelings and physical reactions in a situation to include perceptions and images. Box 11.2 provides an example. Here the client is asked to put a star by the hot perceptions most associated with the feelings and physical reactions. Trainees can teach clients how to complete the worksheet, possibly by working through an example with them on a whiteboard in the counselling room. Clients can be asked to fill out separate worksheets for difficult situations they faced between sessions.

Box 11.2 Worksheet for identifying and rating key feelings, physical reactions, perceptions and images in a situation

Situation
(*Who? What? When? Where?*)
Wednesday, 8.45 a.m.
I was held up due to a traffic accident and arrive late for work and my boss says 'Where on earth have you been?'

Key feeling(s) and physical reaction(s)
(What did I feel? How did I physically react? Rating for each key feeling and physical reaction (0–100%))

Angry	70%
Hurt	80%
Tense	65%

Perceptions and images
(What perceptions and images did I have just before I started to feel and physically react this way? Place a star by any hot perceptions.)

She/he is angry with me.
*She/he never gives me the benefit of the doubt.
I was looking forward to coming to work.
Work is not always as psychologically safe as desirable.
An image of our recent fight about another issue.

A further approach to monitoring thinking is to use the STC framework, which was introduced in Chapter 3 (see pp. 27–8). This framework can be used by trainees and clients alike as a tool for analysing how thoughts mediate between situations and how clients feel, physically react, communicate and act on them. In this framework:

S = Situation (situations I face)
T = Thoughts (my thoughts and visual images)
C = Consequences (my feelings, physical reactions, communications and actions)

The idea is that clients do not go automatically from the situation (S) to the consequences of the situation (C). Instead the consequences of the situation are mediated by what and how they think (T). Their feelings, physical reactions, communications and actions, for good or ill, are mediated by their thoughts and mental processes.

Box 11.3 provides an STC worksheet that clients can use both during counselling sessions and between sessions to monitor and analyse their thoughts in situations. Again, trainees can show clients how to complete the worksheet during a session, possibly using a whiteboard as an aid. The worksheet in Box 11.3 has been filled out for Eva, a 28-year-old college lecturer who is very anxious about an upcoming conference presentation and thinks in negative ways. The worksheet goes beyond identifying the client's thoughts to identify the mind skills that these thoughts represent. Note that the first person singular has been used throughout the worksheet, even though it may have been filled out in a counselling session. This is because clients tend to think in the first person singular.

Box 11.3 STC (Situation–Thoughts–Consequences) Worksheet

Situation

State my problem situation clearly and succinctly.

In two weeks' time I have to make a presentation at a conference.

Thoughts

Record my thoughts about the situation.

'I must do very well.' (creating rules)

'I'm no good at public speaking.' (creating perceptions)

'I am afraid that I will make a mess of the talk.' (creating expectations)

Consequences

What are the consequences of my thoughts about the situation?

My feelings and physical reactions

Feelings: very anxious

Physical reactions: tension in my stomach, not sleeping properly

My communications and actions

In the past I have avoided speaking at conferences whenever possible.

I have started withdrawing from my friends.

Activity 11.1 Assisting a client to identify and rate thoughts and images regarding a situation

Part A: Situation, feelings, perceptions and images

Make up a worksheet similar to that in Box 11.2. Counsel a partner who acts as a client and presents you with a situation in which she/he has experienced and still is experiencing distressing feelings. With the aim of assisting your client to learn how to do this for themselves, assist her/him to fill out the worksheet in which she/he describes the situation, identifies her/his key feelings and physical reactions, rates each of them on a 0–100 scale, lists her/his perceptions and images before and/or when having these feelings/physical reactions, and puts a star by any hot perceptions and images.

Afterwards, discuss and reverse roles.

Part B: STC – situation, thoughts and consequences

Make up a worksheet similar to that in Box 11.3. Counsel a partner who acts as a client and presents you with a situation in which she/he has experienced and still is experiencing distressing feelings. With the aim of assisting your client to learn how to do this for themselves, assist her/him to fill out the STC worksheet in which she/he describes the situation, lists her/his main thoughts and images in relation to it, where appropriate identifies relevant mind skills, and identifies the feelings/physical reactions consequences and the communication/action consequences of these thoughts and images.

Afterwards, discuss and reverse roles.

Form hypotheses about mind skills to improve

For some people all roads lead to Rome and they focus on one important mind skill. For example, rational emotive behaviour therapists focus on altering irrational beliefs or rules and cognitive therapists focus on improving clients' ability to test the reality of their perceptions.

Clients rarely, if ever, tell counselling trainees: 'Look, I've got this poor mind skill I need to improve!' and then proceed to name it. Trainees who think that many clients need to improve more than one mind skill have to make inferences and form hypotheses about possible poor skills. Inferences about thinking may stem from clients' words, feelings and actions. Trainees may obtain clues from how clients use language. For example, use of words like 'should', 'ought' or 'must' may indicate unrealistically rigid rules. Use of verbs like 'I can't' and expressions like 'I had no choice' may indicate insufficient ownership of personal responsibility in explaining cause. Use of terms like 'What will people think of me?' and 'I wonder if I look as stupid as I feel' both represent negative self-talk and also indicate an unrealistic rule about needing others' approval.

Counselling trainees can identify and collect evidence that helps them form hypotheses. As part of the process of assessing thinking, they may collect further information that either supports or negates their hypotheses. Conversely, they may choose not to collect further information about some hypotheses.

In the following case study the counsellor makes hypotheses about which mind skills a client might improve. For didactic purposes, the counsellor in this case makes hypotheses that cover the six central mind skills reviewed in Chapter 3 and mentioned at the start of this chapter. In real-life counselling, counsellor and client might focus on improving the two or three mind skills they consider the most important to change.

Case study: Julia

Forming hypotheses about mind skills Julia needs to improve

Julia, just turned 22, graduated in computer engineering from a prestigious university where she had done very well. Julia was head-hunted by her tutor to join a small, but high-powered computer start-up company with 15 staff. This company, called Infoguru, was financed with private venture capital and run by Dr Sam, a very well known and respected figure in the computing world. Immediately after leaving university Julia started at Infoguru as a website developer and software programmer. Though Julia put in long hours and often voluntarily worked weekends, she was happy in her job and made a promising start to her career.

One Friday afternoon, just before a long weekend, Dr Sam took Julia with him to the offices of an important client to demonstrate a program that Infoguru had been developing for them. When they came to test the program with the client's data, they found some unexpected bugs in the part of the program that Julia had written, so the demonstration was not a success. Later that afternoon in the car on the way back to Infoguru's office Dr Sam let Julia know that he was very displeased about what had happened and that he wanted her to stay in over the long weekend to de-bug her part of the program. Julia became highly anxious at this feedback and later found that she had left her briefcase in Dr Sam's car. Since she had made previous arrangements to visit her out-of-town family, Julia declined to work over the long weekend. On returning after an anxious weekend in her home town, Julia decided to see a counsellor. A very unhappy and hurt Julia told the counsellor that she was seriously thinking of resigning from Infoguru.

The counsellor's assessment is that Julia is disturbing herself through her faulty thinking to the point where she might make the big mistake of resigning prematurely from an excellent first job and then still not know how to cope with similar pressures in succeeding jobs. It is much better for Julia to learn to become mentally more skilful earlier in her career.

- *Creating rules*: Julia can detect, challenge and alter her subconscious demanding rule that her boss must approve of everything she does all the time.
- *Creating perceptions*: Julia can get a more balanced perception of Dr Sam: for instance she can remember that Dr Sam has praised her in the past, drives everyone including himself very hard, and that his angry feelings may be transient.
- *Creating self-talk*: Julia can talk to herself with calming statements and with statements that help her to stay focused on goals that are important both in this particular mini crisis and in her overall career.
- *Creating visual images*: Julia can use visual images both to calm herself down and to rehearse in her imagination how she might communicate more effectively in her future dealings with Dr Sam.
- *Creating explanations*: Julia can regain confidence by explaining to herself that she can assume responsibility for handling this situation to the best of her

ability and that much of Dr Sam's angry reaction could be related to both the realistic and self-inflicted pressures he feels under to make a success of the company.

- *Creating expectations*: Julia can also learn to correct her tendency, when feeling emotionally vulnerable, to create unrealistic expectations about how badly situations are likely to turn out.

Activity 11.2 Forming mind skills hypotheses

As appropriate, do parts of this activity on your own, in pairs or in a group. Look back at the case example of Julia in this chapter for further ideas.

Part A: Hypothesizing about poor mind skills/goals

Read the following case example and answer the questions about how each partner thinks.

Case example
Sally and Duncan have been living together for a year. Both think that their relationship is headed for the rocks.

Sally thinks: Duncan has little respect for me. We moved in together for companionship and now we are in a power struggle. He seems to enjoy putting me down. He is controlling and critical. At times I think that underneath he hates women. When I try to talk with him about our problems, I'm afraid that he will leave the room in a huff. I get anxious just thinking about having a serious talk with him and we never seem to discuss our relationship properly. Good relationships shouldn't have conflict. His family is very cool toward me. I want a boyfriend that I can be proud of and who is fun to be around. Our problems are mainly Duncan's fault.

Example of one of Sally's possible poor mind skills/goals
Poor mind skill: Unrealistic rule
Statement suggesting deficiency: Good relationships shouldn't have conflict.

What are your hypotheses about Sally's poor mind skills/goals and what statement or statements suggests each one as a poor mind skill/goal?

Duncan thinks: Sally is no longer the person I moved in with. We used to have such fun together. She is often late home from work and never does anything around the house. All she cares about is her career. I want a woman who can openly express affection and knows what I want without having to be told. It seems as though I am doing all the giving in our relationship. Sally is uncaring. I think it is Sally's fault that our relationship is in such deep trouble. What is the point of trying to improve it? She will never change.

What are your hypotheses about Duncan's poor mind skills/goals and what statement or statements suggests each one as a poor mind skill/goal?

Part B: Practising forming mind skills hypotheses

Look for evidence of one, two or three poor mind skills/goals.

You counsel your partner for 10 minutes about a specific problem she/he brings to counselling. You may take brief notes. At the end of the 10 minutes, share with your partner any evidence that suggests she/he might possess a poor mind skill/goal in one or more of the following three skills areas.

1 Creating rules
2 Creating perceptions
3 Creating self-talk

Afterwards reverse roles.

Look for evidence of any relevant poor mind skills/goals.

Counsel your partner in relation to a problem for as long as it takes to make an initial assessment of what poor mind skills/goals sustain her/his problems. Do not restrict yourself to focusing on the above three skills. At the end of the session summarize your main conclusions and check these with your partner. Afterwards, reverse roles.

Part C: Group activity on forming mind skills hypotheses

One person acts as client who presents a specific problematic situation to the group. The remainder of the group, say up to six people, sit in a semicircle round the client and counsel the client in such a way as to assess her/his thoughts and images before and during the situation. One approach is for the group members to take brief turns as counsellor. Every now and then stop and discuss both what's happened and where to go next. Before ending, the group shares and discusses their mind skills hypotheses with the client.

The group can repeat this exercise with other 'clients'.

assess communication and actions 12

Chapter outcomes

By studying and doing the activity in this chapter you should:

- know the importance of assessing communication and actions; and
- know some of the main ways of assessing communicaton and actions.

Counsellors and trainees need to pay close attention to communication and actions because, if clients are to manage most problems better, they must change how they behave. Communication and action skills interact with thinking and feeling. Improved thinking is generally insufficient unless it is accompanied or followed by effective communication and action. Furthermore, if clients are to feel better, they frequently need to change how they communicate and act to achieve their goals: for example, developing friendship skills so as to become less lonely.

Generally counselling trainees find it easier to think in terms of communication and action skills than mind skills. However, a common mistake is to focus only on verbal skills. Communication and action skills involve five main message categories: verbal, voice, body, touch and action-taking. The first four message categories usually assume face-to-face contact. The fifth category, action-taking messages, does not require direct contact: for instance, sending flowers to someone you love. Box 12.1 shows different skills of vocal and bodily communication. Before proceeding with this chapter, some readers may find it helpful to refer back to Chapter 2, where these different skills areas were described.

Box 12.1 Skills areas for vocal and bodily communication

Vocal communication	Bodily communication
Volume	Facial expressions
Articulation	Gaze
Pitch	Eye contact
Emphasis	Gestures
Rate	Posture
	Physical closeness
	Clothes
	Grooming

Skills for eliciting and assessing communication and actions

Counsellors and trainees seek both to identify which skills are important and also to evaluate how well clients perform them. Below are some skills for assessing clients' communication and actions and for helping clients monitor and assess themselves.

Build a knowledge base

Counselling trainees require knowledge of the relevant communication and action skills for the client populations with whom they work. As with mind skills, if they do not know what constitutes skilled behaviour in an area they will be unable to assess it with any accuracy. For example, trainees working with the unemployed require knowledge of how to make résumés, seek employment information and handle interviews. Those trainees who work with clients with sexual difficulties require knowledge of the communication and action skills for managing different sexual problems and disorders. Counselling trainees working with school and university students' study and examination problems require knowledge of how to study and sit exams effectively.

Gather information inside and outside of counselling sessions

Trainees can gather information about observable communication and actions either inside or outside of counselling sessions. There are a number of ways in which they can collect such information in interviews. First, there is client self-report. Clients can tell trainees how they behave outside counselling. A limitation of this is that trainees do not observe client behaviour directly and so have to rely on versions of events which may be incomplete and/or inaccurate. Clients may edit what they say to protect their self-image.

Trainees can also observe clients in the counselling room. Depending on the areas of clients' problems, trainees may learn much from observing their verbal, voice and body messages. For example, shy clients may exhibit shyness behaviours in their presence. Trainees can listen to their own experiencing of how they feel when clients communicate in certain ways and use this as additional information for assessment: for instance, a trainee may personally experience the impact of a client's annoying mannerism.

Counselling trainees may wish to supplement interview information with that gathered in clients' natural or home environments. Trainees can go with clients into situations in which they experience difficulty and observe how they behave: for instance, when requesting a drink in a bar or relating to children at home. However, trainees must be sensitive to issues of boundaries for them and their clients.

With permission and being highly sensitive about confidentiality and possible subsequent repercussions, trainees may also collect information about how clients communicate and act from third parties such as spouses, parents, siblings, peers or supervisors. They need to be mindful of, and consider exploring, differences between third parties' and their clients' own observations. Trainees may need to train third parties in what to look for and in how to observe systematically.

Ask questions

Questions about clients' communication and actions aim to elicit specific details of how they behave. Often clients' reports are vague and they require assistance in becoming more specific. However, many trainees are poor at helping clients discover what actually happened in situations and so the vagueness can persist.

Box 12.2 provides some examples of questions focusing on communication and actions. Though they are presented as though asked by counsellors, clients can ask themselves many of the same questions either in counselling sessions or on their own outside of counselling.

Box 12.2 Examples of questions focusing on communication/actions

'How did you behave?'
'What did you say?'
'How did you communicate with your voice?'
'How were you communicating with your body language?'
'How did she/he react when you did that [*specify*]?'
'What is the pattern of communication that develops between you when you row?'
'In what situations do you behave like that?'
'How do you actually behave when you procrastinate about studying?'
'What happened before you did that?'
'What were the consequences of doing that?'
'When does it happen?'
'Where does it happen?'
'How many times a day/week/month do you … ?'
'Over what period were you … ?'
'How long does it take you to … ?'
'How many minutes/hours do you … each day?'

A further question focusing on communications and actions is 'Show me?' Clients can be invited to illustrate the verbal, vocal and body messages they used in an interaction either on their own or in a role-play with the counselling trainee playing the other party. For instance, parents having difficulty in disciplining children can show the student how they attempt this. Role-play allows the possibility of exploring patterns of communication that extend beyond an initial 'show me' response focused on just one unit of interaction. Trainees can also video record role-plays and play them back to clients to illustrate points and develop clients' skill in observing themselves.

Encourage clients to monitor their communication and actions

Counselling trainees can encourage clients to become more aware of how they communicate and act in problem areas. Sometimes trainees and clients agree on between-session homework tasks, for instance telephoning to ask for a date, and clients are asked to record how they behave.

Clients can take away and fill in worksheets. The simplest version of such a worksheet asks clients to describe the situation first and then report how they communicate/act in the situation. When filling in worksheets, clients need to pay attention to vocal and bodily as well as verbal communication. More elaborate worksheets follow a situation, feelings, thoughts and communication/actions format or adopt the STC (Situation–Thoughts–Consequences) format. When using the STC format, clients record how they communicate and act in the consequences section.

Filling out activity sheets or schedules in which clients record what they do throughout the day is another way that they can monitor their communication and actions. When using activity schedules with depressed patients, Beck and his colleagues ask them to provide ratings on 0 to 10 scales for feelings of mastery and of pleasure experienced during each activity (Beck and Weishaar, 2005).

Form hypotheses about communication and action skills to improve

As counselling trainees listen to clients and collect information, they form communication and action skills hypotheses. Trainees may feel confident about some hypotheses at the end of an initial session. They may make other hypotheses more tentatively. Still others emerge as counselling progresses. Clients may also share ideas about unhelpful communication and actions. Such observations always merit attention, not least because clients are assuming some responsibility for their problems and problematic skills.

Trainees may formulate many hypotheses concerning broad areas in which clients may need to develop skills. As was the case with George in Chapter 4, trainees often leave detailed assessment of specific skills deficiencies until subsequent sessions when there is more time to do the job thoroughly. Furthermore, by then, trainees and clients may have decided which skills areas require detailed attention. In the following case study, the counsellor identifies just one communication/action skill to improve and illustrates it with some verbal, vocal and bodily communications that the client might change.

Case study: Julia

Forming hypotheses about communication/action skills Julia needs to improve

This is a continuation of the case study presented in the previous chapter identifying how Julia might improve her mind skills.

Regarding communication/action skills hypotheses, the counsellor considers that Julia needs to improve her assertion skills when relating to Dr Sam. The counsellor has noted the following as actual or potential assertion skills deficiencies.

- *Verbal communication*: Insufficiently using 'I-statements' that briefly and clearly explain her viewpoint on specific issues. Failing to express appreciation for positive actions by Dr Sam in the past.
- *Vocal communication*: Allowing her voice to have a whiney quality about it. Speaking too quickly. Disempowering herself by not speaking sufficiently clearly and firmly.
- *Bodily communication*: Slouching slightly by not having her shoulders sufficiently back. Making insufficient eye contact. Picking at her hair.

Activity 12.1 Gathering information about communication and forming communication skills hypotheses

Complete this exercise with a partner.

Part A: Collect information in interviews

Counsel a partner who discusses a problem entailing how she/he communicates with another person. Your focus in this session is to work with your client in identifying and assessing her/his communication skills. Counsel in an open-ended manner for the first two or three minutes and then intersperse focusing on communication questions with reflective responses. As you proceed, incorporate role-play into your information gathering. Aim to obtain a clear picture of your client's verbal, vocal and bodily communication in the situation and of any unhelpful patterns of communication. During this process form communication skills hypotheses about how she/he may be contributing to her/his relationship problem. End the session by summarizing and discussing with your client your communication skills hypotheses.

Part B: Collecting information in natural settings

Assume that you wish to collect further information to assess the client's communication skills from natural or home settings. Work out with your client how such information might be collected in each of the following ways:

(a) counsellor as observer
(b) client as observer
(c) third party (specify) as observer

Afterwards reverse roles and do both Parts A and B of this activity.

13 agree on a shared analysis of problems

Chapter outcomes

By studying and doing the activities in this chapter you should:

- know how agreeing on shared analyses of problems in skills terms can add value to counselling;
- know the three main steps in agreeing on shared analyses of problems;
- understand some counsellor skills for agreeing on shared analyses of problems; and
- possess some skills for ending initial sessions.

Introduction

The desired outcome of the second stage of the lifeskills counselling model is a clear analysis of the poor skills that sustain a problem, agreed upon by both client and counsellor or counselling trainee. Good shared analyses of problems in skills terms break problems down and identify specific mind skills and communication/action skills areas in which clients can make better choices. During later sessions, problems may be still further broken down into their component skills. However, such detail may be inappropriate for initial sessions. Early analyses of problems in skills terms can pinpoint or flag areas for later work.

Statements of problems in skills terms are sets of hypotheses about poor skills that may be sustaining clients' problems. Though forming the basis for goal setting and intervening, they should be open to modification in the light of feedback and new information. In short, these initial analyses are subject to continuous testing and to major or minor reformulations as counselling progresses.

Shared analyses as adding value

Shared analyses in skills terms, if well done, can add value to counselling. Analyses of problems that use skills language normalize or 'depathologize' counselling. Some clients become visibly relieved when they hear that the object of the initial session is to identify some lifeskills to help them to cope better with their problem. Many clients feel threatened by going to counsellors and counselling trainees – some think they will be psychoanalysed. Furthermore, some clients devalue themselves for not standing on their own two feet. Skills language can reduce threat and self-disparagement. Shared analyses identify the underlying poor skills/goals that sustain them and have more value than descriptive summaries that focus on coping with a current problem. Such summaries may fail to pinpoint poor skills/goals even for managing the current problem, let alone preventing and managing similar problems.

Clarifying problems in skills terms can reduce clients' anxiety and increase their optimism, confidence and motivation for change. Whereas previously clients may have felt stuck, now they gain some glimpses of how to proceed. The process of agreeing on analyses of problems in skills terms involves the mutual identification by counselling trainees and clients of which poor skills/goals sustain problems. Restatements are constructed with clients rather than imposed on them. They are creative constructions of reality that provide meaning for both clients and trainees (Strong et al., 1995). Such analyses can include working on poor skills for dealing with disempowering forces in clients' environments and agreeing on goals. Lifeskills counselling does not assume that clients are the sole source of their problems.

Shared analyses also provide ways of setting goals, intervening and developing lifeskills after counselling. Good shared analyses summarize the past and present in such a way as to provide a crossing to a better future. Value is also added, providing a focus for monitoring and evaluating progress.

Steps in shared analyses of problems

The process of making shared analyses of problems in skills terms can be broken down into three steps.

Step 1: Lay the groundwork

A good shared analysis, clearly summarizing the skills required to address a problem, requires thorough prior preparation. The analysis logically draws together areas covered in earlier work. In addition to good active listening skills, counselling trainees require skills of establishing a focus or setting an agenda. They cannot adequately analyse a problem if they and the client are unclear about which problem they are working on. This may seem obvious, but many trainees allow initial sessions to drift aimlessly. All the skills previously mentioned for clarifying and assessing problems and forming hypotheses are also relevant to laying the groundwork. Students can take notes to refresh their memories.

Step 2: Present shared analyses in skills terms

Having laid the groundwork, the next step is for counselling trainees to present their hypotheses to the client. Together they construct an analysis that rings true and has meaning for them. I always use a whiteboard for this process. I ask clients for a minute or so to go over my notes and pull together the threads of what they have said so that I can suggest a breakdown or 'printout' of poor skills on which they may need to work. I do not get into lengthy explanations of what poor skills are, other than to say that another way of looking at poor skills is that we are establishing goals. Once specific communication/action or mind skills are presented, most clients easily comprehend what constitutes a poor skill/goal. If clients do not understand what is meant, it can be explained more fully. If a poor skill still fails to possess meaning for clients, it can either be reworded in an acceptable form or removed altogether. Once trainees and clients construct mutually agreed analyses of problems on whiteboards, they may then reword poor skills so that they more clearly become goals.

Step 3: Record shared analyses in take-away form

Much of the value of counselling sessions can be lost if clients and counselling trainees fail to memorize information accurately. Consequently, the next step is to make permanent records of shared analyses. When clients are clear about how poor skills can become goals, restatements can be transferred from whiteboards on to standard 'assessment of poor skills/statement of goals' forms (see Box 13.1). In lifeskills counselling, both clients and counsellors or trainees keep records. The client's records consist of the initial assessment of poor skills/statement of goals form, plus additional homework sheets on which they record work performed in subsequent sessions on specific skills.

Box 13.1 Assessment of poor skills/statement of goals form

LIFESKILLS COUNSELLING ASSESSMENT OF POOR SKILLS/STATEMENT OF GOALS

PROBLEM OR SITUATION

____

____

____

ASSESSMENT OF POOR SKILLS/STATEMENT OF GOALS

Mind skills poor skills/goals	Communication/action skills poor skills/goals

Some skills for agreeing on shared analyses of problems

The following are some skills that counsellors and trainees can use during the process of agreeing with clients on shared analyses of their problems in skills terms.

Take notes

It is extremely difficult to make sharp definitions of problems in skills terms unless notes are taken as one goes along. During the clarification and assessment time, clients will provide much valuable information for defining their problems. Why lose much of this by not taking notes? Memory is incomplete, selective and fallible. Counselling trainees cannot do a professional job of defining problems unless they have properly gathered and stored the information on which their analyses are based.

Storing information properly means being able to retrieve it accurately and easily to form the basis of poor skills/goals hypotheses. Clients are much more likely to acknowledge the validity of trainee hypotheses if these are backed up by specific thoughts or communications they have talked about than if the hypotheses appear solely to come from a trainee's external frame of reference. Furthermore, when intervening later, trainees can refer back to the information in their notes. Slavishly taking down everything clients say is not being advocated. But when clients provide important clues as to possible poor skills and statements that illustrate specific poor skills, it makes sense to write them down.

Make a transition statement

When making initial structuring statements, counselling trainees can indicate to clients that later on their problems will be broken down into mind skills and communication/action skills terms. Below are possible transition statements that trainees might make when starting to offer definitions in skills terms.

> 'Well, Karen, for the past 30 minutes or so we've been exploring in some detail the difficulties in your relationship with your mother, Heather. I'm now about to test out on you a way of viewing your problem in skills terms. I'll put this up on the whiteboard. I'll make two columns – one for mind skills poor skills/goals and the other for communication skills poor skills/goals. I call them poor skills/goals because any skill we agree requires development can then become a goal for our work. If possible, we need to agree on the main skills areas in which you experience difficulty. Your feedback is vital since you are unlikely to work on skills where you do not see the point.'

> 'Louise, I've now asked you a number of questions about your problems with going for a senior job interview. Time is moving on and,

if it's all right with you, I'd now like to give you a printout on the whiteboard of some skills that may help you. Can you give me a moment or two to look at my notes and pull together the threads? [*Louise agrees and counsellor looks at notes.*] I'm now ready to make some suggestions. We can discuss each of them as I write them up. If you are unhappy with anything I put up, let me know and I can either reword it or remove it. [*Counsellor starts writing on the whiteboard.*] I use the term poor skills/goals to indicate that poor skills are really goals for developing skills.'

Make clear analyses in skills terms

Counselling trainees should remember that analyses of problems in skills terms are mainly for clients' benefit. Unless clients understand them, analyses of skills are useless. Trainees should always use simple and clear language. They should aim to summarize key mind skills and communication/action skills deficiencies in the targeted problem area or situation. Furthermore, they need to be sensitive to the amount of material clients can absorb. It is better for clients to be comfortable with a small amount of material than to be confused by a lot. It is also far easier for trainees to put up simple analyses of skills than to try to do too much and then do it poorly. In later sessions they can elaborate their skills analysis either by breaking down the skills initially presented or by adding other poor skills/goals.

Besides clarity and brevity, the following are some other characteristics of good analyses in skills terms:

- They bear a clear relationship to information clients provide.
- They are illustrated with material or statements provided by clients.
- They are formulated in conjunction with clients.
- They relate to a problem or problems of high priority to clients.
- They are stated as hypotheses.
- Clients are likely to perceive them as relevant and own them as a basis for working on their problems.
- They lend themselves to setting helpful and realistic goals.

Consider using a whiteboard

Using a whiteboard has many advantages. The discipline of writing up a definition – a column each for poor mind skills/goals and for poor communication/action skills/goals – imposes a degree of discipline. The visual image may increase clients' understanding and retention of what is being communicated. Clients can clearly see the component parts of how counselling trainees break down their problem. They do not have to struggle to remember previous poor skills/goals as students move on to introduce new ones.

The whiteboard provides a useful vehicle for the social construction of analyses of skills, which are not only presented, but negotiated. Having a written definition of skills before their eyes makes it easier for clients to provide feedback. For example, clients can be asked what wording or examples they would like to use when illustrating particular poor skills. Trainees should word the poor skills/goals in language that has meaning for clients. Trainees and clients can openly work together on the whiteboard to formulate their analysis. Trainees should be prepared to remove any poor skill/goal with which clients continue to remain uncomfortable. In addition, once they are agreed, having skills analyses on whiteboards makes it easy for trainees and clients to record them. Such recording may take place either before or after the poor skills have been reworded to become working goals.

Why use the whiteboard instead of other visual aids? Whiteboards are cleaner than blackboards – users do not get their hands chalky. Whiteboards lend themselves easily to erasing material and also to getting a clearer picture. Some modern whiteboards can even provide printouts of what has been written on them. Though notepads are used when collecting information, when presenting analyses in skills' terms they have the huge disadvantage of restricting the degree to which clients can participate in the joint work in progress. Trainees usually control notepads, which often they place on their laps, and when trainees write on them they can lose some contact with clients. It is harder to make changes on notepads than on whiteboards.

Construct shared meaning

Analysing problems in skills terms is a creative process involving translating problems into statements of poor skills/goals that have meaning for both counselling trainees and clients. As they become skilled, trainees accompany clients below the descriptive surface of their problems to the point where they understand the underlying structure of their good and poor skills. Adequate restatements of problems are conceptualizations that trainees and clients can share. Counselling trainees often possess a deep understanding of how poor skills impede clients. If the 'defining problems in skills terms' phase is properly negotiated, clients will have participated sufficiently to construct a shared meaning of their problem with those who counsel them.

The following are some ways in which trainees can enhance the likelihood of success in this. Readers should not feel obliged to follow these suggestions all the time.

- Use the client's material.
- Use the whiteboard to create shared space.
- Use the client's language, where appropriate.
- Explain tactfully and carefully what you mean by suggesting specific poor skills.
- Invite contributions and feedback: for example, by questions like

  Is that clear?
  Do you agree?
  How would you like me to word that?

- Check the client's satisfaction with the skills analysis, for example by asking

  Is there anything that I've left out?
  Are you happy with that analysis in skills terms?
  What do you feel about that way of analysing your problem?

- Allow clients the right to veto what goes into the analysis of skills.
- Acknowledge significant environmental factors.

Where appropriate, trainees can let clients know that they appreciate their problem may include how best to develop skills for dealing with other people's problems and with broader social and organizational structures and constraints. However, trainees need to be careful not to collude with clients who cast themselves as victims.

Attend to feelings

Counselling trainees should always pay attention to clients' feelings. They should look out for any reservations regarding taking a skills approach to their problems. If possible, work through these reservations together. Trainees should be aware that often they are dealing with highly sensitive material and that they always require tact. Often clients find it difficult to accept responsibility for their problems rather than externalizing them. Do not make it harder by being clumsy. Good analyses of problems in skills terms can improve clients' morale and motivation. Whereas previously they may have been stuck, now they have 'handles' with which to work. A glimmer of light appears. Problems experienced as insurmountable may now seem manageable. However, trainees must take note of any signals that clients have not found the analyses of skills useful, either in part or in whole. For example, clients may acquiesce and later sabotage working together. Had the mixed messages contained in their acquiescence been caught earlier, their reservations might have been addressed sooner.

Encourage between-session learning

From the start of lifeskills counselling, trainees can encourage clients to take an active role in learning. Working closely with clients during the initial sessions, including using a whiteboard, has been mentioned. Sessions can be recorded on cassette and clients asked to play them back prior to subsequent sessions. Many clients find this useful for further exploring problems and understanding skills analyses. They find that there is too much material to remember and absorb first time around. Trainees can use the time between sessions to build clients' self-assessing skills. For instance, they may request that clients keep records of how they think, feel and behave in targeted skills areas.

Case study: Dr Sam

Agreeing on a shared analysis of a problem in skills terms

Dr Sam goes to see a counsellor because he feels stressed out by trying to make a success of Infoguru. He also mentions that staff turnover at the company is higher than usual and wonders whether his behaviour might be contributing to this situation. After letting Dr Sam tell his story and then conducting a more thorough assessment, the counsellor and Dr Sam agree on the following shared analysis of his problem(s). The counsellor illustrates each skill briefly.

Mind skills I need to improve	Communication/action skills I need to improve
Creating self-talk/visual images • insufficiently calming myself • insufficiently coaching myself in skilled communication	*Showing appreciation skills to staff* • working on verbal, vocal, bodily and action-taking communication
Creating rules I must be perfect. Others must be perfect.	*Pleasant activities skills* • engaging more in non-work activities that I enjoy
Creating perceptions I tend to perceive myself and others like machines rather than as persons.	*Physical recreation skills* • swimming regularly again
Creating explanations Other people are in the wrong.	

Then the counsellor and Dr Sam each make a written record of this shared analysis on a worksheet that the counsellor has prepared.

Activity 13.1 Using a whiteboard for analysing problems in skills terms

Part A: In pairs

1 *Discussion and practice*
Hold a discussion with your partner who presents a very specific situation that she/he perceives as a problem (for example, getting started with a particular essay or starting a counselling session with a new client). Together clarify, assess and analyse the problem in skills terms. Limit yourselves to up to three poor mind skills/goals and one poor communication/action skills/goal (though for this skill, stipulate verbal, voice and body components, if appropriate). As you go along one of you writes the analysis on the whiteboard and together you discuss how best to go about this. At the end, each of you writes down the analysis in skills terms on an assessment of poor skills/statement of goals form (see Box 13.1).

2 *Counselling practice*
Allow yourself 15–20 minutes in which you counsel your partner who presents a very specific problem or situation. During this period, clarify and assess your client's problem. Using the whiteboard, negotiate a simple analysis of the problem in skills terms. At the very least, identify and illustrate one poor mind skills/goal and one poor communication/action skills/goal. Do not try to do too much in the time. Afterwards discuss the session with your partner. At the end, each of you writes down the analysis in skills terms on the assessment of poor skills/statement of goals form. Playing back a video of the session may help you assess your skills.

Afterwards, reverse roles. You can repeat this activity either with the same or with other partners.

Part B: In a group

1 *Group discussion*
Hold a group discussion on analysing clients' problems in skills terms. Issues that you can focus on include:

- whether or not restating problems in skills terms adds value to counselling
- taking notes
- using a whiteboard
- constructing shared meaning
- what clients remember and take away from initial sessions

2 *Group practice*
One member of the group acts as 'client', while the others act as counsellors or, if it is a large group, some may be observers. The client presents a very specific situation or problem. The group members counsel her/him, clarify and assess the problem, and negotiate an analysis in skills terms (here one 'counsellor' takes responsibility for writing poor mind and communication/action skills/goals on the whiteboard). Keep the analysis in skills terms very simple. During the activity stop every now and then to assess what you are doing, where to go next, and why. At the end of the session, each group member writes down the analysis in skills terms on the assessment of poor skills/statement of goals form.

Afterwards, repeat the exercise with another 'client'.

Ending initial sessions

Counselling trainees need to create a different ending for each initial session depending on the circumstances of the client and the progress that has been made together. For a number of reasons, initial sessions may turn out to be final sessions. Some clients have an immediate issue to address, for example, an exam or meeting with a former spouse, and one session is all they have time for before the event. With such clients, trainees have to fit what they do into this limited time frame. Other clients may decide to end because they lack the motivation to continue or have reservations about the counselling process or the counsellor. On other occasions, mindful of Arnold Lazarus's dictum 'Know your limitations and other clinicians' strengths' (Dryden, 1991: 30), trainees may decide to refer clients.

It goes without saying that counselling trainees need to check with their clients towards the end of initial sessions whether they wish to return. Usually trainees can tell how committed clients are to the counselling process from the degree and quality of the collaboration achieved so far. Sometimes by the end of the first session trainees will not have completed their assessments or agreed with their clients on shared analyses of their problem(s). In these circumstances, they can agree to work with clients on these tasks in the next session. Less frequently, at the end of the initial session, trainees may still be struggling to discover what the real issues are for clients who may not be certain themselves. However, such clients may still be engaged in the counselling process and want to continue despite their confusion.

Most often trainees working in the lifeskills counselling model finish negotiating and agreeing on a preliminary shared analysis of the client's problem or problem situation towards the end of the first session. Clients may then ask 'What next?' or 'Where do we go from here?' If possible, such questions should be answered accurately, but briefly. Before ending the initial session, trainees and clients may agree on between-session homework activities as a prelude to the next session. Sample activities include monitoring feelings, thoughts and communications in a situation and experimenting with changing a specific behaviour. Trainees should always check that clients write out the instructions for any activities accurately and know how to perform them on their own. Trainees can also ask clients for feedback on what happened in the session and how comfortable they are with the counselling relationship.

Before ending, trainees and clients may need to clear up a number of practical matters, for example about times and days to meet, how to cancel or change an appointment, fees, and discussion about communication and feedback to any referrer (Bayne et al., 1999; Miller, 1999). In addition, trainees should let vulnerable clients know how to contact them in an emergency.

Think realistically about initial sessions

Before and during initial sessions, counselling trainees who are thinking realistically can take much pressure off themselves. For example, rather than use negative self-talk like 'I'm only a trainee and may mess things up', trainees can make calming self-statements and gently coach themselves in the skills of competent performance. In addition, prior to conducting initial sessions, trainees can imagine themselves using good counselling skills.

Trainees can challenge and replace demanding rules, like 'I must be perfect', 'I must get quick results' and 'I must have my clients' approval at all costs', that engender anxiety and possible poor communication with clients. Furthermore, they can be realistic about perceiving their strengths and limitations. Many trainees err on the side of underestimating their strengths and ability to offer good counselling relationships. If so, time spent on owning realistic strengths may be time well spent. Unfortunately there are a few trainees who possess insufficient insight into the fact that they are beginners. Such trainees may be reluctant to practise their skills enough, including those of conducting initial sessions well. Matters can become even worse if these trainees react negatively to constructive peer, trainer and supervisor feedback.

Some trainees place pressure on themselves by assuming too much responsibility for the success of initial sessions and of counselling. When interviewing, such trainees are at risk of assuming too much ownership of clients' problems and of being too controlling. These trainees need to remind themselves that their job is to cooperate with clients so that they can help themselves rather than to do it for them. In addition, trainees can create anxiety by creating false expectations, such as 'If I make a mistake, it will be the end of the world.' Unrealistic expectations need to be detected, challenged and modified or abandoned.

Later in the book, two chapters are devoted to interventions for working with how clients think. Counselling trainees can view themselves as their own clients and, where appropriate, follow the advice, 'Counsellor, heal thyself.' Peers, trainers and supervisors can all help trainees to think more realistically about how they counsel and conduct initial sessions. Clients and personal therapists are other possible sources of feedback for trainees.

Activity 13.2 Conducting a full initial session

Work with a partner and practise conducting an initial 40–50-minute counselling session in which you complete stages 1 and 2 of the lifeskills counselling model. 'Clients' can present problems that require breaking down into different component areas, but these problems should not be too complex. If presented with a complex problem, agree with your client to target a specific part of the overall problem or a specific problem situation as an agenda. Once you have agreed on a shared analysis of the client's problem or problem situation, each of you writes it down for your records. Then the counsellor terminates the session by negotiating any homework activities, ensuring that the client knows how to perform them, asking for feedback about the session, and making practical arrangements about subsequent contact. Playing back a video of the session may help you assess your skills.

Afterwards, reverse roles. You can repeat this activity either with the same or with other partners.

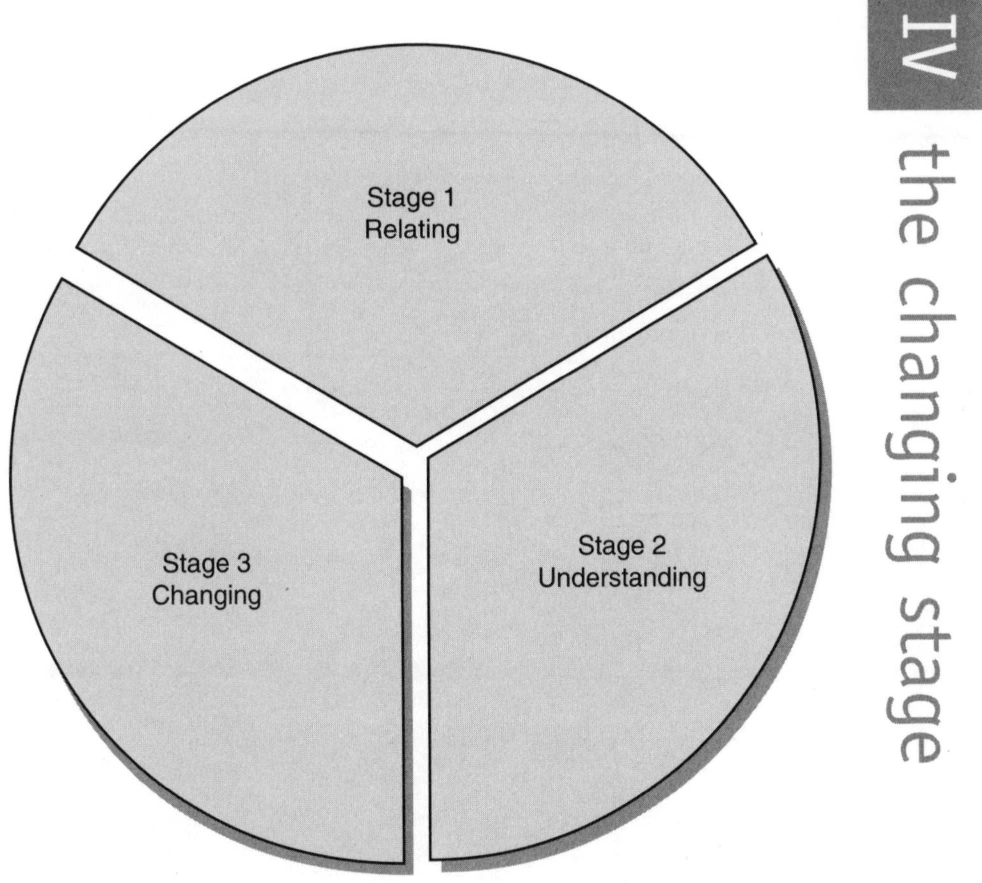

The lifeskills counselling model

The relating stage's main task: to form a collaborative working relationship
The understanding stage's main task: assess and agree on a shared definition of the client's problem(s)
The changing stage's main task: achieve client change and the maintenance of change

plan interventions 14

Chapter outcomes

By studying and doing the activities in this chapter you should:

- know what the terms interventions and plans mean;
- understand issues connected with empirically supported treatment;
- understand counsellor and client considerations in choosing interventions;
- know some different types of plan;
- understand some considerations in developing plans;
- know some skills for working with clients when choosing and planning interventions.

Agreeing on shared analyses of problems in skills terms provides the bridge to choosing interventions. Counsellors and counselling trainees as practitioner-researchers hypothesize not only about goals, but also about ways to attain them. This chapter focuses on some of the many issues and skills in choosing and planning interventions. Though the focus of this chapter is on initial sessions, counsellors and trainees also choose and plan interventions for goals that emerge during counselling.

Some readers might consider that a chapter on choosing and planning interventions might be better placed after the chapters on the different interventions. However, it appears at the start of this section on change for the simple reason that in counselling, choosing and planning interventions comes before intervening. Readers can choose to read or reread this chapter after reading the subsequent chapters on interventions.

Interventions and plans

Counsellors and counselling trainees make choices both concerning specific interventions and also about interventions used in combination. An important distinction exists between interventions and plans.

Interventions

In lifeskills counselling, interventions are intentional behaviours designed to help clients attain problem management and problematic skills goals.

In the context of this and subsequent chapters, interventions mean 'change strategies' (Cormier and Nurius, 2002) or techniques.

Interventions or change strategies can be either counsellor-centred or client-centred. With counsellor-centred interventions, counsellors do something to or for clients: for instance they may give clients advice on how to behave. With client-centred interventions, counsellors develop clients' capacities to intervene in their own problem and problematic skills areas: for instance, they may assist clients in how to monitor their thinking. The object of all counselling trainee interventions should be to strengthen clients' self-helping interventions: 'I as a counselling trainee am of most use to you as a client if I help you to intervene, at first with my assistance but later on your own, to develop and maintain *your* skills to manage *your* problems now and in future.' Trainees require a repertoire of interventions or intervention skills to cover a variety of clients' lifeskills deficiencies. Because of the enormous range of problems and poor skills, sooner or later trainees may need to specialize in the most useful interventions for the client populations with which they deal.

Plans

Plans are overall statements of how to combine and sequence interventions for managing problems and attaining goals. They are the outlines, maps or diagrams that enable counselling trainees and clients to get from where they are to where they want to be. The term 'treatment plan' is sometimes used. A possible risk in employing this term is that it may connote counsellor-centredness rather than trainees developing clients' skills to help themselves. The term 'working plan' may be more appropriate, since plans provide frameworks within which both trainees and clients work. Plans outline interventions beforehand. However, as the Roman writer Publius Styrius observed in the first century BC: 'It is a bad plan that admits of no modification.'

Choosing interventions

Many counselling trainees, after agreeing on a shared analysis of clients' problems, experience a sense of emptiness about their ability to do anything useful to help clients attain them. The requirement to choose and plan interventions creates pressure to 'deliver the goods'. Trainees need time and experience to build a repertoire of interventions that they can apply confidently and competently. Furthermore, even experienced counsellors often find that decisions about interventions are not clear-cut and involve trade-offs between conflicting considerations. Trainees' anxieties about choosing interventions are not in themselves detrimental – how they handle their anxieties is what matters.

This section focuses more on how to choose interventions than on how to implement them. Having stated goals, the next step is to decide on appropriate interventions to attain them. Trainees do not start from scratch in doing this. Even as they clarified, assessed and agreed on a shared analysis of clients' problems in skills terms, they were probably thinking about possible interventions. Now is the time to clarify and refine these hypotheses. Below are some criteria to consider when deciding on interventions.

Empirical support for interventions

The issue of empirically supported or valid treatments is becoming increasingly prominent in counselling circles (Frankland, 2003). Reasons for this include the desire to see that clients get the best and most appropriate treatments and a genuine attempt to economize on the costs of treating clients. However, the costs issue is also influenced by counselling and health care organizations' attempts to reduce service expenses and, sometimes, this economic motivation conflicts with those of counsellors and clients.

Clinical psychologists seem to be at the forefront of the empirically validated treatment movement: for instance, in conjunction with the American Psychological Society's Division of Clinical Psychology, at least three published articles have specified criteria to evaluate treatments as either 'well established' or 'probably efficacious' (Chambless et al., 1996, 1998; Task Force, 1995). However, there is still a long way to go before empirically supported treatments among American clinical psychologists gain widespread acceptance (Barlow et al., 1999).

The American Psychiatric Association's Division of Counselling Psychology also adheres to the scientist-practitioner model. However, its Special Task Group on empirically supported interventions in counselling psychology thought that the traditions of counselling psychology, the nature of the interventions that counselling psychologists deliver, and the state of the empirical literature precluded developing a set of criteria that would lead to a list of empirically supported interventions (Wampold et al., 2002). Instead it formulated seven principles of empirically supported interventions. These represented a first step in the ongoing attempt to recognize the complex relationship between science and practice in counselling psychology. For example, Principle 1 states that 'Level of specificity should be considered when evaluating outcomes', with Level 1 incorporating the broadest, general categories of action, and Level 4 being specific approaches in specific areas for specific populations. In short there is still much debate over empirically supported interventions within APA's clinical and counselling divisions. To date, neither British nor Australian counselling psychologists have addressed the issue in such detail.

Those training to become counsellors can look at the issue of integrating research into counselling practice in terms of three broad models: the reflective practitioner model, the scientist-practitioner model and the practitioner-researcher model.

The reflective practitioner model

The goal of the reflective practitioner can be seen as the provision of a firm basis for a model of the role of research in the work of the counsellor. This model takes one's own practice as its starting point. Whether they think about themselves in this way or not, all practitioners are in fact researchers continually engaged in a process of making and evaluating hypotheses about how they respond to, relate to, assess and intervene with their clients. Furthermore, supervisors are also engaged in researching the processes and outcomes of their supervisees' work.

Criteria for the effectiveness of reflective practitioners include how well they are able to form and carry out hypotheses when working with clients, how systematically they collect and observe data, and how assiduous they are in keeping sources of invalidity, including personal biases, out of the way they interpret these data. Assuming reflective practitioners draw accurate conclusions from their observations, they also need to be able to implement these conclusions in practice. Training in the reflective part of being a reflective practitioner aims to help trainees attain these criteria.

The scientist-practitioner model

Currently, the scientist-practitioner model tends to refer to the training of clinical and counselling psychologists rather than that of counsellors and psychotherapists. Placing the word 'scientist' before the word 'practitioner' indicates a model that takes academic values rather than practitioner values to be pre-eminent. The scientist-practitioner model assumes that practitioners require the skills of conducting as well as of consuming research. Thus, in addition to such subjects as counselling and psychotherapy theory and skills, there is a heavy emphasis on statistical, computer programming, research design and conducting and evaluating research projects skills. Though counselling needs some trainees to be educated as scientist-practitioners, the reality is that most trainees, even those from psychology departments, are going to become practitioners.

The practitioner-researcher model

A third model for linking research to counselling practice is that of the practitioner-researcher. This model can be viewed as building on and upgrading the reflective practitioner model. The main emphasis in both models is on research as a guide to practice rather than on conducting experimental research studies. Starting with basics, all trainees should be taught to regard the conducting of counselling in scientific terms. For example, every time they frame a response to what a client communicates they make a responding hypothesis. Every time they assess a client and decide on how best to intervene they make one or more treatment hypotheses. In both instances, when implementing hypotheses, practitioners need to be open to feedback about their accuracy and usefulness.

Counsellors as practitioner-researchers require the skills and motivation to evaluate their practice systematically, whether it be with individuals, couples or groups. Where appropriate, they can design small self-evaluative studies to this effect. Furthermore they can be trained in relatively straightforward service delivery programme evaluation skills. In instances where higher-level statistical and computing expertise is required, one option is to buy it in. In addition, counsellors as practitioner-researchers need to access competently the professional and research literature on therapeutic processes and outcomes. Lazarus observed that relatively few empirically supported or evidence-based treatments come from outside the area of cognitive-behaviour therapy (Lazarus, 1997), and this state of affairs remains the case.

Where such treatments exist, there is a professional and ethical obligation on the part of counsellors working with the targeted problems and client populations to keep themselves informed. Unless they have good reason for not doing so in terms of particular clients' circumstances, practitioners must seriously consider either implementing the treatments themselves or referring clients to those competent to do so. However, even in areas where empirically supported treatments exist, there may be still better ways of treating clients. Empirically supported treatments do not succeed with all clients who participate in the controlled studies. Furthermore, the concerns of many clients do not fall into circumscribed problem areas and the unavoidable messiness of much of therapeutic practice does not easily lend itself to empirical research studies.

With the move towards empirically supported treatments, hopefully counselling and psychotherapy researchers will become better at presenting material that is accessible and comprehensible to practitioners. Professional associations are likely to play a greater role in providing practitioner-friendly summaries and overviews of research studies about treatments of choice for different problems.

Future directions

Most counselling skills training is likely to focus on the reflective practitioner and the practitioner-researcher models. Including more research-related content on counselling training courses is no guarantee that trainees will want to use this knowledge and these skills afterwards. While avoiding the excesses of the scientist-practitioner model, the counselling professions in Britain and Australia can work towards a model of the effective practitioner than is attainable, perceived as reasonable by most members, and pays more attention to applied research skills and knowledge than currently appears to be the case. As part of this change process, the reflective practitioner identity for counsellors will gradually be superseded by a practitioner-researcher identity. However, those adopting this identity should recognize the limitations as well as the strengths of counselling research and empirically supported interventions.

Importance of maintaining a supportive relationship

Whatever interventions counselling trainees choose in conjunction with clients, they should always offer them within the context of supportive relationships. A risk for some trainees when breaking down problems, stating goals and specifying interventions is that they become too technique oriented. For some vulnerable clients, until they gain more confidence and insight, the emphasis on them as persons derived from supportive counselling relationships may be the major intervention. For all clients supportive relationships will contribute to the working alliance and facilitate motivation. Supportive relationships can assist more task-oriented interventions, for instance by providing better emotional climates for role-plays and coached performance of skills.

Emphasis of interventions on managing problems or altering problematic skills

Counselling trainees and clients may choose to focus more on managing an immediate problem than on altering problematic skills. How trainees intervene will be heavily influenced by such a decision. For example, there may be more emphasis on problem management when clients are in crisis. They may feel overwhelmed by the intensity of their emotions and be in shock, disoriented, highly anxious, extremely depressed, very angry, contemplating suicide and fearing insanity or nervous breakdown. The objectives of interventions in crises include protecting clients, calming them down, and assisting them in here-and-now problem-solving and planning so that they regain a sense of control over their lives. A clear focus on problematic skills is deferred until later, if at all.

Simlarly, clients may be faced with coping with immediate problems: for instance, upcoming tests, public speaking engagements or confrontations with difficult people. Together counselling trainees and clients can develop 'game plans' for dealing with immediate situations rather than emphasize self-helping skills which may warrant consideration later. Or clients may have limited goals: dealing with an immediate problem may be all that they have time or inclination for. One's own schedule as a trainee may be so busy that all one has time to offer is emergency problem management assistance.

Counsellor competence

If one's only tool is a hammer, one will probably treat everything as if it were a nail. Wise counsellors know their limitations and strengths. Counselling trainees need to acknowledge the range of interventions within which they can work effectively. Initially they should focus on building a repertoire of central interventions. For example, helping clients build the thinking skill of identifying, disputing and restating unrealistic personal rules is pertinent to numerous client problem areas (Ellis, 2005). Similarly, helping clients learn skills of delivering verbal, voice and bodily assertive messages has widespread relevance (Alberti and Emmons, 2001). Another criterion for developing a repertoire of interventions is to focus on those of most use to the client populations with which trainees either work or are likely to work. As time goes by, most counsellors acquire a fund of practical knowledge concerning what goals and interventions to use for which kinds of problems and skills deficiencies.

Counselling trainees cannot expect to perform interventions competently without adequate training, practice and supervision. Trainees put much less pressure on themselves if they aim to achieve limited agendas well rather than attempt too much. Though some trainees are overambitious, many underestimate their potential to help. This may lead them either not to suggest interventions or not to implement them confidently. Self-consciousness and a degree of discomfort are inevitable when learning new interventions. Under-confident trainees require good training and supervision coupled with realistic self-appraisal. In addition, they should be open to client feedback about how well they implement interventions. Experienced counsellors too may doubt themselves as they take risks to develop their repertoire of interventions. Nevertheless, it is important that they continue to build their skills.

Client considerations

Numerous client considerations influence both choosing and implementing interventions, including the following.

Anxiety level and sense of worth

Counselling trainees should always take into account how psychologically vulnerable clients are and how badly their anxieties interfere with how they feel, think and act. For example, interventions focused on improving marital communication assume that clients can accept some responsibility for contributing to marital distress. Interventions to assist highly anxious clients to initiate friendships may need to wait until they have sufficient confidence to start implementing them. Specific interventions for building career decision-making skills may be premature for clients badly out of touch with their valuing process.

Motivation and resistance

With its emphasis on developing clients' self-helping skills, motivation is a critical issue in lifeskills counselling. As with goals, clients can say 'yes' to interventions when they mean 'no' or 'maybe'. Counselling trainees can assess clients' motivation for implementing interventions and explore potential difficulties and resistances. Clients need to own interventions both intellectually and emotionally in order to exhibit commitment to attaining them. Interventions that bring early rewards, including relief of psychological distress, can enhance motivation.

Expectations and priorities

Related to motivation is the degree to which interventions are geared to outcomes that clients want and expect from counselling. Always take client expectations and priorities into account. For instance, those who enter counselling wanting to manage an immediate problem may not want interventions focused on longer-term skills building. Clients who see career issues as the main focus for counselling may resist interventions focused on their personal lives.

Age and maturity

Counselling trainees need to adjust interventions to the age of clients. Although friendship skills for adults and pre-teen children have similarities, children and adults require somewhat different skills for relating to peer and friendship groups. Trainees should take into account how much both children and adults know about relationships. Ways in which trainees can deliver interventions according to the age and maturity of clients include varying how they use language.

Intelligence level and ability to comprehend interventions

Depending on their intelligence level, some clients may experience difficulty comprehending certain interventions, for instance the mind skill of identifying possible misperceptions, generating alternatives and choosing best-fit perceptions. Counselling trainees must work with interventions that clients can comprehend. Ultimately clients have to understand the choices involved so that they can implement lifeskills on their own.

Culture

Counselling trainees need to take into account clients' cultures when choosing and implementing interventions. For instance, since the rules for work and personal relationships differ greatly across cultures, relationship skills interventions need to be sensitive to such cultural rules.

Sex and gender

Depending on their biological sex, clients may have learned different skills strengths and deficiencies. Trainees need to be careful to avoid fitting clients into masculine and feminine stereotypes. Nevertheless, they can assess where inappropriate sex-role conditioning interferes with the development of clients' lifeskills and choose interventions accordingly.

Support factors

Families, peer groups, friendship groups and work colleagues can support or interfere with skills acquisition. Sometimes clients can be trained to identify and use environmental supports better. As part of this process they may also learn how to be more supportive to others. On other occasions, interventions may focus on helping clients develop skills to protect themselves from environmental pressures.

Practical considerations

Practical considerations that may influence choice of interventions include pressing current difficulties, threatening upcoming tasks, unexpected challenges and stresses, time available for counselling, whether or not the client lives locally, financial circumstances and so on.

Development of self-helping skills

Some interventions may directly address issues of clients maintaining skills: for instance, helping clients develop realistic expectations and explanations of the reasons they experience difficulty in acquiring and maintaining skills. Trainees can also choose to implement interventions in ways that emphasize self-helping: for instance by ensuring that clients understand and can verbalize the sequence of choices involved in specific skills – an example is that of self-administered relaxation as contrasted with counsellor-administered relaxation.

Appropriateness of group interventions

Some clients might best attain some or all of their working goals by attending one or more lifeskills training groups. Others might benefit from joining longer-term interactional groups, if possible also incorporating a skills focus (Corey and Corey, 2002; Gazda et al., 2001; Yalom, 1995). Considerations relevant to selecting group interventions include: the nature of the clients' problems, availability of appropriate groups, and clients' willingness to participate in group work instead of, concurrently with, or after individual work.

Appropriateness of third-party involvement

Sometimes counselling trainees may choose to work with people who are part of clients' environments. Those working in schools with depressed or acting-out pupils may, with permission, choose to work with parents or families as well. They can also involve third parties as counsellor's aides. For example, trainees can enlist parents, teachers or peers to help shy clients to develop confidence and communication skills. In work settings, trainees can enlist the help of supervisors and managers: for instance, in developing employees' public speaking skills. On other occasions trainees' interventions with third parties may even involve advocacy on clients' behalf.

Appropriateness of referral

When making referrals, counselling trainees generally assess that other counsellors or helping professionals can deal with clients' problems and problematic skills better than they can. Trainees may start making referral hypotheses in stage 1 of the lifeskills counselling model. Whether or not they implement them then or in subsequent stages depends on whether and when they become sufficiently certain that referral is in their clients' best interests.

Activity 14.1 Choosing interventions

As appropriate, complete this exercise on your own, with a partner or in a group.

Discuss the importance of each of the following criteria in choosing interventions. State reasons for your observations.

- Empirical support for interventions
- Maintaining a supportive relationship
- Emphasis on managing problems or on altering problematic skills
- Counsellor competence to administer interventions
- Client considerations:

  anxiety level and sense of worth
  motivation and resistance
  expectations and priorities
  age and maturity
  intelligence level and ability to comprehend interventions
  culture
  biological sex
  support factors
  practical considerations (for instance time, pressing current difficulties)
  other client considerations not mentioned above

- Development of self-helping interventions
- Appropriateness of group interventions
- Appropriateness of interventions involving third parties
- Appropriateness of referral
- Other criteria for choosing interventions not mentioned above

Planning interventions

Almost invariably, counsellors do not use interventions in isolation. Consequently, as well as developing hypotheses about interventions, trainees need to develop hypotheses about how interventions might best be used in combination. In short, they need to develop plans of varying degrees of complexity to attain goals.

Problem management plans

Problem management plans are outlines of interventions and steps required to help clients manage specific problematic situations. Counselling trainees who wish to focus on problematic skills may, for practical reasons, make treatment compromises. Clients may only have time or motivation to plan for managing immediate situations: for instance, requesting pay rises, imminent public speaking engagements, statistics tests or visits from in-laws. Even in longer-term counselling, trainees and clients can develop plans to deal with specific situations, although this is more likely to take place within the framework of altering and improving problematic skills. Below is an example of problem management planning.

> Emily came for counselling with anxieties about being a female engineer. During her second session, Emily and her counsellor, Tony, planned how best to manage a specific current problem in Emily's life. Emily's first job after graduation was with a leading construction engineering company. When hired, she was promised a salary review after her first year's service. The company had not conducted this review three months into her second year. Emily and Tony formulated her overall problem management goal: ask her boss for a salary review before the end of two weeks. Then Emily and Tony developed a plan for how she would make a salary review request when face to face with her boss. This plan included strategies for handling possible counter-moves by her boss. Tony demonstrated, coached and rehearsed Emily in how to carry out the plan.

Problematic skills: structured plans

Counselling trainees and clients may consider a highly structured approach the best way to achieve some goals. Structured plans or programmes are step-by-step training and learning outlines of interventions for attaining specific goals. They are commonly used in lifeskills training groups, for instance in assertion or stress management groups. Structured plans may also be used to train individual clients in skills where working goals are clear and specific. Three variations of structured plans are predetermined programmes, tailor-made structured plans, and partially structured plans.

Predetermined programmes

These are existing, or modifications of existing, packages or programmes to develop skills. Such skills development programmes may be in areas like parenting, career decision-making, and weight control. Below is an example of using a structured programme.

Henry suffered from hypertension. A central working goal was to develop his relaxation skills, both physical and mental. Henry's counsellor decided that the best way to develop his relaxation skills was to use a program based on Bernstein and Borkovec's *Progressive Relaxation Training: A Manual for the Helping Professions* (1973).

Tailor-made structured plans

Structured plans combining interventions can be tailor-made to specific problems or to specific persons. When tailor-made to specific problems, such plans resemble predetermined packages. For instance, when Jim Blake sees the outplacement counsellor Sam Rushton about getting another job, Sam can either fit Jim into an existing job skills program, or design a program specifically to address Jim's skills weaknesses, or combine the two approaches. In the tailor-made approach Sam develops a step-by-step outline of how to attain Jim's working goals. Here Jim can be part of the planning process, with his specific goals, wishes and circumstances taken into account. The structured plan is negotiated rather than prescribed.

Partially structured plans

These plans have elements of structure, yet fall short of step-by-step structured plans. For instance, in the case of the unemployed executive Jim Blake, another option for his counsellor Sam Rushton is to set aside certain sessions for testing to assess interests and aptitudes and also for developing specific action skills, such as résumé writing and interview skills. The agendas for the remaining sessions are open for negotiation at the start of each session.

Problematic skills: open plans

Open plans allow counselling trainees and clients without predetermined structure to choose which interventions to use to attain which working goals, and when. Many considerations influence the decision to adopt an open plan. Some clients may require nurturing relationships to help them get more in touch with their feelings and reduce their anxieties. They may not be able to work effectively on their poor mind skills and communication skills until they feel less vulnerable. In addition, some cases are complex and difficult to understand. Counselling trainees risk prematurely deciding on interventions if they opt for too much structure too soon. Open plans allow trainees and clients to cooperate in setting session agendas. Such agendas can emphasize the material and the skills on which clients and students currently want to work. Open plans have the great advantage of flexibility. Clients may be more motivated to work on skills and material that have relevance at a specific time than being run through existing programmes independent of current considerations.

> The counsellor Richard [the author] and client Louise Donovan decided to use an open plan to address her poor interview skills. In reality her interview skills weaknesses were just the tip of the iceberg in a well-entrenched, cumbersome, pedantic and off-putting style of professional relating. The initial impression given by Louise was that she would be best placed in back rooms well away from important clients. I suggested to Louise that she not only needed to work on specific communication skills, but also on the poor mind skills that contributed to her being highly anxious in interviews.
>
> Near the start of each session Louise and I would establish an agenda for that session's work. Early sessions focused mainly on building Louise's interview skills. Together we made a list of questions she was likely to be asked at interviews and I engaged in cassette-recorded question-and-answer sessions with her. Afterwards we assessed the cassettes and looked for specific evidence to confirm or negate points. During this evaluation, Louise became both more aware of the effect her differing verbal, voice and body messages could have on interviewers and more conscious that in interviews for senior positions how she related was also important alongside what she knew. In the third session, using the whiteboard, I helped Louise to dispute her rule that she must give the perfect answer and then developed with her a statement of a more realistic rule.
>
> Subsequent sessions incorporated the following interventions: more practice in the verbal, voice and body message skills of answering questions; making up a cassette in which I relaxed Louise and then took her through appropriate calming, coaching and affirming self-talk to use when waiting outside the interview room and when going in and answering the first few questions competently; and identifying and listing Louise's competencies and then cassette recording them twice – first using my voice and then with Louise's voice.
>
> During counselling, I negotiated with Louise a series of homework assignments both to prepare for sessions and also to consolidate skills targeted in sessions. I encouraged Louise to practice her skills in her daily professional life, which she did with increasing success. This daily practice was especially important since Louise was not going for interviews then because she did not want to leave her present job, unless it was for a substantial improvement.

Considerations in planning

In the above section varying degrees of structure for plans was emphasized. Here the focus is on the use of plans in helping clients to develop lifeskills from systematic learning sequences. Most considerations mentioned below are also relevant to plans for managing specific problem situations.

Preparation time

If a counselling trainee decides to design treatment plans for individual clients, when do they do it? Though trainees may discuss with clients possible interventions for attaining goals, they may find it difficult to develop systematic plans during the same session. Instead, they should do this before the next session. Some trainees do not develop systematic plans because they are unwilling to spend out-of-session time on this task.

Involvement of clients and others

Counselling trainees need to consider at what stage and how much to involve clients in planning. Trainees' prior discussions of goals provide some protection against formulating plans unacceptable to clients. They should always check that clients understand and are comfortable with proposed plans. Sometimes it helps to involve clients early in the planning process. If they take clients' wishes and priorities into account, clients will be more likely to implement the plans. With clients' permission, trainees may, when planning, sometimes involve significant others such as partners, care givers or parents.

Sequencing of interventions

What is the best way to sequence activities to attain goals? Sometimes the logic in sequencing interventions is clear. For instance, with most unemployed executives there are three logical steps in assisting them in becoming re-employed: (1) evaluation and career planning; (2) developing a job marketing plan; and (3) implementing a job marketing plan (Davidson, 1988). Within an individual intervention like choosing realistic rules, the sequence of sub-interventions is clear: identifying unrealistic rules, disputing them, and restating them in the form of more realistic rules. Here the learning tasks are cumulative. In communication skills interventions, counselling trainees can often use step-by-step graded tasks to develop clients' skills and confidence.

Time frame for plan

Counselling trainees, clients and the learning process may all influence the time allocated for carrying out plans. For instance trainees may have a restricted amount of time to work with clients, and they may want clients to participate in learning activities offered by others, for instance workshops that are only available on specific dates. Client considerations include varying degrees of urgency in acquiring skills and different abilities to pay, if fees are involved. Learning process considerations include the degree to which sessions and planned activities should be intensive rather than spaced out, or a combination of the two. In addition, should one or more follow-up or booster sessions be planned?

Management of learning considerations

What is the best way to put interventions across? For each intervention, when should counselling trainees use the following training and learning methods: assessment and facilitating client self-assessment, facilitation, verbal presentation, demonstration, coaching, and homework assignments? Trainees also need to make decisions concerning the overall balance between facilitation and didactic input. Other considerations include availability of written training materials, such as training manuals and handouts, and of audiovisual materials and equipment. A further set of learning considerations includes sensitivity to the costs and rewards for clients of carrying out plans. How difficult are the plans' various elements? What are the clients' support factors? Are their counsellors supportive? When do clients obtain rewards from implementing planned activities?

Emphasis on maintaining and developing skills

When initially planning interventions, counselling trainees should consider how to help clients take away and maintain trained skills as self-helping skills for later. Both structured and open plans should emphasize clients learning to use skills on their own. Trainees can stress clients' mind skills relevant to maintenance: for instance, realistic expectations about the difficulty of maintaining change and understanding the sequences of choices in targeted skills well enough to instruct themselves and, if necessary, make corrections. Trainees can also plan interventions in ways that help clients maintain communication skills. Ways of doing this include emphasizing over-learning, practice in real-life settings, and anticipating and working through difficulties in applying skills.

Counselling trainees may leave developing more formal maintenance plans to phase 2 of stage 3 of the lifeskills counselling model: Ending. They can then take clients' end-of-counselling skills levels into account as well as their current estimations of obstacles to maintaining skills. In brief counselling, planning interventions, intervening, and consolidating self-helping skills and ending may become compressed into one another. In such circumstances, trainees and clients have to plan for maintenance as best they can.

Monitoring and evaluating outcomes

In Chapters 10, 11 and 12 ways of assessing feelings, physical reactions, thoughts and communication/actions were reviewed. When making plans, it is important to keep in mind the need for clients to develop self-assessment skills and to monitor their progress. When agreeing on a shared analysis in skills terms, counselling trainees have defined the areas in which it is important to observe change. Plans are successful to the extent that they efficiently help clients develop and maintain self-helping skills. If plans do not produce desired results, trainees should closely examine the reasons and, if necessary, modify plans.

Activity 14.2 Making plans for interventions

As appropriate, complete this exercise on your own, with a partner or in a group.

Part A: Choosing and planning interventions

Select a typical problem for a typical 'client' whom you might counsel either when in training or afterwards. For instance, exam anxiety is a common problem among secondary and tertiary students. Answer the following questions.

1 What is the typical problem you have selected for your typical 'client'?
2 What might be up to two mind skills goals for the client's problem?
3 What intervention or interventions would you choose to develop the client's skills for each of these goals?
4 What might be up to two appropriate communication/action skills goals for the client's problem?
5 What intervention or interventions would you choose to develop the client's skills for each of these goals?
6 What type of plan would you choose to help your client attain the above mind skills and communication/action skills goals? Give reasons for your choice.
7 If appropriate, outline your plan.

Part B: Conduct role-play interviews

Conduct a series of role-plays with one or more partners. In each role-play the person acting as counsellor suggests and discusses with the client interventions and plans to attain goals. Skills to bear in mind include:

- Make a transition statement.
- Enlist cooperation and commitment.
- Give simple explanations and answers.
- Discuss counsellor and client role expectations and any contract involved.

After each role-play hold a sharing and feedback session with your 'client'. Afterwards, reverse roles. Playing back video or audio recordings of role-plays may help you learn skills faster.

Skills for working with clients

Make transition statements

Counselling trainees may have signalled moving on to discussing interventions as part of their rationale for stating clients' problems in skills terms: for instance with a sentence like 'Also, stating problems in skills terms gives us a focus for discussing how best to improve the skills you need.' The following are examples of possible transition statements after trainees have finished presenting and checking their client's agreement on skills to improve.

> 'Now that we have agreed on the skills you need to improve, let's spend some time in discussing how best to do this.'
> 'Can we now move on to discuss approaches to building your skills.'
> 'Now let's look at some ways to attain your goals.'

Enlist cooperation and commitment

It is crucial that counselling trainees encourage clients to cooperate. One way of doing this is for trainee and client jointly to develop a plan using a whiteboard. When trainees present plans, they can do so in ways that imply that plans are series of suggestions for discussion that, if necessary, can be modified or fine-tuned. Check clients' comprehension and feelings about proposed plans. Explore reservations and, if necessary, negotiate changes in plans. Trainees can also explore with clients the payoffs and rewards as well as the costs of implementing plans.

Give simple explanations and answers

Without insulting clients' intelligence, counselling trainees can offer clear and simple explanations for suggested interventions and plans.

Trainees can give clients too much information so that they feel confused rather than motivated to work. They should be prepared to answer questions, but again keep their answers simple and to the point. In initial sessions, the purposes of discussing interventions and plans are as much emotional and motivational as instructional. Clients feel better if they perceive counsellors as knowing ways to approach their problems and poor skills. Often describing the detail of interventions is best left until later when clients require this information to develop specific skills.

Discuss expectations and contract

Counselling trainees and clients can discuss expectations of themselves and each other. For instance, a trainee may indicate that they expect regular attendance over a specified number of sessions, with possibly a joint review of progress at the end of this period. They may stress the necessity of the client's diligently carrying out homework assignments. Sometimes trainees give clients written plans. These plans can assume the status of contracts of varying degrees of formality. One approach is to turn the plan into an informational treatment contract. Informational contracts possess five elements: (1) information about interventions; (2) statements about (goal) outcome expectations; (3) client intention statements, in which the client agrees to participate fully in important aspects of interventions; (4) duration (weeks or sessions) of the contract; and (5) an informed consent statement (Cormier and Nurius, 2002).

Start implementing plans

After trainees agree with clients on shared definitions of problems and discuss plans, they can then negotiate homework assignments. One type of assignment is for clients to observe and monitor feelings, thoughts and actions in targeted skills areas. Clients may be instructed to start developing specific skills: for instance speaking louder or taking a few gentle risks in disclosing more information about themselves. Getting clients started on implementing plans right away has many advantages: it reinforces the idea of working rather than simply talking relationships; clients may feel better for working on problems and problematic skills that have worried them for some time; implementing plans may lead to short-term rewards that build motivation and commitment; and getting started enables profitable use of the time between first and second sessions. Ultimately this may mean one or more fewer sessions.

deliver interventions 15

Chapter outcomes

By studying and doing the activities in this chapter you should:

- understand the counsellor's role as trainer;
- know what are reconnect and catch-up skills;
- understand establishing session agenda skills;
- know some speaking skills for presenting interventions;
- know some demonstrating skills; and
- know some coaching and feedback skills.

The counsellor as trainer

This chapter focuses on some central skills of conducting sessions in which the counsellor or counselling trainee delivers interventions. In much of counsellor training the emphasis is on receiver or listening skills rather than on sender skills or training skills. Trainees as developmental educators also require educational or training skills. Counselling is an educational process in which helpers flexibly use both relationship and training skills to assist clients to attain learning goals for now and later. Lifeskills counselling encourages clients to learn for themselves and to understand, retain and use what they have learned.

Clients as learners require counsellors as trainers to guide learning. Counsellors as trainers require not only knowledge of what interventions to provide, but also skills of how to intervene. The *what* of intervening needs to be supplemented by the *how* of intervening.

The following are examples of counsellors who sabotage their effectiveness by showing poor training skills.

Leanne is a counsellor trainee on placement. She attempts to explain the mind skill of creating rules to a client, Chris, who devalues himself with 'musts' about needing to do very well in examinations. Leanne doesn't really understand the skill herself, her presentation is muddled and she answers Chris's questions poorly. She also speaks in a monotone and keeps tugging at her hair. Chris learns nothing that is useful about how to avoid putting unnecessary pressure on himself.

Barbara is a counsellor who tries to teach Sanjay, a recent immigrant from India, assertion skills. Barbara spends a lot of time discussing with Sanjay what he might say when he faces racial discrimination. However, at no stage does Barbara demonstrate the voice and body messages that might accompany Sanjay's assertive verbal messages. Consequently, Sanjay does not really know how to be assertive.

Neil is a careers counsellor who thinks that Lisa requires better interview skills to increase her employability. Neil talks about interview skills and demonstrates some of them. However, he never encourages and helps Lisa to rehearse and practise these skills. Lisa tells her friends that she still goes to pieces in job interviews and devalues herself for not using the skills Neil talks about. However, Neil has never role-played with Lisa how to improve her skills, nor has he suggested that she do specific homework assignments.

Counselling trainees should pay attention to good skills in three broad areas central to most interventions: *tell*, *show* and *do*. In the above examples, Leanne exhibited poor skills in the area of tell, or helping Chris to learn from hearing; Barbara, in the area of show, or helping Sanjay to learn from observing; and Neil, in the area of do, or helping Lisa to learn from doing. Trainees are more likely to impart lifeskills and clients are more likely to learn them if they use all three modes. When initially presenting a lifeskill, 'tell' may be accompanied by 'show' and then 'do'. On many occasions all three modes interact. For example when clients rehearse skills, 'do' may be interspersed with 'show' and 'tell'.

Importance of the counselling relationship

In the training role, both good relationship skills and good training skills are required. Trainees who only possess good relationship skills are unable to impart specific skills clearly and efficiently. For instance, person-centred counsellors operate on the assumption that all clients have lifeskills strengths latent in their repertoires that will be unblocked by empathic helping relationships (Raskin and Rogers, 2005; Rogers, 1975). While such an assumption may be appropriate for some clients, it is not entirely true for most. Imagine trying to learn how to drive a car with an instructor who only provides an empathic relationship. The relationship might support learning, but would be insufficient on its own for acquiring the required skills. Most clients do not have sufficient skills strengths for they and trainees to be able to rely on the quality of the counselling relationship alone.

The majority of clients are stuck and require more active help to provide them with the skills to move forward. The counselling relationship is central to this learning process in many ways, including strengthening the working alliance, helping assessment and client self-assessment, assisting client self-exploration and experiencing of feelings, providing the emotional climate for clients to take risks and also to look more closely at the consequences of their behaviours, and allowing clients to be open about difficulties in implementing skills. Clients are likely to gain most from trainees who both offer good relationships and also impart skills effectively. The counselling relationship needs to be part of an active approach to training and learning.

Reconnect and catch-up skills

When counselling trainees meet clients for sessions in stage 3 of the lifeskills counselling model, they need to start by re-establishing their relationship with them. In other words, they reconnect and catch up with one another. Trainees might engage in minimal small talk with clients as they usher them into their office. Then they ask an open-ended question that checks 'where the client is at'. They deliberately give some control of the content of the first part of the session to clients. Sample opening questions are 'How's your week been?', 'How have you been getting on?' and 'Where would you like to start today?' When the client responds, trainees should use active listening skills to show their understanding. In addition, they can use questioning skills to show their interest and elicit relevant information.

Why is such a 'softly, softly' approach to starting post-initial sessions advocated? First of all, counselling trainees need to re-establish that they offer person-to-person relationships. Clients' views and agendas are important and need to be treated with respect. Trainees also re-establish their influence base as a rewarding person for clients. Right from the start, trainees encourage clients' active participation by valuing their contribution. They allow clients the psychological safety and space to bring them up to date with information that they select as important. By not 'pushing the agenda', trainees avoid talking over or suppressing significant events that clients may wish to share with them. The opportunity is provided for amending the session's agenda in the light of new information provided by clients. Trainees also help create a safe emotional climate for subsequent more focused work on developing specific lifeskills. They also minimize the chance of resistances arising through clients feeling unheard and/or misunderstood.

Once counselling trainees have allowed clients some initial session space, they may still require further information to help assess clients' progress regarding specific skills and homework assignments. As appropriate, trainees can ask additional questions pinpointing feelings, physical reactions, thoughts, communications and interactive patterns to illuminate the picture already provided.

There are no easy answers to how long this reconnect and catch-up phase of post-initial sessions should last. It is possible to err on the side of being both too brief and insufficiently rigorous. The kind of relationship the client expects and is comfortable with needs to be taken into account (Lazarus, 1993). Assuming there have been no significant new developments or crises, a rough guide is to spend the first five to ten minutes of 45–50-minute sessions on this phase. This suggestion can be adjusted upwards or downwards as circumstances warrant. Often in practice the dividing line between re-establishing relationships and delivering interventions becomes blurred.

Establishing session agenda skills

Near the start of each session in the interventions stage, it is generally desirable for counselling trainees and clients to establish an agenda for the session's work. Often the best time to do this is immediately after trainees have reconnected and caught up with their clients. If trainees are working with a highly structured plan, the session agenda might be outlined in the plan. When conducting sessions with an open plan, each session requires an agenda. Agendas may be for all or part of sessions. Trainees may decide where they will begin working and then, later, make another decision regarding the next agenda area. Alternatively, as part of the initial agenda-setting discussion, trainees may target one area to start and then agree to move on to another area. However, even when session agendas have been established, it is important to remain flexible and respond to developments during sessions.

An issue in establishing session agendas is how client-centred or how counsellor-centred to be. I favour paying considerable attention to clients' wishes since I want their involvement and motivation. For instance with a client like Louise Donovan, when establishing a second session agenda, I might say:

> 'In the last session we stated a number of goals for developing your interview skills. For instance, your mind skills goals were to develop skills of choosing a more realistic rule about giving perfect answers, perceiving interviews and yourself more accurately, and using coping self-talk. Your communication skills goals were to develop your verbal,

voice and body messages skills for interviews. Where would you like to work first?'

If I thought there was some important reason for starting with a particular skill, I would share this observation with clients. However, my inclination would be to allow clients the final say in where work was done. If necessary, I set limits: for instance, not participating in long, unfocused conversations.

In third and subsequent sessions, often at least part of an agenda will flow or feed forward from previous sessions. For example, at the end of a previous session a counselling trainee may have broken off working on a skill and wants to continue now. Another variation is that a trainee agreed on a homework assignment that would provide information for working on a specific skill in this session. A further option is to ask clients where they would like to work. Still another option is for counselling trainees to make some suggestions themselves.

Speaking skills

The main delivering intervention skills of tell, show and do are now presented in turn. Whether counselling trainees are listening actively or training clients they require effective speaking skills. For instance, when listening, trainees need to communicate reflections and summaries. Here I emphasize using speaking skills when training clients in specific lifeskills. The following are some occasions when trainees might require speaking skills for doing this:

- When offering reasons for developing a skill.
- When initially describing component parts of skills.
- When providing commentaries for skills demonstrations.
- When coaching clients as they rehearse skills.
- When answering client questions about skills.
- When negotiating homework assignments.

Speaking skills for training are somewhat different from those used for active listening. Some counselling trainees experience difficulty switching from the more passive role of active listening to the more active role of imparting information. They cannot feed off their clients' most recent utterances. Without overwhelming clients, they need to communicate information as clearly and as interestingly as possible. Furthermore, they should remain conscious that the best learning requires clients to develop their own self-talk about how to implement skills.

Manage speech anxiety

Whether presenting to individuals or groups, counselling trainees may suffer from debilitating speech anxiety. As beginners they still need time to become comfortable in their knowledge of the skill. Their delivering interventions skills require developing, and they may also possess some poor mind skills that interfere with the relaxed concentration required to present lifeskills well.

Speech anxiety has many dimensions. Feelings that may be associated with speech anxiety include tension, insecurity, vulnerability, embarrassment and confusion. Physical reactions include nausea, a dry mouth, butterflies in the stomach and one's mind going blank. Verbal messages include using confused and rambling sentences. Voice messages that can convey anxiety include speaking too quickly or softly. Body messages that may be inappropriate include hair tugging, scratching and excessive smiling.

The following are some illustrative poor mind skills associated with trainees becoming anxious over their speech when counselling.

- *Creating rules.* Trainees may place unrealistic 'musts', 'oughts' and 'shoulds' on themselves and clients: for instance, 'I must be an excellent presenter of skills immediately', or 'Clients must always understand me.'
- *Creating perceptions.* Trainees may overemphasize their poor skills in presenting lifeskills and inadequately acknowledge their skills strengths. They may be hypersensitive to any cues of negative feedback from clients.
- *Creating self-talk.* Trainees may either use negative self-talk or fail to use coping self-talk, or both. Negative self-talk statements include: 'I can't cope', 'I can't do anything right' and 'I feel totally confused.' Trainees may fail to use the calming, coaching and affirming dimensions of coping self-talk.
- *Creating visualizing.* Trainees may be visualizing the worst about how they describe skills to clients. Negative and catastrophic imagery may interfere with competent performance. Much better is to use their imagination to rehearse and practice relaxed competence (Lazarus, 1984).
- *Creating explanations.* Trainees may assume too much responsibility for clients' learning. They may also wrongly attribute the causes of their speech anxiety, for instance to their genes or to unfortunate previous attempts to present skills to clients. Some counselling trainees inadequately attribute the cause of their anxiety about presenting lifeskills to their own lack of preparation.

- *Creating expectations.* Trainees may be beset by undue pessimism, or undue optimism, or oscillate between the two regarding presentation skills.
- *Creating realistic goals.* If trainees suffer from anxiety when presenting lifeskills to clients, they can make overcoming this anxiety a goal. Some trainees increase their anxiety by having unrealistic goals about what is attainable in counselling.

The skills that counselling trainees require to handle speech anxious thinking are the same skills clients require to manage their poor mind skills. The next two chapters will describe ways in which trainees and clients can work to develop their mind skills.

Prepare clear content

Clients cannot be expected to comprehend poorly presented skills, let alone know them well enough to instruct themselves once counselling ends. Many counselling trainees experience difficulty in explaining skills clearly. Some are aware of this, others less so. In some cases, anxiety is a factor. Unfortunately, all too often neophyte counsellors do not properly understand skills they present. Consequently, their explanations are either muddled or clearly inaccurate. On other occasions, trainees may understand the skills, but communicate them insufficiently well.

Individual counselling lends itself to a more informal and interactive approach than is sometimes possible in training groups. Nevertheless, counselling trainees still require the skills of introducing and describing the key points of any lifeskills they impart. Systematic preparation is desirable, especially for beginners. Such preparation should not lead to rigid presentations. Rather, when clear in their own minds, trainees can better address individual clients' needs and learning rates.

Counselling trainees' presentations of lifeskills should focus on the mechanics of how to perform a skill or sub-skill. They are not academic discourses. In addition to preparing clear content, trainees should use clear language: for instance *active listening* is better than *empathic listening*. They should be concise, specific and aim to describe skills as simply as possible so that clients can easily describe the skills to themselves. Trainees should avoid long sentences – the language of speech uses shorter sentences than written language (Bernstein, 1988). The longer the sentences, the fewer are the clients who can comprehend them.

The language of lifeskills counselling is not the language of boredom. If rightly used, humour can illustrate points and make learning fun. It can relax clients and lower defensiveness and resistances. However, if wrongly used, humour can divert both clients and trainees from attaining goals.

Counselling trainees should consider using visual as well as aural presentation. Audiovisual aids, for instance the whiteboard, may help them to present information more clearly. Trainees need to think carefully about how to integrate audiovisual aids into their presentations so that they are not disruptive.

Develop delivery skills

If counselling trainees prepare clear content they are only part-way to introducing and describing skills effectively. They still need to put the message across. Presenting information to individuals or couples does not require the theatrical performance skills of presenting information to larger numbers. Nevertheless, even in individual counselling, trainees' voice and body are delivery tools for holding interest, emphasizing points and enlisting motivation.

Send effective voice messages

Counselling trainees, perhaps even more when they send messages than when they receive them, need to develop an awareness of their voice as a delivery tool. For better or worse, their voice messages frame their verbal messages. Let's take the VAPER acronym and suggest how volume, articulation, pitch, emphasis and rate can be used when delivering content rather than responding to clients.

Volume

When presenting skills, trainees are under less obligation to adjust their volume to reflect that of clients than when responding as a listener. Without overwhelming clients, trainees need to speak reasonably loudly, possibly more loudly than when responding. Some trainees may be better at being gentle listeners than outgoing talkers. If so, they may need to project their voices when presenting skills in counselling.

Articulation

Clear articulation may be more important when presenting information than when responding. If counselling trainees enunciate poorly when sending listening responses, clients at least are able to put what is said in the context of their previous utterances. Clients do not have this opportunity when information is presented for the first time. Instead they may be struggling to understand both content and delivery. The longer speakers talk, the more poor enunciation distracts.

Pitch

Any pitch errors that counselling trainees possess – for instance uncomfortable highness, lowness or narrowness of range – may be more pronounced when they present information. When responding, trainees may modify their pitch to match the client's pitch, but when presenting information, trainees may be less conscious of pitch because they are thinking of what to say. They have more scope for pitch errors since they are likely to speak for longer when presenting material than when responding.

Emphasis

When as listeners trainees use reflections, they emphasize the same words and phrases that clients emphasize. As a presenter of information trainees emphasize words and phrases that highlight their own main points. Their use of emphasis should convey interest and commitment.

Rate

As with responding, when describing skills, counselling trainees should speak fairly slowly. A slow, but comfortable, speech rate gives them time to think and gives clients time to comprehend. Effective use of pauses can both clarify and emphasize what they say and also allow clients to ask questions. Pause errors include having too many or too few, or making them too long or too short. Making extraneous sounds such as 'uhms' and 'ers' is also unhelpful.

Send effective body messages

Sending effective body messages when describing a lifeskill is partly a matter of avoiding interfering messages and partly a matter of sending good messages. Unlike when presenting skills in training groups, in individual sessions counselling trainees are likely to be seated. Many body messages for attending to clients when listening are still appropriate when delivering content: for instance relaxed body posture, physical openness, sensitivity to physical proximity and height, appropriate clothing and grooming, and appropriate facial expressions. The following are some additional suggestions for using effective body messages when trainees present information.

Gestures

Counselling trainees should use gestures economically to help explain what is being said. Fischer (1972) states there are three main types of gesture: *emphatic* gestures, such as pointing the finger, designed to make it clear that what is being said is important; *descriptive* gestures, for instance stretching one's arms out when saying that marital partners are poles apart, designed to help illustrate points; and *symbolic* gestures to which a commonly understood meaning has been ascribed, for instance shaking the head to say no. Another broad category of gestures is that of *distracting* gestures: touching one's head, scratching one's nose, pulling lint off one's cuff, waving one's arms around, tugging one's hair and so on. Trainees can learn to use gestures to work for rather than against their training messages.

Gaze and eye contact

Talkers tend to use much less gaze and eye contact than listeners. Nevertheless, when presenting information, trainees require an adequate gaze level to read clients' reactions. Trainees should present lifeskills as though conversing with clients rather than talking at them. Their use of gaze and eye contact is a most important way of relating directly to clients when making learning points. Gaze and eye contact errors include looking down too much and turning away when writing on the whiteboard rather than checking for clients' reactions.

Put content and delivery together

So far the focus has been on managing speech anxiety, preparing clear content, and using good voice and body message delivery skills. Counselling trainees may have practiced long and hard to develop their active listening skills so that clients want to talk to them. They need to show the same conscientiousness in developing sender skills of imparting information so that clients want to hear them. An analogy may be made with effective parenting: parents not only need to listen so that their children will talk, they also need to talk so that their children will listen (Gordon, 1970). Trainees may need to rehearse and practice in order to gain fluency in describing different lifeskills to clients. Effective counsellors combine talking and listening skills in such a way that clients feel they are valued parts of the training process and not just receptacles of another's knowledge – the so called *jug-and-mug* approach. Skilled counsellors develop an emotional climate so that clients are motivated to learn, ask questions, and take risks.

At risk of repetition, trainees should use speaking skills to help clients develop self-instruction skills. Ideally, when learning new skills, clients start by being receptive to the trainee's voice in their heads. However, they then need to replace the trainee's voice with their own voice. During this process, the trainee's public speech becomes the client's private speech.

Activity 15.1 Developing speaking skills

As appropriate, do the parts of this activity on your own, with a partner or in a group. Work through those parts that you find useful.

Part A: Prepare clear content

Choose a skill or sub-skill to present to a client. Thoroughly prepare the content of your initial presentation of the skill. Pay attention to the following guidelines:

- Know your material.
- Outline your presentation.
- Use appropriate language.
- Where appropriate, use humour.
- Consider using the whiteboard.

Part B: Develop delivery skills

1 Either on your own or with a partner acting as client, practice your voice message delivery skills as you present your content. Pay attention to your volume, articulation, pitch, emphasis and rate.
If possible, obtain feedback from audio recording your efforts and from your client.
2 Either on your own or with a partner acting as client, practice your body message skills as you present your content. Pay attention to your gestures, facial expressions, posture, gaze and eye contact.
If possible, obtain feedback from video recording your efforts and from your client.

Part C: Put content and delivery together

Practice your speaking skills as you give initial descriptions of skills to partners who act as clients. Focus on:

- managing speech anxiety;
- preparing clear content;
- using appropriate audiovisual aids;
- sending effective voice messages;
- sending effective body messages.

Playing back audio recordings or video recordings of how you perform may assist learning.

Demonstrating skills

By demonstrating skills, effective counsellors and counselling trainees add 'show' to 'tell'. One of the main ways in which people learn is observational learning or learning from models (Bandura, 1986). In real life, much modelling is unintentional. However, trainees can consciously promote observational learning of desired skills and sub-skills. Here the more everyday word *demonstrating* is used instead of modelling.

Goals for demonstrating

Demonstrating may be used to initiate new skills strengths, develop existing skills strengths, disinhibit existing skills strengths, and inhibit and weaken existing skills deficiencies. Goals for demonstrating and observational learning can be viewed in the following categories.

Mind skills

Mind skills include creating rules, perceptions and self-talk.

Nicole, a human relations consultant, works with Ross on his public speaking skills. As part of her plan, she aims to train Ross to use coping rather than negative self-talk before, during and after speaking situations. Nicole demonstrates coping self-talk by verbally giving examples of appropriate coping self-talk statements and also by giving Ross a handout with examples of public speaking coping self-talk statements.

Communication/action skills

Communication and action skills demonstrations focus on observable behaviours. For instance, when demonstrating communication, counselling trainees should emphasize voice and body as well as verbal messages.

Nicole and Ross have working sub-goals: (a) speaking at a comfortable rather than a rapid rate, (b) being easy to hear rather than too quiet, (c) making good gaze and eye contact with the audience, and (d) using gestures to emphasize points. Nicole demonstrates one skill at a time then coaches and rehearses Ross in it before moving on to the next skill. Ultimately Nicole demonstrates and coaches Ross in all four skills together. She also encourages Ross either to audio record or, if possible, to video record his own competent performance of the skills so he can use himself as a model in future. In addition, she encourages Ross to observe good public speakers and assess how they use the targeted skills.

Communication/action skills with accompanying self-talk

Here the demonstrator focuses both on communication/action skills and on accompanying self-instructions.

To speak effectively in public, Ross needs to combine mind and communication skills. Nicole demonstrates to Ross in slow motion how he can use calming and coaching self-instructions when speaking. Nicole's demonstration intersperses 'think aloud' self-instructions with demonstrating communication skills.

Methods of demonstration

Counselling trainees have many options when presenting demonstrations. These options, which are not mutually exclusive, are summarized in Box 15.1.

Written

Mind skills in particular lend themselves to written demonstration. Trainees can demonstrate mind skills on whiteboards and clients can record these examples on homework sheets. In addition, trainees can demonstrate lifeskills on the written page – whether handouts or passages in books and training manuals. Written demonstrations, which can be supplemented by visual images such as cartoons, are easily stored and retrieved by trainees and clients. Written examples can introduce subsequent written or live exercises.

Box 15.1 Methods of demonstrating lifeskills

Methods of demonstrating lifeskills	Mind skills	Skills areas Communication/ action skills	Communication/ action skills plus self-talk
Written demonstration	✓	Difficult	Difficult
Live demonstration	✓	✓	✓
Recorded demonstration	✓	✓	✓
Visualized demonstration	Less suitable	✓	✓

Live

Probably most counselling demonstrations are live. Counselling trainees may demonstrate live when initially presenting skills, when coaching clients afterwards and when working with current material that clients bring into later sessions. Live demonstrations have the advantage of here-and-now communication. Clients can receive verbal, voice and body messages as they occur. Trainees can interact with clients and, if appropriate, show different or simpler ways to enact skills.

Live demonstrations do have limitations. Unless they are recorded, clients have no copies to listen to or watch on their own. It can be difficult to portray scenes involving more than one or two persons in live demonstrations.

A variation of live demonstration is to encourage clients to observe good and poor demonstrations of targeted skills in their everyday lives. For instance, clients with public speaking problems can monitor the skills of good and poor public speakers. Clients with difficulty initiating contact with others can look out for how socially skilled people do this. Clients with poor parenting skills can be asked to observe parents they admire.

Recorded

Recorded demonstrations can use audio cassettes and videotapes either as integral parts of initial skills demonstrations or for homework assignments. Some advantages of such demonstrations are that they can be reproduced, loaned to clients, and lend themselves to playback and to repeated viewing.

Audio cassettes are particularly useful for demonstrating mind skills. With audio cassettes, clients can be taken through the sequences of choices entailed in targeted skills without visual distractions. Initial audio cassette demonstrations of mind skills are best done by trainees: it is unreasonable to expect clients to demonstrate skills that they do not properly understand. Later in the learning process, trainees can help clients make up their own demonstration cassettes. If clients switch to using themselves as demonstrators during counselling, they may be more likely to maintain skills afterwards. Clients probably require repeated listenings to their demonstrations for the mind skills to become part of their everyday repertoire. Some disadvantages are that audio cassette demonstrations are not as spontaneous as live demonstrations and that they may be insufficiently geared to individual clients' needs. Often a combination of audio cassette, written and live demonstration is the most effective way of training clients in mind skills.

A major advantage of videotape demonstration over audio cassette demonstration is that it enables clients to observe body messages. During sessions counselling trainees can use videotapes to demonstrate communication skills: for instance, making an assertive request for a behaviour change, demonstrating attention and interest when listening, or answering questions at job interviews. Clients can also make use of demonstration videotapes on their own. Many lifeskills training videotapes are already on the market. However, commercial videotapes may not suit individual needs. When trainees make their own demonstration videotapes, they have the choice of whether or not to bring in outside resources.

Visualized

Visualized demonstration is sometimes called covert modelling (Cautela, 1976; Cormier and Nurius, 2002; Kazdin, 1994). Counselling trainees ask clients to close their eyes and visualize or imagine the demonstration scenes that they describe. Depending on the instructions, clients visualize either themselves or persons similar to themselves demonstrating targeted action skills. Visualized demonstration has the advantage of flexibility. Different situations can be readily presented to clients' imaginations, depending on their needs and how fast they learn. Clients can follow this up with visualized demonstration and rehearsal at home. There are some disadvantages. It is only appropriate for clients who can visualize scenes adequately. Clients never actually see skills demonstrated and, as a consequence, even when instructions are well given there may be significant gaps between what is described and what clients imagine.

In general, clients visualize best when relaxed. Counselling trainees can develop different visualized demonstrations around targeted skills. For instance, visualizations may be graded by threat or difficulty. In addition, clients can visualize themselves coping with different consequences when using targeted skills.

Demonstrator skills

Beyond speaking well, the following are some demonstrator skills. Live demonstrations require adequate preparation. Counselling trainees must know their material thoroughly if they are to integrate good demonstrations into skills presentations. One issue is whether to demonstrate incorrect as well as correct behaviours. Trainees may plan briefly to demonstrate negative behaviours as a way of highlighting positive ones. However, they should make sure not to confuse clients and should always place the major emphasis on correct rather than incorrect skills.

Counselling trainees should take care how they introduce demonstrations. Their initial demonstration of a skill is likely to be part of a 'tell', 'show', 'do' sequence. They can increase clients' attention by telling them what to look out for and also by informing them that afterwards they will perform the demonstrated behaviours.

During and at the end trainees may ask clients whether they understand the points that they have demonstrated. In addition, clients may summarize the main points of demonstrations. Research suggests that observers who actively summarize the main points of demonstrations are better able to learn and retain this information (Bandura et al., 1966; Perry and Furukawa, 1986). Probably, the best way to check clients' learning is to observe and coach them as they perform demonstrated behaviours.

Activity 15.2 Demonstrating mind skills

As appropriate, do the parts of this activity on your own, with a partner or in a group. Work through those parts that you find useful.

Part A: Write out a demonstration

Think of a specific mind skill or sub-skill you might like to demonstrate to a client. Write out an instructional handout for your chosen mind skill or sub-skill, in which you:

- state the targeted skill;
- identify the key learning points to observe in your demonstration;
- provide one or more demonstrations of the targeted mind skill or sub-skill.

Part B: Record a demonstration

Either for the mind skill or sub-skill you worked on above or for another mind skill or sub-skill, make a demonstration cassette, in which you:

- state the targeted skill;
- identify the key learning points to observe;
- provide one or more demonstrations.

Before making your recording, develop a script (or use the script from Part A) and then rehearse it using either your own or someone else's voice(s). When ready, audio record your script, play back your cassette, and modify it as many times as necessary to attain a polished performance. Think through how you might incorporate a recorded cassette demonstration into your overall presentation of your chosen mind skill or sub-skill.

Part C: Demonstrate live

Work with a partner. Either for a mind skill or sub-skill for which you prepared a script above or for another mind skill or sub-skill, rehearse and give a live demonstration. Afterwards obtain feedback from your partner on the effectiveness of your demonstration.

Assess the main advantages and disadvantages, when initially presenting lifeskills, of live over written and recorded mind skills demonstrations.

Activity 15.3 Demonstrating communication/ action skills

As appropriate, do the parts of this activity on your own, with a partner or in a group. Work through those parts that you find useful.

Part A: Video record a demonstration

Think of a specific communication/action skill or sub-skill that you might want to demonstrate to a client. Make up a videotape demonstration that focuses on the verbal, voice and body message dimensions of your chosen skill or sub-skill. You may make your videotape either with one demonstrator (probably yourself) or with two demonstrators using dialogue. Perform the following tasks:

- Set clear verbal, voice and body message goals for your demonstration videotape.
- Develop a brief script that indicates the verbal skills you want to convey – in the margin indicate appropriate voice and body messages.
- If appropriate, coach and rehearse your demonstrator(s) in the verbal, voice and body aspects of your demonstration.
- Make at least one pilot videotape and then, if necessary, keep altering and re-recording your demonstration until satisfied with it.

Indicate how you might incorporate instructions in your videotape demonstration so that clients know what to observe: for instance, will you pre-record instructions?

Part B: Demonstrate live

Work with a partner. Either for the communication/action skill or sub-skill that you worked on above or for another communication/action skill or sub-skill, rehearse and give a live demonstration either with or to your partner. Afterwards, obtain feedback from your partner.

Part C: Use visualized demonstration

Work with a partner. Either for a communication/action skill or sub-skill that you have worked on above or for another communication/action skill or sub-skill, give a visualized demonstration. Perform the following tasks:

- Develop a visualized demonstration involving an interaction between two people. The demonstration should
  - set the scene
  - describe the appropriate communication/action skill(s)
  - depict favourable consequences for using the skill.
- Rehearse your visualized demonstration.
- Ask your partner to visualize your scene as you describe it. Afterwards get feedback regarding how realistic she/he found your demonstration.

Part D: Demonstrating a communication/action skill with accompanying self-talk

Rehearse and practice a live demonstration in which the demonstrator talks herself/himself through a communication/action skills sequence. You may use a partner as an assistant in your demonstration.

Coaching skills

Here the focus is on coaching clients to perform skills after initial presentations. Learning from hearing and observing must be translated into learning from doing. I have listened to the supervision tapes of many counselling trainees who describe and demonstrate mind skills and communication skills, but then omit to coach clients in how to perform them. The following are some skills for coaching clients in lifeskills.

Balance didactic and facilitative coaching

In *didactic* coaching, counselling trainees give a series of explicit instructions to clients on how to perform skills. The trainee's comments take the form: 'First you do this. Then you do that. Then you do that', and so on. The trainee is the expert taking clients through sequences of performance choices.

In *facilitative* coaching, trainees have two important objectives: first, to draw out and build upon clients' existing knowledge and skills; and, second, to help them acquire the skills of self-coaching. Trainee comments may include: 'I'm going to ask you to perform the skill now and then get you to evaluate your performance. Afterwards, I'll give you some feedback too', and 'How did you think that went in practice?'

When coaching, trainees require both facilitative and didactic skills. For example, trainees might start with trying to build on the existing knowledge and skills of learners, but then intersperse didactic instructions when clients go badly wrong. Didactic coaching alone can produce resistances. Furthermore, coaching without using facilitative skills lessens the likelihood of targeted skills being owned and integrated into clients' daily routines.

Give clear instructions

In initial presentations and demonstrations of skills, include clear instructions for coached performance. Then, when coaching, trainees still need to give specific instructions, tips and prompts that build targeted skills. Coaching should emphasize ways in which clients can help themselves, for instance by translating clear instructions into clear self-instructions.

Break tasks down and consider number of trials

When getting clients to perform skills, counselling trainees may decide to start by breaking these down into sub-skills. Consider how much clients can assimilate in each learning trial. For example, with a teenager wishing to return a defective compact disc to a shop, one trial might focus on verbal messages, another on voice messages, another on body messages, and another on putting it all together. Another way of breaking learning trials down is to include graded steps. Here trainees coach clients in how to use targeted skills in progressively more difficult situations. With or without graded steps, clients may require many coached attempts before they can perform skills competently within, let alone outside, counselling sessions.

Use behaviour rehearsal and role-play

By definition, when trainees coach they also rehearse clients in targeted skills. Behaviour rehearsal and role-play are not always the same. Clients can rehearse action skills on their own without role-plays, for instance rehearsing relaxation skills. Furthermore, they can mentally rehearse mind skills. Role-plays are especially useful for rehearsing communication skills. Behaviour rehearsal and role-play skills are covered in more detail in Chapter 18.

Use feedback skills

When coaching, counselling trainees are managers of the feedback that they give. The following are some feedback dimensions to bear in mind (Egan, 2002; Gazda et al., 2001; Kazdin, 1994):

- *Client self-feedback or counsellor feedback.* Throughout, trainees should encourage clients to develop skills of monitoring and assessing their behaviour and its consequences for them and others. As a guideline, after each role-play clients should be the first to comment on their learnings and should give their own reactions to their performance. Nevertheless, trainee feedback is still essential, especially when they have special knowledge of targeted skills.
- *'I' message or 'You' message feedback.* Trainees should take responsibility for their feedback and send, or at least imply, 'I' messages. For example, 'Wendy, I think Denis would appreciate your request to go out for a meal together more if your voice were louder' is different from 'Your voice should have been louder when asking Denis out for a meal.'
- *Specific or non-specific feedback.* Feedback should always be specific and concentrate on targeted thoughts, communications and actions. For instance, in the previous example, suggesting to Wendy that her voice might be louder is far preferable to saying that her voice quality is poor.
- *Verbal or demonstrated feedback.* Feedback may be given largely by means of words. Often, however, trainees may communicate feedback even more clearly if they accompany verbal description with demonstration. For instance, in the Wendy and Denis example, the trainee could demonstrate Wendy's present voice loudness and then demonstrate a more appropriate volume.
- *Confirmatory or corrective feedback.* Confirmatory feedback reinforces correct behaviours, whereas corrective feedback lets clients know which specific behaviours require altering and in what ways. Much feedback is both confirmatory and corrective: for example, 'Wendy when you asked Denis to go out I thought that you gave a good verbal 'I' message [confirmatory], but that your voice was too quiet [corrective].' Persistent corrective feedback, without some confirmatory feedback, can weaken clients' motivation to work and change.
- *Audiovisual feedback.* Audio cassette feedback may be especially useful when trainees are coaching verbal messages, voice messages and mind

skills. Putting how clients think on whiteboards can also provide useful visual feedback since it highlights clients' thought processes. Videotape feedback is especially beneficial when coaching body messages. Audiovisual feedback lends itself to client self-assessment and provides a factual basis for trainees' discussions with clients.

- *Feedback or reward.* Trainees can say 'good' or 'well done' in response to specific behaviours that clients implement well. They can also use non-verbal forms of reward such as nods and smiles. However, trainees need to beware of clients performing targeted behaviours only under conditions of external reward rather than of self-reward.
- *Verbal or non-verbal feedback.* Much feedback, for good or ill, is non-verbal. Uninterested looks and voice messages can greatly interfere with good verbal coaching messages. Conversely, good voice and body messages when giving feedback increase the likelihood of clients receiving the verbal message positively. Whether or not trainees speak, they should show interest when clients perform demonstrated skills.
- *Cultural feedback considerations.* Counselling trainees who come from different cultural backgrounds from clients require sensitivity to differences in cultural rules concerning giving and receiving feedback. They can give clients permission to relate how feedback is handled in their cultures.

Activity 15.4 Developing coaching skills

As appropriate, do the parts of this activity on your own, with a partner or in a group. Work through those parts that you find useful.

Part A: Considerations in coaching

Imagine that you have just given to a client a verbal presentation of a specific lifeskill or sub-skill, followed by a demonstration. You are now about to coach the client in how to perform the skill. How might you take into account each of the following considerations?

- Balancing didactic and facilitative coaching.
- Giving clear instructions.
- Breaking tasks down.
- Choosing the number of learning trials.
- Using behaviour rehearsal and role-play.
- Using feedback skills.

Part B: Rehearsing and practising how to coach

1 Work with a partner. Give her/him a verbal presentation that includes demonstration of a specific skill or sub-skill. Do not attempt too much. Afterwards, coach her/him to the point where, within the limits of this activity, she/he performs the skill competently. Playing back videotapes of your coaching efforts may enhance learning.
2 Work with one or more partners. Repeat the activity until you have coached another person in (a) a mind skill, (b) a communication/action skill, and (c) a communication/action skill plus self-talk.

Some readers may not have sufficient knowledge of interventions to do the activities in this chapter properly. If this is the case, before doing the activities for this chapter, read Chapters 16–19, which review specific interventions.

interventions for thinking – 1 16

Chapter outcomes

By studying and doing the activities in this chapter you should:

- understand why it is important that clients think about how they think;
- understand why counsellors should attend to feelings when focusing on thinking;
- know some interventions for creating rules;
- know some interventions for creating perceptions;
- know some interventions for creating self-talk; and
- know some interventions for creating visual images.

Abraham Maslow reportedly said that most clients were not sick, but just cognitively wrong. In other words they possessed poor mind skills. The importance of focusing on how clients and counsellors think is a major theme of this book. Counselling trainees should focus on their own as well as their clients' thinking. Unless they develop skills in understanding and working with how they think, they risk ignorance and ineffectiveness when focusing on how their clients think. To paraphrase the old adage, 'Physician, heal thyself' – 'Counselling trainee, think realistically yourself.'

Both trainees and clients are hypothesis makers and testers who have the reflective capacity to think about how they think. Why do both trainees and clients need to develop such skills? Unless clients can think about how they think they risk condemning themselves to repetitive patterns of poor mind skills. They need to learn how to take responsibility for how they think. If they develop a language that categorizes different mind skills, they can target specific skills for development. For example, those capable of understanding how their thinking has been affected by parental and cultural rules can free themselves from unwanted 'voices in the head'.

Counselling trainees and clients capable of thinking about how they think are better able to define themselves and shape their lives by learning and instructing themselves in how to think more effectively.

Attend to feelings

Working with clients' mind skills should not be an arid intellectual exercise. An important part of cultivating collaborative working relationships is to attend closely to clients' feelings. Counselling trainees need to remain sensitive to their own feelings and to use them in clients' best interests. The following are some ways of attending to clients' feelings.

- *Assess readiness and motivation.* Trainees need to take into account client readiness to work on mind skills. For instance, vulnerable clients may wish to use the early phases of counselling to discharge and discuss feelings of hurt and pain. Some clients may be so anxious and distort information so badly that they have insufficient insight to explore thinking difficulties until they become less anxious. Clients take differing lengths of time to trust counsellors. Until trust is established, they may be neither willing nor able to deal with their faulty thinking choices.
- *Elicit thoughts and feelings.* Working with clients' thinking can be a delicate process in which trainees create a safe emotional climate for clients' thoughts and feelings to emerge. Trainees and clients collaborate in unearthing and detecting both poor mind skills that sustain unwanted feelings and self-defeating actions. Insufficient trainee empathy can block clients from experiencing, identifying and exploring their feelings and thoughts.
- *Distinguish clients' own thoughts.* Trainees need to attend closely to clients' feelings to help them distinguish what they think from what they have been taught to think. They should permit clients to articulate their thoughts and, where necessary, support them through the pain and guilt of going against significant others' ways of thinking.
- *Acknowledge defences and resistances.* Trainees require awareness of barriers and resistances to acknowledging and working with specific thoughts and poor thinking skills. Frequently, clients do not readily share their worlds. Clients may feel threatened if trainees focus on certain areas of clients' lives, and trainees need to be sensitive to this. Then, they have various options: for example helping clients acknowledge and work through resistances or backing off, either temporarily or permanently.
- *Check the emotional validity of mind skills hypotheses.* Counselling trainees' hypotheses about clients' thoughts and poor mind skills must have emotional validity if they are to enlist clients' motivation for change. Clients may overtly agree, but covertly disagree, with trainees' hypotheses. Trainees should check this emotional validity with clients. Furthermore, they can help clients do their own work.

Hypotheses that clients arrive at for themselves are more likely to feel right for them.

- *Offer support during learning, rehearsal and practice.* Trainees should attend to clients' feelings as they train them in mind skills. Client feelings requiring attention include confusion, insecurity and disappointment – for instance, when unsuccessfully practising the skill during homework.

When working to develop clients' mind skills, active listening skills are central. The desirable counselling relationship is one of mutual co-operation in pursuit of goals. Counselling trainees can support clients in many ways: emotionally, by facilitating exploration, helping them to analyse information, and encouraging their learning.

Creating rules

As George Bernard Shaw said: 'The Golden Rule is that there are no golden rules.' Albert Ellis has been particularly prominent in highlighting the importance of creating realist rules or what he calls rational as contrasted with irrational beliefs (Ellis, 2001, 2003, 2005; Ellis and Dryden, 1997). Counsellors and trainees can help clients replace their demanding rules with ones that are more realistic. All people possess rulebooks that provide them with ready-made guidelines for leading their lives so that they do not have to think through all emerging situations from scratch. Most of the rules of well-functioning people are rational, realistic and based on their preferences for themselves, others and the environment. However, many clients contribute to disturbing themselves and making themselves unhappy because, often unawares, they possess some significant or rigid rules that are based on making irrational and unrealistic demands on themselves, others and the environment.

Detect demanding rules

Trainees can help clients develop the skills of identifying danger signals which indicate that they may possess one or more demanding rules.

Attend to inappropriate language

Rigid demanding rules are characterized by 'musts', oughts', 'shoulds' and 'have to's'. Such language signals absolutistic 'musturbatory' thinking. Ellis has identified three major clusters of irrational beliefs or demanding rules that create inappropriate feelings, physical reactions, communication and action consequences. The first cluster focuses on the individual: 'I absolutely *must* do well and win approval for all my performances, or else I am a rotten person.' The second cluster focuses on others: 'Others absolutely *must* treat me considerately and kindly, in precisely the way I want them to treat me; if they do not, society should severely blame and damn them.' The final cluster focuses on environmental circumstances: 'The conditions under which I live absolutely *must* be arranged so that I get practically everything I want comfortably, quickly, and easily, and get virtually nothing that I do not want.'

Counselling trainees can also help clients to identify when they are using language which signals they are telling themselves the derivatives of demanding rules or irrational beliefs. As we saw in Chapter 3, the three main derivatives of such rules and beliefs are:

1 *Awfulizing*: 'If I don't have my important goals unblocked and fulfilled as I must, it's awful!' In this context, 'awful' means totally bad or more than bad.
2 *I can't stand-it-itis*: 'If I don't have my important goals unblocked and fulfilled as I must, I can't stand it!'
3 *Damning oneself and others*: 'If I don't have my important goals unblocked and fulfilled as I must, I'm a stupid, worthless person.' 'Others are bad people for blocking my important goals.'

Attend to inappropriate feelings and physical reactions

Inappropriateness might be signalled by feelings that are out of place in specific situations, feelings that are too strong or too weak, feelings that persist beyond a reasonable time, and feelings that lead to self-defeating communications and actions. Clients can ask themselves questions like: 'Is this feeling and/or physical reaction appropriate for the situation?', 'Am I over-reacting?' and 'To what extent does this feeling and/or physical reaction have unnecessary negative consequences for me and for others?'

Attend to inappropriate communications and actions

Clients can become more skilled at backtracking from counter-productive communications and actions in order to detect and understand the demanding rules or beliefs that may be driving them. Clients can ask themselves questions like: 'Are my actions helping or harming me and others?' and 'Is my communication self-defeating?'

Detect the real agenda

Counselling trainees and clients need to be able to detect the real agenda. Trainees can assist clients in the skills of identifying which rules are most important. For example, it may be more important for clients, whose anger at home is related to self-induced stress at work, to focus on stress rules rather than anger rules.

Help clients to use the STC framework

In detecting demanding rules, clients need to understand the relationships between thoughts, feelings, physical reactions, communications and actions. Using aids such as whiteboards and self-help forms, counselling trainees can train clients in putting demanding rules into the STC framework. Assuming adequate initial explanation, trainees should encourage clients to do their own work rather than spoon-feed them. Below is an example of a demanding rule at T placed into the STC framework.

Case example: Workaholic Pat is a stressed-out middle manager

S Pat reaches her/his 40th birthday and becomes highly anxious.

T(1) Demanding rule
I must devote all my energies to my job.

C(1) *Negative feelings consequences* include anxiety, feeling very stressed, irritability and low self-esteem.
Negative physical reaction consequences include mental exhaustion, brownouts (memory losses due to exhaustion), hypertension, migraine headaches and lower back pain.
Negative communication/action consequences include spending excessive time at work – not always very productively – neglecting one's home life, and taking inadequate recreation.

Dispute demanding rules

Ellis (2005) considers disputing to be the most typical and often used method of his rational emotive behaviour therapy (REBT). Disputing involves using reason to challenge demanding and absolutistic rules. Counselling trainees may approach disputing using either a didactic or a Socratic style. In a didactic or lecturing style, trainees can provide explanations and illustrations. In a Socratic or scientific questioning approach, through a series of leading questions trainees attempt to pinpoint where clients' thinking, feeling and behaving is becoming problematic. Such questions are intended to help clients develop skills of questioning themselves. When clients start practising disputing, it is important that they do so outside of stressful situations to give them the chance to build up and fine-tune their skills for the actual situations.

Counselling trainees can help clients use reason, logic and facts to support, negate or amend their rules. Questions students can ask clients and then teach clients to ask themselves include: 'Can I rationally support this rule?' 'What evidence exists for the truth of this rule?' 'What evidence exists for the falseness of this rule?' 'Why is it awful?' 'Why can't I stand it?' 'How does this make me a rotten person?' See Box 16.1 (Ellis and McLaren, 1998).

Box 16.1 Four methods of disputing demanding rules

Functional disputing
Functional disputing aims to point out to clients that their rules may be preventing them from attaining their goals. Typical questions are:

- Is it helping you?
- How is continuing to think this way (or behave, or feel this way) affecting your life?

Empirical disputing
Empirical disputing aims to help clients evaluate the factual components of their rules. Typical questions are:

- Where is the evidence that you must succeed at all important tasks you want?
- Where is the proof that it is accurate?
- Where is it written?

Logical disputing
Logical disputing aims to highlight illogical leaps clients make when thinking irrationally, from desires and preferences to demands. Typical questions are:

- How does it follow that just because you'd like this thing to be true and it would be very convenient, it *should* be?
- Where is the logic that because you sometimes *act* badly that makes you a *bad person*?

Philosophical disputing
Philosophical disputing aims to address the meaning of and satisfaction in life issues. Often clients get so focused on identified problems that they lose perspective on other areas of life. A typical question might be:

- Despite the fact that things will probably not go the way you want some/most of the time in this area, can you still derive some satisfaction from your life?

In the following example, I am working with Louise Donovan, a very highly qualified accountancy executive who keeps getting turned down at job interviews. Usually demanding rules contain realistic as well as unrealistic parts. For example, it is realistic for Louise to want to give highly competent answers at job interviews, but unrealistic to strive for perfection. Consequently, Louise and I need to focus on discarding the 20–30 per cent of the rule that is unrealistic rather than getting rid of it altogether. The client and I list not so much the disputing questions as the answers that challenge the client's demanding rule 'I must give the perfect answer.'

Case example: Assisting Louise Donovan to dispute a demanding rule

Richard, the counsellor, and Louise Donovan, the client, agreed that the first item on their agenda for a particular session was to dispute her demanding rule for interviews that 'I must give the perfect answer.' I encouraged Louise to challenge her own thinking, but also gave feedback and made suggestions along the way. Sometimes, my feedback was aimed at helping Louise to be more specific. Sometimes, I suggested additional challenges. Throughout, I wrote on the whiteboard the information shown below. Afterwards, Louise and I each wrote down everything that was written on the whiteboard.

Demanding rule
I must give the perfect answer.

Challenges/disputations
In my application I've already demonstrated meticulous attention to detail, so I need to add value with human relating skills.
There is no perfect answer.
The panel at my level is more concerned about style than substance.
I may have to sacrifice detail for conciseness.
I need to keep communication two-way, but also allow each panel member to have their allocated time.
Pressure for perfection lowers performance.
Excessive attention to technical detail lowers perception of personal relations skills.
I'm limiting my opportunity to gain marks on other questions.

State preferential rules

Vigorously and repeatedly challenging key demanding rules should have the effect of loosening their hold on clients. An added way of reducing the hold of demanding rules is to restate them succinctly as preferential rules. Clients' disputations or challenges can be too many and varied to remember easily. Together counselling trainee and client can create a revised rule easy to record, remember and recall.

In creating revised rules, it is particularly important that clients develop skills of expressing preferences rather than demands. An example is 'I'd PREFER to do very well but I don't HAVE TO' (Sichel and Ellis, 1984). Clients can replace rules about mastery and perfection with rules incorporating competence, coping and 'doing as well as I can under the circumstances'. These rules should be appropriately flexible and amenable to change and updating. However, since such flexibility is based on inner strength, the clients can still hold firmly to well thought through core beliefs and values.

Instead of rating themselves as persons, clients should evaluate how functional their specific communications are. Their underlying thinking is 'I am a PERSON WHO acted badly, not a BAD PERSON' (Sichel and Ellis, 1984). Clients can attempt to avoid awfulizing by accepting that the world is imperfect and by refraining from exaggerating negative factors and possibilities. In addition, they can endeavour to eliminate 'I can't stand-it-itis'. They can tell themselves that they *can* stand the anxiety and discomfort arising from the fact that they, their partner and the environment are not as they would prefer them to be. Indeed, even in genuinely adverse work and personal circumstances, clients may have many strengths as well as people who can support them.

The case example of Louise Donovan is extended below to demonstrate replacing a previous demanding rule (T1) with a preferential rule (T2). Revised consequences C(2) for successfully adhering to the preferential rule then follow.

Case example: Assisting Louise Donovan to create a preferential rule

Continuing using the whiteboard, Louise and I worked together to create a more realistic and preferential rule. Afterwards each of us wrote down this revised rule for our records.

Though the example here is in the STC format, in the counselling session only the attempts to create a preferential rule (T2) appeared on the whiteboard.

S Going for job interviews for senior positions

T(1) Demanding rule: I must give the perfect answer.

T(2) Preferential rule: I'd prefer to give highly competent technical answers, but to achieve my goals it is also very important for me to come over well as a person.

C(2) *Positive feelings and physical reactions consequences* include reduced anxiety and tension.

> *Positive communication consequences* include a more interactive interview style and, when answering questions, stopping lecturing interview panels in a booming voice.

Homework assignments

Unrealistic rules tend to be deeply ingrained habits whereby clients relate to themselves, others and the world (Ellis, 1998, 2005). Clients usually have to fight hard both to lessen their influence and also to avoid losing any gains they have made. As we know, there is no concept of cure in overcoming demanding rules. Counselling trainees need to remind clients that maintaining restated rules requires PRACTICE, PRACTICE, PRACTICE. They can point out to clients that, since they possess well-established habits of re-indoctrinating and recontaminating themselves, they need to practice challenging and restating the same rule again and again.

Clients can use appropriate self-help forms to practice their skills of challenging demanding rules and restating them as preferential rules. They can make cassettes of their challenges and restatements and keep playing them back until they sink in. Clients can also post in prominent positions reminder cards with their revised rules. In addition, they can use visual rehearsal in which they imagine themselves in a specific situation experiencing the negative consequences arising from their demanding rule. Then they can imagine switching over to their preferential rule and visualize the positive consequences of so doing.

Counselling trainees can use rewards and penalties to encourage clients to do homework and to implement self-change programmes (Ellis and Dryden, 1997). They can recommend relevant self-help books to clients (for example Ellis, 1999, 2003; Ellis and Crawford, 2000; Ellis and Harper, 1997).

Trainees should help clients to change how they communicate and act in line with their changed rules. The new rules may make it easier for clients to communicate effectively. For example, Louise finds it easier to develop interview skills now she no longer puts pressure on herself to give the perfect answer. In turn, communicating and acting effectively is perhaps the most powerful way of generating evidence with which to dispute self-defeating rules. For instance, if Louise changes the way she thinks and behaves and then obtains positive consequences, she has collected invaluable evidence to combat her rule, 'I must give the perfect answer.'

Ultimately there is no substitute for real-life practice. Sometimes, latent in their repertoires, clients already possess the relevant communication and action skills to handle specific problem situations better. If so, by changing their rules, clients can free themselves to use these skills. On other occasions, changing their rules is insufficient and clients also need to improve their communication and action skills.

Activity 16.1 Improving skills at creating rules

Counsel a partner who either uses a personal concern or role-plays a client. The counsellor's goal is to help the 'client' to create one or more preferential rules to manage a problem situation better. Within the context of a collaborative working relationship and, possibly, using a whiteboard during the process:

- use speaking skills to describe the difference between demanding and preferential rules;
- use demonstrating skills;
- cooperate with the client to identify any major demanding rules;
- use coaching skills to assist the client to dispute and challenge the main demanding rule;
- use coaching skills to assist the client to create a preferential rule to replace the main demanding rule;
- use negotiating homework assignment skills.

During the above process, both counsellor and client make written records, including challenges to the main demanding rule and the preferential rule created to replace the main demanding rule.

Afterwards discuss and reverse roles. Playing back audio recordings or video recordings of skills-building sessions may assist learning.

Creating perceptions

A Chinese proverb states: 'Two thirds of what we see is behind our eyes.' Aaron Beck is a prime advocate of helping clients to influence how they feel by choosing more realistic perceptions. Beck has focused on the thinking that is associated with depression, anxieties, phobias and anger in relationships (Beck, 1988; Beck and Weishaar, 2005). Numerous clients with a wide range of problems can be helped to develop the skill of testing the reality of their perceptions. Here Beck's approach is viewed as encouraging 'propositional thinking' as contrasted with Ellis's approach, which encourages 'preferential thinking'.

Understand how perceptions influence feelings

Counselling trainees can let clients know that they may have a tendency to jump to unhelpful conclusions that contribute to negative feelings. Beck uses the example of instructing a male client to imagine that a person was at home one night and heard a crashing noise in another room. When asked how the person might react to the first interpretation, 'there's a burglar in the room', the client replied that he would feel 'very anxious, terrified', and that he might hide or phone the police. The client thought that the person might react to the second interpretation, 'the windows have been left open and the wind has caused something to fall over', by not being afraid, but possibly sad if something valuable had been broken. The person would probably go and see what was the problem. Beck explained to the client that this example illustrates that there are a number of ways that people can interpret situations and that this affects how they feel and behave (Beck et al., 1979).

Clients need to become more aware of the thinking that accompanies how they feel. Clients can use the STC framework to monitor the relationship between situations, perceptions and feelings. Ideally, they should monitor situations as they happen. Trainees can get clients to set aside some time each day to monitor and record perceptions related to negative feelings. Clients can fill in a log with the following three column settings. They rate the intensity of their feelings for each perception on a 0 to 10 or 0 to 100 scale. In addition they can place a star by any 'hot' or particularly significant perception.

S The situation	T My perceptions	C My feelings

Understand the difference between fact and inference

Related to showing the influence of perceptions on feelings and behaviour, counselling trainees can also teach clients to understand the difference between fact and inference. Clients may believe that their perceptions of themselves, others and the world are their subjective 'facts'. Often, however, they fail to realize that these perceptions are based on inference rather than fact. See Box 16.2.

Box 16.2 Examples of the difference between fact and inference

Example 1

Fact: My parents fail to congratulate me effusively on the news that I have just received some very good grades.

Inference: My parents are not proud of me.

Example 2

Fact: My partner comes home late from work three evenings in a row.

Inference: She/he is more concerned with her/his career than with me.

In each of the above examples the facts and evidence did not justify the inferences.

The distinction between fact and inference is stressed because it is a theme that underlies how clients create and persist in creating inaccurate perceptions. Clients may jump to conclusions yet remain unaware that they have taken the leap. Illusion then becomes their reality, in whole or in part.

Elicit and identify automatic perceptions

To change their thinking, clients first need to become aware of their automatic perceptions. Automatic perceptions reflect deeper beliefs and assumptions. In normal functioning, self-appraisals and self-evaluations operate more or less automatically to help people stay on course. However, when things go wrong, certain automatic perceptions operate to ensure that people stay off course.

The following are some salient characteristics of such perceptions. Automatic perceptions:

- are part of people's internal monologue – what they say to themselves and how they say it;
- can take the form of words, images, or both;
- occur very rapidly and usually at the fringe of awareness;
- can precede and accompany emotions, including feelings and inhibitions – for instance, people's emotional responses to each other's actions follow from their interpretations rather than from the actions themselves;
- are generally plausible to people who assume that they are accurate; and
- have a recurring quality, despite people trying to block them out.

These are sometimes hard to identify, but counselling trainees can teach clients to pinpoint automatic perceptions with great accuracy. Below are some specific interventions for assisting clients to elicit and identify their automatic perceptions.

- *Questioning.* Clients may be questioned about automatic perceptions that occur during upsetting situations. If clients experience difficulty in recalling thoughts, then imagery or role-playing may be used. When questioning, trainees should observe clients carefully for signs of emotion that may offer leads for further questioning.
- *Using a whiteboard.* When clients see their initial thoughts written up on the board, this may trigger them to reveal less obvious and more frightening thoughts.
- *Encouraging clients to engage in feared activities.* During sessions, trainees can encourage clients to engage in anxiety-evoking activities: for instance making phone calls or writing letters they had been

putting off. As they perform the activity, trainees can ask, 'What is going through your mind right now?' Trainees may also go with clients into real-life situations where they experience difficulty, for instance crowded places, and get them to verbalize what they think.

- *Focusing on imagery.* Gathering information about imagery can be an important way of accessing automatic perceptions. Though individual differences exist, clinical observations suggest that many people visualizing scenes react to them as though they are real.
- *Self-monitoring of perceptions.* Clients may be set homework assignments in which they record their thoughts and perceptions. Clients can complete daily worksheets in which they record in separate columns:

  - *situation(s)* leading to negative emotion(s)
  - *feelings and physical reaction(s)* felt and their degree on a 0–100 scale
  - *automatic perceptions and image(s)* and a rating of how strongly they believed the automatic perception(s) on a 0–100 scale. In addition, they can star any particularly hot perceptions.

  Counselling trainees may request that clients fill in worksheets identifying and rating key feelings, physical reactions, perceptions and images for specific problem situations they encounter between sessions. Trainees can also encourage some clients to use wrist counters to help them learn to recognize automatic perceptions as they occur.

Test the reality of automatic perceptions

Counselling trainees can emphasize to clients the importance of testing the reality of perceptions rather than continuing to jump to conclusions. They can train clients to acknowledge that they have choices in how they perceive. When clients become aware that they are feeling and communicating, or are at risk of feeling and communicating, in inappropriate ways, they can run a reality check on the accuracy of their information base. They can calm themselves down and ask themselves questions such as 'Where's the evidence?' and 'Are there any other ways of perceiving the situation?'

Where's the evidence?

Greenberger and Padesky observe: 'When we have negative automatic thoughts, we usually dwell on data that confirms our conclusions' (1995: 67). Clients can systematically bias how they process information by emphasizing confirmatory evidence when creating negative perceptions and by maintaining them once made. Counselling trainees need to teach clients to take a more balanced approach to searching out and processing information.

Greenberger and Padesky ask clients to identify hot thoughts or perceptions and then write out 'Evidence that supports the hot thought' and 'Evidence that does not support the hot thought.' For example, a grandfather, Ben, felt very sad and attributed this feeling to the hot thought that 'The kids and grandkids don't need me any more.' Ben then wrote down evidence that supported the hot thought: for instance, 'Amy, the 15-year-old, left at 7.00 p.m. to be with her friends.' However, Ben was also able to find evidence that did not support the hot thought: for instance, 'I made my 5-year-old granddaughter laugh often throughout the day', and 'Amy seemed to enjoy my stories about her mom as a teenager.' Ben experienced a positive shift in mood as a result of finding evidence that did not support his hot thought or perception (Greenberger and Padesky, 1995: 66–9).

Are there any other ways of perceiving the situation?

Clients can also jump to inaccurate or negative conclusions because they possess poor skills of generating and evaluating alternative ways of perceiving situations. In real life, clients do not always have to decide how they perceive on the spot. Instead they can take their time to mull over whether there are alternatives. Counselling trainees can teach clients to be more creative and flexible in how they perceive. The following is an example:

S Charlie says to his wife Fiona: I've decided we need a new car.
T(1) *Fiona's automatic perception:* Charlie doesn't respect my judgement.
C(1) Fiona *feels* hurt, gets angry and *communicates*: I don't see why we need a new car. What's wrong with the one we've got?

When Fiona cools down and reflects upon the matter, she says to herself: 'Are there any other ways I might perceive Charlie's remark about deciding to get a new car?' This time Fiona acknowledges she has choices in how she perceives and looks for alternative perceptions, which include the following:

- Charlie is really suggesting that we now have two cars, so we can each have one of our own.
- Charlie is trying to make me happy by suggesting we get a new car.
- I wish Charlie had worded his statement differently, but I know he will listen to my opinion if I state it assertively.

- Just because Charlie wants a new car, it doesn't mean that we have to rush out and buy it immediately.
- What about the new carpet and curtains for the living room? He is ignoring that they are more important to me.
- Just like a man to want to have a new, expensive toy. I can treat that as humorous rather than serious.

Conduct experiments to test the reality of perceptions

In addition to asking questions, counselling trainees and clients can together set up experiments that encourage clients to test the reality of their perceptions. See Box 16.3 (Beck, 1988: 224).

Box 16.3 Example of an experiment to test the reality of a perception

The client
Marjorie, who was afraid to make a mental commitment to her spouse, Ken, because she was afraid she might find out that she could not trust him.

Marjorie's underlying perception
I must never allow myself to be vulnerable.

Consequence of Marjorie's distorted thinking
Marjorie's aloof behaviour and fault-finding created distance in her and Ken's relationship.

The experiment
Beck and Marjorie set up a three-month experiment for her to test the hypothesis: 'If I totally commit myself to the relationship, look for the positive instead of the negative, then I will feel more secure.' During the experiment, Marjorie was to change how she thought and communicated.

Result of the experiment
Marjorie discovered that she was more secure and had fewer thoughts about leaving Ken.

Assist clients to form more accurate perceptions

After identifying their automatic perceptions and questioning their reality, counselling trainees can teach clients how to state more accurate perceptions. The following are some approaches they can use.

Creating balanced perceptions

When clients answer the question 'Where's the evidence?', as in the earlier example of sad grandfather Ben, they can generate evidence both to support and not to support their hot thought or hot perception. Where the evidence is mixed or doubtful clients can replace it with more balanced perceptions. When Ben reviewed the evidence for and against his perception 'The kids and grandkids don't need me any more', he decided that the evidence only partially supported it. Ben then created two balanced perceptions: 'Even though my children and grandchildren don't need me the same way that they used to, they still enjoy my company and they still ask for my advice' and 'They paid attention to me throughout the day although the attention was not the same as it has been in the past' (Greenberger and Padesky, 1995: 96–7). After Ben wrote down his balanced perceptions the intensity of his sadness lessened from 80 per cent to 30 per cent.

Choosing the 'best fit' perception

In instances, such as in the example of Fiona and Charlie, where clients generate a number of alternative perceptions, they are then left with the task of choosing the perception that best fits the available facts. Keeping the distinction between fact and inference clearly in mind, clients can evaluate each of the perceptions. The following is the result of Fiona's deliberations:

S Charlie says to his wife Fiona: I've decided we need a new car.

T(2) *Best fit perception*: I wish Charlie had worded his statement differently, but I know he will listen to my opinion if I state it assertively.

C(2) *Feelings consequences*: Fiona is not angry with Charlie and in turn Charlie does not get angry with Fiona.
Communication consequences include: not starting a fight, Fiona's acknowledging Charlie's wish for the car but saying they need to talk about it more since she wants some new curtains and carpets, and both agreeing to set aside a time to talk the issue through.

Forming rational responses

Counselling trainees can teach clients how to form more rational responses to their automatic perceptions. Again, questioning is an important way to help clients learn to use their inner speech for rather than against themselves. Box 16.4 gives an example of a client providing a counteracting rational response to herself (Beck, 1988: 264). Finding a rational response can help clients see their automatic perceptions as interpretations rather than as 'the truth'.

Box 16.4 Example of forming a rational response

The situation

Wendy was phoned by her husband Hal to say he was tied up at the office.

Emotional reaction:	Anger
Automatic perception:	It's not fair – I have to work too. If he wanted to, he could be home on time.
Rational response:	His job is different. Many of his customers come in after work.

Homework assignments

All of the above approaches lend themselves to homework assignments. Once trained in what to do, clients can write down evidence for and against their hot perceptions and then create more balanced perceptions. Using worksheets, clients can generate and evaluate different perceptions and then choose the best-fit perceptions. On worksheets they can also record their perceptions and develop rational responses to those that appear inaccurate. Filling out worksheets may be a stepping-stone to, but is no substitute for, creating improved perceptions in daily life, which is the ultimate homework assignment.

Activity 16.2 Improving skills at creating perceptions

Counsel a partner who either uses a personal concern or role-plays a client. The counsellor's goal is to help the 'client' to create one or more accurate perceptions to manage a problematic situation better. Within the context of a collaborative working relationship and, possibly, using a whiteboard during the process:

- use speaking skills to describe the importance of reality-testing perceptions rather than jumping to conclusions;
- use demonstrating skills;
- cooperate with the client to identify and rate the main feelings and physical reactions associated with a recent incidence of the problem situation;

- cooperate with the client to identify inaccurate automatic perceptions and images and place a star by the main hot perception;
- use coaching skills to help your client to reality-test the evidence for the main hot perception by addressing the questions:

  - Where is the evidence?
  - Are there any other ways of perceiving the situation?

- use coaching skills to assist the client to create a balanced or best-fit perception to replace the main automatic perception;
- use negotiating homework assignment skills.

During the above process, both counsellor and client make written records, including the evidence supporting and not supporting the hot perception and any alternative perceptions generated; and the balanced or best-fit perception created to replace the main hot perception.

Afterwards discuss and reverse roles. Playing back audio recordings or video recordings of skills building sessions may assist learning.

Creating self-talk

Training in coping self-talk is an intervention applicable to most clients. Meichenbaum and others have trained many groups of clients in coping self-talk. Targeted problems include managing anger, managing stress, being creative, curbing impulsiveness, managing pain, and controlling weight (Meichenbaum 1977, 1983, 1985; Meichenbaum and Deffenbacher, 1988). One way to help clients understand that they engage in self-talk is to ask them to close their eyes for 30 seconds and think of nothing. Most become highly aware that they cannot rid themselves of self-talk.

Let's assume that a trainee and a client have targeted developing coping self-talk skills to manage a particular situation as one of their counselling goals. When the time comes to intervene, what can be done?

Highlight negative self-talk

As part of the assessment the counselling trainee may have noted or elicited negative self-talk statements from the client. They can retrieve these statements from their notes. For example, Val, 56, is a client with public speaking anxiety who used the following negative self-talk statements in the 30 to 60 seconds before she was due to speak:

Don't be so stupid.
My anxiety may get out of control like two years ago.
I may have a heart attack.

A trainee can work with the client, possibly using the whiteboard, to identify further negative self-talk statements that engender anxiety and/or disrupt performance in the specific situation they have targeted. They can use the STC framework to emphasize the consequences of using negative self-talk.

Educate clients about coping self-talk

Clients can be educated in the skill of coping self-talk. Below is an example of the kind of statement introducing the skill of coping self-talk to a client like Val.

> 'Coping self-talk is a useful thinking skill for managing public speaking anxiety. The idea is that during your waking hours you continuously engage in an internal dialogue, or perform self-talk. The goals of coping self-talk are to calm your anxieties and to help you deal effectively with the task at hand. Thus, coping self-talk contains three major elements: calming, coaching and affirming. Coping self-talk is about coping or 'doing as well as I can' rather than about mastery or 'being perfect' and 'having no anxiety'. Coping is a much more realistic goal than mastery. You can use coping self-talk before, during and after public speaking.'

This example points out to the client that calming, coaching and affirming statements tend to be interspersed in coping self-talk.

- *Calming statements*. Simple statements include 'keep calm', relax' and 'take it easy'. In addition, clients can instruct themselves to 'take a deep breath' or 'breathe slowly and regularly'.
- *Coaching*. Coaching statements involve breaking tasks down and identifying the steps needed to attain goals. Clients then instruct themselves in the specific elements of competent behaviour.
- *Affirming statements*. Clients may have strengths and prior successes about which they can remind themselves. Furthermore, they can focus on support factors in specific situations, and they can make statements like 'I can handle this situation.'

Elicit coping self-talk from clients

Frequently, for each main category of coping self-talk, I ask clients to supply their own statements that I then write on the whiteboard. Box 16.5 shows an example of how to do this.

Box 16.5 Eliciting coping self-talk statements

Val's counsellor first put the word 'calming' on the whiteboard and then helped Val to identify statements she would find useful to calm herself down in the 30 to 60 seconds before speaking in public. The counsellor and Val repeated this process for coaching and affirming self-statements. They ended with the following categories and statements written on the whiteboard.

Calming
Calm
It's not the end of the world
Coaching
Rehearse my opening ideas and remarks
No last minute changes
My anxiety is a signal for me to use my coping skills
I can retrieve mistakes
Affirming
I've done this very well many times before

Emphasize homework and practice

The following are some ways whereby clients can consolidate their coping self-talk skills. They can write down on lifeskills counselling homework sheets their *tailor-made statements* from the whiteboard. Counselling trainees can make *cassettes* in which they relax clients and then take them through guided imageries of competently dealing with targeted stressful situations by using their coping self-talk skills. Clients can play these cassettes as often as necessary to learn the skills thoroughly. In addition, they have the cassettes available for use in future, should they need them. Clients themselves can make *cue cards,* or *reminder cards,* that they can carry with them and read just before they face their specific anxiety-evoking situations. Trainees can set clients *homework assignments* in which they seek out and practice their coping self-talk skills in real-life situations.

Activity 16.3 Improving skills at creating self-talk

Work with a partner who either uses a personal concern or role-plays a client. The counsellor's goal is to help the 'client' to improve her/his creating self-talk skills to manage a specific problem situation better. Within the context of a good collaborative working relationship and using either a whiteboard or notepad, as appropriate:

- use speaking skills to describe the skill of creating self-talk;
- use demonstrating skills;
- help the client to identify any current negative self-talk before, during or after the problem situation;
- use coaching skills to assist the client in formulating and rehearsing improved self-talk statements with which to replace the current negative self-talk;
- use skills of assisting the client to record and remember important work conducted during the session; and
- use negotiating homework assignment skills.

Afterwards discuss and reverse roles. Playing back audio recordings or video recordings of skills building sessions may increase learning.

Creating visual images

Counselling trainees should not underestimate the importance of working with clients' visual images (Beck and Weishaar, 2005; Ellis and MacLaren, 1998; Lazarus, 1984, 2005a). One way of looking at clients' minds is to see them as movie cameras that have been and are continually recording images of what they see. These images get stored in the movie vaults or picture albums of their memories and may be accompanied by sounds, tastes, touch and smells.

Some clients possess well-developed powers of imagery or can develop the skills of visualizing vividly. Others may experience great difficulty and the trainee may need to concentrate on alternative ways of controlling their thinking. In general, the more clients can experience the senses and feelings attached to their images, the better they can use visualizing as a self-helping skill.

Assist clients to develop an awareness of visualizing

Some clients may need to become more aware of the role of visual images in sustaining their problems. The following are ways that counselling trainees can highlight the importance of visualizing.

Questions

Trainees can encourage clients to ask themselves questions to elicit and increase the power of their images, including: 'What visual images do I have about the situation before, during and after it?' 'Are people moving?' 'Do I hear anything?' 'Do I smell anything?' 'Do I taste anything?' 'Do I have any tactile sensations?' 'How vivid is my image?' 'What feelings accompany my visual images?' Another method for increasing the vividness of imagery is for clients to verbalize what they see. For instance, they can imagine a past, present or future situation and describe the scene as they are doing so either aloud or to themselves. Clients can also be asked to close their eyes and recount specific instances as though they were describing a slow-motion replay of a movie.

Explanations

Trainees can incorporate visual images into the STC framework used to explain problematic situations. For instance, the T in the STC framework can emphasize visual images as well as thoughts:

S the situation
T your thoughts and *visual images*
C your feelings, physical reactions and action consequences

Activities

Trainees can use activities to illustrate various aspects of visualizing. One simple exercise is to ask clients to think of someone they love. Almost invariably they will create a visual image. Trainees can show the relationship between visualizing and feelings by getting clients first to visualize something that 'makes' them feel happy and then something that 'makes' them feel afraid.

Enhance relaxation

When clients visualize, it is best if they are relaxed. In addition, relaxation can be a useful skill for clients to develop if they suffer from such problems as tension headaches, hypertension, excessive stress, anxiety (Deffenbacher and Suinn, 1988; Wolpe, 1990) and anger (Deffenbacher et al., 2000). The most common helping approach to relaxation is probably the Jacobson progressive muscular relaxation technique (Jacobson, 1938), more fully described in Chapter 21. Visual imagery may be used independently of as well as in conjunction with muscular relaxation. Counselling trainees may assist clients in the following elements of visual relaxation.

Identifying relaxing scenes

Trainees can encourage clients to identify one or more favourite scenes conducive to their feeling relaxed, for instance looking at a valley with lush green meadows, lying on a beach on a warm sunny day, or sitting in a comfortable chair at home.

Developing self-instructions

Though trainees may initially relax clients, the idea is for clients to develop visual relaxation as a self-helping skill. First, trainees can demonstrate how clients can instruct themselves in visual relaxation. Then trainees rehearse clients as they use their own instructions. Clients may wish to record their self-instructions for playback outside of counselling sessions. For example:

> 'I'm lying on an uncrowded beach on a pleasant, sunny day, enjoying the sensations of warmth on my body. There is a gentle breeze. I can hear the peaceful noise of the sea steadily lapping against the nearby shore. I haven't a care in the world, and enjoy my feelings of peace, calm, relaxation, and well-being.'

Using visual relaxation in daily life

Trainees can help clients to identify opportunities for taking 'time out' in their daily lives to use visual relaxation. They can encourage clients to keep monitoring logs of their daily practice and use of the skill. Clients can also record the consequences of using visual relaxation skills.

Enhance competent performance

Though they overlap, visualized rehearsal and practice and visualizing attaining goals are two important skills for clients wishing to perform tasks more competently.

Visualized rehearsal and practice

Counselling trainees can encourage clients to use visualized rehearsal to prepare for more distant scenarios. Clients may have limited opportunity to rehearse and practice certain targeted skills in real life, for instance going for a job interview or speaking in public. However, they have virtually unlimited opportunity to use visualized rehearsal and practice. Although it is no substitute for the real thing, visualized rehearsal has many advantages: it can help clients to break tasks down and focus on the processes of skilled performance, to identify potential setbacks and ways of coping with them, and to rehearse and practice coping self-talk along with their visualizing skills. I have often made up cassettes to assist clients in visualized rehearsal: for instance, waiting outside an interview room, then going in, sitting down and answering the first question competently.

The following are instances of clients using visual rehearsal and practice.

Gillian, 43, an executive, has an interview coming up with Nicole, 27, whose work has been poor recently. Gillian visually rehearses the best way to do this, including how she might respond if Nicole is uncooperative.

Martin, 37, a printing company foreman, visualizes different ways he can tell employees when their work is good.

Visualizing attaining goals

Visualized rehearsal and practice focuses on the *processes* of skilled performance. However, clients may also enhance their performance if they visualize themselves being successful in attaining goals (Lazarus, 1984). For example, if clients rehearse hard and then visualize themselves performing very competently when speaking in public, they are more likely to do so than if they visualize lack of success. Often clients are far too good at visualizing the worst. They need to be able to counteract this tendency. Counselling trainees can, however, encourage clients, even when imagining the worst possibility, to visualize how they can cope successfully.

Break bad habits

As Oscar Wilde said: 'I can resist everything except temptation.' Visualizing can be a useful skill when trying to overcome bad habits. Instead of dwelling on negative consequences, clients often switch to dwelling on short-term rewards. If they sincerely wish to break bad habits, the time to reward themselves is when they have resisted temptation, not when they have given in to it. Visualizing realistic negative consequences and visualizing exaggerated negative consequences are two ways counselling trainees can assist clients to break bad habits.

Visualize realistic negative consequences

How can trainees help clients to visualize the realistic negative consequences of such activities as smoking and engaging in unsafe gay sex? One way is to encourage them to collect visual images of negative consequences, for instance coloured medical photographs either of the effects of smoking on lung tissue or of AIDS-related symptoms, such as Kaposi's sarcoma and malignant lymphomas. In addition, clients can be encouraged to develop visualizations, possibly including photographic images, of negative consequences of bad habits: for instance, the ability to call up on their memory screens pictures of AIDS-related symptoms. Clients can develop the following self-helping skill. When tempted, they can shout to themselves 'Stop!' and then strongly visualize the negative consequences of giving in to the temptation. Clients may then engage either in distracting activities or in substitute rewarding activities that involve little or no risk.

Visualize exaggerated negative consequences

Cautela (1967b) developed what he termed a 'covert sensitization' approach to undermining and resisting temptations. Clients are encouraged to visualize exaggerated negative consequences whenever an unwanted temptation is anticipated or experienced. For instance, if clients wish to break overeating, and they have targeted rich cakes as a food to avoid, they might practice visualizing the following sequence:

> 'I am at home, sitting around the table at dinner, and a rich cake is being served. As I see it I start getting nauseous. I accept a piece. As I take my first bite, I vomit all over the table and my clothes. I throw up all my dinner in a disgusting smelly mess. Seeing and smelling my vomit makes me retch even more violently. I feel very weak and faint. Everybody is looking at me in disgust. As I get up from the table, having made up my mind to eat no more, I feel better. I wash, change and feel great to have stopped eating rich food.'

I prefer encouraging clients to visualize realistic rather than exaggerated negative consequences. Realistic consequences can be horrific enough. However, some clients may find that exaggeration increases the power of their negative imagery, with a beneficial effect on willpower.

Activity 16.4 Improving skills at creating visual images

Work with a partner who either uses a personal concern or role-plays a client with a goal of improving her/his creating visual images skills to manage a specific problem situation better. Within the context of a good collaborative working relationship:

- use speaking skills to describe the skill of creating visual images;
- use demonstrating skills;
- help the client to identify any current negative visual images before, during or after the problem situation;
- use coaching skills to assist the client in formulating and rehearsing improved visual images and coping self-talk with which to replace the current negative visual images;
- use skills of encouraging the client to record and remember important work conducted during the session; and
- use negotiating homework assignment skills.

Afterwards discuss and reverse roles. Playing back audio recordings or video recordings of skills building sessions may increase learning.

interventions for thinking – 2 17

Chapter outcomes

By studying and doing the activities in this chapter you should:

- know some interventions for creating explanations;
- know some interventions for creating expectations;
- know some interventions for creating realistic goals;
- know some interventions for creating realistic decisions; and
- understand more about managing problems and altering problematic skills.

Creating explanations

This section focuses on helping clients to develop better skills at assuming personal responsibility for and in their lives. The first section focuses on assuming responsibility for choosing and the second section examines creating more accurate explanations in a number of different areas.

Assume responsibility for choosing

An aspect of mind that is related to creating explanations is that of creating responsibility for choosing. In their waking hours people are always choosers. Counselling trainees and clients can make choices in relation to themselves, others and the environment. Within limits they can choose how they think, feel and act. All people can be the authors or architects of their lives (May and Yalom, 2005; Yalom, 1980). Often, however, they are unaware of the full extent of their existential responsibility to shape their lives. Additionally, they may knowingly or unknowingly relinquish some of this responsibility. They may possess an illusion of autonomy that masks a constricted approach to life. Trainees as well as clients may need help to become more aware that (1) they are always choosers, (2) their choices always have costs and consequences, and (3) within the constraints of reality, they can develop skills to increase the odds that their choices will have good rather than bad results.

Very frequently counselling trainees assist clients indirectly rather than directly to realize that they are responsible for their choices. For example, in the lifeskills counselling model, clients who agree upon a shared analysis of skills they need to improve to address a problem also agree implicitly that they are responsible for maintaining their difficulties and for changing the way they think and communicate/act. Clients are often quite willing to assume more responsibility for their lives if they are helped to see how they can do so. There follow some suggestions for ways in which trainees can help clients to create the fundamental explanation that they are responsible for their lives and for the choices they make. This list is far from exhaustive.

Raise consciousness about being a chooser

Some clients may need to be told in simple language that they are personally responsible for creating their lives through their choices. They may require help in seeing that they can choose not only how they act, but also how they think and feel. In the past they may have taken a passive stance to life and waited for things to happen to them. Counselling trainees can encourage them to see that they can be active agents in shaping their lives.

Skilled trainees can also assist clients in exploring their choices or options and their consequences. They should be careful not to make clients' choices for them, but to help them to choose for themselves. Spending time exploring choices is a valuable way of developing clients' understanding of how they can assume more personal responsibility for the authorship of their lives.

Encourage the language of choosing

Clients can become more aware of how their use of language can either restrict or enhance their choices. Trainees can encourage clients to send 'I' messages in which they speak for themselves, to use verbs that acknowledge choice, for example 'I won't' rather than 'I can't'; and to avoid static self-labelling, for example, 'I am a poor letter-writer' rather than 'I choose to be a poor letter-writer'.

When clients make statements like 'I had no choice but to … ' trainees can either challenge such statements or help clients to challenge themselves. In specific situations where clients fail to see that they can be choosers, for instance in resisting peer group pressure, trainees can assist them to feel less powerless by helping them to see that they still have choices. Sometimes trainees may need to train clients in relevant communication skills, for instance assertion skills for saying 'no'.

Borrowing from reality therapy (Glasser, 1998; Glasser and Wubbolding, 1995), counselling trainees can encourage clients to use active language when describing their feelings: for instance clients are not depressed but 'depress-ing'. Other active language terms for feelings include: 'anxiety-ing', 'guilt-ing', 'phobic-ing', 'compuls-ing', headach-ing' and 'sick-ing'. Glasser considers that using active language helps clients to own that they are creating their feelings and to take responsibility for controlling them.

Exploring and lessening use of defences

Counselling trainees can assist clients in acknowledging the impact of any characteristic 'security operations' or 'defensive processes' they adopt (Arlow, 2005; Clark, 1991; Freud, 1936; Sullivan, 1954). Defensive processes diminish clients' ability to assume personal responsibility for their choices in the interest of making life more psychologically comfortable in the short term. Illustrative defensive processes include denying or distorting information, rationalizing, and projecting unwanted aspects of oneself on to others. Assisting clients to explore and lessen their use of defences requires skill and caution, since these defences alleviate their anxiety and may protect highly sensitive areas.

Identify inaccurate explanations

Often clients' explanations of cause convert partial truths into whole truths. For instance, a partial cause of Olivia's difficulties with men friends could be that she was rejected by her father. However, Olivia can immobilize herself from changing if she attributes her difficulties only to her father's past behaviour. Counselling trainees can use the STC framework to help clients identify not only explanatory errors, but their negative consequences. The following are some explanatory errors for different areas.

Causes of problems

Explanation of cause errors can contribute to clients remaining unnecessarily stuck with problems.

- *It's my genes.* Though genetic endowment does limit capacities, clients also limit themselves. For instance, clients who say that they are 'naturally' lazy obscure their own role in sustaining their laziness.
- *It's my mental illness.* The medical profession has done ordinary people a huge disservice by fostering the concept of mental illness. For most psychological problems, the explanation of mental illness overemphasizes the role of heredity and physical factors and underemphasizes the role of learning and choice.
- *It's my unfortunate past.* As shown in the example of Olivia, unfortunate pasts may contribute to problems and to poor skills. However,

clients are unlikely to change unless they assume responsibility for how they sustain problems.

- *It's my poor environment.* Adverse social, economic and psychological environments may make it more difficult for clients to fulfil themselves. However, even in Nazi concentration camps, people were able to change and grow psychologically (Frankl, 1963).

Feelings of depression

Clients' explanations of the causes of positive and negative events in their lives affect their self-esteem. The following are some inaccurate explanations that may contribute to depression.

- *I am the cause of all negative events.* Clients may overemphasize their role in negative events in their own and others' lives (Beck et al., 1979).
- *I am never the cause of positive events.* Clients can deny and distort their roles in positive events in their own and others' lives.
- *I am unable to act on my environment in such a way as to produce desired results.* Depressed people often think of themselves as powerless to influence their environments.

Relationship problems

Often clients require help in acknowledging their contributions to sustaining relationship problems. The following are some common explanatory errors.

- *It's all your fault.* Instead of looking at conflicts from the inside to the outside, clients view them from the outside to the inside. Disliking what they see outside provides a convenient excuse for not looking at their own behaviour.
- *It's because of her/his poor personality.* A permanent and pervasive negative label may be attached to one's partner. Why should anyone change if they perceive themselves, despite their own best efforts, as victims of another's personality problems? One of the values of thinking in skills terms is that it encourages specificity rather than talking in vague and general terms about 'personality'.
- *You must change first.* Here clients allow their feelings, thinking and actions to be dependent on their partner's behaviour. Unwittingly clients give up some control over their lives.
- *You deliberately want to hurt and humiliate me.* 'Hostile explanatory or attributional bias' means a tendency to interpret the intent of others as hostile when social cues are ambiguous. Biased explanations of hostile intent can lead to increases in anger and aggression (Epps and Kendall, 1995). People explain to themselves that malicious

intentions stimulate another's negative behaviour and so justify anger toward her or him. Beck observes: 'The attribution of negative intent is a marital barometer. When spouses consistently ascribe negative motives, especially malice to one another, their relationship is troubled' (1988: 166). Beck acknowledges that insidious motives do exist. However, people in distressed relationships often exaggerate one another's negative motives and sanitize their own.

- *You do not love me.* A partner may say 'If you loved me, you would not act like that.' This level of explanatory simplification can ignore interactive patterns – for instance your unlovable behaviour may be in response to mine. It also assumes that love is a black-and-white phenomenon rather than an emotion difficult to define, fluctuating and frequently tinged with ambivalence. In addition, partners may fail to understand differences between them in the symbolic meaning they attach to certain behaviours – for example, remembering birthdays and anniversaries.
- *I cannot trust you.* Irrational jealousy or misplaced mistrust is a clear case of explaining cause inaccurately. Here, rather than locating the cause of insecure feelings in oneself, one projects cause on to a partner and then punishes her/him for one's own disloyal fantasies.

Becoming and staying unemployed

Depending on clients' specific situations, the following explanations may be inaccurate.

- *It was my fault.* Numerous external reasons contribute to unemployment: for instance, recessions, takeovers, restructurings, downsizings and technological change. Clients may genuinely not be responsible for their job loss, or only partially so.
- *It was their fault.* Some clients fail to acknowledge that they may have some poor personal and work-related skills that increase the chances of their being fired.
- *The state should provide for me.* Whatever clients' political persuasions, the reality is that they are likely to receive limited welfare payments.
- *My work skills are adequate.* Clients may need to review the accuracy of this assumption. For example, their work skills may be in demand, but they perform them poorly. Alternatively, their work skills may be, in varying degrees, obsolete.

Academic successes and failures

Counselling trainees can assist both underachieving and over-striving students to be more realistic about their explanations of cause for their academic successes and failures. The following are some ways by which students may explain academic success and failure. Needless to say, there is a subjective element in what students perceive as success or failure.

- *Aptitude.* Aptitude is an internal and stable explanation.
- *Effort.* Effort is an internal explanation largely within a client's control.
- *Task difficulty.* Task difficulty is composed of the task's realistic level of difficulty and any perceiving errors, for example magnifying or minimizing.
- *Luck.* Academic results due to chance are outside clients' control. Unfortunately some clients attribute their academic successes to luck, but are quick to blame themselves for their academic failures.
- *Anxiety.* Anxiety can both help and hinder academic performance. The effects of debilitating anxiety may be inadequately recognized.
- *Staff competence.* Good or poor teaching and supervision may help or hinder achievement.
- *Student group norms.* The degree to which the student peer group values or does not value academic success.
- *Student group attraction.* The degree to which the student group is attractive to a person and they like studying with their peers.
- *Socio-economic considerations.* Some students need to take outside work to support themselves. Some live in inadequate housing, and so on.

Alter inaccurate explanations

Counselling trainees can use some of the skills already described in the section on creating perceptions to help clients become more realistic in explaining cause. For example they can encourage clients to examine the evidence for their explanations and see how closely they fit the facts. Then clients can generate and evaluate alternative explanations. In addition, clients can dispute explanations and restate them into more realistic ones. For example, the explanation in a relationship conflict that 'It's all my partner's fault' can be restated to 'Even though I may not like how my partner behaves, I may be happier if I examine how I behave to my partner and, if necessary, change how I act rather than wait for her/him to change first.' Furthermore, trainees can assist clients to conduct behavioural experiments in which, for specified periods, they change their actions in line with altered explanations. For example, a husband's 'It's all my partner's fault' explanation can be disproved if he communicates more positively with his wife, who in turn communicates better with him.

Counselling trainees can provide new information that challenges existing explanations: for example, informing clients wrongly diagnosing themselves as schizophrenic that they do not exhibit any of its key symptoms. Trainees can also encourage clients to test the accuracy of their explanations by collecting additional information. For instance, clients explaining their maths problems as the result of insufficient aptitude can collect additional information by taking a maths aptitude test.

Emphasize homework

Ways discussed previously for consolidating other mind skills as self-helping skills are relevant to consolidating the skills of creating explanations: namely, copying work from the whiteboard, using reminder cards, making cassettes, and encouraging clients to discipline themselves to practise the skills in daily life. In addition, where clients are in relationships, they can demonstrate creating explanations skills to one another and reward each other's honesty. To avoid repetition, it will be assumed that readers understand the importance of emphasizing homework, so it will not be highlighted for the remaining mind skills covered in this chapter.

Activity 17.1 Improving skills at creating explanations

Work with a partner who either uses a personal concern or role-plays a client with the goal of using creating explanations skills to manage a specific situation better. Within the context of a good counselling relationship:

- use speaking skills to describe the skill of creating explanations;
- use demonstrating skills;
- cooperate with the client to identify any current inaccurate or partially inaccurate explanations;
- use coaching skills to assist the client to question and restate inaccurate as more accurate explanations; and
- use negotiating homework assignment skills.

Afterwards discuss and reverse roles. Playing back audio recordings or video recordings of rehearsal and practice sessions may assist learning.

Creating expectations

Clients lead their lives into the future rather than into the past. Expectations are thoughts and images forecasting the future. George Kelly took a rational approach to expectation when he wrote: 'The two factors from which predictions are made are the number of replications already observed and the amount of similarity which can be abstracted among the replications' (1955: 53). Invariably clients experience disorders of expectation of varying degrees of intensity. Anxiety is a disorder of expectation (Beck and Emery, 1985). Distorted predictions play a large part in depression, for instance creating predictions of hopelessness (Beck et al., 1979).

Become aware of style of expectation

Counselling trainees can help clients to become more aware of their styles of creating expectations of risk and reward. The following are the four main options.

Predict risk inaccurately

Underestimating bad consequences

Some research in the health area indicates that people tend to underestimate their own, relative to other's, susceptibility to various illnesses and negative life events (Weinstein, 1980, 1984). Many people underestimate their risk of HIV infection. For example, a large-scale study of nearly 6,000 men entering gay bars in 16 small American cities found that, excluding those in long-term exclusive relationships, 27 per cent reported engaging in unprotected anal sex during the previous two months (Kelly et al., 1995). Compulsive gamblers and stock-market speculators have similar tendencies to underestimate risk.

Overestimating bad consequences

Fear of change, failure and success can be powerful motivators for clients to overestimate negative consequences of actions. Many clients engage in catastrophic predictions and overestimate loss through creating unrealistic expectations both about their chances of failing and about the negative consequences of so doing. For example, when shy clients start to date they often create exaggerated expectations about not being liked and about their inability to deal with any form of rejection. Such shy people may talk to themselves pessimistically as though their expectations are both permanent ('It will always happen in future'), and pervasive ('It will happen across many situations and with many different people').

Predict reward inaccurately

Overestimating good consequences

Overestimating good consequences frequently accompanies underestimating bad consequences. It can have disastrous consequences for clients' health, happiness and financial security if they engage in rash actions based on these false expectations, for instance in compulsive gambling.

Underestimating good consequences

Nothing ventured, nothing gained. Many clients underestimate the good consequences of communicating and acting differently. Instead, they create expectations focusing far more on risk than reward. Two trends are common in underestimating reward: clients are poor at identifying rewards; and even when they do identify rewards, they minimize their significance.

Acting in this way can be risky. For instance, in relationships, clients can underestimate the good consequences of using such communication skills as showing more gratitude and solving differences cooperatively rather than competitively. Consequently they lose out on the potential gains from communicating differently.

Link erroneous explanations and expectations

Clients can create and reinforce their own pessimism by the permanence and pervasiveness of certain erroneous explanations. Counselling trainees can work with clients to help them see how their explanatory styles often create self-fulfilling prophecies. For instance, spouses who think their partner will never change because of their poor personality may themselves sustain their partner's negative behaviour by failing to do anything positive. By ascribing a permanent cause to their partner's negative behaviour, the spouse continues to reinforce the negative outcomes contained in the expectation.

Where necessary, trainees can enable clients to reality-test the pervasiveness of their explanations. For instance, they can challenge a client who, after one unsatisfactory date with a man/woman, then makes negative predictions about their abilities in other areas, for instance study or work.

Become aware of current expectations and their consequences

A simple two-column technique can be useful for eliciting clients' assessments of risks and rewards in specific situations. For example, using the STC framework, the S or situation is that Sean is a shy 30-year-old bachelor wondering whether to ask Suzanne for a date. Sean's counselling trainee places the following two column headings on the whiteboard to elicit Sean's thoughts or expectations at T.

Risks (–s)	Rewards (+s)

Then the trainee helps Sean to articulate his fears about asking Suzanne out: for instance, 'This might contribute to keeping me depressed.' and 'I could get hurt.' At this stage, Sean has difficulty expecting that there will be any rewards for his actions.

Counselling trainees can go beyond pinpointing expectations to exploring their consequences for clients and for others, at C. For instance, Sean's overemphasis on the risks rather than the gains may lead to persistent loneliness. Or drug-addict Jessica may need to see more clearly the dangers for others of sharing her needles.

Create better expectations

The following are some interventions that counselling trainees can use to help clients to create better expectations.

Assess probability better

This involves clients in reviewing their assumptions concerning the likelihood of risks or rewards occurring. They may erroneously assign high probability to low-probability events and low probability to high-probability events. Counselling trainees can encourage clients to use their skills of distinguishing fact from inference and seeing that their expectations are related as closely as possible to the available facts.

When assessing probability, questions that trainees can ask clients and encourage clients to ask themselves fall into two categories. First, 'What *rational* basis do I have for creating particular expectations about events?' Clients can use the number and similarity of previous events as a basis for creating expectations about future events. They can also collect further information which may help in this process. In addition, they can try to identify relevant factors that are not immediately apparent and allow for the unexpected.

The second category of question is 'What *irrational* considerations might interfere with the accuracy of my expectations?' Strong emotions can bias the accuracy with which clients create expectations, as can their physical condition, for instance being very tired. If they are conscious that they are agitated, they can instruct themselves to 'STOP ... THINK ... and calm down.' They may then be in a better position to create more rational expectations. In addition, clients can monitor their style of creating expectations, for instance their tendency to overestimate or underestimate gain and loss.

Increase expectations about performing competently

The most effective way for clients to increase their confidence in their competence at potentially rewarding tasks is to experience success in performing them. Success tends to raise expectations about levels of competence, whereas failure tends to lower them.

Observing other people behaving competently and gaining rewards for doing so can also increase clients' expectations about their own competence. For example, partners can learn from observing one another's communication skills strengths. Demonstrations of competent communication transmit knowledge and teach effective skills and strategies for managing various situations. However, the effects of observing another's performance tend to be weaker than first-hand success. Clients can also increase their competence expectations by obtaining support when learning to communicate and act in improved ways. They also imagine themselves, or even others, performing relevant communication tasks competently and successfully.

Identify coping skills and support factors

Clients' may predict on the basis of inaccurate assessments of their skills. They may focus on their poor skills and need to counteract this by searching for and affirming their good skills and personal resources. In addition, clients may possess many support factors that they inadequately acknowledge: for example, people who can help them prepare for prospective tasks, friends and relatives to provide emotional support, and opportunities to attempt failed tasks another time. Counselling trainees should encourage clients to create more confident expectations by identifying, using and developing appropriate supports.

Use time projection

Time projection, which entails imaginary mind-tripping into the future, is a useful visualizing skill that clients can use to create more accurate expectations (Lazarus, 1984). Clients can both visualize how the present might look from the vantage point of the future and also visualize looking into the future. Furthermore, they can visually project how to deal with worst-case scenarios.

An example of using time projection is for clients to visualize relationship difficulties from a vantage point three, six, or twelve months 'down the track'; it may then be easier for them to see their true significance. Visualizing in this way may also help clients to create more accurate expectations now, so that they can feel and communicate more appropriately in the present. For instance, a client may be reeling from the fact that their partner has walked out on them. However, if this client takes a mind trip six months into the future and looks back on the break-up, she/he can get much more perspective on it. For instance, she/he will probably realize that, although sometimes life can be painful, this setback is one with which she/he has the resources to cope.

Clients can attempt reality checks by mind tripping into the future. For example, a client thinking of forging a permanent commitment with someone they are still getting to know can visualize how it might be to spend each hour of a representative day with that person at some stage in the future, say five years from now. They can then imagine this representative day repeated, with minor variations, day after day.

Visualizing the worst possibility is another form of time projection that may help clients to create more accurate expectations. Counselling trainees can ask clients 'So what if the worst were to happen?' , and then encourage them to visualize it happening at some stage in the future, and ask them to imagine how they might cope with their worst-case scenario. Once they actually face in their imagination having to deal with their worst fears, clients may find that they have sufficient resources to cope if this situation were to arise in real life.

Create and evaluate additional gains or losses

If, when creating expectations, clients err more in the directions of overestimating the potential for gain and underestimating the potential for loss, counselling trainees may need to assist them to develop skills of generating ideas about additional risks. However, clients frequently overestimate potential risks. If so, trainees can help them develop their skills of creating and evaluating additional gains.

Sean, aged 30, had little experience of dating women, his longest experience lasting three dates. In his church group, Sean was on a committee with Suzanne who had been friendly to him and he wondered if he should ask her out. Sean questioned, 'Why bother to take the risk of seeking the gain?' With his counsellor, Sean generated both the potential risks and gains of taking this initiative. He was already expert at acknowledging risks and needed to learn that it was in his interests to look at gains as well as risks in his decisions. Sean's list of potential gains for asking Suzanne out included the following:

I might have a chance of a strong relationship.
I might gain more experience in developing relationships.
This might contribute to helping me become happier.
I might gain confidence and a more positive self-image.
I might develop my ability to express my feelings more.
I might give myself the opportunity of enabling Suzanne to take some of the initiative too.

Test the reality of expectations

In the above example, Sean evaluated that the gains of asking Suzanne out outweighed the risks. He then acted on his revised expectation that if he communicated differently there was a good chance that Suzanne would want to spend more time with him. Subsequently, Suzanne became Sean's first steady girlfriend. Counselling trainees should remember that the most conclusive way of encouraging clients to assess the accuracy of their expectations is for them, like Sean, to put them to the test.

Activity 17.2 Improving skills at creating expectations

Work with a partner who either uses a personal concern or role-plays a client with the goal of developing creating expectations skills to manage a specific situation better. Within the context of a good counselling relationship:

- use speaking skills to describe the skill of creating expectations;
- use demonstrating skills;
- collaborate with the client to identify any unrealistic expectations;
- use coaching skills to assist the client to identify, assess and, where appropriate, alter unrealistic expectations; and
- use negotiating homework assignment skills.

Afterwards discuss and reverse roles. Playing back audio recordings or video recordings of rehearsal and practice sessions may assist learning.

Creating realistic goals

Bandura observes: 'Human motivation relies on *discrepancy production* as well as *discrepancy reduction*. It requires both *proactive control* and *reactive or feedback control*' (1989: 1179–80). Initially, people motivate themselves through setting standards or levels of performance that create a state of disequilibrium and then strive to maintain them. Goals act as motivators by specifying the conditions of self-satisfaction with performance. Feedback control involves subsequent adjustment of efforts to achieve desired results.

Clients' goal-setting errors vary. Some clients may possess goals that are unrealistically high or low. Furthermore, their goals may be based on how others think they should be rather than on their own valuing process. Other clients may lack clear goals. Still more may require assistance in stating their goals clearly. Some of the rewards for clients of setting realistic goals include increased authorship of their lives, clarity of focus, finding increased meaning, and gaining increased motivation. However, risks to clients setting themselves unrealistic goals include: self-alienation, overemphasizing doing as contrasted with being, putting too much pressure on themselves, and compromising their health.

Assisting vulnerable clients to formulate clear goals may entail long-term counselling. Such clients can lack a clear sense of their identity. Counselling trainees may need to help them to get more in touch with their feelings, wants and wishes. Furthermore, they may need to caution clients against making major decisions until they are less anxious.

Many other mind skills are relevant to assisting clients in setting realistic goals. Clients' goals need to be based on creating realistic rules. Where clients' goals involve another person, for instance in getting engaged or married, they need to perceive this person reasonably accurately. In addition, clients can use visualizing skills to formulate goals. When setting goals, they can also engage in the steps of rational decision-making.

State goals clearly

Clients are more likely to attain goals that they state clearly. Counselling trainees can make clients aware of the following criteria for effective goals:

- *Do your goals reflect your values?* Clients' goals should reflect what they consider to be worthwhile in life.
- *Are your goals realistic?* Clients' goals are realistic when they adequately acknowledge both external and personal constraints. Trainees should encourage clients to set goals reflecting potentially attainable standards.
- *Are your goals specific?* Trainees should assist clients in stating goals as specifically as possible. Ideally, clients' goals should be stated so that they can easily measure the success of attempts to attain them. For instance, when Lucy makes a goal statement, 'I will introduce myself to three new people in my ballroom dancing class', this statement is much preferable to the more general 'I want to meet some new people.'
- *Do your goals have a time frame?* Goals can be short-term, medium-term, or long-term. Vague intentions are insufficient. Assist clients in stating a realistic time frame for attaining goals: for instance, Lucy might set as a goal 'By the end of this month, I will introduce myself to three new people in my ballroom dancing class.'

Once goals are stated, counselling trainees may need to work with clients to identify the mind skills and communication/action skills required to attain them. In the above example, her counsellor could assist Lucy in articulating the mind skills and communication skills helpful for meeting three new people in the ballroom dancing class. Then, the trainee might need to train her in some or all of these skills.

Set sub-goals

Where appropriate, assist clients to break goals down into sub-goals. Particularly useful are progressively difficult short-term sub-goals. These both provide incentives for action and, when attained, produce confidence to persist. In the above example, an initial goal might be for Lucy to meet one new person at her next ballroom dancing class, followed by a second goal of meeting two new people by the middle of the month, with the third goal being meeting three new people by the end of the month.

Sometimes, striving for high goals may provide evidence that clients have made significant gains. However, on other occasions, clients are at risk of relapsing into previous poor skills because they attempt too much too soon. Then trainees may need to support them as they work through any negative reactions to not doing as well as they would like. In addition, trainees can reaffirm or renegotiate appropriate goals and sub-goals.

Paul Fleming, a client with golf swing anxiety, was building his confidence and skills by gradually and systematically succeeding in more difficult tasks. As part of this gradual approach, both in the office and on various golf courses, I would assist him through any mental and technical difficulties he faced. One day, when I was not present, Paul had a particularly good score. Three weeks later Paul, with my knowledge, entered a Pro-Am tournament that was way beyond his experience, since entering counselling, of playing in public. He fared disastrously and came off the course physically drained and mentally depressed. Paul was afraid that he had undone all his progress to date. When we next met, Paul and I discussed how his Pro-Am experience showed he had tried too much too soon. We then negotiated some more realistic short-term, medium-term and longer-term goals for consolidating his skills.

Activity 17.3 Improving skills at creating realistic goals

Work with a partner who either is unclear as to her/his goals in one or more areas of her/his life or who role-plays a client with the goal of developing creating realistic goals skills in one or more areas of her/his life. Within the context of a good counselling relationship:

- use speaking skills to describe creating realistic goals skills;
- use demonstrating skills;
- cooperate with the client to identify any current unrealistic goals;
- use coaching skills to assist the client in developing setting realistic goals skills; and
- use negotiating homework assignment skills.

Afterwards discuss and reverse roles. Playing back audio recordings or video recordings of rehearsal and practice sessions may assist learning.

Creating realistic decisions

Frequently clients are faced with decisions. Such decisions include making choices about jobs and career, major area of study, further education, recreational activities, getting married or divorced, and whether or not to give up a bad habit. Decisions produce conflict and anxiety. Clients may fear the consequences of making the wrong decision. Additionally, they may be under stress at the time of making the decision: for instance, leaving university. How can counselling trainees assist clients to make better decisions and, even more important, to become better decision-makers? The main thrust of all counselling interventions is to help clients to make better choices. Here two areas are reviewed, decision-making styles and realistic decision-making, in which counsellors specifically focus on clients' decision-making processes.

Explore decision-making styles

Clients have styles of making decisions that may be helpful or harmful. In reality, each client possesses a profile of decision-making styles. They may make different decisions in different ways, and their styles may alter when making decisions in conjunction with other people.

Though far from an exhaustive listing, the following eight styles describe how people make individual decisions:

- *Rational.* A person dispassionately and logically appraises all important information and then selects the best option in the light of their criteria.
- *Feelings-based.* Though different options may be appraised and generated, the basis for choice is what intuitively feels right. This style characterizes a person getting in touch with what they truly feel.
- *Impulsive.* A person makes decisions rapidly, based on sudden impulses. They act on initial and surface feelings rather than exploring and evaluating options.

- *Hyper-vigilant.* A person tries too hard. They become so anxious and aroused by the conflict and stress triggered by the decision that their decision-making efficiency decreases. They may become indecisive and fail to see the wood for the trees.
- *Avoidant.* A person copes with decisions by refusing to confront them, hoping they will go away, or by procrastinating over them.
- *Conformist.* A person conforms to what others expect of them. They allow their decisions to be heavily influenced, if not made, by others.
- *Rebellious.* A person rebels against what others expect of them. Their decisions are dependent on what others think, though in an oppositional way.
- *Value-based.* The framework for a person's choice is a code of values and ethics, whether religious or secular.

Sometimes counselling trainees can help clients to become more aware of their styles of joint decision-making. Many clients are in situations where they have differences and potential conflicts of interest with others, for instance partners. Here are three main styles of joint decision-making:

- *Competitive.* People operate on an 'I win – you lose' basis and view decisions as competition for scarce resources. They think and, possibly, behave aggressively.
- *Collusive.* People are non-assertive and either go along with or give in to each other. This can be an 'I lose – you win' style. Alternatively, they both avoid decisions and problems, which may end up as an 'I lose – you lose too' solution.
- *Cooperative.* Two people assertively search for a solution that best meets each person's needs. They search for an 'I win – you win too' solution. If necessary, they make rational compromises in the interest of the relationship.

Some clients may need to think through the consequences of their decision-making styles more thoroughly: for instance, impulsively choosing friends or buying goods on credit. Trainees require skills such as active listening and challenging when clients explore decision-making styles and their consequences. In addition, they may need to challenge clients who distance themselves from responsibility for decisions and who do not perceive their consequences accurately.

Develop realistic decision-making skills

Some clients require assistance in learning to make decisions systematically. Realistic or rational decision-making can be viewed as taking place in two main stages: first, confronting and making the decision;

second, implementing and evaluating it. The following is a seven-step framework for realistic decision-making within the context of these two main stages:

Stage 1: Confronting and making the decision

Step 1: Confront the decision. Component skills include acknowledging the need for decisions and clearly stating what is the decision to be made.

Step 2: Generate options and gather information about them. Some clients may be poor at generating options and thus restrict their decision-making effectiveness. Other skills weaknesses include inability to identify and gather relevant information.

Step 3: Assess the predicted consequences of options. Clients need accurately to perceive and evaluate positive and negative short-term and long-term consequences both for themselves and others.

Step 4: Commit yourself to a decision. Clients need to go beyond making rational decisions and commit themselves to implementing them. Clients may have various barriers to commitment, including post-decisional anxieties and conflict.

Stage 2: Implementing and evaluating the decision

Step 5: Plan how to implement the decision. Component skills of planning include stating goals and sub-goals clearly, breaking down tasks, generating and assessing alternative courses of action, anticipating difficulties and setbacks, and identifying sources of support.

Step 6: Implement the decision. Clients need to consider when best to implement decisions and be open to feedback during implementation. They may require skills of rewarding themselves for performing targeted behaviours: for instance by positive self-talk or more tangible rewards, such as a new item of clothing or some special entertainment.

Step 7: Assess the actual consequences of implementation. Realistic decision-making requires accurate perception of feedback and a willingness to act on it. Clients may stick with original decisions or modify or discard them.

Especially if they work in a decision-related area, for instance as career advisers, counselling trainees can make clients more aware of the steps of realistic or rational decision-making. One approach is to go through the steps, possibly using a whiteboard and then giving clients handouts. In addition, trainees can request clients to identify their decision-making strengths and weaknesses. They should take into account previous decision-making skills weaknesses. Clients can work through current decisions following the steps of realistic decision-making. Here trainees should focus on developing clients' skills rather than doing the work for them. For example, rather than saying 'Your options seem to be ...', a trainee might ask, 'What are your options and what information do you require to assess them adequately?'

Activity 17.4 Improving skills at creating realistic decisions

Work with a partner who either has a real decision to make or role-plays a client whose goal is to develop her/his decision-making skills in relation to a specific decision. Within the context of a good counselling relationship:

- use speaking skills to describe creating realistic decisions skills;
- use demonstrating skills;
- cooperate with the client to identify any decision-making skills weaknesses;
- use coaching skills to assist the client to develop realistic decision-making skills; and
- use negotiating homework assignment skills.

Afterwards discuss and reverse roles. Playing back audio recordings or video recordings of rehearsal and practice sessions may assist learning.

Preventing and managing problems and altering problematic skills

Decision-making and problem management overlap. The previous section focused on making decisions at major and minor turning points where clients needed to decide between different options. Here the focus is on helping clients use mind skills to prevent and manage thoughts, feelings, behaviours and situations that are problematic for them.

Assist clients to prevent problems

Counselling trainees can assist clients to recognize the preventive function of thinking skilfully in their daily lives. When thinking effectively, clients may be less disposed to a range of problems. Skilled thinking can make them more confident and less prone to upset themselves with imaginary, as opposed to real, difficulties. Clients can also learn to anticipate problems and 'nip them in the bud'. For example, clients able to anticipate when they are at risk of excessive stress are in a better position to take preventive actions than those less aware. Once aware of the risk of allowing themselves to be excessively stressed, clients may still need to use a range of mind skills, for instance creating realistic rules about achievement, to prevent them from giving in to bad habits. In addition, clients who have come to counselling with stress-related problems are never totally cured. They still need to think skilfully to prevent recurrences.

Assist clients to manage problems and alter problematic skills

Managing problems effectively requires clients to use many of the same skills as for making decisions. Nevertheless, there are important differences, for instance in how problems are assessed and restated. The lifeskills counselling model is basically a self-helping model. Counselling skills students can train clients in how to use the model to manage future problems and problematic skills. The model can be simplified to CASIE when used for client self-helping purposes.

C *Confront* and clarify my problem.
A *Assess* and restate my problem in skills terms.
S *State* goals and plan self-helping interventions.
I *Implement* my plan.
E *Evaluate* the consequences of implementing my plan.

Because of limited exposure, clients in brief counselling are unlikely to learn how to apply the lifeskills counselling model to future problems. Clients in longer-term counselling will acquire some knowledge of the model as they and their counselling skills students work with the problematic skills underlying their problems. Trainees may also identify characteristic poor mind skills. Consequently, longer-term clients have a start in knowing where to look when assessing future problems. In addition, trainees can systematically teach clients how to prevent and manage problems. In doing so they may use clients' anticipated problems as case material for developing skills in preventing and managing problems. Counselling trainees require both good relationship and good training skills to impart the CASIE self-helping model effectively.

Activity 17.5 Improving skills at preventing and managing problems

Work with a partner who has come for counselling over a specific problem and now wishes to learn how to take a systematic approach to preventing and managing future problems and altering the problematic skills associated with them. Within the context of a good counselling relationship:

- use speaking skills to describe how to use the CASIE model;
- use demonstrating skills;
- use coaching skills to assist the client to develop skills in how systematically to prevent and manage problems using the CASIE model; and
- use negotiating homework assignment skills.

Afterwards discuss and reverse roles. Playing back audio recordings or video recordings of rehearsal and practice sessions may enhance learning.

interventions for communication and actions – 1

18

Chapter outcomes

By studying and doing the activities in this chapter you should:

- understand some issues in when to intervene for communication and actions;
- know how to develop clients' skills for self-monitoring;
- be able to raise clients' awareness of their vocal and bodily communication;
- know how to use rehearsal and role-play; and
- know some ways of timetabling desired activities.

Introduction

However well clients feel and think, unless they communicate and act more effectively they are unlikely to attain personal goals. Communication and action skills provide the link from the inner to the outer world, from self to others and the environment. Counsellors, trainees and clients cannot afford to ignore communication and action skills. Whereas the last two chapters focused on how to develop clients' mind skills, their inner game, this chapter focuses on how to develop clients' communication and action skills, their outer game. These skills entail verbal, voice, body and touch messages. They relate to how clients communicate and act when on their own and also with others. Though the two are interrelated, in this and the next chapter I focus more on learning new skills and on developing existing skills strengths rather than on lessening and/or extinguishing communication and action skills weaknesses.

Counsellors and trainees who have inadequately assessed clients may fail to intervene, or do so inadequately, for communication and action skills. The following is an example of inadequate assessment:

Daniel, a counselling trainee, brought a cassette of an initial interview with Charlotte, aged 17, to a supervision session. Daniel allowed Charlotte to talk at great length about how angry she was with her parents' behaviour toward her. Every now and then Charlotte would make remarks about how she behaved toward her parents, for instance when she came home from school she would spend most of her time in her room, and would make no effort to socialize with her parents' friends. By allowing Charlotte's main focus to be on how her parents treated her and never focusing on how Charlotte behaved toward her parents, Daniel lost the opportunity to assess Charlotte's communication skills properly. Instead, he probably colluded in keeping Charlotte stuck in her present way of communicating.

When to intervene to develop communication/action skills

Basically, there are three main options for when counselling trainees can intervene to develop clients' communication/action skills: communication/action skills before mind skills; mind skills before communication/action skills; and mind skills and communication/action skills together.

Communication/action skills before mind skills

Without necessarily using skills language, a counselling trainee can focus at an early stage on getting clients to change how they communicate or act. A reason for intervening on communication/action skills first is that many clients understand the need to change how they communicate more easily than the need to change how they think. Throughout counselling, some clients work better with an approach focused on overt communications and actions rather than on covert thoughts. Furthermore, some counsellors consider that 'It is much easier to change concrete actions, or to introduce new ones, than it is to change patterns of thinking' (Beck, 1988: 208). Early successes in changing communications and actions can instil confidence. For example, when working with severely depressed patients, Beck initially attempts to restore their functioning to pre-morbid levels through interventions such as scheduling activities (Beck et al., 1979). Early changes in communication can also engender goodwill in others. For instance, distressed couples who see some immediate positive changes in one another's behaviour may have created a better emotional climate in which to work on deeper issues (Beck, 1988; Stuart, 1980).

Mind skills before communication/action skills

Sometimes both counselling trainees and clients may wish to intervene with mind skills prior to communication and action skills. For example, clients may have numerous fears about changing their outer behaviour. Changing private thoughts may seem less risky than altering outer behaviour, which is mostly public. Trainees may have to work with clients' fears about: performing skills adequately; coping with the consequences of failure; coping with the consequences of success; and reluctance to give up rewarding 'secondary gains'. Often in relationship conflicts, clients may externalize problems by projecting them on to their partners. Trainees can enable them to see their need for change prior to working with relevant communication skills.

Mind skills and communication/action skills together

Counselling trainees can simultaneously intervene with mind skills and communication/action skills. For example, with clients whose fears of change are not excessive, they can work to overcome such mental fears when training them in relevant communication/action skills. Trainees can also focus on both types of skills when targeting unwanted feelings such as anxiety, anger, shyness and stress. Sometimes using a mind skill contributes to learning a communication skill – for example, using visualized rehearsal to develop assertion skills. Mind skills invariably play a part in maintaining communication/action skills: for instance, having realistic expectations about maintaining and developing skills after counselling. Clients also need to develop the capacity for self-instruction through the sequences of choices entailed in implementing communication/action skills. Then these skills more clearly become self-helping skills.

Develop monitoring skills

The following are examples of clients engaging in systematic monitoring of their communication and actions.

Jim, 17, is trying to stop smoking. As part of his programme, he not only keeps a daily tally of how many cigarettes he smokes, but also keeps a log of the time, antecedents and consequences of each time he smokes.

Ellie, 53, is receiving help for depression. Ellie has a goal of increasing the number of times she engages in pleasant activities. She keeps a daily chart of each time she engages in a number of specific pleasant activities (Lewinsohn et al., 1986).

Thomas, 48, has had heart problems and is on a weight loss programme. He keeps a chart listing his daily weight. Also each time he eats between meals, he records the time, what happened immediately before, what he eats, and the consequences of his behaviour.

Jack, 26, is an unemployed client searching for a job. He keeps a daily record of each time he engages in specific job search activities: for instance, making phone enquiries and written applications.

Systematic self-monitoring or self-observation enables clients to become more aware of their thoughts, feelings and actions. Here the main focus is on monitoring communication and actions. Systematic monitoring can be important at the start of, during and after interventions focused on developing specific skills. When commencing interventions, monitoring can establish baselines and increase awareness. During interventions, it can act as a reminder, motivator and progress check. After an intervention, monitoring is relevant to maintaining gains, though clients may not collect information as systematically as during counselling. Monitoring is best thought of as an adjunct to other interventions. As an intervention on its own, the effects of monitoring often do not last (Kazdin, 1994).

Monitoring methods

The following are some methods whereby clients can monitor how they communicate and act.

Diaries and journals

Keeping a diary or journal is one way of monitoring communication/action skills. Clients can pay special attention to writing up critical incidents where skills have been used well or poorly. Although diaries and journals may be useful, some clients find this approach too easy to ignore and too unsystematic.

Frequency charts

Frequency charts focus on how many times clients enact a specific behaviour in a given time period, whether daily, weekly or monthly. For example, clients may count how many cigarettes they smoke in a day and then transfer this information to a monthly chart broken down by days. Take the earlier example of unemployed Jack recording his job search behaviours. Jack's counselling trainee gives him a Job Search Activity Chart and suggests that he fill it out for the next two weeks. The chart has activities on the horizontal axis and days on the vertical axis (see Box 18.1). Where clients are only monitoring single communications or actions, they may use wrist counters or pocket counters. However, they still need to transfer information gathered by such methods on to frequency charts.

Box 18.1 Jack's chart for recording job search activities

Activity	1 M	2 T	3 W	4 Th	5 F	6 Sa	7 Su	8 M	9 T	10 W	11 Th	12 F	13 Sa	14 Su	15 M
Written application															
Phone application															
Letter enquiry															
Phone enquiry															
Cold canvass															
Approach to contact															
Employment centre visit															
Interview attended															

Stimulus, response and consequences logs

To become more aware of their behaviour and its consequences, clients can fill in three-column stimulus, response, consequences logs.

Stimulus (What happened?)	Response (How I acted?)	Consequences (What resulted?)

For example, clients who work on managing anger skills might record each time they feel angry, what they did, and the consequences for themselves and others

Situation, thoughts and consequences (STC) logs

Filling in three-column situation, thoughts and consequences (STC) logs can help clients to see the connections between how they think and how they felt and communicated or acted.

Situation (What happened and when?)	Thoughts (What I thought)	Consequences (How I felt and communicated)

Use of targeted skills logs

Counselling trainees and clients need to go beyond monitoring communication/actions to monitoring skills. During the intervention stage, clients can usefully monitor and evaluate use of targeted skills. For instance, a trainee works with a teenager, Kim, on how to make assertive requests to her parents. Together, trainee and client agree on verbal, voice and body message sub-skills for each time Kim makes such a request. Kim's trainee asks her to complete an Assertive Request Monitoring Log after each request to her parents (see Box 18.2). In particular, the trainee asks Kim to record how she uses the sub-skills they have targeted.

Box 18.2 Kim's log for monitoring assertive requests

Kim's assertive request skills

Verbal messages: make 'I' statements, say 'please'
Voice messages: speak calmly and firmly
Body messages: use good eye contact, avoid threatening gestures

Date and situation	How I communicated		
	Verbal messages	Voice messages	Body messages
1.			
2.			
3.			
4.			
5.			
6.			
7.			
8.			

Assist clients to develop monitoring skills

Below are some ways counselling trainees can assist clients to monitor themselves and to develop self-monitoring skills.

Offer reasons for monitoring

Clients are not in the habit of systematically recording observations about how they act. Trainees need to motivate them to do so. For instance, they can explain: 'Counting how many times you perform a behaviour daily not only indicates how severe your problem is but also gives us a baseline against which to measure your progress in dealing with it.' Or, 'Systematically writing down how you send verbal, voice and communication messages after each time you go for an interview provides us with information to build your skills.'

Train clients in discrimination and recording

Clients are not naturally accurate self-observers (Thoresen and Mahoney, 1974). Counselling trainees need to educate them in how to discriminate and record specific behaviours. Clients require clarity not only about what to record, but about how to record it. They also require awareness of any tendencies they have to misperceive or selectively perceive their actions: for instance, being more inclined to notice deficits than strengths.

Design simple and clear recording logs

Counselling trainees should always supply the logs themselves. Do not expect clients to make up their own logs. They may not do so in the first place and, if they do, they may get them wrong. Simple recording systems enhance comprehension and recording accuracy.

Use reward skills

Trainees can reward clients with interest and praise when they fill in logs. This guideline is based on the basic behavioural principle that actions that are rewarding are more likely to be repeated.

Encourage clients to evaluate monitoring information

When clients share monitoring logs with trainees, the trainees can help them to use this information for self-exploration and evaluation. Assist clients to understand the meaning of the information they have collected. However, do not do their work for them. When counselling ends, trainees will not be around to assess the implications of their frequency counts and monitoring logs. Train clients to do this for themselves.

Use other skills-building strategies

Trainees should not expect clients to develop communication/action skills on the basis of self-observation alone. They are likely to require other interventions, for example behaviour rehearsals and self-reward, to develop these skills. Furthermore, they require work and practice to acquire and maintain skills.

Activity 18.1 Developing clients' monitoring skills

Part A: Assisting a client to monitor her/his communications/actions

Role-play a counselling session with a partner who has a goal of wanting to alter a specific communication/action skills weakness. You decide that it would help both you and your client if she/he were to observe systematically the frequency of this weakness over the next week. Within the context of a good counselling relationship, use the following skills:

- Offer reasons for monitoring.
- Train the client in discrimination and recording.
- Design a simple and clear recording log.

Afterwards discuss with your partner and reverse roles.

Part B: Assisting a client to record use of targeted communication/ action skills

Conduct a further counselling role-play with a partner. You are now training the client in the verbal, voice and body dimensions required to develop a specific communication/action skills strength, for example making an assertive request. Make a recording log using the format below and make sure that your client knows how to fill it out for each time she/he attempts to use the targeted skill.

Targeted skill______________________________

____

Verbal message sub-goal(s) ____________________

Voice message sub-goal(s)____________________

Body message sub-goal(s) ____________________

Date and	How I communicated		
situation	Verbal messages	Voice messages	Body messages
1 2			

Afterwards, discuss with your partner and reverse roles.

Raise awareness of vocal and bodilycommunication

Many clients have a poor understanding of how they come across to others. They may lack awareness both of various aspects of their vocal and bodily communication and of the fact that that they can choose to gain more control over the messages that they send to others. Fritz Perls (1973) regarded the simple phrase 'Now I am aware' as the foundation of the Gestalt approach. The 'now' because it keeps therapists and clients in the present and reinforces the fact that experience can only take place in the present; the 'aware' because it gives both therapists and clients the best picture of clients' present resources. Awareness always takes place in the present and opens up possibilities for action.

If necessary, counselling trainees can assist clients in becoming aware not only of what they say, but of how they communicate with their voices and bodies. Sometimes trainees may need to teach clients about the various dimensions of communication: for example, raising awareness of how they might control the volume, articulation, pitch, emphasis and rate of how they speak. Below are some examples taken by Dolliver of Perls directing the client Gloria's attention to her non-verbal behaviour taken from the *Three Approaches to Psychotherapy* film series (Dolliver, 1991: 299; Perls, 1965).

> What are you doing with your feet now?
> Are you aware of your smile?
> You didn't squirm for the last minute.
> Are you aware that your eyes are moist?
> Are you aware of your facial expression?

Exaggeration, which may focus on either movement and gesture or on verbal statements, is another way of heightening clients' awareness of how they communicate. In each instance, clients are asked progressively and repeatedly to exaggerate the behaviour. Examples of exaggeration requests from Perls's interview with Gloria are as follows (Dolliver, 1991: 300, Perls, 1965).

> Can you develop this movement?
> Now exaggerate this.
> What you just said, talk to me like this.
> Do this more.

Yet another way of heightening clients' awareness of their here-and-now communication is to ask them to use the phrase *'I take responsibility for it.'* For instance, 'I am aware that I am moving my leg and I take responsibility for it' or 'I am aware that I am speaking very slowly and quietly and I take responsibility for it.'

Similarly, clients can be asked to focus on either their bodily or vocal communication or both and to say *'I choose to.'* For instance, 'I choose to put my right hand on my right knee', or 'I choose to raise my voice', or 'I choose to remain still.'

When using awareness techniques, counselling trainees may self-disclose and provide here-and-now feedback about how they see the client communicating. Trainees can judiciously share how they are affected when the client communicates in a particular way.

Activity 18.2 Raising awareness of vocal and bodily communication

Work with a partner, with one person acting the role of counsellor and the other that of client.

Part A: Vocal communication

The counsellor

1 asks the client to say 'Now I am aware' as she/he becomes aware of each aspect of her/his vocal communication;
2 instructs the client to exaggerate one or more aspects of her/his vocal communication;
3 asks the client to say 'I take responsibility for it' in conjunction with her/his changed vocal communication; and
4 asks the client to say 'I choose to' in regard to maintaining or changing aspects of her/his vocal communication.

Afterwards hold a sharing and discussion session and reverse roles.

Part B: Bodily communication

The counsellor

1 asks the client to say 'Now I am aware' as she/he becomes aware of each aspect of her/his bodily communication;
2 instructs the client to exaggerate one or more aspects of her/his bodily communication;
3 asks the client to say 'I take responsibility for it' in conjunction with her/his changed bodily communication; and
4 asks the client to say 'I choose to' in regard to maintaining or changing aspects of her/his bodily communication.

Afterwards hold a sharing and discussion session and reverse roles.

Rehearse and role-play

Learning any skill generally requires repeated performances of targeted behaviours. Rehearsals may take place immediately after initial coached performance of skills, later in counselling, and before, when and after clients apply targeted skills in their daily lives. In role-plays, clients rehearse communication and action skills in simulated or pretend situations involving one or more others. Most often counselling trainees play the part of the other person, but sometimes trainees and clients switch roles.

Skills for assisting rehearsal

Many counsellor skills for assisting clients in rehearsing communication/action skills overlap with those of coaching: for example giving clear instructions, breaking tasks down and using feedback skills. The following are some skills for role-play rehearsals.

Explain reasons for role-plays

Some clients find the idea of role-playing off-putting. For example, they may be self-conscious about their acting skills. Trainees can explain reasons for role-plays to ease clients' anxieties and help motivate them. Here is a rationale for using role-play rehearsal with a client, Bill, who gets excessively angry when his teenage daughter, Julie, comes home late.

> 'Bill, I think it would be helpful if we role-played how you might use your new skills to cope better with Julie next time she comes home late. I realize that it may seem artificial acting the scene here. However, role-playing gives us the chance to rehearse different ways you might behave – your words, voice messages, and body messages – so that you are better prepared for the real event. It is safer to make mistakes here where it doesn't count for real. There is no substitute for learning by doing. What do you think about this approach?'

Set the scene

Trainees can elicit information about the physical setting of proposed scenes, what other characters are involved, and how they behave. If they are to role-play someone, for instance Julie, they should collect sufficient information about Julie's verbal, voice and body messages so that they can get into the role. Depending on what sort of office trainees have, they may be able to move the furniture around to create a 'stage', for instance a family living room.

Assess current communication/action skills

Trainees can usually spend time well if they conduct assessment role-plays in which clients demonstrate how they currently act in problem situations. They can elicit much relevant information about non-verbal communication that may not be apparent if clients only talk about how they communicate and act. Assessment role-plays can also reveal how clients think in situations.

Formulate changed communications/actions

Trainees can cooperate with clients to formulate new and better ways of communicating that both use targeted lifeskills and yet feel 'comfortable'. They should facilitate clients' contributions to the discussion prior to making you their own suggestions. For instance, they can ask: 'How might you use your new skills to behave differently in the situation?' Together with clients they can generate and review alternative scripts and appropriate voice and body messages. As part of this process trainees can demonstrate the different verbal, voice and body message components of appropriate communication and action skills. Trainees can also explore with clients how to cope with different responses by others.

Rehearse changed communications/actions

Once clients are reasonably clear about their new roles and counselling trainees understand their 'parts', trial enactments or rehearsals can take place. Trainees should avoid trying to do too much or anything too difficult too soon. They may allow role-plays to run their course. Alternatively, they may intervene at one or more points along the way to allow client self-assessment and provide feedback and coaching. Rehearsal role-plays are dry runs of how to use communication and skills in specific situations. Video feedback may be used as part of coaching both during and after role-plays. Trainees may require a number of rehearsals to build clients' skills. Some role-plays may involve responding in different ways to clients. For example, clients asking for dates may get accepted, postponed or rejected in separate role-plays.

Role reversal and mirroring are psychodrama techniques that counselling trainees may use (Blatner, 2005; Moreno, 1959). In role reversal, trainees get clients to play the other person in interactions. Role reversals force clients to get some way into another's internal viewpoint. With mirroring, trainees 'mirror back' clients' verbal, voice and body messages. Clients see themselves as others experience them.

Rehearse mind skills

Trainees may rehearse clients' mind skills alongside their communication/action skills. They can rehearse clients in the calming and coaching dimensions of appropriate self-talk to accompany new communication skills, as well as in other relevant mind skills.

Process role-plays

Processing involves spending time dealing with clients' thoughts and feelings generated by role-plays. Together counselling trainees and clients can discuss what has been learned, and make plans to transfer rehearsed skills to daily life. They can ask clients processing questions like: 'How were you feeling in that role-play?' 'How well do you think you used your skills in that rehearsal?' 'What have you learned in that role-play that is useful for real-life?' 'What difficulties do you anticipate in implementing your changed behaviour and how can you overcome them?' After processing the previous role-play, trainees and clients may move on to the next role-play either with the same or with another problem situation.

Case example: Louise Donovan

In Chapters 14 and 15, I mentioned using an open plan and how I might establish a second-session agenda with Louise Donovan, the client who was repeatedly having unsuccessful interviews for senior positions, when training her in interview skills. Here, I elaborate on how I rehearsed Louise in communication skills for job interviews. This training concurrently addressed the mind skills required by Louise to support her communication skills.

In restating Louise getting consistently bad feedback from job interviews problem in skills terms, her poor communication skills/goals were to develop good interview skills. In particular her poor communication skills/goals were: verbal messages – answers too long, unfocused and lecturing; voice messages – too booming and overpowering; and body messages – too stiff, eyes glaring, unsmiling (not user-friendly).

When building Louise's interview skills, Louise and I first developed a list of questions that she was likely to be asked or that might cause her difficulty. I wrote each question down as Louise suggested it. Illustrative questions were:

Why have you applied for this position?
Why did you leave your previous position?
How would you go about supplying leadership to professional accountants who work for this company?
What is your approach to the supervision of support staff?

Then, for assessment purposes, Louise and I conducted a cassette-recorded mini interview. When playing back this interview, I asked Louise to evaluate her skills and made some suggestions of my own. As a result of this assessment, I wrote six answering question rules on the whiteboard (these were also taken down by Louise):

1 Home in on questions by paraphrasing/repeating their crux/key words.
2 Place conclusion at front of answer.
3 Give reasons for conclusion in point form.
4 Be brief.
5 Voice messages – comfortable, avoid booming.
6 Body messages – smile, look relaxed, use some gestures – but not too many.

Leaving these rules clearly visible on the whiteboard, Louise and I then conducted a series of cassette-recorded mini interviews and played them back. Louise first monitored herself and then I provided her with feedback on her performance, and coaching to improve it. Louise rehearsed body as well as verbal and voice messages. These rehearsals, in which I represented an interview panel, took place in two subsequent sessions as well.

Louise was given the homework assignments of practising her interview skills in her present job (when interviewing clients and attending meetings) and listening to the most recent cassettes of her counselling session rehearsals. Later, I made Louise a homework cassette in which I relaxed her and guided her through the imagery of waiting outside an interview room, being called in, sitting down, and answering the first question competently, using all her rehearsed skills. I asked Louise to listen to this cassette a number of times to help the skills 'sink in'. Louise also now had a cassette available to help her rehearse the targeted skills in periods just before future interviews.

Activity 18.3 Developing role-playing and rehearsing skills

Conduct a session with a partner as 'client' in which you aim to help her/him use one or more targeted communication/action skills in a specific problem situation in her/his life. Conduct one or more role-play rehearsals of the targeted communication/action skills with your client using the following skills:

- explaining the reasons for role-playing;
- setting the scene;
- assessing current communications/actions;
- formulating changed communications/actions;
- rehearsing changed communications/actions;
- processing each role-play rehearsal; and
- encouraging your client to rehearse in her/his imagination competent performance of the communication/action skill(s) rehearsed in the counselling session.

Afterwards discuss and get feedback on your use of role-play rehearsal skills from your partner. Then reverse roles.

Timetable activities

Counsellors and trainees can work with clients to timetable desired activities and to build clients' skills in this area. How to assist clients in timetabling activities varies according to their needs.

Areas for timetabling

The following are some areas in which timetabling may help clients to perform desired activities and to build communication and action skills. Box 18.3 shows a blank weekly timetable that can serve numerous purposes.

Box 18.3 Weekly timetable

Date							
Time	Monday	Tuesday	Wednesday	Thursday	Friday	Saturday	Sunday
6.00							
7.00							
8.00							
9.00							
10.00							
11.00							
12.00							
1.00							
2.00							
3.00							
4.00							
5.00							
6.00							
7.00							
8.00							
9.00							
10.00							

Timetable daily activities

Beck and his colleagues (Beck and Emery, 1985; Beck et al., 1979; Beck and Weishaar, 2005) stress the usefulness of developing daily activity schedules for clients who are immobilized by depression and anxiety. Counsellors and clients collaborate to plan specific activities for one day at a time. These are recorded on a weekly timetable, with days represented by columns and hours represented by rows. As clients develop skills and confidence, they can do their own activity scheduling, with the last activity for one day being the scheduling of the following day. To ease pressure, trainees can instruct clients to state what rather than how much they will accomplish and to realize that it is OK not to complete all activities – the important thing is to try.

Timetable minimum goals

Some clients get extremely anxious about performing certain tasks and then engage in avoidance behaviour. For instance, Sue is a college student who is very distressed because she is not studying. She has lost all sense of control over her work. One approach to Sue is to assist her to timetable some minimum goals that she feels prepared to commit herself to keeping before the next session. Her minimum goals may be as little as three half-hour study periods during the week. For each study period, Sue needs to write down time, task and place. This does not mean that she cannot spend more time studying if she wishes. With certain highly anxious clients, counselling trainees need to be very sensitive to avoid becoming just another source of pressure. The idea of timetabling minimum goals is to show clients that they can be successful in achieving modest targets rather than large goals. Later on Sue may increase her study periods.

Timetable to create personal space

Many clients require timetabling skills to prioritize and create personal space. Such clients include housewives who are trying to stop being at everyone's beck and call, stressed executives who need to create family and relaxation time, depressed people who need to timetable more pleasant activities, and students who need to plan their study time so that they know when they can say 'yes' rather than 'no' to requests to go out. Trainees can assist clients to define personal space goals and to allocate time accordingly.

Timetable to keep contracts

Clients make commitments to perform certain activities, to themselves, to counsellors and to third parties, for instance their spouses. Trainees can help clients to develop skills of keeping commitments by getting them to timetable when they are going to carry out these activities. For instance, Todd is a teenager who has been resisting doing any of the household chores. He finally decides he is prepared to mow the lawn each week. Todd may be more likely to keep this commitment if he timetables when he is going to perform this task.

Timetable homework assignments

Certain homework assignment activities lend themselves to being timetabled at regular times: for instance, practising progressive muscular relaxation or planning an activity schedule for the next day. Other assignments do not lend themselves so easily to regular scheduling, but are more likely to be performed if clients timetable them. For instance, the homework assignments of Joan, an unemployed executive, include developing an effective résumé, a task she has avoided. Joan is more likely to complete this assignment and to develop résumé-making skills if she blocks out specific periods of time to do it properly.

Some skills for timetabling

As shown above, many reasons exist why counsellors, trainees and clients use timetabling. Below are some counsellor skills in using timetabling to develop communication and action skills.

- *Provide timetables.* Trainees should not expect clients to have easy access to made-up timetables or to make the effort to develop their own.
- *Offer reasons for timetabling.* For some clients the need to timetable activities and goals is obvious. Other clients require explanations. Trainees can tactfully challenge certain clients with the negative consequences of their failure to timetable.
- *Be sensitive to anxieties and resistances.* Timetabling can be very threatening to highly anxious clients – they feel failures if they do not do as agreed. Trainees need to be very sensitive about how much pressure timetabling creates for vulnerable clients. They should also be aware that a few clients may play timetabling games: either consciously or unconsciously they have little intention of keeping their commitments.
- *Do not overdo timetabling.* Even with less vulnerable clients, trainees may overdo timetabling. Clients can spend too much time scheduling activities and too little time carrying them out.
- *Review progress.* At the next session, trainees should check with clients on progress in adhering to timetabled activities and find out about any difficulties that they experienced.

- *Work with mind skills.* Often non-adherence to timetables shows that clients have one or more poor mind skills, for instance perfectionist rules about achievement. Trainees can identify and work with any relevant poor mind skills.
- *Help clients to develop timetabling skills.* Trainees should always work closely with clients to decide what goes in the timetable. Trainees can aim to help clients develop their own timetabling skills so that they can 'fade' from assisting them.

Activity 18.4 Developing timetabling skills

Part A: Thinking about timetabling

For each of the following areas, assess if, with what kinds of clients, and why you might use timetabling to develop communication/action skills:

- scheduling daily activities
- setting minimum goals
- creating personal space
- keeping contracts
- performing homework assignments

Part B: Helping a client to timetable

Conduct a counselling session with a partner as client. Your client has a communication/action skills weakness for which you decide that it will benefit her/him to use timetabling between sessions. Help your partner to timetable in the following ways:

- Provide the timetable.
- Offer reasons for timetabling.
- Be sensitive to anxieties and resistances.
- Ensure your client knows what to do.

Afterwards discuss the activity with your partner and obtain feedback on your use of skills when assisting timetabling. Then reverse roles.

interventions for communication and actions – 2

19

Chapter outcomes

By studying and doing the activities in this chapter you should:

- know about planning sub-goals and sequencing graded tasks;
- know about communication/action skills experiments:
- be introduced to designing activities and games;
- know some ways of using self-reward; and
- be introduced to using counsellor's aides.

Plan sub-goals and sequence graded tasks

When counsellors and trainees attempt to develop clients' communication and action skills, planning sub-goals and sequencing graded tasks overlap. Counselling trainees may plan sub-goals in two main ways.

Sequence sub-skills

When assisting clients to learn complex skills, counselling trainees can break the skills down into their component parts. Then they can decide in what order they wish to train the components. For example, William and his trainee, Chloe, have the overall goal of enabling William to make assertive requests to his boss, Jody. William and Chloe decide during their sessions to focus first on verbal messages, second on voice messages, third on body messages, and finally on putting all three messages together.

Sequence graded tasks

Sequencing graded tasks is sometimes called graded task assignment (Beck and Weishaar, 2005) or setting proximal sub-goals (Bandura, 1986). A useful distinction is that between setting distant and proximal or nearer goals. The research evidence is equivocal regarding the effectiveness of setting distant goals. More certain appears the desirability of setting proximal goals or sub-goals. Bandura observes that 'Subgoals provide present guides and inducements for action, while subgoal attainments produce efficacy information and self-satisfactions that sustain one's efforts along the way' (Bandura, 1986: 475).

The following is an example of sequencing graded tasks to develop communication skills.

Ricky is a shy college student with a communication skills goal of developing his dating skills. Together Ricky and his counsellor draw up a sequence of graded tasks that Ricky thinks he can complete before their next session:

1. Say 'hello' to the girls in my class when I see them on campus.
2. Sit down in the student union with a group of classmates of both sexes and join in the conversation.
3. Sit next to a girl in my class and initiate a very brief conversation in which I ask her what she thinks about the class.
4. Sit next to a girl in class and hold a slightly longer conversation in which I make a personal disclosure at least once.

Near the start of the next session, Ricky and his counsellor review progress in attaining each task. The counsellor encourages Ricky to share his thoughts and feelings about progress. The counsellor emphasizes that Ricky achieves his sub-goals as a result of his willingness to take risks, his effort and his skill. As a result of feedback Ricky gets both from others and gives himself about his growing skills, the counsellor and he develop further graded tasks for the next period between sessions. At progress reviews the counsellor rewards Ricky for working to develop his skills whether or not he is successful. For instance, when Ricky eventually asks a girl for a date, the counsellor will reward him, even if she refuses. The counsellor encourages Ricky to view as learning experiences all attempts to attain graded tasks.

Skills for sequencing and reviewing graded tasks

The following are some counsellor and trainee skills for sequencing and reviewing graded tasks.

Relate graded tasks to targeted skills

Always make links between tasks and skills. The purpose of graded tasks is not only to assist clients to manage specific problems, but also to help them develop specific skills. Encourage clients to view graded tasks as ways of developing skills for handling not just immediate but future problems.

Sequence graded tasks in cooperation with clients

Work with clients to assess whether they feel willing and able to work on graded tasks. Discuss with them the tasks that are important for them.

When sequencing tasks, go at a comfortable pace. Start with small steps that clients think they can achieve. Be prepared to build in intermediate steps if clients think the progression of tasks is too steep. As depicted in Box 19.1, graded tasks should be stepping-stones for clients to develop skills and confidence.

Box 19.1 Graded tasks as stepping-stones for developing skills and confidence

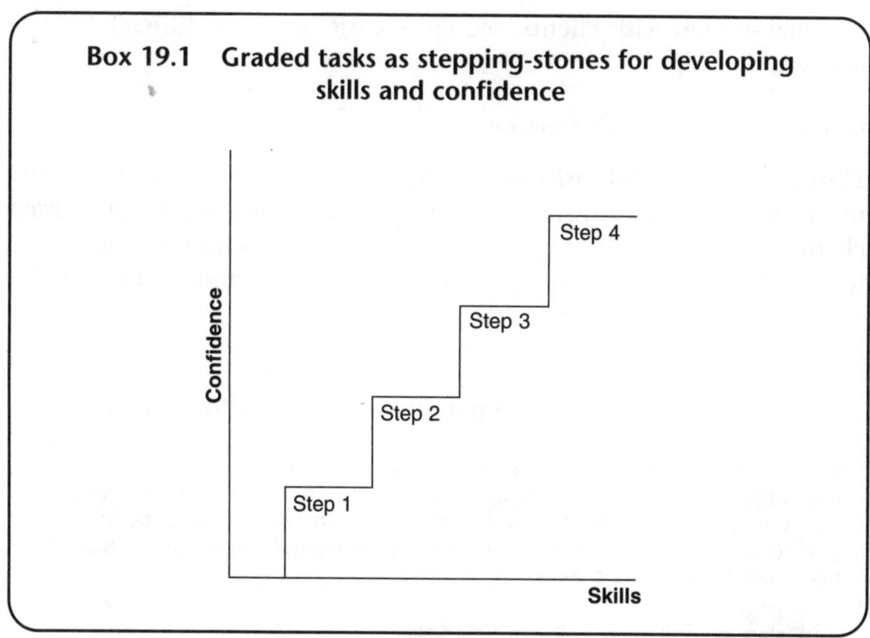

Encourage realistic evaluation of skills

Before they attempt graded tasks, encourage clients to assess what skills they need to attain them. When reviewing progress, help clients to evaluate their use of targeted skills.

Encourage clients to view themselves as practitioner-researchers

To avoid connotations of failure, encourage clients to view each task as an experiment in which they gain valuable information about themselves. Even if they are unsuccessful, attempting tasks provides clients with useful learning experiences about how they think, feel and act.

Pay attention to feelings and thoughts

Help clients to share feelings and thoughts about attempting graded tasks. Where necessary, work with clients' poor mind skills.

Assist clients to own successes

Encourage clients not only to acknowledge their successes, but also to realize that success results from willingness to take risks, expending effort and using targeted skills.

Sequence new and different tasks as appropriate

In collaboration with clients, sequence easier or more difficult tasks as necessary.

Encourage homework and practice

Though some graded tasks are performed within counselling sessions, most are performed outside of counselling. Where feasible, encourage clients to rehearse and practise graded tasks before trying them. Repeated success in specific tasks consolidates skills and confidence.

Activity 19.1 Arranging a graded task plan for a client

Conduct a counselling session with a partner as a 'client' with the goal of developing a specific communication/action skills strength. You decide that the best way to help your client is for her/him to work through a sequence of graded tasks between sessions. Sequence progressively more difficult graded tasks using the following skills:

- Relate graded tasks to the targeted skill.
- Sequence graded tasks in cooperation with the client.
- Encourage realistic assessment of existing skills.
- Encourage the client to adopt a practitioner-researcher approach.
- Pay attention to feelings and thoughts.
- Encourage homework and practice.

Afterwards discuss your counselling session with your client, including obtaining feedback on your skills in assisting sequencing of graded tasks. Then reverse roles.

Assist clients to use changing communication/action skills experiments

A major concern of all skilled counsellors is how best to help clients take the risks of changing how they behave. Another major concern is how best to help them transfer trained skills to their worlds outside of the counselling room. Communication and action skills experiments provide an excellent way to approach both concerns. Clients in conjunction with counselling trainees can hypothesize about the consequences of using outside the skills they learn inside the counselling room. Then clients implement the skills and evaluate the consequences of their changed behaviour.

An advantage of viewing changing communication and action skills in experimental terms is that it helps clients to be detached about what they do and its results. When experiments do not work out quite as planned, clients do not have to think they have failed. Rather, each experiment can be seen as a learning experience.

Often experiments simultaneously focus on changing both mind skills and communication/action skills. For instance, Dang wants to increase his skills at showing affection to his girlfriend, Kylie. An experiment focused solely on communication skills might target improving Dang's verbal, vocal and bodily communication skills of showing affection. An experiment focused solely on mind skills might target Dang's skills of creating more helpful self-talk before, during and after he communicates affection. An experiment focused on both types of skill would target improving both. In this section, for the sake of simplicity, I focus solely on designing and implementing experiments for changing communication/action skills.

Steps in communication/action skills experiments

Experiments focus on the use of targeted skills in specific situations or relationships. There are six main steps in designing, conducting and evaluating communication/action skills experiments.

1 *Assess.* Counselling trainees collaborate with clients to assess their good and poor communication/action skills in problem situations.
2 *Formulate changed communication/action skills.* Trainees and clients work out how to behave differently in situations by using improved skills, paying attention to vocal and bodily as well as verbal communication.
3 *Make an 'If ... then ... ' statement.* The 'If' part of the statement relates to clients rehearsing, practising and then using their changed skills. The 'then ... ' part indicates the specific consequences they predict will follow from using their changed skills.
4 *Rehearse and practice.* Probably with assistance from their counselling trainees, clients need to rehearse and practice their changed skills if they are to have a reasonable chance of implementing them properly outside of counselling.
5 *Try out changed communication and action skills.* Clients implement changed skills in actual problem situations.

6 *Evaluate*. Initially clients should evaluate their use of changed skills on their own. This evaluation should focus on questions like: 'How well did I use my changed skills?' 'What were the positive and negative consequences of using the targeted skills for myself and for others?' 'Have my predictions been confirmed or negated?' 'Do I want to use my changed skills in future?' Afterwards trainees can assist clients in processing what they learned from their experiments. Some clients may just require encouragement to keep persisting in their changed behaviours, while others may require additional rehearsing. Sometimes, trainees and clients may decide to modify the client's use of these skills.

Box 19.2 Provides an example of designing a communication skills experiment.

Box 19.2 Example of designing a communication skills experiment

In this outline for an experiment, Dang addresses the question: 'What happens when I use improved communication skills to express affection to Kylie?'

Part A: Assessment

1 For a period of a week, monitor on a worksheet how I communicate affection to Kylie. Focus on strengths and deficiencies in each of the following sub-skills of expressing affection: verbal, vocal, bodily, touch and action-taking communication. Use the following column headings on my worksheet.

Situation (What? When? Where?)	Expressing affection communication (Verbal, vocal, bodily, touch, action)

2 List all the positive thoughts and feelings that I either fail to or inadequately convey in our relationship.

___

___

___

___

3 Based on the answers to questions 1 and 2 above, assess my good and poor communication skills in expressing affection to Kylie.

Expressing affection to Kylie (my good skills)	Expressing affection to Kylie (my poor skills)

Part B: Make an 'If … then … ' statement

Make an 'If … then' statement along the lines:

'**If** I use the following changed communication skills [specify] to express affection to Kylie during the next week, **then** these specific consequences are likely to follow' [for instance, (a) I will feel better about myself for being honest, and (b) Kylie will feel and act more positively toward me].

If______________________________________

____

then

(a)______________________________________

(b)______________________________________

(c)______________________________________

(d)______________________________________

Part C: Implement and evaluate using my changed communication skills

During the coming week, try out my changed communication skills in expressing affection to Kylie. What are the positive and negative consequences for Kylie and me? Have my predictions been confirmed or negated? Have I learned anything useful from this experiment? If so, what?

____

____

____

____

Activity 19.2 Designing a changing communication skills experiment

Review the section of this chapter on assisting clients to use changing communications and actions experiments. Collaborate with a partner who acts as client to design an experiment in which she/he will try out changing how she/he communicates for a specified period of time. Together you conduct the first four steps involved in designing, conducting and evaluating experiments:

- Assess.
- Formulate changed communication skills.
- Make an 'If ... then ... ' statement.
- Rehearse and practice.

Afterwards, discuss and reverse roles.

Use activities and games

Activities are structured exercises designed with a specific learning purpose. This book contains numerous activities that I designed to build readers' lifeskills counselling skills. Whether for children or adults, activities involving play are called *games*. Counselling trainees may help clients to develop communication/action skills, mind skills and communication/action skills with accompanying self-talk by using activities and games. Clients may use these materials both within counselling sessions and also as take-away assignments.

There are two main sources of activities and games: using other people's or making up one's own. In the relationship skills area, for example, numerous books contain activities – for example, Johnson's *Reaching Out: Interpersonal Effectiveness and Self-actualization* (2002). However, other people's material may not be appropriate either for the clientele or for specific clients with whom counselling trainees work. If so they may need to construct some activities. These are particularly cost-effective if they can be used repeatedly. For instance, trainees who work with clients, many of whom have relationship difficulties, might often use activities about how to make assertive requests to change others' behaviours. I encourage readers not only to use existing material, but also to tap their creativity in designing learning material tailor-made to their clients' needs.

Design activities

The following are guidelines for designing activities and games.

- *Set clear, specific and relevant goals.* Clients should be clear about the targeted skills they are expected to work on in the activity.
- *Emphasize homework skills.* Activities should be highly practical and focused on learning by doing. Avoid vague activities unrelated to the

development of specific skills. Many counselling trainees start by designing activities that are insufficiently practical.

- *Make written instructions available.* Ensure that clients are clear about and remember an activity's instructions. Written instructions lessen the chance of slippage when clients perform activities.
- *Demonstrate the activity.* Demonstrate activities between giving instructions and asking clients to perform them. Such demonstrations go beyond demonstrating skills or sub-skills to show how to do the activity.
- *Coach and provide feedback.* Where necessary, coach clients on how to do the activity.
- *Process the experience.* When clients have completed the activity, give them the opportunity to share their thoughts and feelings about it. Ensure that they understand the main points to be learned from the activity.
- *Pilot activities.* If possible, trainees should pilot activities to see if they work. If necessary, refine activities or even discard them and try again.

Activity 19.3 Designing an activity or game

Part A: Designing an activity and developing written instructions

Design an activity or game you can use for helping either individuals or couples with whom you either currently work or would like to work. Use the following skills:

- Set clear, specific and relevant goals.
- Emphasize 'doing it on your own' skills.
- Write out a set of instructions to give as a handout to the client or clients covering the following points:

  (a) goal of activity or game
  (b) main learning points
  (c) instructions for each step of the activity or game

Part B: Counselling a client using an activity or game

Work with a partner who acts as a client typical of those for whom you have designed the activity in Part A above. Demonstrate how to do the activity and, if necessary, coach the client not only in the targeted skills but also in how to do your particular activity. Afterwards discuss and obtain feedback on your 'designing and presenting an activity or game' skills. Then reverse roles.

Assist clients to use self-reward skills

Counsellors and trainees may choose to use reinforcement or reward to help develop communication/action skills. Such rewards include praise, encouragement, smiles and nods. However, ultimately clients have to learn to perform targeted communication/action skills independent of their counsellors' rewards so they may also influence and administer their own rewards. Approaches to using counsellor-administered and client-administered rewards are based on operant conditioning (Skinner, 1953, 1969). The word 'operant' emphasizes the fact that behaviour operates on the environment to produce consequences as well as being influenced by or contingent upon that environment. When clients find responses to their improved communication/action skills rewarding, the probability of their using these skills again increases, but the reverse is also true.

Basic concepts concerning rewards

Here, I use the everyday word 'reward' in preference to the more technical term 'reinforcement'. Reward better suits the language of self-helping. Some basic reward concepts are listed below.

- *Positive reward.* This entails presenting stimuli that increase the probability of responses occurring: for example, money increases the probability of work responses. Positive rewards can be verbal, material and in the imagination.
- *Negative reward.* This increases the probability of a response occurring by removing something from the situation: for example a loud noise, a very bright light, extreme heat or cold, or electric shock. Negative reward is distinguished from punishment. Sometimes punishment can increase rather than lessen the probability of a response, whereas negative reward always increases the probability.
- *Contingencies of reward.* To consider adequately the contingencies or circumstances involved in the provision of rewards, counselling trainees and clients should take into account: (1) the occasion upon which a response occurs; (2) the response itself; (3) the rewarding consequences.
- *Schedules of reward.* Basically there are three main reward schedules: reward each response; do not reward any response; and intermittently reward responses. Intermittent rewards can be very powerful: for instance they can strongly help to sustain gambling behaviour.
- *Self-reward.* Here clients influence how they act by administering their own rewards.

- *Prompting and fading.* Prompts are verbal, physical or environmental cues that direct clients' attention to desired actions. Fading entails progressively eliminating prompts.
- *Shaping.* Communication/action skills may be shaped by rewarding successive approximations to targeted goals – for example, breaking an assertive response down and rewarding clients as they successfully enact progressively more difficult parts of the response and/or as they learn to use the response in progressively more difficult situations.
- *Covert conditioning.* Using clients' imaginations to envisage the consequences of varying degrees of reward. For example, getting a client to imagine doing a task or part of a task successfully and then to imagine receiving a reward for so doing.

Identify suitable rewards

In many instances, clients find the use of targeted communication/action skills intrinsically rewarding. They discover, too, that they bring about rewards from others. For instance, clients who use their improved expressing appreciation skills may enjoy giving and receiving pleasure. On other occasions clients may need to strengthen their motivation by self-administering rewards. The basic idea in using self-reward to improve communication and action skills is that clients make the administration of rewards contingent upon the implementation of target behaviours (Watson and Tharp, 2001). Rewards should be accessible and potent (Cormier and Nurius, 2002). Counselling trainees may need to assist clients in identifying suitable rewards. There are several ways of doing this, including asking them directly, getting them to monitor what they find rewarding, asking others who know them, while being sensitive to issues of confidentiality, observing them, and asking them to fill out reward questionnaires.

Some self-report questionnaires exist for assessing rewards. Cautela (1967a) has devised a 'Reinforcement Survey Schedule' to identify possible reinforcing stimuli together with their relative values. Another self-report questionnaire is MacPhillamy and Lewinsohn's 'Pleasant Events Schedule' (Lewinsohn et al., 1986; MacPhillamy and Lewinsohn, 1971). This instrument consists of 320 events and activities generated after an extensive search of possible 'pleasant events'. Subjects rate each item in the schedule on a five-point scale of pleasantness. A shortened version of the 'Pleasant Events Schedule' has been derived from 49 items associated with improved mood for a substantial proportion of people.

For children, pictures may portray rewards. An example is Daley's 'Reinforcement Menu' for finding effective rewards for 8-year-old to 11-year-old mentally retarded children (Daley, 1969). Daley enclosed 22 high-probability rewarding activities drawn in colour in a single book or 'menu' with one activity per page. Children identified rewarding activities from the 'menu' book.

Assist clients to deliver self-rewards

Counselling trainees can assist clients in learning how to deliver positive self-rewards. There are two main categories of reward that clients can self-administer: external and internal.

- *External reward* includes (1) self-administration of new rewards that are outside the client's everyday life, such as a new item of clothing or a special event, and (2) initial denial of some pleasant everyday experience and later administration of it once a desired action has been carried out. Wherever possible a positive self-reward should be relevant to the targeted goals: for instance clients achieving weight loss goals can reward themselves by buying slimmer fitting clothes.
- *Internal reward* includes self-talk statements like 'That's great', 'I did it', or 'Well done' that clearly indicate the client's satisfaction at performing a sub-goal or goal. Clients can also use their imagination to visualize significant others praising their efforts.

Counselling trainees can collaborate with clients to determine the precise conditions for administering rewards to themselves as they work to improve their communication and action skills. In making positive self-reward plans, pertinent considerations can include identifying rewards, sequencing progressive tasks, and making the connections between achievements and rewards very clear. Clients should know that, in general, it is best that they reward themselves either immediately or shortly after performing targeted action skills or sub-skills.

Trainees can encourage clients to draw up contracts that specify the relationship between self-rewards and developing targeted skills. Contracts should establish clear-cut criteria for achievement and specify the means whereby behaviour is observed, measured and recorded. Contracts can be unilateral or bilateral. In unilateral contracts clients commit themselves to personal change programmes independent of contributions from others. Bilateral contracts, which are commonly used in relationship counselling, stipulate obligations and rewards for each of the parties. For example, partners can contract with one another to increase their exchange of caring behaviours for a specified time period.

Not all clients like self-reward plans or follow them. Some consider the use of self-reward too mechanical. Furthermore, counselling trainees may introduce self-reward ideas too soon, before clients are sufficiently motivated to change. Trainees should assess how well clients accept the idea of self-reward and their motivation for change. Often trainees and clients also need to work with one or more of the poor mind skills by which clients sabotage their capacity to change.

Stimulus control

Thoresen and Mahoney (1974) indicate that there are two general self-control strategies that clients can use to influence their actions. First, they can try modifying their environments to control target actions *prior to* their execution. Second, they can self-administer a reward *following* or *contingent upon* an action or series of actions that achieves either a goal or a sub-goal.

Counselling trainees can assist clients to use stimulus control as one form of environmental modification. This entails either modifying in advance the stimuli or cues associated with maladaptive responses and/or establishing cues associated with adaptive responses. If we take the earlier example (on p. 313) of Thomas, 48, who is badly overweight and recovering from a minor heart attack, the following are some ways in which a medical counsellor can suggest that, as part of his weight reduction programme, he modify his environment to control his food intake: ensuring that food is placed out of sight and easy reach, equipping his refrigerator with a time lock, only keeping as much food in the house as can be consumed in a short period of time, and, where appropriate, avoiding contact with people he associates with excessive eating.

Stimulus control can also be used to enhance adaptive actions. For example, students can learn to associate their desks with work if they use them only for that purpose. Morawetz (1989) uses stimulus control in treating sleep disorders by having insomniac clients only associate their beds with sleep.

Self-punishment

So far I have mainly emphasized positive self-reward and stimulus control. However, though less frequently used, counselling trainees can encourage clients to self-administer aversive consequences. For example, weight-loss programme clients can give to charity a specified sum of money for every 100 calories in excess of a daily intake limit or they can present themselves with a noxious odour after each extra snack (Thoresen and Mahoney, 1974).

Ellis uses self-administered penalties as one of the behavioural interventions in rational emotive behaviour therapy (Ellis and MacLaren, 1998). For example, when Ted was attempting to give up smoking he accepted the penalty of writing out a $20 cheque to tobacco lobbyists each time he did not complete his homework assignment. Another example is that of Barbara, whose penalty was to call up a boring and obnoxious acquaintance and converse with her for 20 minutes each time she failed to comply with a mutually agreed homework assignment. When clients use penalties as well as rewards, they can receive a 'double whammy' if they fail to complete targeted communications and actions in that they must self-administer the penalty *and* forgo the reward.

Covert sensitization

Often clients who engage in negative communications/actions deny or rationalize the negative consequences of their behaviour. Counselling trainees can help clients to gain greater awareness of the consequences of such communications/actions. Covert sensitization, sometimes known as covert conditioning, is an intervention for stopping or lessening clients' unwanted behaviours (Cautela, 1967b). Here counsellors administer and help clients to self-administer aversive consequences in their imagination: for instance imagining the sight and smell of puking all over themselves if they eat a piece of chocolate cake.

Activity 19.4 Assisting a client to use self-reward

Conduct a counselling session with a partner in which together you design a plan for helping her/him use self-reward to improve a specific communication skill. Your plan should contain the following elements:

- an overall goal;
- a sequence of at least three graded steps to develop the communication skill;
- what reward(s) the client intends using;
- the precise conditions for self-administering reward(s); and
- a time frame.

Afterwards discuss and obtain feedback on your counselling skills. Then reverse roles.

Use counsellor's aides and help clients to obtain support

Counselling trainees can both use third parties to develop clients' action skills and also assist clients to identify and use third parties to support change attempts.

Use counsellor's aides

Reasons why counsellors and trainees may enlist others as aides include pressure of work and the opportunity to extend interventions into clients' home environments. Counselling trainees may use a variety of people as aides: teachers, parents, paraprofessionals, supervisors and friends. Here are two examples:

> Rudy, aged 8, is referred by his teacher, Rob, to Pat, the school counsellor, because he is very shy and does not participate in class. As part of Rudy's treatment plan, Pat enlists Rob's help both to ask questions that draw Rudy out and also to reward him when he participates in class. In addition, Pat asks Rob to monitor any changes in how well Rudy relates to the other children in the playground.
>
> Rachel, 21, volunteers to be a student paraprofessional 'companion therapist' in a programme to support anorexic and bulimic fellow students undergoing professional treatment at the university counselling service (Lenihan and Kirk, 1990). Rachel undergoes a 25-hour training program. She then maintains daily personal or phone contact with her allocated client. In addition, she engages in such activities as joint exercise, walking and lunching. Rachel also helps her client monitor nutrition and assists with meal planning and shopping.

The following are some skills for selecting and using counsellor's aides.

Identify suitable aides

Carefully select and screen counsellor's aides. They have the potential to do harm as well as good.

Obtain client permission

It is always essential to obtain adult clients' permission to discuss their behaviour with 'non-professional' third parties. Clients need to recognize and accept the potential usefulness of counsellor's aides if they are to work with them. Sometimes it may be inappropriate to obtain children's permission: for instance, in the above example of Rudy's teacher helping him.

Involve aides in planning interventions

Counsellor's aides such as teachers, parents and supervisors may have special knowledge of how best to support clients in developing communication skills. Furthermore, if consulted, aides may be more motivated to participate in treatment plans than if they think plans are imposed on them.

Train aides

Some counsellor's aides work with many different clients. Where this is the case, effort put into training them may reap rich rewards. Even where aides work with single clients, it is essential that they understand their roles and can carry them out competently.

Support and debrief aides

Keep in touch with aides and make sure that they perform their functions as agreed. Give them the opportunity to share thoughts and feelings about clients and about their contribution to treatment programmes. Where necessary, revise agreements on how your aides should assist.

Withdraw or fade counsellor's aide assistance

Clients need to learn how to perform communication skills without others' assistance. Consider how best to withdraw an aide's assistance. One option is to withdraw all assistance at once. Another option is to progressively withdraw or fade assistance.

Assist clients to identify and use supports and resources

Counselling trainees may need to raise some clients' awareness about the importance of identifying and using supports and of lessening contact with unsupportive people. Trainees and clients can work together to identify people in home environments who can support a client's efforts to develop targeted skills. For example, university students with poor study skills can seek out sympathetic lecturers and tutors to help them develop specific skills, for instance how to write essays or prepare for examinations. Unemployed people can approach friends and relatives who may not only offer them emotional support, but also be sources for job leads. Women working on developing assertiveness skills can seek out women's groups where they may find others with similar objectives. Those in business who feel burnt out can associate with colleagues who are relatively happy with their lot rather than those who perpetually complain. Furthermore, they can develop self-care skills by engaging in recreational activities with people unconnected with work.

An inverse approach to support is for counselling trainees and clients to identify unsympathetic or counter-productive people. Clients are then left with various choices: getting such people to accept, if not support, their efforts to change; seeing less of them; or stopping seeing them altogether. If these people are family members, avoiding them altogether may be difficult, especially if clients are financially dependent on them. Here, trainees and clients may discuss damage control strategies. However, clients can often choose their friendship and membership groups. For example, if juvenile delinquents want to develop communication skills that integrate them into the wider community, they may need to change the company they keep.

Counselling trainees can also assist clients to identify and use resources for helping them attain and maintain communication/action skills goals. Such resources include workshops and short courses, self-help books and manuals, instructional audio cassettes, videotapes and CD-ROMs, appropriate voluntary agencies, peer support groups and networks, telephone hot-lines and crisis information outlets.

Trainees should familiarize themselves, and establish contact, with the human supports and educational and information resources of most relevance to the client populations with which they work. Access to suitable supports and resources may be of tremendous assistance to some clients as they take positive steps towards changing how they communicate and act in problem areas.

interventions for feelings 20

Chapter outcomes

By studying and doing the activities in this chapter you should:

- understand the difference between assisting clients to experience, express and manage their feelings;
- improve clients' skills at experiencing their feelings;
- improve clients' skills at expressing their feelings;
- improve clients' skills at managing their feelings; and
- be introduced to the use of medication in counselling.

Introduction

The lifeskills counselling approach attaches great importance to influencing clients' feelings and physical reactions so that their underlying biological nature works for them rather than against them. All clients' problems involve feelings in one way or another. This chapter builds on the previous chapters by showing how to influence the way clients feel by intervening with their mind skills and communication/action skills. The topic of feelings is complex. I have subdivided it into three main areas: experiencing feelings; expressing feelings; and managing negative feelings. Box 20.1 depicts the interrelationships of these areas. The chapter also briefly reviews the use of medication in conjunction with counselling.

Box 20.1 Interrelationships of experiencing, expressing and managing feelings

Broadly speaking, counsellors and trainees can take two main approaches to clients' feelings. First, there is the *facilitative approach* in which they use active listening skills to help clients experience, disclose and explore feelings. They assume that if clients truly experience their significant feelings and self-actualizing drives they think rationally and act appropriately. Second, there is the *training approach* in which they use training skills to help clients to make better choices in how they feel. The facilitative approach emphasizes experiencing feelings; whereas the training approach emphasizes expressing and managing feelings. Rogers's person-centred therapy, and cognitive-behavioural therapy are prime examples of the facilitative and training approaches, respectively.

Lifeskills counselling draws on both approaches to feelings. Lifeskills counsellors flexibly use both helping relationship and training skills to assist clients to experience, express and manage feelings (see Box 20.2).

Box 20.2 Clients with problems experiencing, expressing and managing feelings

Experiencing feelings
Dave, 27, feels emotionally flat much of the time. He seems not to know what he wants to do with his life.

Expressing feelings
Hannah, 31, is in a relationship that is heading for the rocks. She has great difficulty expressing both positive and negative feelings to her boyfriend, Julian.

Managing feelings
Paul, 43, is the boss of a factory with huge staff morale problems. Over the past few weeks, Paul has been getting increasingly tense, anxious and depressed about his work and life.

Assist clients to experience feelings

Experiencing feelings has at least three dimensions. First, clients need the actual sensation of experiencing feelings rather than blocking them off or distorting them. Second, clients require the skills of exploring feelings and of following feelings trails to see where they lead. Clients can gain useful insights from getting in touch with their wants, desires and wishes. Third, clients require the skill of labelling feelings accurately. The following are some interventions to enable clients to improve these three skills.

Encourage clients to acknowledge feelings and physical reactions

Counsellors and trainees can help some clients if they legitimize the importance of focusing on feelings. How they do this depends upon the needs of individual clients. Let's take the example of Jude, a 17-year-old, whose school counsellor, Helen, discovers that he relies on others' thoughts and feelings to guide his choice of university and course. Here, Helen has a number of choices, albeit not mutually exclusive. She can keep using active listening skills in the hope that Jude will become more inner than outer directed. Or she can challenge him along the lines of: 'Jude, you seem to be saying a lot about what your parents and teachers want for you, but I'm wondering what *you* think and feel about *your* choice of university and course?' Note the emphasis on you and your. She can also suggest to Jude that he takes an occupational interest inventory to assist self-exploration. And she can offer Jude reasons for acknowledging his own feelings more fully.

> 'Jude, you seem to say a lot about what your parents and teachers want for you. However, I get the impression that you inadequately attend to *your* feelings about what *you* want to do. Though not the only source, your feelings can provide you with a rich source of information about what might be the right choices for you. Learning to acknowledge and listen to your feelings is a skill. If you inadequately listen to your feelings, you risk making choices that you may later regret. I think you need to improve your skills of listening more to your feelings and inner voices. What do you think?'

Explaining reasons for focusing on feelings may lead to a discussion with clients about how much they think they are in touch with feelings and their fears about expressing them. As an intervention for aiding emotional responsiveness, it needs to be accompanied by other interventions. However, explaining reasons may encourage some clients to take feelings more seriously as a basis for future work on becoming more emotionally literate.

Another approach is to assist those who are either showing moderately strong feelings or may have strong feelings near the surface to experience these feelings more intensely. The counsellor 'openly and directly welcomes, encourages, appreciates, lauds, enjoys, or is pleased with the client's undergoing of strong feelings' (Mahrer et al., 1999: 43). Such strong feelings include defiance, anger, laughter and love.

Related to acknowledging feelings, counselling trainees can also stress the importance of clients improving their skills at tuning into their bodies and listening to their physical reactions. Take the examples of workaholic students or stressed executives who fail to listen to the messages they are receiving from their bodies and so risk psychological or physical breakdown of one sort or another. Another example is that of helping service professionals who fail to tune into their physical and mental exhaustion, suffer from burnout, and are less helpful to clients than they might otherwise have been.

Improve mind skills

Counselling trainees can assist clients to improve the mind skills that are conducive to experiencing feelings. The following illustrations are of poor mind skills that can block or interfere with clients' experiencing feelings and physical reactions. Readers can turn to the previous two chapters on how to help clients to improve these mind skills.

- *Creating rules.* Clients can possess demanding rules that get in the way of experiencing feelings. Examples of such rules are: 'I must never have strong feelings', 'Christians [or members of any other religion] must always be self-effacing', 'I must not have strong sexual feelings because they are dirty and animal', and 'I must never acknowledge that I deeply care for another person.' Trainees can assist clients to detect rules unhelpful to experiencing feelings and dispute and restate them as more realistic rules.
- *Creating perceptions.* Clients have much more choice in how they feel than most of them realize. Trainees can enable clients to make links between how they perceive and how they feel. Clients can learn not to restrict themselves to the first feeling they experience. Instead they can generate and evaluate alternative perceptions that in turn lead to alternative feelings. Clients can then choose the 'best fit' perceptions and feelings. Trainees can also help clients to feel less negatively about themselves and others. Searching for strengths in oneself and in others is one skill for attaining this outcome.
- *Creating self-talk.* Clients can talk to themselves in ways that enhance their capacity to get in touch with feelings. They may make calming self-statements like 'Relax', 'Calm down', 'Take a deep breath.' In addition, they can make coaching self-statements, like: 'Let's clear a space to truly get in touch with what I feel', 'Remember, my feelings are important and I need to spend time getting in touch with them', or 'Don't rush into a decision, let's feel and think this one through.' Furthermore, clients can make affirming self-statements, for example: 'I have a right to acknowledge my feelings' and 'My feelings are important.' Often calming, coaching and affirming self-statements can be combined: 'Relax. Take time to get in touch with how I feel about this. My feelings are important.'

- *Creating visual images.* Counselling trainees can elicit current feelings and also the experiencing of past feelings by asking clients to visualize the situations in which they occurred. They can also use visualizing to help clients experience feelings about the future, for instance taking them through a guided imagery about getting married or moving house. Trainees can enhance clients' feelings of competence by getting them to visualize themselves performing competently.
- *Creating explanations.* Counselling trainees can help clients to explain more accurately how they create their feelings. For instance, depressed clients may attribute the cause of all negative events to themselves (Beck, 1991; Beck and Weishaar, 2005). Challenging these explanations may help such clients to feel better. Others may project negative feelings about themselves on to others – for instance, jealous clients who are hypersensitive about another's jealousy may require help in getting more in touch with how they truly feel.
- *Creating expectations.* Disorders of expectation permeate how people experience negative emotions and fail to experience genuinely positive feelings. For example, distorted expectations of hopelessness and pessimism play a large part in depression (Beck and Weishaar, 2005; Seligman, 1991). Unrealistic expectations of physical or psychological danger characterize clients suffering from anxiety disorders.

Train clients in inner listening

So far in this book I have emphasized the need for counsellors to be rewarding listeners to clients. However clients also need to develop skills of being rewarding listeners to themselves. They need to become aware of, experience, explore and label their own feelings. Assuming clients have a moderate degree of insight, one can teach inner listening as a self-helping skill.

The following are elements of inner listening training.

Explain reasons for focusing on inner listening

Assist clients to realize that this is a useful skill for understanding both themselves and others. Clarify what experiencing feelings, exploring them, and labelling them accurately means.

Stress creating sufficient time and psychological space

To practise inner listening, clients must give it sufficient priority in their lives. This may mean that they spend a certain amount of time with themselves each day or that they make sure that they clear a space when something bothers them or needs deciding.

Present and demonstrate the skill

Much of the active listening material in Chapters 6 and 7 is relevant here, but with modification. For instance, the concept of internal frame of reference in this context becomes that of getting inside one's own rather than another's internal viewpoint. In inner listening, it is vital that clients tune into feelings, flow with them, try to understand their messages and label them accurately. Counselling trainees may help clients to understand the skill if they demonstrate it by verbalizing their feelings and thoughts when attempting to listen to themselves.

Coach and negotiate homework assignments

Coach clients to ensure that they understand the skill of inner listening. Homework assignments, in which clients practise the component parts of the skill, act as a bridge between counselling and clients relying on their own resources.

Use feelings and physical reactions questions

Counselling trainees can use feelings questions to encourage clients to experience and share feelings and physical reactions. Be careful not to get clients talking about feelings in distant ways rather than experiencing them. Another danger is that clients will respond to counsellors rather than get in touch with themselves. However, if skilfully used, feelings questions can give clients useful practice in listening to and becoming more aware of their feelings. Feelings and physical reactions questions and statements include:

- 'How do you feel about that?'
- 'What is the emotional impact of that on you?'
- 'Could you describe your feelings more fully?'
- 'I'm hearing that you're feeling ... ?'
- 'You seem to have conflicting feelings. On the one hand ... , on the other hand ... ?'
- 'What are your physical reactions?'
- 'How does your body experience the feeling?'

Be authentic and appropriately self-disclose

The ability of counsellors to be real is very important in aiding clients to experience feelings. Rogers used terms like 'congruence' and 'genuineness'

(Rogers, 1957, 1975). Existential psychologists use terms like 'presence' and 'authenticity' (Bugental, 1981; May and Yalom, 2005). Bugental views presence as consisting of an intake side called accessibility, allowing what happens in situations to affect one, and an output side called expressiveness, making available some of the content of one's subjective awareness without editing. If one is alive and present in relating to clients one demonstrates experiencing feelings and creates the climate for them to do so too. Clients may perceive counsellors who are able to experience and express feelings and share personal information as more similar to themselves (Edwards and Murdock, 1994). Showing involvement and sharing information may make it easier for clients to experience feelings: for instance, feminist counsellors with women clients, gay counsellors with gay clients, and former drug addicts with substance abuse clients.

Challenge inauthenticity

Counselling trainees can use their here-and-now experiencing as guides to whether clients communicate what they really think and feel. Clients may wear masks and play roles that interfere with their experiencing and expressing what they truly feel. Such roles include playing the clown, playing dumb or playing helpless. Trainees may make clients aware of such tendencies: for example, 'I get the impression that whenever you get close to your deeper feelings, you use humour to avoid revealing them.' Trainees can also challenge clients who externalize their own feelings by projecting them on to others. In addition, trainees can challenge inconsistencies between verbal, voice and body messages. For instance: 'You say you don't feel hurt by his behaviour, yet you speak with a sad tone of voice and your eyes seem weepy.'

Use role-play methods

In Chapter 18 I discussed role-play as a method of rehearsing action skills. Role-plays can also be used to allow clients to experience feelings. Role-play methods can be powerful ways of releasing and exploring feelings in various kinds of personal relationship, past, present or future. This unburdening may in turn generate further self-exploration and deeper understandings of underlying feelings. Clients may play both people in a relationship either by visualizing with eyes closed or by switching chairs as they play each part. Alternatively, counselling trainees may play one of the parts in the relationship, for example a parent, spouse, boyfriend or girlfriend. In role reversal, trainees and clients switch roles. Trainees may heighten clients' awareness by mirroring their feelings-related verbal, voice and body messages. After, as well as during, role-plays, they can enable clients to experience, articulate and explore feelings uncovered by and associated with what happens.

Use empty chair dialogue

The resolution of 'unfinished business' can be a key task in counselling. Unfinished business refers to lingering negative feelings towards significant others. If unresolved, these may contribute to anxiety and depression, and be transferred into other relationships where they are inappropriate. Drawing on Gestalt therapy's empty chair technique (Perls et al., 1951), Greenberg and his colleagues have devised an empty-chair dialogue intervention (Greenberg et al., 1993). This intervention, 'in which the client engages in an imaginary dialogue with the significant other, is designed to access restricted feelings allowing them to run their course and be restructured in the safety of the therapy environment' (Pavio and Greenberg, 1995: 419).

The empty chair dialogue technique, which can be used in individual or group work, helps clients experience feelings both of unresolved anger and also of weakness and victimization. During the successful application of the intervention, clients feel a greater sense of self-empowerment. Clients either view the significant other with greater understanding or hold them accountable for harm. Some promising research findings indicate that, both at the end of counselling and after a four-month follow-up, clients who received the empty chair intervention gained considerable relief from distressing symptoms and that their perceptions of resolution of unfinished business improved greatly (Pavio and Greenberg, 1995).

Assist clients to express feelings

Expressing feelings well requires clients to be skilled at experiencing, exploring and accurately labelling feelings. When clients reveal feelings they put themselves very much on the line. Some feelings are difficult for most clients to express, especially when they do not feel safe with another person: for example, feelings of worthlessness, incompetence and unattractiveness. Some may be more difficult for female clients to express, though male clients can have difficulty expressing them too: for example, feelings of ambition, leadership and assertion. Some feelings may be more difficult for male than female clients to express, though again differences exist within each sex: for instance vulnerability, sensitivity and affection. Many clients find it difficult to express specific feelings well: for instance altruism. Within the context of good relationships, counselling trainees enabling clients to express feelings need to focus on both mind skills and communication/action skills.

Improve mind skills

Mind skills may interfere with or assist appropriate expression of feelings. Mind skills deficiencies blocking experiencing of feelings overlap with those hindering appropriate expression of feelings.

Creating rules

Many personal and relationship rules interfere with appropriate expression of feelings:

Unrealistic personal rules
I must have approval all the time.
I must always express feelings smoothly.
Men must keep a stiff upper lip.

Unrealistic relationship rules
We must never have conflict in our relationship.
Wives must always be sexually available to husbands.
Children should be seen and not heard.

Creating perceptions

Many clients need to learn how to allow their feelings toward others to be based on more accurate perceptions of self and others so that the feelings they express are what they truly feel. For instance, personal insecurity or 'having a bad day' frequently triggers unnecessary anger against others. Once clients are in touch with their feelings, they still require flexibility in perceiving various options for expressing them.

Creating self-talk

As well as calming themselves down, clients can develop skills of coaching themselves through sequences of choices involved in the skilled expression of feelings. For example, those who feel strongly about obtaining promotion might use the following self-statements before and during interviews with their bosses: 'Stay calm. Remember to be polite and state my case in the positive. Speak firmly and make good eye contact.'

Creating visualizing

Clients can use visualizing skills to rehearse how to express feelings appropriately. They can visualize themselves attaining their goals if they use good expressing feelings skills. Clients can also visualize negative consequences stemming from the lack of these skills.

Creating explanations

Without realizing it, some clients may wait for others to make the first move in expressing feelings: for example, they may explain to themselves, 'I cannot express positive feelings about her/him until she/he expresses positive feelings about me.' Counselling trainees may need to assist clients to take an active rather than a passive stance in explaining and expressing feelings. Trainees can also challenge clients who blame others for their feelings.

Creating expectations

Many clients do not express certain feelings either at all or well enough because they create false expectations in their own minds. For instance, many shy clients are reluctant to initiate social contacts because of fear of rejection. Clients in relationships may be unwilling to bring up differences because of catastrophic expectations about the consequences. These expectations may cause them either to under-react or to over-react when they eventually discuss differences.

Improve communication/action skills

When assisting clients to express feelings, always pay attention to verbal, voice and body messages. Trainees may also focus on touch and action messages. In what follows I illustrate different communication messages for showing caring skills. Needless to say, clients need to be sensitive to what others perceive as caring messages and not make unwarranted assumptions.

Verbal messages

Verbal messages of caring include statements like 'I love you', 'I care for you' and 'I want to help you.' Clients can also pay compliments. They can also show caring if they use good verbal skills when listening.

Voice messages

If clients' voice messages are wrong, they contradict their verbal messages. Characteristics of caring voice messages include warmth and expressiveness. Clients' voices should convey kindness and interest, not harshness and lack of interest.

Body messages

When clients send caring verbal messages, their gaze, eye contact, body orientation and facial expressions all need to demonstrate interest and concern for the other person. Similarly, clients need to show good attending and listening body message skills when others share problems with them.

Touch messages

Touch can be a wonderful way to express caring. Clients can express caring by a hug, a half-embrace, an arm over the shoulder, a touch on the arm, or a hand on top of or holding a hand, among other ways. However, with all touch messages clients are in the close intimate zone and consequently must be very sensitive about another's willingness to be touched.

Taking action messages

Taking action messages indicating caring include making the other person a cup of tea or coffee in the morning, being prepared to do one's share of the household chores, giving birthday cards and presents, initiating pleasant events such as going out to dinner, showing affection through flowers and other spontaneous gifts, and being available to help out in times of need.

Activity 20.1 Using role-playing to assist a client to experience and express feelings

Work with a partner.

1. Partner A encourages partner B, who acts as a client, to describe a two-person encounter in which he or she felt strongly, but did not experience and hence show the full extent of her/his feelings.
2. Partner A and partner B then role-play the scene,(1) first as it was and then (2) with partner B being encouraged to experience what she/he inhibited, and to express with verbal, vocal and bodily messages what she/he left unsaid.
3. Then partner A uses active listening skills to process partner B's feelings and thoughts concerning the role-play. If necessary, do repeated role-plays and debriefings.
4. Afterwards hold a sharing and feedback session, before reversing roles. Playing back videotapes of role-plays may assist learning.

Activity 20.2 Assisting a client to improve her/his skills at expressing feelings

Work with a partner who is a client with difficulty expressing a feeling (if possible, use real-life material). To further distinguish this activity from the next one, the client might choose a positive feeling that she/he finds difficult to express.

1 Form a collaborative working relationship and facilitate your client's disclosure of the problem.
2 Together with your client assess the 'expressing a feeling' problem and agree upon a shared analysis of it, using the following two-column format.

Mind skills I need to improve	**Communication skills I need to improve**

3 Discuss with your client some interventions for improving her/his skills and, if appropriate, start implementing one or more interventions and negotiate a homework assignment.
4 Afterwards discuss and, after an appropriate interval, reverse roles. Playing back video recordings of your counselling work may enhance learning.

Assist clients to manage feelings

Many clients come to counselling wanting release from painful and negative feelings. Often they lack confidence in themselves, and are also subject to such feelings as excessive anger, depression and anxiety. In reality, feelings tend to overlap: clients can be simultaneously depressed, anxious and excessively angry. Success in managing one of these feelings better is likely to enhance self-esteem and lead to handling the others better too. Clients may use the skills learned for managing one feeling for managing other feelings.

Here I use anger, depression and anxiety to show how to develop clients' skills of managing feelings. The discussion of pertinent mind and communication/action skills is illustrative rather than comprehensive. In practice, skills analyses should be tailor-made to clients' particular poor skills and unique circumstances. When assisting clients to manage feelings always use active listening skills at the same time.

Managing anger

Clients can identify and manage anger without necessarily attempting to rid themselves of it altogether. Anger can have positive uses. It can be a signal indicating something is wrong and requires attention. It can be an energizer motivating clients to take appropriate action. In some instances, anger may also be a purge: after expressing it, clients may calm down and be more rational. Part of managing anger is to be able to experience, explore and accurately label angry feelings. Box 20.3 shows some further skills, each of which I discuss in turn.

Box 20.3 Illustrative mind skills and communication/action skills for managing anger

Mind skills	Communication/action skills
Creating rules e.g. avoid demandingness Creating perceptions e.g. avoid misinterpreting Creating self-talk e.g. calming and coaching Creating visualizing e.g. relaxing and rehearsing Creating explanations e.g. owning responsibility	Assertion skills – request behaviour changes Handling aggressive criticism skills Relaxation skills Managing stress skills Helping one another skills

Mind skills

Creating rules

Ellis (1977) regards childish demandingness as the central mind skills weakness of people who get angry. Clients make 'musturbatory' demands on themselves, for instance 'I must never make mistakes'; on others, for instance 'Others must always let me have my way'; and on the environment, for instance 'Life must be fair' and 'I must never have hassles.'

Creating perceptions

Clients need to learn not to jump to superficial negative conclusions about others. Beck (1988) observes of relationship difficulties that much of the friction is due to misunderstandings that stem from differences in perspective and not from meanness or selfishness.

Creating self-talk

Simple self-instructions like 'Calm down' and 'Cool it' can often give clients more time and space to get feelings under control. Clients can also use longer self-statements, for instance, 'I can handle this situation if I don't let my pride get in the way' (Novaco, 1977; Meichenbaum, 1983).

Creating visualizing

Clients can rehearse how to express angry feelings appropriately, relaxing themselves by visualizing restful scenes, and perceiving others' perspectives more accurately.

Creating explanations

Clients have choices in how they experience, express and manage anger. Until they own responsibility for their anger, they will have insufficient motivation to develop the skills to manage it effectively.

Communication/action skills

Assertiveness

Skills for expressing anger assertively include using 'I' statements, speaking in a clear and firm voice, and maintaining good gaze and eye contact. Clients can also develop skills of requesting others to alter their behaviour before rather than after they have become thoroughly fed up with it (Alberti and Emmons, 2001).

Handling aggressive criticism

Clients have numerous choices, other than impulsive knee-jerk reactions, in dealing with aggressive criticism. For instance, they can tell themselves to relax, calm down and breathe more slowly until they feel more under control. They can also choose from a number of verbal strategies: for example, reflecting another's anger, or partly agreeing with another's point and then putting their own, or asking another to be more specific about what they have done to upset them. Clients may also back off now and react to criticism at a later date – either requesting or, on their own initiative, taking a 'cooling off' period.

Relaxation

Clients can develop skills of muscular and visual relaxation to manage anger (Deffenbacher et al., 1995). I describe relaxation skills in the next chapter.

Managing stress

Frequently inability to handle life's stresses makes clients prone to anger. As well as using muscular and visual relaxation, clients may manage stress better if they develop recreational outlets, actively look after their health, and develop adequate support networks. Since much stress is internally generated, counselling trainees and clients also need to review relevant mind skills.

Helping one another

Clients can learn to work with their partners to help each other to manage anger. Relevant communication skills for clients are disciplining themselves to watch their tongues, expressing anger assertively, showing an awareness of what partners experience before, during and after they receive clients' expressions of anger, and using active listening and questioning skills to help partners express angry feelings. It helps if partners possess realistic relationship rules, for instance: 'Where either of us expresses anger is our relationship it is a signal to explore our own thoughts, feelings, and actions, and not just those of the other person.'

Managing depression

Depressed clients can be very sensitive to the quality of the counselling relationship. Experiencing difficulty in affirming themselves, they seek affirmation from outside. Trainees require good counselling relationship skills both initially, when clients may feel dependent on them, and also later, as they develop skills for emotional independence (see Box 20.4).

Box 20.4 Illustrative mind skills and communication/action skills for managing depression

Mind skills	Communication/action skills
Creating rules e.g. avoid demanding approval Creating perceptions e.g. own strengths Creating explanations e.g. avoid unnecessary self-blame Creating expectations e.g. avoid unnecessary pessimism	Relationship skills • initiating contact • self-disclosing Assertion skills • setting limits and saying 'no' Pleasant activities skills

Mind skills

Creating rules

Clients can create and sustain their depressed feelings when striving to attain and failing to live up to unrealistic rules (Ellis, 2005). Depressogenic unrealistic rules include: 'I must be perfect' and 'I must always gain others' approval.'

Creating perceptions

Beck observes of his cognitive theory of depression: 'Of all the hypotheses, pervasiveness of negative thinking in all forms of depression, symptomatic or syndromatic, has been the most uniformly supported' (1991: 372). Depressed clients tend to jump to negative conclusions about how others perceive them. They are also skilled at blocking out positive information about themselves (Beck, 1991; Beck et al., 1979; Beck and Weishaar, 2005).

Creating explanations

Depressed clients may overemphasize their responsibility for negative events (Beck et al., 1979). They may also see negative events not only as more due to themselves, but also as more due to permanent and pervasive causes than is warranted (Seligman, 1991). Furthermore, clients can contribute to depressing themselves by underemphasizing their contribution to positive events in their own and others' lives.

Creating expectations

Depressed clients tend to predict the future negatively. They are more prone to feelings of hopelessness (Beck et al., 1979), helplessness (Abramson et al., 1978), perceived self-inefficacy (Bandura, 1986), and pessimism (Seligman, 1991) than non-depressed people.

Communication/action skills

Depressed clients may have good communication and action skills in specific areas, but under-rate them. The following discussion assumes their communication/action skills genuinely require development.

Relationship skills

Many depressed clients are lonely because they have insufficient as well as insufficiently high quality social contacts. Initiating contact and appropriately self-disclosing are among the relationship skills such clients may need to develop.

Assertion skills

Frequently depressed clients lower their self-esteem through inability to use assertion skills. Those who do not stand up for themselves may feel doubly bad: first, they have the outer negative consequences of having to do extra work, pay extra money or whatever else follows from their lack of assertion; and second, they have the inner negative consequences of devaluing themselves because of their weakness.

Pleasant activities skills

Lewinsohn and his colleagues state: 'If you feel depressed, it is very likely that you are not involved in many pleasant activities' (1986: 73). Depressed clients can develop skills of identifying activities they find rewarding and then develop and implement plans to participate more in them. As the old adage says: 'A little of what you fancy does you good.'

Managing anxiety

Anxiety is a normal survival reaction. However, many, if not most, clients suffer from excessive or debilitating anxieties that interfere with happiness and fulfilment. Beck and Weishaar (2005) consider that the anxious person's perception of danger is either excessive or based on false assumptions, while the normal response is based on a more accurate assessment of the risk and magnitude of the danger. Normal individuals can correct their misperceptions using logic and evidence. It is vital to offer anxious clients a good counselling relationship, as many are threatened by meeting new people, including counselling trainees. Clients can also become anxious when talking about their anxieties.

Assisting clients to manage anxiety invariably involves focusing on how they think.

Sometimes anxious clients have good communication/action skills, but let their anxieties get in the way of using them. For instance, some students perform well when examinations do not count, but poorly when they count. Some otherwise good to passing students have genuinely poor examination skills. Box 20.5 shows some common mind skills for managing anxiety. The requisite communication and action skills are less easy to list, since they vary with clients' problems. For example, clients require different communication skills for attending job interviews than for developing intimacy.

Box 20.5 Illustrative mind skills and communication/action skills for managing anxiety

Mind skills	Communication/action skills
Creating rules e.g. avoid perfectionism Creating perceptions e.g. perceive danger accurately Creating self-talk e.g. calming, coaching and affirming Creating visualizing e.g. calming, rehearsing Creating expectations e.g. avoid catastrophizing	Skills required for specific situations (verbal, voice, body messages) Relaxation skills

Mind skills

Creating rules

Anxious clients tend to have personal rules that engender both fear of failure and self-devaluation (Ellis, 2005). Making perfectionist demands on self and others is a central characteristic of such rules. Anxious clients can be far too self-conscious because they possess 'musturbatory' rules about needing, as contrasted with preferring, approval.

Creating perceptions

Anxious clients overemphasize the degree of threat in situations. They selectively perceive what might go wrong and insufficiently perceive what might go right. They possess poor skills in assessing evidence for the reality or otherwise of their perceptions. In addition, anxious clients underestimate both their ability to cope and also the supports available to them (Beck and Emery, 1985; Beck and Weishaar, 2005). Defensiveness, in which clients deny or distort aspects of themselves they find threatening, is another way that anxiety interferes with perception.

Creating self-talk

Anxious clients engage in much anxious self-talk (Beck et al., 1988; Kendall and Hollon, 1989). Their anxiety symptoms are signals for telling themselves that they cannot cope or do anything right. In social situations, their self-talk may be about making fools of themselves. Often clients with panic disorders tell themselves that a vital system, for instance the cardiovascular or nervous system, may collapse (Beck and Weishaar, 2005).

Creating visualizing

Most anxious clients experience negative visual images prior to and concurrent with anxiety attacks (Beck et al., 1974). Clients may have poor skills for using visualizing both to relax and also to rehearse communication and action skills.

Creating expectations

Frequently anxious clients possess catastrophic thoughts and images about the future and their ability to cope with it. They are pessimists rather than optimists, either in general (pervasive anxiety), or with regard to the specific situations in which they become anxious (situational anxiety).

Communication/action skills

Skills required for specific situations

Anxiety may either be the cause of poor communication and action skills, their consequence, or a mixture of the two. Some clients may have good communication/action skills, but experience difficulty implementing them under pressure. Other clients may need to develop specific skills: for instance, in public speaking, asking for a date, driving a car, managing a company, policing an angry crowd, and so on. Increased competence in these skills lowers anxiety.

Relaxation skills

Many anxious clients are poor at relaxing because they engage in insufficient pleasurable and relaxing activities. In addition, they may have poor muscular and mental relaxation skills.

Activity 20.3 Assisting a client to improve her/his skills at managing feelings

Work with a partner who is a client with difficulty managing an unwanted feeling (if possible, use real-life material).

1. Form a collaborative working relationship and facilitate your client's disclosure of the problem.
2. Together with your client assess the 'managing a feeling' problem and agree upon a shared analysis of it, using the two-column format (see Activity 20.2).
3. Discuss with your client some interventions for improving her/his skills and, if appropriate, start implementing one or more interventions and negotiate a homework assignment.
4. Afterwards discuss and, after an appropriate interval, reverse roles. Playing back video recordings of your counselling work may enhance learning.

Use of medication

When aiding clients to manage feelings, counselling trainees often require familiarity with psychotropic drugs – drugs that act on the mind. Trainees attached to general practices and working in other medical settings are especially likely to require knowledge about the use of such drugs.

Counselling trainees may find it difficult to assess how clients feel unless they take into account the effects of any medication they are on. If medication seems advisable, trainees need to refer clients to physicians. When working with clients on medication, trainees may need to discuss appropriate levels of dosage, both amounts and frequency, and any side-effects. In addition, clients themselves may wish to discuss their use of medication. Though trainees should not get out of their depth, their clients may feel reassured if informed discussion can take place.

There are four major types of psychotropic medicine: anxiolytics/hypnotics, otherwise known as minor tranquillizers; antipsychotics, also known as neuroleptics or major tranquillizers; antidepressants; and lithium (Sexton, 1999; Sexton and Legg, 1999). All psychotropic drugs have possible toxic or unwanted side-effects. Even minor tranquillizers can affect some clients with drowsiness, lessened muscular coordination, lowered sex urge, and dependency. Furthermore, being on tranquillizers can make it more difficult for clients to learn anxiety management skills. To develop these skills properly, clients need to feel anxious and then learn how to reduce the emotion (Greenberger and Padesky, 1995). A drug like lithium carbonate, used for mania and depression, is highly toxic and requires close medical monitoring. If counselling trainees require information about drugs, they can ask physicians or look it up in the latest editions of regularly updated medical prescription reference sources, such as *MIMS* (latest edition) in Britain and Australia.

Counselling trainees may need to explore their own and clients' attitudes to the use of psychotropic drugs. Some trainees have prejudices against any use of drugs and, sometimes, also against the medical profession. Other trainees, like some clients, may treat medication as a crutch. Clients' attitudes toward psychotropic drugs vary from viewing taking them as personal weakness to willing dependence on them (Padesky and Greenberger, 1995).

Though it is sometimes difficult to achieve, counselling trainees should aim for clients to become psychologically self-reliant in managing feelings, including taking as little medication as possible. However, on occasion, using medication may be appropriate, for instance with seriously disturbed clients (American Psychiatric Association, 2000) or those clients who require relief to tide them through crises. As counselling progresses, often in consultation with their physicians, clients may choose to wean themselves off drugs, possibly at first by taking smaller and less frequent dosages. For quick-acting drugs, another option is for clients to use them only in emergencies.

systematic desensitization 21

Chapter outcomes

By studying and doing the activities in this chapter you should:

- be able to use progressive muscular relaxation with clients;
- know about brief relaxation procedures;
- know how to construct systematic desensitization hierarchies; and
- know how to present items from hierarchies to clients.

Systematic desensitization is an approach that is relevant not only to managing feelings, but to experiencing and expressing them as well. Systematic desensitization helps clients to manage and lessen their experiencing of unwanted feelings so that they can replace these with more appropriate feelings and hence communicate and act more effectively. Counselling trainees can consider intervening with systematic desensitization when clients have specific anxieties and phobias rather than general tension. Some counsellors consider that the use of systematic desensitization is most appropriate when clients have the required communication and action skills in their repertoires, but avoid situations or perform less than adequately because of anxiety (Kalodner, 1998).

The version of systematic desensitization developed by its originator, the late Joseph Wolpe, involved three elements: (1) training in deep muscular relaxation, (2) the construction around hierarchies of anxiety-evoking situations, and (3) asking clients, when relaxed, to imagine items from the hierarchies (Wolpe, 1958, 1990; Wolpe and Wolpe, 1988). Wolpe's 'reciprocal inhibition' or counter-conditioning explanation, was that the pairing of anxiety-evoking stimuli with the relaxation response brings about a lessening of the anxiety response, in effect weakening the bond between anxiety-evoking stimuli and anxiety responses. Other explanations exist for systematic desensitization's effectiveness and it is increasingly presented as a self-control skill. Such an approach emphasizes coping with anxiety rather than mastering it, which was Wolpe's goal.

Progressive muscular relaxation

Counselling trainees can start systematic desensitization by briefly explaining all three elements. They should also explain to clients why they think this intervention might be helpful for them. Presumably, the client has some specific anxiety management problem or problems for which desensitization seems the preferred intervention. Trainees should emphasize that it is helpful for clients to regard it as a coping skill rather than as a cure.

Once clients agree that systematic desensitization might be useful in helping them to change how they feel, think and communicate or act, trainees can start teaching them progressive muscular relaxation skills. The physical setting of trainees' offices should be conducive to relaxation. This involves absence of disruptive noise, interior decoration that is restful, and lighting which may be dimmed. Clients may be taught to relax in recliner chairs, or on mattresses or, at the very least, in comfortable upright chairs with headrests.

From the start trainees can teach relaxation training as a useful skill for daily life. Clients should understand that success in learning relaxation, just like success in learning any other skill, requires practice and that relaxation homework will be required. Before starting relaxation, trainees should suggest that clients wear loose-fitting, comfortable clothing both during interviews and when doing relaxation homework, and that it is helpful to remove items such as glasses and shoes.

Bernstein and Borkovec (1973) observe that in teaching muscular relaxation there is a succession of events that must be observed with each muscle group. Clients should go through a five-step tension–relax cycle for each muscle group:

1 *focus* – focus attention on a particular muscle group;
2 *tense* – tense the muscle group;
3 *hold* – maintain the tension for five to seven seconds;
4 *release* – release the tension in the muscle group; and
5 *relax* – spend 20 to 30 seconds focusing on letting go of tension and further relaxing the muscle groups.

Clients need to learn this *focus–tense–hold–release–relax* cycle so that they may apply it in their homework.

Having explained the basic cycle, counselling trainees may then demonstrate it by going through the cycle in relation to their own right hand and forearm, at each stage asking their clients to do the same. Thus, 'I'm focusing all my attention on my right hand and forearm and I'd like you to do the same' progresses to 'I'm clenching my right fist and tensing the muscles in my lower arm ... ', then on to 'I'm holding my right fist clenched and keeping the muscles in my lower arm tensed ... ', followed by 'I'm now releasing as quickly as I can the tension from my right fist and lower arm ... ', ending with 'I'm relaxing my right hand and forearm, letting the tension go further and further and letting these muscles become more and more relaxed ...'. The final relaxation phase tends to last from 20 to 60 seconds, and is frequently accompanied by relaxation 'patter' about letting the tension go and acknowledging and experiencing feelings of deeper and deeper relaxation as they occur. Having been through the tension–relax cycle once, especially in the initial sessions the client may be instructed to go through it again, thus tensing and relaxing each muscle grouping twice.

Trainees are then likely to take clients through the muscle groups, demonstrating them as necessary. Box 21.1 shows 16 muscle groups and suggested tensing instructions. The arms tend to come at the beginning, since they are easy to demonstrate. For most clients, relaxing parts of the face is particularly important because the most marked anxiety-inhibiting effects usually originate there.

Box 21.1 Relaxation training muscle groups and tensing instructions

Muscle group	Tensing instructions*
Right hand and forearm	Clench your right fist and tense the muscles in your lower arm.
Right biceps	Bend your right arm at the elbow and flex your biceps by tensing the muscles of your upper right arm.
Left hand and forearm	Clench your left fist and tense the muscles in your lower arm.
Left biceps	Bend your left arm at the elbow and flex your biceps by tensing the muscles of your upper left arm.
Forehead	Lift your eyebrows as high as possible.
Eyes, nose and upper cheeks	Squeeze your eyes tightly shut and wrinkle your nose.
Jaw and lower cheeks	Clench your teeth and pull the corners of your mouth firmly back.
Neck and throat	Pull your chin down hard towards your chest chest yet resist having it touch your chest.
Chest and shoulders	Pull your shoulder blades together and take a deep breath.
Stomach	Tighten the muscles in your stomach as though someone was about to hit you there.
Right thigh	Tense the muscles of the right upper leg by pressing the upper muscle down and the lower muscles up.

Right calf	Stretch your right leg and pull your toes towards your head.
Right foot	Point and curl the toes of your right foot and turn it inwards.
Left thigh	Tense the muscles of the left upper leg by pressing the upper muscle down and the lower muscles up.
Left calf	Stretch your left leg and pull your toes towards your head.
Left foot	Point and curl the toes of your left foot and turn it inwards.

*With left-handed people, tensing instructions for the left side of the body should come before those for the right.

Once clients have learned how to tense the various muscle groups, they are instructed to keep their eyes closed during relaxation training and practice. Towards the end of relaxation sessions, counselling trainees may ask clients for a summary, along the lines of 'Well, how was your relaxation today?' and discuss any issues that arise. Ending relaxation sessions may be achieved by trainees counting from five to one and when they get to one asking their clients to wake up pleasantly relaxed as though from a peaceful sleep.

The importance of practising muscular relaxation may be further stressed at the end of the initial relaxation session. Clients are likely to be given the homework assignment of practising muscular relaxation for one or two 15-minute periods a day. Trainees should ask clients whether they anticipate any obstacles to practising, such as finding a quiet place, and help them to devise strategies for ensuring good homework. Trainees can also either make up cassettes of relaxation instructions that clients can take away for homework purposes or recommend existing relaxation training cassettes. There is some evidence that clients who monitor their relaxation practice are much more likely to continue doing it (Tasto and Hinkle, 1973). Consequently, it may be helpful for trainees to give clients logs for monitoring their homework.

Brief muscular relaxation skills

These skills aim to induce deep relaxation with less time and effort than the 16-muscle group relaxation procedure. When clients are proficient in full progressive muscular relaxation, trainees can introduce such skills. Brief relaxation skills are useful both in counselling sessions and in daily life. The following are two examples.

Sequential brief relaxation

Here counselling trainees first instruct clients and then get them to give themselves the following instructions focused on tensing and relaxing in turn four composite muscle groupings:

> 'I'm going to count to ten in units of two. After each unit of two I will instruct you to tense and relax a muscle grouping. One, two ... focus on your leg and feet muscles ... tense and hold the tension in these muscles for five seconds ... release ... relax and enjoy the sensations of the tension flowing from your legs and feet. Three, four ... take a deep breath and focus on your chest, shoulder and stomach muscles ... tense and hold the tension in these muscles for five seconds ... release ... relax and enjoy the sensations of the tension flowing from your chest, shoulders and stomach. Five, six ... focus on your face, neck and head muscles ... tense and hold the tension in these muscles for five seconds ... release ... relax and enjoy the sensations of the tension flowing from your face, neck and head. Seven, eight ... focus on your arm and hand muscles ... tense and hold the tension in these muscles for five seconds ... release ... relax and enjoy the sensations of the tension flowing from your arms and hands. Nine, ten ... focus on all the muscles in your body ... tense all the muscles in your body together and hold for five seconds ... release ... relax and enjoy the sensations of the tension leaving your whole body as your relaxation gets deeper and deeper ... deeper and deeper ... deeper and deeper.'

Simultaneous brief relaxation

As at the end of the previous example, counselling trainees instruct clients to tense all muscle groupings simultaneously. They also can say:

> 'When I give the signal, I would like you to close your eyes very tightly, take a deep breath and simultaneously tense your arm muscles, your face, neck and throat muscles, your chest, shoulder and stomach muscles, and your leg and foot muscles. Now take a deep breath and tense all your muscles ... hold for five seconds ... now release and relax as quickly and deeply as you can.'

Mental relaxation skills

Often clients visualize restful scenes at the end of progressive muscular relaxation. Such a scene might be 'lying in a lush green meadow on a warm, sunny day, feeling a gentle breeze, watching the clouds'. Clients can visualize such scenes independent of muscular relaxation. In addition, they can use the 'counting to ten in groups of two' as a mental relaxation procedure. For example: 'One, two ... focus on your leg and feet muscles ... relax and enjoy the sensations of the tension flowing from your legs and feet.' As a mental relaxation procedure, clients edit out the tense, hold and release instructions.

Relaxation training considerations

Counsellors differ in the number of sessions they use for relaxation training. Furthermore, clients differ in the speed with which they learn how to relax. Wolpe (1990) taught progressive muscular relaxation in about six lessons and asked his patients to practice at home for two 15-minute sessions per day. Wolpe and Wolpe observe: 'It is crucial to realize that the aim of relaxation training is not muscle control per se, but emotional calmness' (1988: 42). Bernstein and Borkovec (1973) suggest a 10-session relaxation training timetable, with the first three sessions devoted to training in relaxing all muscle groups, the next four sessions to brief muscular relaxation, and the final three sessions to verbal relaxation procedures. Again, daily homework practice is assigned. Trainees may vary their relaxation-training timetable according to their clients' needs and their own workload. Nevertheless, it is important that clients have sufficient sessions to learn relaxation adequately.

Borkovec and Sides (1979) reviewed 25 controlled studies using progressive muscular relaxation and found that 15 studies reported the superiority of, and 10 studies its equivalence to, control group outcomes. However, of the seven studies that consisted of three or more training sessions, live rather than taped training, and clinical as contrasted with normal subjects, only one failed to report that progressive muscular relaxation was superior to control group conditions.

Activity 21.1 Assisting a client to develop progressive muscular relaxation skills

Review the section of the chapter on assisting clients to use progressive muscular relaxation skills. Conduct a counselling session in which partner A's task is to train partner B, who acts as client, in progressive muscular relaxation skills. During the session, partner A:

(a) offers reasons for using progressive muscular relaxation;
(b) provides a live demonstration of tensing and relaxing the first muscle grouping in Box 21.1;
(c) makes up a progressive muscular relaxation cassette as she/he relaxes partner B using the five-step tension–relax cycle (readers can alter the Box 21.1 tensing instructions to self-instructions by substituting 'my' for 'your' throughout);
(d) presents a mental relaxation scene at the end of the muscular relaxation;
(e) checks how relaxed the client became and provides further relaxation instructions for any muscle group which s/he still feels is tense; and
(f) negotiates a progressive muscular relaxation homework assignment with the client.

Afterwards hold a sharing and discussion session and, after an appropriate interval, reverse roles.

Construct hierarchies

Hierarchies are lists of stimuli centred around themes and ordered according to the amount of anxiety they evoke. Counselling trainees can identify with their clients one or more suitable themes and give priority to themes or areas that are either the most debilitating or of most immediate importance to clients. They can then assist clients to generate items around the theme or themes. Items need to be described in such a way that clients can imagine them. Sources for hierarchy items include information gathered during assessment, homework assignments involving self-monitoring, and suggestions from clients and counsellors. Some counsellors and trainees ask clients to write items on index cards to make for ease of ordering.

Once generated, items are then ranked to form one or more hierarchies, each centred on a theme. Ranking items involves clients rating those for each theme on a subjective anxiety scale and ordering them accordingly. A common way to check the anxiety-evoking potential of items is for counsellors to say that 0 represents no anxiety and 100 is the maximum anxiety possible for that theme. Wolpe calls such a 0–100 scale a 'subjective units of disturbance' or *sud* scale, with each item having a *suds* rating (Wolpe, 1990: 91–2). In general, items should be arranged so that there are no gaps of over 10 units. If necessary, trainees and clients can generate intervening items. As treatment progresses, they may need to reorder, reword, or generate further items. Box 21.2 illustrates a hierarchy.

Box 21.2 Hierarchy for client with maths exam anxiety

Rank	Rating	Item
1	5	Thinking about a maths exam when revising at my desk 1 month before
2	10	Thinking about a maths exam when revising at my desk 3 weeks before
3	15	Thinking about a maths exam when revising at my desk 2 weeks before
4	20	Thinking about a maths exam when revising at my desk 1 week before
5	25	Thinking about a maths exam on the night before
6	30	Waking up on the morning of the maths exam
7	40	Driving my car on the way to the maths exam
8	50	Waiting outside the exam room
9	60	Going into the exam room
10	70	Sitting down at my desk in the exam room
11	80	Looking at the maths exam paper for the first time
12	90	Sitting in the exam room looking at everybody else working hard
13	100	Having a panic attack during the maths exam

A basic assumption of systematic desensitization is that clients are capable of imagining hierarchy items or scenes. Counselling trainees need to check their clients' ability to imagine. It they find this difficult, one option is for trainees to describe the scenes more fully and check out their authenticity with the client. Some clients imagine items or scenes better if they, rather than their counsellors, describe them aloud.

Present hierarchy items

A desensitization session starts with counselling trainees relaxing clients. When they are sure that clients are deeply relaxed, trainees can present items along the lines of 'Now I want you to imagine you are sitting at your desk revising for a maths exam one month before the exam ...' They start with the least anxiety-evoking item and often ask clients to raise their index finger if experiencing anxiety. If clients experience no anxiety, trainees then ask them to switch the scene off and go back to feeling pleasantly relaxed. After 30–50 seconds trainees can ask clients to imagine the item again. If this causes no anxiety, trainees withdraw the item, possibly spend further time relaxing clients and move on to the next item.

If clients indicate anxiety with items, counselling trainees have two main choices. First, they can withdraw the item immediately, relax the client again, and then present the item a second time. Second – and a preferable option for developing self-helping skills – they can both instruct clients to continue imagining the item and also encourage them to relax away their anxiety by calming and coaching self-talk and taking slow deep breaths (Goldfried and Davison, 1976; Meichenbaum, 1977). If clients repeatedly experience anxiety with an item, trainees can intersperse less threatening items.

Systematic desensitization assumes that once a low anxiety-evoking item, for example 10 units or *suds*, ceases to stimulate anxiety, all other hierarchy items become less anxiety-evoking by 10 units. Thus the 100-unit item becomes 90 units, and so on. Consequently, trainees only present weak anxiety-evoking items to clients.

Counselling trainees should keep records of all item presentations and their outcomes. Wolpe's (1990) desensitization sessions lasted 15 to 30 minutes. Initially, he might present a total of 8 to 10 items, possibly from different hierarchies. In later sessions, he might make as many as 30 to 50 presentations. Goldfried and Davison (1976) suggest covering from 2 to 5 items each session. Trainees can also cassette-record items, and get clients to work through them as homework assignments.

Counselling trainees should also encourage clients, when either preparing for or facing anxiety-evoking situations in daily life, to develop self-helping skills for relaxing away tensions, breathing slowly and deeply, and using coping self-talk. Where appropriate, trainees can give clients logs to monitor their use of anxiety management skills.

Real-life desensitization

Real-life desensitization sometimes goes by the name of exposure therapy (Donohoe and Ricketts, 2000). Many visualized desensitization considerations – such as using relaxation, constructing hierarchies, and the level of anxiety within which to present items – still apply to real-life desensitization. There are two main reasons why real-life or *in vivo,* rather than visualized, desensitization may be the preferred intervention. First, clients may have difficulty imagining items. However, items for real-life desensitization need to be readily accessible and this is frequently not the case. Second, where items are readily accessible, desensitization can be more powerful if counselling trainee and client work with real rather than with imaginary items.

An example of real-life desensitization is its use in the treatment of agoraphobia, fear of open spaces or public places. Counselling trainees can prepare clients to anticipate fearful reactions and teach them appropriate coping skills. Furthermore, trainees can accompany clients into the real-life exposure situations, providing encouragement, support and coaching. Wilson (2005) observes that, once clients enter feared situations, it is important for them not to leave until their anxiety has decreased. After clients have had a successful exposure with counsellor support, they can consolidate their learning and gains with appropriate homework assignments conducted in their own time.

Activity 21.2 Conducting systematic desensitization

This activity builds upon Activity 21.1. Work with a partner who is a client wanting help to manage a specific anxiety (if possible real; otherwise role-played) and complete the following tasks.

1 *Explain systematic desensitization.* Explain systematic desensitization to your client and offer reasons for suggesting it as an intervention. Present systematic desensitization as a coping skill.

2 *Construct a hierarchy.* Box 21.2 is an example of a systematic desensitization hierarchy for a client with maths exam anxiety. Work with your partner to construct a hierarchy around the theme of her/his phobia. On a scale from 0–100 units of anxiety, have no items further apart than 10 units.

3 *Present hierarchy items.* Use progressive muscular relaxation to relax your partner who closes her/his eyes. When she/he is deeply relaxed, present items along the lines of 'Now I want you to imagine you are sitting at your desk revising one month before the exam ... If you experience any anxiety, raise your index finger.' Let the client imagine the item for about 10 seconds. If she/he experiences no anxiety, ask her/him to switch the item off and go back to feeling pleasantly relaxed. After about 30 seconds, you may present the item again. If your client experiences anxiety in either presentation, instruct her/him to continue imagining the item and encourage her/him to relax away the anxiety, take slow deep breaths, and use coping self-talk. If the client repeatedly experiences anxiety with an item, intersperse a less threatening item. If possible, during this activity, take your client through at least the first three items on her/his hierarchy.

End by encouraging your client, when preparing for or facing the anxiety situation in daily life, to use self-helping skills of relaxing away tensions, taking slow deep breaths, and using coping self-talk.

Afterwards hold a sharing and feedback session with your partner and then reverse roles.

negotiate homework 22

Chapter outcomes

By studying and doing the activity in this chapter you should:

- recognize the importance of setting homework;
- be able to start negotiating realistic assignments;
- begin giving clear instructions in take-away form;
- possess some skills of increasing clients' compliance;
- be able to anticipate some difficulties and setbacks; and
- signal a joint progress review.

After presenting, demonstrating and coaching clients in new skills, counsellors and trainees can negotiate relevant homework assignments. Homework assignments or between-session activities include completing self-monitoring sheets and filling out worksheets for developing mind skills that influence feelings, communications and actions. Other assignments can entail reading self-help books, listening to cassettes, watching videotapes, observing people with good communication skills, and trying out improved communication and action skills in real life (Dryden and Feltham, 1992; Greenberger and Padesky, 1995).

Many reasons exist for asking clients to perform homework assignments (Cormier and Nurius, 2002; Egan, 2002). These include speeding up the learning process and encouraging clients to monitor, rehearse and practise changed thinking and communications and actions. Homework activities can help the transfer of trained mind skills and communication/action skills to real life, which may uncover difficulties in applying them in specific problem situations. Homework assignments can increase clients' sense of self-control and of personal responsibility for developing targeted mind skills and communication/action skills.

Skills for negotiating homework

The following central skills can increase the chances of clients actually performing agreed-upon activities.

Offer reasons for assignments

Counselling trainees can often enhance clients' motivation for completing homework assignments if they explain their importance. At the start of tell, show and do sequences, they can introduce the idea of outside counselling practice.

> 'Now, Grant, first I am going to describe —— [specify which] skill, then I am going to demonstrate it for you, then I am going to coach you in it, and then, if agreeable, we will discuss some ways to practice your —— [specify which] skill in real life. To gain competence in developing any skill requires practice.'

Negotiate realistic assignments

I use the word 'negotiate' to highlight the importance of client participation in homework assignment decisions. I assume that clients are more likely to comply with assignments that they have had a say in designing. The following are three key aspects of realistic assignments:

- Such assignments either consolidate earlier learning or set the stage for the learning activities of the next session. Do not introduce any new skills and ideas that clients will have insufficient time to assimilate before the session ends.
- The assignments are of appropriate difficulty. The tasks take into account clients' understanding of and readiness to perform targeted skills. Where appropriate, suggest graded steps.
- The amount of work is realistic for the client's circumstances and motivation. It is preferable for clients to make a definite commitment to a small amount of homework than to make a vague commitment to a larger amount.

Encourage clients to view homework in terms of learning contracts not just with the counsellor but, more importantly, with themselves.

Give clear instructions in take-away form

How can clients know precisely what to do? What? When? How often? How recorded? are all pertinent questions. Sometimes clients have already received handouts summarizing the main learning points of a skill. Where possible, give instructions in take-away form. Counselling trainees can design their own homework assignment forms. Box 22.1 shows four possible formats. Either trainee or client should write down clear instructions for homework assignments on these forms. Writing instructions on scraps of paper is generally not good enough. Trainees should always check what clients write to make sure they have taken down the instructions correctly. If trainees want clients to fill out forms such as monitoring logs, they should provide these forms themselves. This practice ensures clear instructions and saves clients the extra effort of having to write out forms before filling them in.

Box 22.1 Formats for homework assignment forms

Format 1

Homework assignment form

In order to gain the most from your counselling session(s) you are encouraged to engage in the following between-session activities.

Format 2

To follow up

In order to gain the most from your counselling session(s) you are encouraged to perform the following tasks.

Format 3

Take-away sheet

Use this sheet for writing down (1) your main learnings from counselling and (2) any instructions for between-session activities.

Format 4

Learning contract

I make a learning contract with myself to perform the following activities before the next counselling session.

Aim to increase compliance

One of the central problems in assigning homework activities is getting clients to do them. Often as a trainer I have observed trainees rush through negotiating homework assignments at the end of counselling sessions in ways that virtually guaranteed client non-compliance. Common mistakes included not leaving enough time, inviting insufficient client participation, giving vague verbal instructions, and not checking whether clients clearly understood what they were meant to do. Box 22.2 lists nine guidelines recommended by psychologists Christine Padesky and Dennis Greenberger (1995: 24–7).

Box 22.2 Guidelines for increasing clients' compliance with homework assignments

1 Make assignments small.
2 Assign tasks within the client's skill level.
3 Make assignments relevant and interesting.
4 Collaborate with the client in developing learning assignments.

5 Provide a clear rationale for the assignment and a written summary.
6 Begin the assignment during the session.
7 Identify and problem-solve impediments to the assignment.
8 Emphasize learning, not a desired outcome.
9 Show interest, and follow up in the next appointment.

Anticipate difficulties and setbacks

Explore with clients their motivation for completing homework assignments. Where possible, identify and help clients work through resistances. In addition, identify rewards for completing assignments. If counselling trainees have negotiated realistic amounts of homework, hopefully clients will comply. Sometimes, implementing a skill requires asking clients to give up long-established habits. Here, it can be especially important not to assign too difficult an assignment too soon. Where possible, trainees and clients should try to build in some early successes to encourage clients to keep working on their skills.

Some clients return to unsupportive, if not downright hostile environments. Here trainees may need to prepare clients more thoroughly prior to suggesting they implement targeted skills in real-life settings. Such preparation is likely to include devising strategies for coping with negative feedback.

Signal a joint progress review

Counselling trainees should signal a joint progress review by letting clients know that at or around the start of the next session, they will ask them how they fared in their homework assignments. Clients who know that their counsellors are interested in and supportive of their attempts to complete homework assignments are more likely to be motivated to do so, that is so long as trainees avoid becoming controlling and judgemental.

Activity 22.1 Developing negotiating homework skills

Part A: Considering negotiating homework assignments

Imagine that you have just coached a client in a specific skill or sub-skill that you have presented and demonstrated. You are now thinking about setting the client one or more homework assignments. How might you take into account each of the following considerations?

- Offering reasons for assignments.
- Negotiating realistic assignments.
- Giving clear instructions in take-away form.
- Anticipating difficulties and setbacks.
- Signalling a joint progress review.

Part B: Rehearsing and practising negotiating homework assignments

Work with a partner acting as client to improve a specific mind skill and/or communication skill in her/his work or personal relationships. Now rehearse and practice how to negotiate one or more homework assignments so that your client can use the time before the next counselling session to good effect. To increase your client's chances of compliance, observe the guidelines provided in Box 22.2.

Afterwards hold a sharing and discussion session focused on your use of negotiating homework assignments skills. If necessary, practice more until you consider that you have obtained some competence in negotiating homework assignments. Then reverse roles.

23 conduct middle sessions

Chapter outcomes

By studying and doing the activities in this chapter you should:

- possess some skills for the preparing phase of middle sessions;
- possess some skills for the starting phase;
- possess some skills for the working phase;
- possess some skills for the ending phase;
- understand some issues about length, frequency and number of sessions; and
- understand some methods of monitoring and evaluating progress in middle sessions.

Counsellors and counselling trainees can conduct the relating and understanding stages of the lifeskills counselling model with most clients in the first one or two sessions. The end product involves agreeing with clients on the mind skills and communication/action skills they need to improve. In phase 1 of stage 3, the changing stage, the focus changes to intervening to improve these targeted skills, which is the task of the middle sessions.

Middle counselling sessions

Counselling sessions have four phases: preparing, starting, middle and ending. Box 23.1 describes some illustrative skills for each of these phases when conducting middle sessions.

Box 23.1 The four phases of middle counselling sessions

Phase 1: The preparing phase

Illustrative skills

Reflecting on previous and next session(s)
Consulting with trainers, supervisors and peers
Ensuring understanding of interventions to be used in upcoming session

Practising delivery of interventions, if appropriate
Preparing and having available relevant handouts and homework assignment sheets
Arriving on time
Setting up the room
Relaxing oneself

Phase 2: The starting phase

Illustrative skills

Meeting, greeting and seating
Re-establishing the collaborative working relationship
Reviewing homework assignments
Establishing session agendas

Phase 3: The middle phase

Illustrative skills

Actively involving clients in the process
Client-centred coaching
Delivering specific interventions
Checking clients' understanding
Refining session agendas
Keeping sessions moving

Phase 4: The ending phase

Illustrative skills

Structuring to allow time for ending
Reviewing sessions
Negotiating homework assignments
Enlisting commitment and checking difficulties in carrying out assignments
Scheduling the next appointment

The preparing phase

Time spent on preparing sessions is often time well spent. When counselling trainees are on placements, they can assign themselves between-session homework activities. One such activity is to play back a tape of the previous session and review how well they conducted each phase of the session, how the client responded, what progress she or he made, and the quality of the collaborative working relationship. In addition, trainees may be required to keep 'professional logs' in which they record details of each supervised placement session.

Counselling trainees' trainers, supervisors and peers can also help them to review the previous session to gain insights into how they might approach the next one. In addition, trainees can revise the interventions they intend using, in order to understand their content thoroughly. Furthermore, they can practise delivering these interventions. Trainees can also use between-session time to ensure that they have any written material, such as handouts and homework assignment sheets, readily available. However, they should be careful not to be too rigid in how they plan to approach the next session. It is vital that they consult with clients as part of establishing strong collaborative working relationships rather than imposing their ideas.

As with initial sessions, counselling trainees should arrive early for middle sessions, set up the room, check any recording equipment they might use and, if necessary, relax themselves. They should not allow clients into the counselling room before they are ready to devote their full attention to them.

The starting phase

The four main tasks are listed in Box 23.1. The meeting, greeting and seating skills for subsequent sessions are similar to those counselling trainees require for initial sessions. If required for supervision and not done previously, trainees should obtain permission for recording sessions.

Once clients are comfortably seated, they will sometimes start talking of their own accord. On most occasions, however, counselling trainees need to make opening statements (see Box 23.2). I advocate a 'softly, softly' approach that starts by checking 'where the client is at' rather than moving directly into delivering interventions. Clients should be allowed the psychological safety and space to bring the trainee up to date with information important to them. Trainees who hold back and do not push their agendas avoid taking over sessions or suppressing significant information that clients may wish to reveal, for instance a promotion or unexpected piece of bad luck. In some instances, clients may bring up new or emergent material that can markedly change the course of their treatment. Trainees should always use active listening skills to help clients know that they are still concerned and interested in how they see the world and their problems.

When counselling trainees have allowed clients air time, and if clients have not brought up the topic of their own accord, they can check to find out how any homework assignments were managed. Box 23.2 provides some statements trainees might make, if they have not already reviewed progress in performing homework assignments. As appropriate, trainees can ask additional questions that clarify and expand their own and clients' understanding of progress made and difficulties encountered.

In the lifeskills counselling model, counselling trainees encourage clients to acknowledge their own agency in bringing about positive changes. For example, Pat, a shy 19-year-old student, says that 'Things are going better in making friends with other students.' Here, the trainee can help Pat to acknowledge that by using his better skills, for instance by replacing negative with calming self-talk, he has helped to bring about the improvement. Pat might now say to himself, 'If I use my self-talk skills, then I am in a stronger position to break the ice and make friends with other students.'

Near the start of each middle session, counselling trainees should consult with clients to establish session agendas. Such agendas may cover all or part of sessions. For example, together they may decide where they will first focus attention and then, later, make another decision regarding where to work next. Alternatively, as part of their initial agenda-setting discussion, they may target one area to start with and then agree to move on to another area. Even when implementing structured plans and following treatment manuals, trainees should remain flexible so that they can respond to developments during sessions. Achieving such flexibility can be difficult for over-anxious trainees.

When establishing session agendas, I pay considerable attention to clients' wishes, since I want to encourage their motivation and involvement. If I thought there were important reasons for starting to improve a particular mind skill or communication/action skill, I would share this reflection with clients. However, I would still be inclined to allow clients the final say in where we worked. Box 23.2 illustrates the kind of agenda-setting statement that a counsellor might make near the start of a second session. Agendas for subsequent sessions tend to be heavily influenced by work done and homework assignments negotiated in the previous session.

Box 23.2 Examples of counsellor statements for the starting phase

Opening statements

'How's your week been?'
'How have you been getting on?'
'Where would you like to start today?'

Reviewing homework assignments statements

'How did you get on with your homework assignment(s)?'
'What happened when you tried out your changed thoughts/communications?'
'Things didn't just happen, you made them happen by using your improved skills of [specify what].'

Establishing a session agenda

'In our first session we agreed upon two mind skills you need to improve for developing your job interview skills: using coping rather than negative self-talk and challenging and then replacing your demanding rule about giving perfect answers. We also agreed upon the importance of improving aspects of your verbal, voice and body communication. Where would you like to work first?'

Activity 23.1 Starting middle sessions

Part A: Formulating statements

Using Box 23.2 as a guide, formulate at least one additional starting phase statement in each of the following categories:

- opening statements
- reviewing between-session activities statements
- establishing a session agenda

Part B: Practising the starting phase

One partner acts as counsellor, another as client, with possibly a third person acting as observer. The client chooses a problem of relevance to her/him. Assume that you have conducted an initial session in which counsellor and client have completed the relating and understanding stages of the lifeskills counselling model. You and your client have identified at least one mind skill and one communication/action skill to be improved during the changing stage, which may last for at least one more session after this one. Discuss how each participant can best get into their roles. Then conduct the starting phase of a second counselling session up to and including the establishment of a session agenda.

Afterwards hold a sharing and feedback discussion. Then, if appropriate, change roles and repeat this activity.

Using audio cassette or videotape recording and playback may add value to the activity.

The middle phase

Once session agendas are established, however informally, counselling trainees can deliver interventions to assist clients to improve one or more skills. One way of viewing this middle phase is that it is the primary working phase of the session. However, I resist using the term 'working phase' here because it may seem to detract from work performed in the preparing, starting and ending phases.

I have already emphasized the importance of client-centred coaching when delivering interventions and I have reviewed numerous interventions. Counselling trainees should be sensitive to the communication patterns or interaction processes they establish with clients. For example, trainees may have a tendency to establish communication patterns which are insufficiently client-focused. If so, they can learn from their clients' reactions to become aware of clues indicating that they are doing most of the talking or taking most of the responsibility for session content. Another unhelpful interaction pattern is if trainees allow relationships with clients to become too cosy. Dryden and Feltham (1992) point out that the purpose of counselling is usually to effect concrete changes in clients' attitudes and lives and that counsellors should avoid allowing themselves to get into collusively superficial relationships.

In the middle phase counselling trainees should involve clients in choices that take place when delivering particular interventions, for instance how many rehearsals they require to improve a specific communication skill prior to experimenting with implementing it outside the counselling room. Furthermore, trainees can involve clients in decisions about moving on to different items in the session agenda and refining agendas as appropriate. Frequently trainees and clients will make trade-offs and compromises: for instance, curtailing time spent working on one mind or communication skill so that they have time available for another.

Counselling trainees need to keep sessions moving at an appropriate pace, neither too fast nor too slow. There are risks in both directions. Trainees may rush through delivering interventions in ways that confuse clients and leave them little of value after sessions end. Furthermore, trainees can put too much pressure on clients to reveal themselves and to work at an uncongenial pace, thus possibly creating resistances. Sometimes, too, clients have important agendas that either they were not emotionally ready to address at the start of counselling or that emerge during counselling and they require encouragement and space to share them.

Alternatively counselling trainees can allow 'session drift' – sessions that drift along rather aimlessly with little tangible progress being achieved. Sometimes this occurs because trainees are poor at balancing relationship and task considerations, at the expense of the latter. They may need to develop assertiveness skills to curtail long and unproductive conversations. Furthermore, trainees require a repertoire of checking out and moving on questions and statements. Box 23.3 provides some examples.

Box 23.3 Examples of checking out and moving on statements

'Do you want to spend more time now working in this area or are you ready to move on?'

'I sense that we've taken working on changing your (specify) as far as we can go for now. What do you think?'

'Do you want another rehearsal for communicating better in that situation or do you think you can manage all right?'

'Before we move on, we can both write down the work we have done on the whiteboard for our records.'

Though the responsibility should be shared, ultimately it is the counselling trainee's responsibility to see that session time is allocated productively. Trainees should be careful not to make moving on statements that allow insufficient time to deal with the next agenda items properly. Generally, it is better to avoid getting into new areas towards the end of sessions rather than to start working on them in a hurried way.

The lifeskills counselling model predominantly takes a psychological education approach to clients' problems. In middle sessions, trainees require training skills focused on 'tell', 'show', 'do' and 'practise'. However, the model also stresses forming and maintaining good collaborative working relationships. When delivering interventions, trainees can sometimes fruitfully vary the nature of the relationship they offer, for instance by showing tough love rather than colluding with clients in settling for less than they might achieve. Lazarus (2005b) makes a similar point when he concludes his case study of George, a 32-year-old client with multiple fears and an extensive prior therapeutic history, by saying the treatment exemplified the way in which the 'right' relationship blended with the 'correct' techniques to produce a salubrious result.

In the earlier chapters on interventions, I presented each of them in a systematic way. However, in middle sessions there is often a tension between adopting a task orientation and maintaining a relationship orientation. Counselling trainees need to be flexible since, in some instances, the psychological education tasks of counselling are best approached indirectly or gradually rather than in an open and systematic manner. Some clients learn skills better with a softly, softly approach integrated into a relationship where they control much of what is talked about. As in the following example, counsellors and trainees can take the material clients present in their everyday language and translate it into a skills framework for educational purposes.

Ken, a worker at a small-sized printing factory, originally came to see the counsellor with numerous stress symptoms. By the tenth session, Ken was feeling better, including being less irritable at work and at home with his wife and kids. Sometimes the counsellor worked systematically on improving Ken's mind and communication/action skills. However, much of the time the counsellor allowed Ken a lot of space to talk because he sensed that Ken would resist a heavily task-oriented approach. In the following excerpt, the counsellor rewords what Ken says to highlight that he is using his improved mind skills to behave differently at work.

Ken: I'm now setting limits on how late I stay at the factory. The boss still takes on extra work and negotiates unrealistic deadlines, but now I feel much better about not staying there after 8 p.m.

Counsellor: Let's put that another way. You are now using your skills of no longer making perfectionist demands on yourself that you can personally supervise all the work done there to the highest standard. You are also using your skills of not assuming total ownership of the problems caused by your boss taking on more orders with shorter deadlines than the company can reasonably handle.

Another aspect of the lifeskills counselling model's psychological education emphasis is that client record-keeping is considered as important, if not more so, than counsellor or trainee counsellor record-keeping. In middle sessions, clients are encouraged to keep written records of all significant work during sessions. This is frequently a matter of writing down work done together on the whiteboard. In addition, clients can keep their completed homework assignment sheets and refer to them later, if necessary. Trainees often make up cassettes that help clients retain material covered during sessions, for example making up cassettes of the appropriate self-talk skills that clients can use both to calm their anxiety and to remember how to communicate/act skilfully in the few minutes before they are due either to give a public speech or to take an examination.

The ending phase

There are various tasks involved in ending sessions competently in the middle sessions. Counselling trainees and clients need to bring closure to any work on a targeted skill in process during the latter part of a session's middle phase. If clients have not done so already, this may be an opportunity for them to write down any work still remaining on the whiteboard. In addition, trainees should leave sufficient time to negotiate and clarify homework assignments.

To allow time to perform the tasks of the ending phase properly, it is often a good idea to make an early structuring statement that allows for a smooth transition from the middle to the ending phase of the session. Counselling trainees might make such a statement about 5 to 10 minutes before the end of a 40–50 minute session. The first two statements in Box 23.4 are some statements trainees might make in this regard.

Box 23.4 Examples of counsellor statements for the ending phase

'I notice that we have to end in about ten minutes ... and, perhaps, we should spend some of this time looking at what you might do between sessions.'
'Before we end it might be a good idea to review what we've done today and see how you can build upon it before we next meet.'
'Is there anything you would like to bring up before we end?'
'Do you have any feedback you would like to share about the session or about our counselling relationship?'

Counselling trainees may want to review work done in the sessions themselves or allow clients to do this. Sometimes reviewing a session may help clients clarify and consolidate work performed during a session. However, session reviews are not always necessary, especially if the relevant skill training has been thoroughly performed in them. When trainee and client negotiate and clarify homework assignments, they may cover some of the same ground anyway.

In Chapter 22 I mentioned some ways of increasing clients' compliance in performing homework assignments. These ways include giving clear instructions in take-away form, collaborating with the client to develop assignments, beginning assignments during the session, and discussing with clients any difficulties they anticipate in carrying out the assignments.

When ending sessions, counselling trainees may also check whether clients have any unfinished business, queries or outstanding items that they would like to mention. Some counsellors like to check how clients have experienced the session and whether they have any feedback they would like to share with them (Padesky and Greenberger, 1995). Before ending a session, trainees should always make clear agreements with clients about the next appointment. They can also inform vulnerable 'at risk' clients how they can contact them between sessions. However, trainees should always maintain boundaries and not let working relationships slide into social relationships.

Activity 23.2 Conducting middle sessions

Part A: Formulating statements

Using Boxes 23.3 and 23.4 as guides, formulate at least two additional statements in each of the following categories:

- middle phase statements
- ending phase statements

Part B: Practising conducting middle sessions

One partner acts as counsellor, another as client, with possibly a third person acting as observer. Using the same assumptions, either for the problem started on in Activity 23.1 or for another problem, conduct a counselling session consisting of the following four phases:

- preparing phase (this may include addressing issues connected with your respective roles)
- starting phase
- middle phase
- ending phase

Afterwards hold a sharing and feedback discussion. Then, if appropriate, change roles and repeat this activity.

Using audio cassette or videotape recording and playback may add value to the activity.

Length, frequency and number of sessions

Perhaps it is most common for counselling sessions to be around 45 to 50 minutes long, the so-called '50-minute hour', with the remaining 10 minutes being left for writing up notes, relaxing and preparing for the next client. However, there are no hard and fast rules. Many considerations determine the length of sessions, including the counsellor's workload, agency policy and the purposes of the session.

Some counsellors conduct first sessions for longer than 45 to 50 minutes, say 90 minutes to two hours, because they are trying to complete the relating and understanding stages of the skilled client model thoroughly in one session. Sometimes subsequent sessions are shorter than 45–50 minutes, say 20–30 minutes, because counsellors are focusing on delivering specific interventions and checking on client progress in homework assignments.

When counselling trainees state that a session is going to be of a certain duration, they should try to adhere to this limit. Reasons for doing so include encouraging clients to speak up within their allotted time, having a break between clients, and not keeping subsequent clients waiting.

Frequency of sessions can range from daily to weekly to fortnightly to monthly or to *ad hoc* arrangements when clients come to see counselling trainees only when in special need. The most usual arrangement is for a weekly appointment at the same time to be scheduled. Advantages of this degree of certainty are that it is easier for clients and counsellors to arrange and remember regular sessions and that vulnerable clients have a weekly island of security on which they can rely. As counselling progresses, sessions may become more spaced out. Furthermore, trainees and clients can schedule one or more booster sessions after terminating their regular meetings.

Counselling trainees require flexibility in arranging and spacing sessions with clients and need to keep the time frames of clients' problems and problem situations in mind. For instance, a partner who is distraught and possibly suicidal over the break-up of an intimate relationship or a spouse who has to attend a potentially acrimonious child custody hearing in ten days' time may require more frequent meetings than once weekly.

There is great variation in the number of counselling sessions. Probably most counselling is short-term, say from one to eight or ten sessions. Medium-term counselling might last from about 11 to 20 sessions, with anything over that regarded as long-term counselling. For instance, though severely emotionally deprived clients might still be helped by short- or medium-term counselling, they often require long-term counselling. In addition, some clients may return for counselling on an *ad hoc* basic when they have crises, decisions and problems that they need to handle skilfully.

Many considerations influence how many sessions a counselling process contains. Clients' considerations include their goals, motivation, progress in counselling and how much counselling they can afford. Counsellors' considerations include their workload, preferred method of working, and how skilled they are at not wasting time (Lazarus, 1997). Contextual considerations include time constraints – for instance the length of terms and semesters in educational contexts; agency policy – for instance some medical settings require that each client is seen for the same number of sessions (Parrott, 1999); and the maximum number of sessions for which health care providers and insurance companies will provide funds. Needless to say, some of these considerations have ethical ramifications.

Counselling trainees can also make contact with clients between sessions. Lazarus (1997) makes extensive use of faxes, email, telephones and letters. Reasons for such contact include making a sympathetic enquiry during a critical situation, changing a homework assignment, or making a point based on reviewing his notes or musing over a session. Lazarus considers that this tendency to 'go the extra mile' models conscientiousness, inspires hope and usually pays huge dividends in expediting counselling progress. On rare occasions he needs to set limits, for instance with clients who want to engage in long Internet conversations for free instead of coming in for billable sessions.

Monitoring and evaluating progress

During the intervening phase of the changing stage of the lifeskills counselling model, counselling trainees and clients collaborate to monitor and evaluate progress in addressing problems and in improving targeted skills. During the middle sessions of counselling, this information is relevant to making decisions about how long to keep working with specific skills and when to move on to improving other skills. Monitoring progress also entails identifying where clients experience difficulty in implementing their skills outside the counselling room and reacting in counselling accordingly. Monitoring progress may lead counsellors and clients to identify impasses in the counselling process that they can then address (Dryden and Feltham, 1992).

Some information concerning progress comes from how clients say they are feeling and communicating or acting. They may feel more confident and less prone to negative emotions. Another source of information comes from clients' reports about how well they fare when performing homework assignments and where their difficulties lie. This information is relevant to establishing session agendas, including working to address specific out-of-counselling difficulties. In addition, clients may report comments made by third parties, such as family members or superiors and colleagues at work, that indicate how well they are progressing. Counselling trainees can form their own impressions about clients' progress by observing for themselves how well clients perform in role-play rehearsals, their ability to comprehend the skills they are learning, and any changes in their demeanour.

Sometimes both counselling trainee and client can assess progress in terms of measurable goals, for instance amount of weight lost, reductions in the number of cigarettes smoked, and only spending a certain amount of money each week. Here clients can monitor and record their behaviour. Another approach is to ask clients to fill out inventories on a regular basis. Greenberger and Padesky (1995) ask depressed clients to fill out the 19-item 'Mind Over Mood Depression Inventory' (p. 155) and anxious clients to fill out the 24-item 'Mind Over Mood Anxiety Inventory' (p. 178) each week. The instruction for both inventories is 'Circle one number for each item that best describes how much you have experienced each symptom over the past week.' Counsellors and clients can then chart clients' progress in improving how they feel. However, trainees should remember to distinguish between charting progress in attaining outcomes, for instance weight loss or improved mood, and monitoring progress in how well clients are actually understanding and using their skills.

end and client self-helping 24

Chapter outcomes

By studying and doing the activity in this chapter you should:

- understand some issues regarding when to end counselling;
- know about some formats for ending counselling;
- know about some tasks entailed in ending counselling; and
- understand some ways of client self-helping.

When should counselling end?

The boundaries for ending counselling are imprecise. In a sense, lifeskills counselling has its ending built into its beginning. To look at it another way, the ending of formal counselling is the beginning of independent self-helping. Counsellors and trainees should start termination discussions before the final sessions and aim for convergence either then or by the final session. Throughout counselling, trainees and clients collect information relevant to termination decisions. The following are sources of and kinds of relevant information.

Client self-report

Clients may perceive themselves as better able to cope with problems. They may think they have attained their mind skills and communication/action skills goals. They may feel more confident and less prone to negative emotions. They perceive they no longer require the support of counsellors and can maintain skills.

Counsellor observation

Over a series of sessions, counselling trainees may notice improvements in how well clients use targeted mind skills and communication/action skills. These observations come from various sources: the counselling conversation, role-plays and other structured activities, and from probes about how well clients use skills outside counselling. Trainees may observe clients feeling happier and more relaxed. They no longer have symptoms that brought them to counselling – for instance excessive anxiety. Problems that previously seemed insurmountable now seem manageable in that clients now can use better skills in responding to such problems. In addition, they seem to understand the targeted skills well enough to maintain them.

Feedback from significant others

Significant others in clients' lives give clients feedback that they are different, or have changed, or make comments such as 'You never used to do that before.' Sometimes the feedback may come direct to a counselling trainee: for instance, from counsellor's aides, spouses, bosses or parents.

Attainment of measurable goals

Clients can have easily measurable goals. For example, they may pass an examination or driving test. Other examples include losing a stipulated amount of weight and maintaining the loss over a given period, cutting down on smoking and maintaining the reduction, keeping off alcohol, or only spending a certain amount of money each week. Clients' goals can be both objective and subjective, for instance making a given number of friends in a set period of time. The given number and set period are objective, whereas the definition of friends is subjective.

If trainees and clients consistently obtain positive information from all four of the above sources, their decision about when to end is easy. However, if positive changes are recent, it may pay to 'wait and see' whether clients maintain them. Inconsistent information, either from within or between different sources, merits further exploration.

Formats for ending counselling

Sometimes counselling trainees and clients have limited choice over when to end counselling, for example when clients leave town, when terms end, and when counselling addresses specific forthcoming situations such as important examinations or a wedding speech. On other occasions, trainees and clients have more choice about when to end. The following are some possible formats for ending counselling.

Fixed ending

The counselling trainee and client may have a contract that they work for, say, eight sessions in one or more problem or problematic skills areas. Advantages of fixed termination include lessening the chance of dependency and motivating clients to use counselling to best effect. Potential disadvantages include restricting coverage of problems and insufficient thoroughness in training.

Open ending when goals are attained

With open endings, counselling concludes when counselling trainees and clients agree that clients have made sufficient progress in attaining their main goals. Such goals include managing specific problems better and developing improved skills to address current and future problems. An advantage of open endings is that of flexibility, such as when counsellors and clients uncover deeper or different issues to address than the ones for which clients originally came for counselling.

Faded ending

Here the withdrawal of counselling assistance is gradual. For example, instead of meeting weekly, the final sessions could be at fortnightly or monthly intervals. Faded endings have much to recommend them when clients are learning mind skills and communication/action skills since they provide more time to ensure that clients have adequately internalized their changed skills.

Ending with booster session(s)

Booster sessions, say after three months, are not to teach new skills, but to check clients' progress in consolidating skills, to motivate them, and help them work through difficulties in taking away and using trained skills in their home environments.

Scheduling follow-up contact after ending

Counselling trainees can schedule follow-up phone calls or postal and email correspondence with clients. This performs some of the same functions as booster sessions, enabling trainees to obtain feedback on how successful counselling was in assisting clients to maintain their skills. Then, where necessary, they can take appropriate action.

Premature ending

Clients can and do leave counselling before counselling trainees think they are ready to do so. Sometimes clients just do not come to their next appointment with or without warning. However, under-confident trainees should be careful about automatically interpreting this as a wish to end counselling. There may be good reasons why a client misses an appointment. When clients build up a track record of good attendance, they almost invariably have sound reasons for missing an appointment. Where trainees have yet to amass sufficient evidence to interpret missed appointments accurately, after waiting for an appropriate period for clients to make contact, one option is to enquire tactfully if they wish to schedule another appointment.

What may seem premature ending to counselling trainees may seem different to clients. Beck and his colleagues cite as reasons for premature ending rapid relief of symptoms, negative reactions to the therapist, and lack of sustained improvement or relapse during treatment (Beck et al., 1979). Premature ending may also take place where there is a mismatch between the kind of counselling relationship that counsellors offer and the kind that clients expect (Lazarus, 1993). Trainees who clumsily handle clients' doubts about and resistances to counselling increase the likelihood of premature termination.

Further reasons why clients leave prematurely include pressure from significant others, laziness, defensiveness, lack of money and fear of being trapped by counsellors or by trainees unwilling to 'let go' or who have their own agendas such as mixing religious proselytizing with counselling. In addition, counselling sometimes ends prematurely because trainees are insufficiently invested in their clients. Reasons for this include fatigue and burnout, personality clashes and finding certain clients unattractive or uncongenial.

Counselling trainees may consider it premature if clients leave counselling feeling able to cope with immediate problems, but having insufficiently consolidated the relevant mind and communication/action skills for dealing with future problems. Sometimes clients initiate this kind of end. However, increasingly counsellors and clients are under pressure from managed care providers and/or agency policies to engage in time-limited counselling that may lead to training in targeted skills being insufficiently thorough. Nevertheless, counsellors and clients may still have done some useful work together. Former clients may now possess insights about the skills needed to cope with future problems and also be more inclined to seek assistance in future, if needed.

Sometimes clients reveal their decision to end to counselling trainees who are of the opinion that this is not the wise thing to do. Dryden and Feltham (1992) assert that counsellors should respect the right of clients who wish to end abruptly to do so, and avoid trying to persuade or coerce them to change their minds. When a trainees and client have developed a good collaborative working relationship, they can calmly discuss the advantages and disadvantages of terminating at that time and still leave the final decision entirely to the client.

Prolonged ending

For various reasons, either counselling trainees or clients or both may be reluctant or unwilling to end counselling. Here I focus on trainee reasons for extending counselling longer than might be justified. Though unlikely in the lifeskills counselling model, some trainees insufficiently prepare clients throughout counselling to face the fact of its termination, thus making it harder to end counselling when the time comes. Sometimes trainees waste time and allow the counselling process to drift rather than stay sufficiently focused on appropriate tasks.

There are also many 'shadow' reasons why counselling trainees may consciously or unconsciously prolong counselling. Such reasons include appreciative and admiring clients who feed the trainee's narcissism, trainees being erotically attracted to clients, and financial considerations attached to extending counselling. Sometimes trainees and clients establish and maintain patterns of communication that can lengthen the counselling process, for example powerful trainees breeding passive clients or both parties becoming friends rather than engaging in a professional relationship.

Consolidating skills when ending counselling

The main task in ending counselling is 'the consolidation of what has been achieved in terms of some durable benefit for the interviewee' (Sullivan, 1954: 41). Many skills that counselling trainees use in the ending phase build on skills that they have used earlier. With clients who come for brief, focused counselling, trainees and clients may be forced to compromise in what they achieve in the ending phase of stage 3 of the lifeskills counselling model. The following are some skills for enhancing consolidation of self-helping skills when ending counselling.

Make transition statements

During counselling, counselling trainees may make statements indicating its finiteness: for instance on the usefulness of homework assignments for developing self-helping skills to use after counselling. Such comments may encourage clients to make the most of their regular sessions and the time between them. Trainees can also introduce the topic of termination with one or more transition statements which clearly signal that counselling is coming to an end (see Box 24.1).

Box 24.1 Examples of transition statements for ending counselling

'We only have a few more sessions left. Perhaps we should not only discuss an agenda for this session, but think about how best we can spend our remaining time together.'

'Our next session is the final session. Would it be all right with you if we spent some time discussing how to help you retain and build on your improved skills for managing your problem?'

'Perhaps the agenda for this final session should mainly be how to help you use the skills you've learned here for afterwards. For instance, we can review how much you've changed, where there is still room for improvement, how you might go about it, and plan how to deal with any difficult situations you anticipate.'

Prevent and retrieve lapses

Two issues that become important after ending counselling are how clients can deal with difficult situations on their own and how they can get back on track if they have a lapse.

During counselling, clients will often have anticipated and coped with difficult situations in their outside lives. Where necessary, in the ending phase, they can identify future difficult or high-risk situations where they might fail to use their improved skills and consequently become discouraged. Counselling trainees and clients can then conduct role-play rehearsals in how to deal with these difficult situations.

Clients can learn the distinction between lapses and relapses. Where appropriate, trainees can help them to develop retrieval skills so that if they make a mistake or have a lapse they can revert to using their improved skills rather than relapse. When clients use poor skills, this is not the time for self-denigration and engaging in black-and-white thinking in which they tell themselves they have lost their improved skills for all time. Sometimes trainees can work with clients to develop appropriate self-talk for handling lapses, underachievement and failure. Box 24.2 provides an example of self-talk for a client working on managing his temper at home that could be put on a reminder card or recorded on cassette.

Box 24.2 Example of self-talk for retrieving a lapse

'OK, on that occasion I went back to my former ways and lost my temper. Now that I have calmed down, this is a signal for me to use my retrieval skills. What is important is that I learn that I can overcome lapses and failure and get back to using my improved mind and communication skills again. I can use my creating rules skills to challenge and restate any demanding rule that has contributed to my anger. In addition I can use my calming self-talk skills and coach myself in making my points more assertively and less aggressively. Where appropriate, I can also apologize for the hurt I have caused and let my family know I really am serious about working to keep on top of my temper. Life at home has been happier for all of us now that I am behaving more reasonably and I am determined to keep my family intact.'

Review progress and summarize learnings

Clients can become not only their own counsellors, but their own trainers. In the final session, counselling trainees and clients may review the client's progress to date and discuss ways of maintaining and improving clients' skills after termination. Furthermore, trainees should emphasize the importance of clients continuing to monitor how well they use their targeted skills. They should also inform clients that learning can continue after the end of counselling, just as it can continue after leaving school or university.

Counselling trainees can encourage clients to persist with their changed thinking and behaviour by continuing to point out associations between attaining wished-for outcomes in real life and using their improved skills. With some clients, trainees may engage in cost-benefit analyses, possibly on the whiteboard.

Throughout counselling, trainees can check clients' understanding of the skills they are learning by asking them to summarize their principal aspects. During the ending phase, trainees and clients may use summaries to review the skills taught during counselling. Where appropriate, trainees can ask clients to record their summaries on cassette as reminders. Another idea is for clients to keep cassette recordings of their final sessions.

Explore arrangements for continuing support

Self-support is the main way that clients can receive continuing help. However, given the likelihood of difficulties and lapses in maintaining targeted skills, counselling trainees should think through how clients might receive ongoing support. The following are some options.

Further contact with the counsellor

Possibilities include scheduled booster sessions, follow-up sessions at clients' request, and either scheduled or unscheduled phone calls and emails. Trainees can discuss with clients how they view further contact with them.

Referral for further individual counselling

Though clients may have made considerable progress with the problems and problematic skills for which they came to counselling, they may still require further professional assistance. For many reasons counselling trainees may decide to refer such clients to other counsellors: for instance, their time may be limited or another counsellor has special expertise in an emerging problem area.

Using outside supports

In Chapter 19 I mentioned the counsellor skill of assisting clients to identify and use supports as they improve their mind skills and communication/action skills. Many of the supports clients identify during counselling should be available afterwards. In addition, in the middle and ending sessions of counselling, trainees can encourage clients to view identifying and using supports as a useful self-helping skill. One way of using others as supports is to encourage them to give honest feedback in non-threatening ways. Such feedback can be either confirmatory, indicating that former clients are on track in using their improved skills, or corrective, informing them that they have wandered off course and need to get back on track (Egan, 2002). Open acknowledgement by others of positive behaviour changes can motivate clients to keep improving their skills.

Continued support from counsellor's aides

During the ending phase, counselling trainees can contact their aides to receive assessments of clients' progress outside counselling. Trainees can also work with aides to identify ways in which they can continue supporting clients once counselling ends. Sometimes three-way meetings between counsellors, clients and aides are desirable. For example, at the end of a series of counselling sessions designed to help an elementary school child become more outgoing, teacher, child and trainee school counsellor might together plan how the teacher could continue supporting the child.

Group counselling and training

Some clients might benefit from joining groups in which they can practise and develop targeted skills. Peer self-help groups provide an alternative to professionally led groups. Counselling trainees can also discuss opportunities for client participation in courses or workshops run by themselves or others.

Further reading and audiovisual material

Some clients appreciate the support provided by further reading, self-help audio cassettes and videotapes. On their own initiative or by request, counselling trainees can suggest appropriate sources.

Further ending counselling tasks and skills

In addition to the major task of consolidating self-helping skills, there are other tasks when terminating counselling. How counselling trainees handle them varies with length of counselling, the nature of problem(s) and problematic skills, and the counsellor–client relationship.

Deal with feelings

When using the lifeskills counselling model, most counselling contacts are short to medium term. Because collaborative working relationships are very important, the relationship is not the central feature of counselling and there is less likelihood of clients feeling angry, sad, anxious and abandoned than when ending longer-term relationship-oriented counselling. Instead clients often feel better able to cope with problems because of their improved skills, and experience a sense of accomplishment and optimism.

Clients' feelings when ending counselling fall into two main categories: feelings about how they are going to fare without counsellors and feelings toward counsellors and the counselling process. Many clients are ambivalent about how they will cope after counselling. On the one hand, they feel more competent, yet on the other hand they still have doubts about their ability to implement skills. Counselling trainees can facilitate open discussion of clients' feelings about the future. Looking at how best to maintain skills also addresses the issue of clients' lingering doubts. Other clients will feel confident that they can cope now on their own, which is hopefully a sign of work well done.

Clients may also wish to share feelings about the counselling process. However, they should not allow themselves to get involved in lengthy discussions of unfinished emotional business. Nevertheless, trainees should allow clients the opportunity to share feelings about their contact with them. They may obtain valuable feedback both about how they come across and about clients' reactions to different interventions and aspects of the counselling process. Trainees may humanize terminating by sharing some of their feelings with clients: for instance, 'I enjoyed working with you', or 'I admire the courage with which you face your situation', or 'I'm delighted with your progress.'

End counselling ethically

Saying goodbye or the formal leave-taking 'should be a clean-cut, respectful finish that does not confuse that which has been done' (Sullivan, 1954: 216).

Last as well as first impressions are important. Counselling trainees should aim to say goodbye in a businesslike, yet friendly way, appropriate to professional rather than personal relationships. By ending counselling sloppily, trainees may undo some of their influence in helping clients to maintain their skills.

There are a number of key ethical issues surrounding ending counselling. For example, counselling trainees need to think through their responsibilities to clients after counselling. Too much support may engender dependency, too little may fail to carry out professional obligations. Each case must be judged on its merits. Another ethical issue is what trainees should do when they think clients have other problems on which they need to work. I suggest tactfully bringing such views to clients' attention.

A further set of ethical issues surrounds the boundary between personal and professional relationships. Most professional associations have ethical codes about providing counselling services. Counselling trainees who allow their personal and professional wires to get crossed when terminating are not only acting unethically, but can make it more difficult for clients to be counselled by them if the need arises in future. When considering any post-counselling personal relationships with clients, trainees should be guided by ethical codes, their conscience, the advice of their supervisors and respected colleagues and, above all, by their own view of the client's best interests.

Evaluate one's counselling skills

When counselling ends, counselling trainees have many sources of information for evaluating their counselling skills. These include attendance, intentional and unintentional feedback from clients, perceptions of client progress, session notes, possibly videotapes or audio cassettes of counselling sessions, clients' compliance and success in carrying out homework assignments, and feedback from third parties such as supervisors.

Counselling trainees can make a final evaluation of their work with each client soon after ending regular contact. Questions trainees can ask include: 'To what extent did the client manage her/his problem(s) better and improve her/his skills?' and 'How well did I use the skills for each stage and phase of the skilled client model?' If trainees defer such an evaluation for too long, they risk forgetting valuable information. When evaluating their counselling skills trainees should beware of their characteristic perceiving errors; for example, they may be too hard or too easy on themselves. What they seek is a balanced appraisal of their good and poor skills to guide their work with future clients.

Client self-helping

Phase 3 of the changing stage of the skilled client model is that of client self-helping. Even where counselling has only addressed how to manage a forthcoming problem, clients can still use their insights to manage other problems once counselling ends. Where counselling has focused on improving mind skills and communication/action skills to manage current and future problems more successfully, clients should have a reasonable grasp of how to keep using their improved skills, monitor their progress, retrieve lapses and, where possible, integrate their improved skills into their daily lives.

The process of consolidating skills in the middle and ending sessions of counselling can continue when clients are on their own. Since this is much more likely to occur if clients use good mind skills, I briefly review here some pertinent mind skills.

Creating rules

Former clients are more likely to keep using their improved mind skills and communication/action skills if they can challenge any demanding rules that may weaken their resolve and restate them as preferential rules. Clearly, those clients who have worked on their demanding rules during counselling are in a strong position to do so. Box 24.3 provides some examples.

Box 24.3 Creating preferential rules about maintaining improved skills

Demanding rule: 'Maintaining my improved skills must be easy.'
Preferential rule: 'There is no such thing as cure. I need to keep practising my improved skills so that using them may then become easier.'
Demanding rule: 'After terminating counselling, I must never go backwards.'
Preferential rule: 'Maintaining any skill can involve mistakes, uncertainty, and setbacks. All I can do is to learn from and retrieve mistakes and cope with setbacks as best as possible.'
Demanding rule: 'Others must support and approve of my efforts to improve my skills.'
Preferential rule: 'Though I might prefer to have others' approval, what is important is that I keep my skills development goals in mind and work hard to attain them.'

Creating perceptions

Former clients should strive to perceive their good and poor skills accurately. They will discourage themselves if they pay disproportionate attention to setbacks rather than to successes. When lapses occur, former clients should try to avoid the perceiving error of over-generalizing them into relapses: 'Since I have gone back to my old behaviour once, I have permanently relapsed and can do nothing about it.' Lapses should stimulate the use of retrieval or 'getting back on the track' skills rather than giving up. Box 24.2 earlier in the chapter provides an example of some self-talk for getting back on track after a lapse.

Creating self-talk

Former clients can use coping self-talk to deal with 'hot' thinking connected with temptations such as food, alcohol, drugs or high-risk sex. Watson and Tharp advocate that as soon as former clients become aware of high-risk situations they should say: 'Danger! This is risky. I could have a lapse here', and then give themselves specific instructions of what to do (Watson and Tharp, 2001). A similar approach is to say: 'Stop ... think ... calm down', and then instruct themselves what to do. Further instructions include telling themselves that cravings will pass, engaging in distracting activities or thoughts, and reminding themselves of the benefits of resisting temptation and the costs of giving in.

When former clients do have lapses they can say to themselves: 'Now is the time for me to use my retrieval skills.' One former client of mine, who became extremely anxious about performing his golf down-swing correctly, learned to replace his anxiety-engendering self-talk when his golf ball ended up in awkward situations by telling himself 'No upheaval, just retrieval.' This retrieval self-talk empowered him to cope with rather than be overwhelmed by difficulties.

Former clients can also use affirming self-talk to maintain their improved skills. They can encourage themselves with internal rewards like 'Well done', 'I hung in there and made it', and 'I'm happy that I'm maintaining my skills.'

Creating visual images

Former clients can visualize anticipated high-risk situations and develop strategies for coping with them. They can also visualize the negative consequences of engaging in or relapsing into unwanted behaviours. Some may need to exaggerate the negative consequences to strengthen their willpower (Cautela, 1967b; Lazarus, 1984).

Creating explanations

Former clients require accuracy in explaining the causes of positive and negative events as they implement and maintain their improved skills.

For instance, where justified, they can attribute the cause of their successes to factors such as effort, willingness to take reasonable risks, and use of targeted skills.

Successful former clients assume personal responsibility for their lives. When in difficulty, looking at the adequacy of their own thinking, communicating and use of targeted skills is the best place to start. They ask themselves questions such as: 'What are my goals and how is my behaviour blocking me from attaining them?' 'What are my characteristic poor mind and communication/action skills in relation to this problem?' 'How well am I using the skills I have learned and how can I improve?'

Creating expectations

Creating realistic expectations can help former clients to maintain skills in a number of ways. Those able to predict high-risk situations that present a greater than usual temptation to lapse into unwanted behaviour can develop strategies to deal with them. Characteristics of high-risk situations include feeling emotionally upset, being under considerable stress, feeling lonely, social pressure from others, and losing control under the influence of alcohol.

Former clients will strengthen their resolve to maintain their improved skills if they are able to predict the benefits of continuing to use them and the costs of giving them up. They can maintain skills in specific situations where realistic risk-taking is desirable if they focus on the gains of action as well as on potential losses. By so doing, they challenge and counterbalance their excessive expectations of danger.

Activity 24.1 Conducting a final session

Conduct a final session with a partner who role-plays a client with whom, for at least four previous sessions, you have worked. The aim now is to improve at least one mind skill and one communication/action skill. In the final session, as appropriate, use the following skills:

- Make transition statements.
- Prevent and retrieve lapses.
- Review progress.
- Summarize learnings.
- Explore arrangements for continued support.
- Deal with feelings.
- Say goodbye.
- End ethically.

At the end of the session, discuss and receive feedback. Playing back an audio cassette or videotape of the session may assist learning. Afterwards, reverse roles.

V further considerations

ethics in practice and training 25

Chapter outcomes

By studying and doing the activities in this chapter you should:

- appreciate some of the main principles underlying ethical behaviour;
- be aware of some important ethical codes and guidelines;
- know about some important ethical issues and dilemmas in counselling and helping practice;
- know about some important ethical issues and dilemmas in counselling and helping training; and
- possess some knowledge and skills for ethical decision-making.

All counselling practitioners and trainees develop personal systems of ethics for how they work with clients. The word 'ethics' is sometimes defined as the science of morals in human conduct. Morals are concerned with the distinction between right and wrong and with accepted rules and standards of behaviour. Thus, ethical codes or ethical guidelines for counselling and helping attempt to present acceptable standards for practice within the profession.

Sometimes it is obvious when there has been an ethical lapse, for instance engaging in sexual relations with clients. However, in the complexities of counselling practice, ethical issues are often unclear. Consequently counsellors and trainees are faced with ethical dilemmas involving choices about how best to act. Given the prevalence of such dilemmas, trainees require the skills of ethical decision-making since they should not just slavishly follow ethical codes.

Ethical principles of counselling and helping

The British Association for Counselling and Psychotherapy's *Ethical Framework for Good Practice in Counselling and Psychotherapy* (BACP, 2002) presents six ethical principles which should, insofar as possible, be followed by counsellors and counselling trainees. Sometimes, ethical issues arise in which it is not possible to reconcile each of these principles and the trainee, with appropriate support, may be forced to make a choice between principles. Nevertheless, trainees are obliged to make all ethical decisions with as much care as is reasonably possible.

- *Fidelity.* Fidelity pertains to honouring the trust placed in the practitioner. Counselling trainees should act in accordance with the trust placed in them and regard confidentiality as an obligation arising from such trust.
- *Autonomy.* Autonomy relates to respect for the client's right to be self-governing. Elements of autonomy that counselling trainees need to adhere to include seeking freely given and adequately informed consent and also letting the client know about actual or potential conflicts of interest as soon as possible.
- *Beneficence.* Beneficence means a commitment to promoting the client's well-being based on professional assessment. Counselling trainees should work strictly within the limits of their competence, based on training and experience, and monitor their practice and outcomes carefully. Trainees and counsellors alike have an obligation to be appropriately supervised and to commit themselves to updating their practice by continuing professional development.
- *Non-maleficence.* Non-maleficence is founded on the commitment of avoiding harm to clients. This includes sexual, financial, emotional or any other form of exploitation. Harm may also be caused by incompetence, malpractice, or be due to personal circumstances such as illness or intoxication. Non-maleficence extends to include counsellors and trainees having a professional responsibility to challenge, where appropriate, the incompetence or malpractice of others. In most instances, trainees should first discuss such matters with their trainers and/or supervisors.
- *Justice.* The principle of justice means the fair and impartial treatment of all clients and focuses on providing adequate services. Legal requirements need to be considered, as do potential conflicts between these requirements and ethical obligations. Justice in the provision of services is important, including allocating services between clients and avoiding discrimination on the basis of personal or social characteristics.
- *Self-respect* Counselling practitioners need to foster their self-knowledge and to care for themselves. They should seek counselling and other forms of personal development as needed. They are under an ethical obligation to use supervision for appropriate professional and personal support and to engage in suitable opportunities for continuing professional development. BACP's statement on ethical principles also encourages 'active engagement in life-enhancing activities and relationships that are independent of relationships in counselling or psychotherapy' (BACP, 2002: 4).

Ethical codes and guidelines

Professional ethical codes and guidelines are an important source for counselling trainees as they develop personal systems of ethics for their counselling practice. Such codes of conduct can provide a starting point for a process of ethical decision-making since they lay out what is generally considered acceptable behaviour in the profession. Since they influence counsellors to behave ethically, codes of conduct help protect the public from potentially unethical counsellors, and such counsellors from themselves. Furthermore, in cases of unethical behaviour, codes of practice form part of the process of hearing complaints against counsellors, something that would be difficult to do in their absence. Where counsellors and trainees have behaved ethically, adherence to an accepted professional code can protect them against charges of malpractice.

There is some question as to whether ethical codes actually do foster and elicit ethical awareness and behaviour. One reason they may lose some of their power is that they tend to be rather boring documents emphasizing 'don'ts' rather than 'do's'. Another reason is that some counsellors and trainees may consider that such guidelines are for other ethically vulnerable counsellors rather than for themselves. It should be stated, however, that individuals' powers of self-deceiving rationalization may take over when facing the temptation of certain unethical behaviours.

A further reason that ethical codes may insufficiently foster and elicit ethical awareness and behaviour is that their existence may engender passivity and even apathy. Such codes can be used as prescriptions that do counselling trainees' ethical thinking for them rather than assisting them in developing their own skills of thinking critically about ethical issues and dilemmas. Pattison observes: 'As an ethicist my main anxiety about professional codes is that they do little to develop or support the active independent critical judgment and discernment that should be associated with true moral responsibility, and indeed, good professionalism' (1999: 375). He states that ethical codes are largely unaccompanied by case studies and detailed explanations that would help trainees and practitioners develop skills of exercising judgement in the light of universally important moral principles and concerns. However, some ethics casebooks do exist, for instance the American Counseling Association's *ACA Ethical Standards Casebook* (Herlihy and Corey, 1996).

Another reason why ethical codes may have had less impact than desirable is that, to date, they have been geared solely to counsellors rather than to counselling trainees. Counsellor training abounds in ethical issues and there is a strong case for developing a code of ethical conduct specifically designed for counselling trainees. Developing ethically aware trainees is a good entry point for developing ethically aware counsellors rather than, as may sometimes happen, having a main emphasis on professional ethics after training.

Box 25.1 lists some illustrative professional codes. Always look out for the most recent copy. Each of these codes is fully referenced in the bibliography at the end of the book. Readers may note that none of these ethical codes and guidelines applies directly to counselling trainees.

Box 25.1 Illustrative British and Australian ethical codes and guidelines relevant to counselling

Britain

British Association for Counselling and Psychotherapy (BACP)
Ethical Framework for Good Practice in Counselling and Psychotherapy (2002)

British Psychological Society (BPS)
Division of Counselling Psychology, *Guidelines for the Professional Practice of Counselling Psychology* (1998)
Division of Counselling Psychology, *Guidelines on Confidentiality and Record Keeping* (2002)

United Kingdom Council for Psychotherapy (UKCP)
Ethical Requirements for Member Organizations (2003)

Australia

Psychotherapy & Counselling Federation of Australia (PACFA)
Ethical Guidelines (2001)
Australian Psychological Society (APS)
Code of Ethics (2002)
Guidelines for Psychotherapeutic Practice with Female Clients (1996)

Activity 25.1 Sources of counselling and helping ethics

Critically discuss the role of each of the following sources in developing your personal system of counselling and helping ethics:

- your personal ethics
- the ethics implicit in the theoretical model(s) that you use
- the policies of the agency or agencies in which you counsel
- insights from moral philosophy
- professional codes and guidelines, and
- any sources not mentioned above.

Ethical issues and dilemmas in counselling and helping practice

Ethical issues and dilemmas permeate counselling and therapy practice. To use legal language, counsellors and trainees always have a duty of care to their clients. Virtually everything counselling trainees do can be performed ethically or unethically. In Box 25.2 the ethical issues and dilemmas connected with enacting this duty of care are divided into five main areas, which overlap: counsellor competence, client autonomy, confidentiality, client protection, and professional monitoring and development. I now overview each area in turn.

Box 25.2 Ethical issues and dilemmas in counselling and helping practice

Counsellor competence

- relationship competence
- technical competence
- readiness to practice
- fitness to practice
- recognizing limitations and making referrals

Client autonomy

- respect for client self-determination
- accurate pre-counselling information
- accurate statements about professional competence
- honest statements about counselling processes and outcomes
- clear contract negotiated in advance
- informed consent to interventions
- respect for diverse values

Confidentiality

- any limitations communicated in advance
- consent for communication with third parties
- issues of disclosure to save life or to prevent serious harm to others
- issues of permission and parental involvement with minors
- permission to record sessions
- permission and anonymity in research projects
- security of all client records

Client protection

- maintaining clear boundaries to the counselling relationship
- avoidance of financial exploitation
- avoidance of emotional and sexual exploitation
- protection of clients' physical safety
- adequate indemnity insurance
- knowledge of relevant law

Professional monitoring and development

- regular and ongoing supervision/consultative support
- continuing professional development
- keeping abreast of research and other relevant literature

Counsellor competence

How competently are many counsellors and therapists performing? When introducing the case of George, noted psychotherapist Arnold Lazarus, the originator of multimodal therapy, highlights the issue of competence in the counselling and psychotherapy profession (Lazarus, 2005b).

> When George first saw Lazarus he was 32, the only child of an alcoholic father and an abusive mother. When George was 20 his father died and he became the 'man of the house' who looked after his mother and widowed aunt, even though never leaving the house without his mother.
>
> Starting age 21 George had spent over $50,000 on being psychoanalyzed several times a week over six years, eventually concluding that he was not being helped. Subsequently, George received behaviour therapy, drug therapy, electroconvulsive therapy, primal therapy, transactional analysis, transcendental meditation and existential therapy.
>
> Despite the above treatments, George still continued to suffer from anxiety, panic, withdrawal, hypochondriasis, agoraphobia, other phobias, nightmares, temper tantrums, bathroom rituals, and obsessive-compulsive habits.

With so many approaches to counselling and helping, the issue arises as to what is competence. In Box 25.2 I distinguish between relationship competence, offering a good counselling relationship, and technical competence, the ability to assess clients and to deliver interventions. There is far greater agreement between the different therapeutic approaches on the ingredients of relationship competence, such as respect and support for clients as persons and accurately listening to and understanding their worldviews, than there is on technical competence. Suffice it for now to say that technical competence is what leading practitioners in a given approach would agree to be competent performance of the technical aspects of that approach. I provided the example of George not to advocate the superiority of multimodal therapy over other approaches – there may be some poor multimodal therapists too – but to indicate that some counsellors and trainees may fall below acceptable levels of either relationship competence or technical competence or very possibly both. If so, this is a challenge to the counselling profession to raise its standards of selection, training and practice.

Readiness to practice means that counsellors and trainees require appropriate training and practice before they are ready to see clients and to use their counselling skills competently. Fitness to practice assumes that counsellors and trainees have satisfactory counselling skills in their repertoires and it only becomes an ethical problem when they are precluded in some way from using these skills competently. An example of readiness to practice as an ethical problem is when trainees take on cases, for example anorexic clients, who are beyond their level of training and competence. An example of fitness to practice as an ethical problem is that of a trainee who drinks at work and so fails to maintain competence. Trainees can avoid ethical issues concerning readiness to practice if they are prepared to refer certain clients to others more qualified to help them. Furthermore, where trainees do not possess the requisite competence to help some categories of clients, they can discourage colleagues from referring such people to them.

Client autonomy

Respect for the client's right to make the choices that work best for them in their lives is the principle underlying client self-determination. Counselling trainees should seek to support clients' control over and ability to assume personal responsibility for their lives. When, for example, trainees provide inaccurate pre-counselling information or make false statements about their professional qualifications and competencies they are stopping potential and actual clients from making informed choices about whether to commence and/or continue in counselling with them.

Most often it is unnecessary and unrealistic for counselling trainees to provide lengthy explanations to clients about what they do. Nevertheless, before and during counselling, they can make accurate statements concerning the counselling process and about the their respective roles. Furthermore, trainees can answer clients' queries about counselling honestly and with respect.

Counselling trainees should also make realistic statements about the outcomes of counselling and avoid making claims that might be disputed both outside and inside of court. Throughout counselling, clients should be treated as intelligent participants who have a right to explanations about why trainees suggest interventions and what is entailed in implementing them.

An issue in client autonomy arises where the values and backgrounds of clients differ from those of their counsellors, for instance as a result of cultural or religious influences. Counselling trainees should not impose their values on clients and, where appropriate, should be prepared to refer clients on to others who may more readily understand their concerns. It is highly unethical for trainees to assess and treat clients as pathological on the basis of judgements determined by culture, race, sex or sexual orientation, among other characteristics.

Confidentiality

Sometimes it is said that all people have three lives: a public life, a private life, and a secret life. Since frequently counselling deals with material from clients' secret lives, their trust that their confidences will be kept is absolutely vital. However, there may be reasons connected with matters such as agency policy and sometimes the law why counselling trainees cannot guarantee confidentiality. For example, when counsellors work with minors – whether in private practice, educational or medical settings – there are many ethical and legal issues surrounding the boundaries of confidentiality and their obligations to parents, teachers and significant others.

Counselling trainees should endeavour to communicate pertinent limitations on confidentiality to clients in advance. Furthermore, other than in exceptional circumstances, trainees should seek clients' permission for any communication to third parties. Having said this, the issue of whether or not to disclose to third parties is at the forefront of ethical dilemmas for counsellors, especially where risks to children are involved. Lindsay and Clarkson (1999) grouped into four areas the answers of a sample of British psychotherapists who reported ethically troubling incidents concerning confidentiality:

- risk to third parties – sexual abuse;
- risk to the client – threatened suicide;
- disclosure of information to others – particularly to medical agencies, other colleagues, the client's close friends, relatives; and
- careless/inappropriate disclosure – by the psychotherapist or others.

Confidentiality assumes that clients have the right to control the disclosure of their personal information. In instances where counselling trainees require tapes for supervision purposes, they should refrain from putting pressure on clients to be recorded. Most clients will understand the request and, provided they are assured of the security of the tapes, will give their permission. Clients who have reservations are often reassured when told that they may stop the recording any time they wish. In instances where trainees want clients to participate in research projects, not only should their permission be sought, but when reporting findings clients' anonymity must be protected.

Clients' records, whether they are case notes, tapes or research information, need to be held securely at all times. A final word about confidentiality is that counselling trainees, when talking socially with colleagues, relatives or friends, should learn to keep their mouths shut about details of their clients' problems and lives. Silence is the best and only ethical policy for those trainees tempted to show off at the expense of their own integrity and in clear breach of their clients' gift of trust.

Client protection

The category of client protection encompasses looking after clients as persons. Counselling trainees require sufficient professional detachment to act in clients' best interests. Dual relationships are those where, in addition to the counselling relationship, counsellors or trainees may already be in, or consider entering, or enter other kinds of relationships with clients: for instance as friend, lover, colleague, trainer or supervisor among others. Whether a dual counsellor–client relationship is ethical, unethical or presents an ethical dilemma depends on the circumstances of the relationship. In small communities, some contact between counsellors and their clients may be hard to avoid and is not, of itself, unethical. Sexual contact with clients is always unethical. In a large-scale study of British clinical psychologists, under 4 per cent of the sample reported that they had engaged in sexual contact with their patients who were either in therapy or discharged. However, nearly 23 per cent had treated patients who had been sexually involved with previous therapists from a range of professions (Garrett, 1998).

Instead of or as well as sexual exploitation, clients may also be subject to emotional and financial exploitation. Emotional exploitation can take many forms, but has the underlying theme of using clients in some way for the counsellor's personal agenda, for example encouraging dependent and admiring clients rather than fostering autonomy. Financial exploitation can also take many forms including counsellors charging for services they are unqualified to provide, overcharging and prolonging counselling unnecessarily.

Counselling trainees need to ensure that all reasonable precautions are taken to ensure clients' physical safety. In addition, counsellors and counsellor training organizations should consider protecting their clients and themselves by carrying adequate indemnity insurance covering such matters as professional indemnity (malpractice, errors and omissions) and public liability (including occupier's liability). Counsellors and trainees will be better placed to protect their clients, and sometimes themselves too, if they have adequate knowledge of pertinent aspects of the law.

Professional monitoring and development

Counselling trainees have a responsibility to current and future clients to keep monitoring their performance and developing their skills. Since these matters form the topic of Chapter 27, suffice it for now to say that trainees need to take care to evaluate and reflect upon what they do, receive either supervision or consultative support to gain insights into good skills and pinpoint other skills that they can improve, and be prepared to engage in a range of activities that expand their knowledge and understanding of how to perform better. Furthermore, trainees have an ethical responsibility to keep abreast of relevant literature both about counselling processes and outcomes and also about social, professional and ethical issues that can impact on their clients and themselves.

Activity 25.2 Ethical issues and dilemmas in counselling and helping practice

Critically discuss how each of the following areas contains important ethical issues, and possibly dilemmas, for counsellors and helpers:

Counsellor competence
- relationship competence
- technical competence
- readiness to practice
- fitness to practice
- recognizing limitations and making referrals

Client autonomy
- respect for client self-determination
- accurate pre-counselling information
- accurate statements about professional competence
- honest statements about counselling processes and outcomes
- clear contract negotiated in advance
- informed consent to interventions
- respect for diverse values

Confidentiality
- any limitations communicated in advance
- consent for communication with third parties
- issues of disclosure to save life or prevent serious harm to others

- issues of permission and parental involvement with minors
- permission to record sessions
- permission and anonymity in research projects
- security of all client records

Client protection
- maintaining clear boundaries to the counselling relationship
- avoidance of financial exploitation
- avoidance of emotional and sexual exploitation
- protection of clients' physical safety
- adequate indemnity insurance
- knowledge of relevant law

Professional monitoring and development
- regular and ongoing supervision/consultative support
- continuing professional development
- keeping abreast of research and other relevant literature

1 In what areas do you consider yourself most at risk of acting unethically when you counsel?
2 What can you do to protect your clients and yourself from your potential to act unethically in the areas you have identified?

Ethical issues and dilemmas in counselling and helping training

Since students counsel clients on placements, counsellor training involves the ethical issues and dilemmas associated with counselling practice. There are additional ethical issues and dilemmas attached to training. Individual students and staff tend to see counsellor training from their own perspectives, but in reality there are numerous parties with varying interests in the conduct of training and hence in how ethical issues and dilemmas are addressed. Box 25.3 lists some of those who may be affected by how ethical training takes place.

Box 25.3 Ethical issues in counselling and helping training: ten interested parties

1 **Individual trainees.** Trainees on counselling and helping courses who interview clients on placements.
2 **Other trainees.** Other course members participating in training, placement and supervision situations.
3 **Trainers.** Those responsible for training trainees in counselling and helping skills.

4 **Supervisors.** Those responsible for supervising the counselling work of trainees conducted on placements.
5 **Placement agencies.** The agencies that sponsor the client contact of trainees.
6 **Current clients.** Clients counselled by trainees when on placement.
7 **Future clients.** Clients whom trainees will counsel later on in training and when they become counsellors and helpers.
8 **Academic department.** The academic department in which the counselling and helping training course is located and which assumes administrative responsibility for it.
9 **Academic institution.** The college or university in which the academic department is located and which has ultimate responsibility for the counselling and helping course.
10 **Professional association.**The professional association responsible for maintaining training and practice standards, that accredits the counselling and helping course.

Competence in performing multiple roles

A theme throughout this chapter is that staff members and trainees are each vulnerable to ethical issues and dilemmas, some similar and others differing according to their roles. For example, both staff and trainees face inevitable role conflicts that create ethical dilemmas if they are to give sufficient time to teaching and to learning essential counselling and helping skills. The basic role of any academic staff member includes teaching, research and administration. In addition, counselling course staff members need to arrange and monitor trainee placements. They should also be maintaining and developing their own counselling skills by continuing to see clients. On top of this, some will be playing important roles in their professional associations. In addition, staff members have private lives that ideally provide nourishment for performing strongly in their professional lives.

Counselling course staff can allow the ethical dilemmas involved in juggling multiple roles to become ethical lapses when they allow insufficient time and energy to perform their training and supervision duties competently. For example, they may be earning extra income from private practice and consulting activities and, hence, be insufficiently prepared for their training duties or less than desirably available to trainees. Another example of an ethical lapse is that of staff members who allow their research interests and promotion ambitions to dominate their time at the expense of trainees. However, with the increasing demands on staff members in higher educational institutions, there is also an increasing risk that fully responsible training can no longer either be offered or expected since trainers need immense dedication and exceptional physical and mental energy to perform their roles well.

Most trainees learning counselling and helping skills are mature. Many courses are part-time or evening courses. All professional courses require supervised placements and attendance at supervisions in addition to regular academic and practical requirements. Where academic requirements involve learning statistical, computing and research design skills and then conducting a detailed research project, trainees may find that the competing demands of academic and practical work create a particularly difficult ethical dilemma in relation to time management. In addition, all trainees have private lives, some have children to look after, and many are in part-time or full-time employment.

When counselling trainees commit themselves to coming on counselling courses, they are also committing themselves to spending sufficient time to learn the skills and to counsel clients on placements properly. Unless there are exceptional mitigating circumstances, it is an inexcusable ethical lapse for trainees to devote insufficient time and attention to developing competence in the required counselling skills. Negligent trainees sacrifice the interests of all the interested parties listed in Box 25.3, including their own interests. Usually trainees' ethical lapses in regard to giving sufficient time to developing skills represent shades of grey rather than being black-and-white matters. I write the above passage with passion because, fortunately only on rare occasions, I have suffered from trainees who unquestioningly expected me to arrange placements where they would counsel genuine clients when all they had been doing in their skills training groups was the bare minimum to continue on the course.

Confidentiality

On counselling courses, trainers and supervisors can build and reinforce trainees' awareness of the need for confidentiality. Already, by participating in introductory skills training groups, trainees should be aware of such issues as not putting pressure on others to disclose more than they are comfortable with, protecting one another's secrets, seeking permission to reveal information to third parties, and safe storage of any written and taped records.

Before commencing their placements trainees need to familiarize themselves with any limitations on confidentiality the agency or institution requires, so that then they can communicate these limitations to clients in advance. Often new clients have been informed when being referred that they are seeing counselling trainees who are required to discuss their counselling work with supervisors both to provide a better service and as part of their training. Already, I have dealt with the issue of recording sessions. I have also stressed that, in any social contacts, total discretion about clients is mandatory.

Trainees may face ethical dilemmas concerning confidentiality in instances of conflicting requirements between ethical codes and agency policies. Most, if not all, of the ethical dilemmas concerning confidentiality with which counsellors in practice wrestle, trainees on placement may encounter too: for example, risk to third parties, such as child abuse, and risk to the client, such as the contemplation of suicide. It is essential that trainees bring to the attention of and discuss with their supervisors any such ethical dilemmas and most trainees are only too happy to do so. Failure to discuss ethical dilemmas concerning confidentiality is a serious ethical lapse in itself, since both supervisors and sponsoring agencies have assumed responsibility for the quality of the trainee's work and for protecting the clients they counsel.

Dual relationships and sexual contact

Dual relationships are those where the participants engage in a relationship that has a different agenda from their professional relationship. In counsellor training there are two main types of dual relationship that can take place: those between trainees on placement and their clients and those between trainees and staff. Though there is a variety of other agendas that may arise in dual relationships, such as business or social, here my emphasis is on intimate emotional and sexual relationships. Box 25.4 provides illustrations of two such unethical relationships.

Box 25.4 Examples of sexual relationships related to counsellor training

Trainee on placement and client

Andy, 41, a counselling skills trainee, counsels Jen, 38. Recently divorced after a marriage lasting nearly ten years, Jen is adjusting again to being single. Jen shares with Andy her feelings of having been unappreciated in her marriage and her current feelings of loneliness and hunger for an intimate relationship with a suitable man. Jen also talks about how unsatisfactory the sex was in her marriage and how she would like to experience her sexuality with a sympathetic and skilled lover. Andy lives with a partner, but also has 'affairs' with other women. Andy starts a sexual relationship with Jen and they collude in keeping the knowledge of it from Andy's supervisor.

Supervisor and trainee
Jody, 38, is a staff member who supervises the counselling work on placement of Don, 24. Jody, who was recently divorced, currently feels vulnerable and lonely. Don has a history of seeking out older women for romantic relationships. As time goes by, despite Don still being under supervision from Jody, an emotional and sexual relationship develops between them.

The case of Andy and Jen in Box 25.4, in which a trainee on placement develops a 'hidden' sexual relationship with a client, contains numerous breaches of trust. First and foremost, the client may be damaged by the relationship. Most clients report harm as the result of sexual contacts with their counsellors. Corey and Corey (2003) observe that they typically become resentful and angry at having been sexually exploited and abandoned. Furthermore, they generally feel stuck with both unresolved problems and unresolved feelings relating to the traumatic experience. Sexual relationships with clients can also have serious legal ramifications for counsellors. The trainee has breached trust with his supervisor, the placement agency, his counsellor training course and with the professional association accrediting the course. Trainees on placements who find themselves sexually attracted to clients can protect all concerned if they raise such issues with their supervisors. Their sexual feelings are not wrong in themselves and, during their careers, many counsellors experience sexual attraction to one or more of their clients. It is how these sexual feelings are handled that can lead to serious ethical misconduct.

In the case of Jody and Don in Box 25.4, Jody as a supervisor had a clear ethical responsibility to keep the supervisory relationship as a professional one. In one American study, in which just under 500 American former female clinical psychology graduate trainees were surveyed, the overall rate of sexual contact between trainees and staff members was 17 per cent. Among trainees separating or divorcing during graduate training this figure rose to 34 per cent (Glaser and Thorpe, 1986). Another study found that clinical psychology trainees who had sexual contact with their supervisors during postgraduate training were more likely to go on to become sexually involved with their patients (Garrett, 1998). Thus the damage of inappropriate staff–trainee relationships can spread well beyond counselling and helping training courses into trainees' subsequent professional practice.

Especially since most trainees are of mature age, they have a responsibility not to engage in staff–trainee relationships that may have negative consequences for their fellow trainees, the staff and probably for themselves. In most instances trainees, who receive messages from staff members that the training relationship might be accompanied by an emotional or sexual one, should use assertiveness skills to nip such advances in the bud. In rare instances, they might suggest to the staff member that any possibility of a personal relationship should be put on hold, pending the end of their course. If sexually harassed, counselling trainees of both sexes can go to people like heads of department, students' rights officers and counselling services, and should consider using institutional sexual harassment procedures, assuming they exist.

Counselling course staff also may need to take appropriate action in instances where trainees sexually harass them. Once when I was a course tutor, I was the recipient of unwanted sexual advances from a trainee, including a letter with visually suggestive images, such as a small picture of a motel room, pasted in it. I immediately shared the letter with my administrative superior. The whole episode raised numerous issues over how best to proceed in a way that would protect all involved. For a year or so after the trainee completed the course, I continued to receive unwanted correspondence, fortunately infrequent.

Ethics and staff–trainee relations

On counselling courses, it is preferable if staff and trainees can develop a set of ethical group norms regarding how they treat one another and clients. When it comes to ethical decision-making, it is undesirable to have an 'us-versus-them' tussle either explicit or implicit in staff–trainee relationships. Both parties have a responsibility to act ethically, to treat one another with respect, and to assume responsibility for the maintenance of ethical standards on the course. For example, if a trainee shirks their responsibilities to learn counselling skills properly by not attending some sessions for no legitimate reason, the trainer deserves support from other course members in explaining why it is neither in the trainee's nor the course's best interests that this situation continue.

Trainees also need to be mindful that counsellor training, with its practical as well as academic components, is resource intensive at a time when higher education budgets are getting squeezed. Furthermore, if the course is located in a traditional psychology department, the professional values of the course and its staff may well be in conflict with the predominantly academic values of most of the remaining staff, including the department's head or chair. In the pressure cooker of counsellor training, trainees both individually and collectively need to be very careful about playing the victim, casting one or more staff members as persecutors, and then seeking support from third parties. If counselling course staff members always have a duty of care to act ethically towards trainees, trainees also have a duty of care to act ethically towards the staff. Trainees should not engage in any behaviour that weakens the position of the course staff or the course itself in the department or institution. In the intense scrambling for resources and frenzied politics of academic life, course staff and trainees should work together to protect the long-term interests of the counselling profession.

Activity 25.3 Ethical issues and dilemmas in counselling and helping training

1 Critically discuss the ethical issues and dilemmas for students on counselling and helping courses in each of the following areas:

- competence in performing multiple roles
- confidentiality
- dual relationships and sexual contact
- staff–student relations

2 What other areas for ethical issues and dilemmas are important in counsellor training, and why?
3 If you were to develop a 'Code of Ethics and Practice for Students on Counsellor Training Courses', what would be its main provisions?

Making decisions about ethical issues and dilemmas

Counsellors and therapists require both ethical awareness and the skills of ethical decision-making. Bond (2000) states that he has become increasingly aware of the need to encourage ethical mindfulness rather than an unquestioning adherence to ethical principles. Being ethically mindful consists of both wrestling with the issues involved in ethical decisions and dilemmas in a systematic and considered way and assuming personal responsibility for acting ethically.

Bond and leading American counselling ethics writers Marianne and Gerald Corey (2003) assert that possessing a systematic step-by-step way of approaching difficult ethical dilemmas increases counsellors' chances of making sound ethical decisions. Box 25.5 presents two models of ethical decision-making: first, Bond's ethical problem-solving model; and second, the Coreys' ethical decision-making model. Models such as these are valuable in listing important considerations and in assisting counsellors to think and act rationally when confronted with ethical dilemmas. Not surprisingly, readers will notice considerable overlap between the two models.

Box 25.5 Decision-making models for ethical issues and dilemmas

Bond's ethical problem-solving model

1 Produce a brief description of the problem or dilemma.
2 Decide 'Whose dilemma is it anyway?'
3 Consider all available ethical principles and guidelines.
4 Identify all possible courses of action.
5 Select the best possible course of action.
6 Evaluate the outcome.

Corey and Corey's ethical decision-making model

1 Identify the problem.
2 Apply the ethical guidelines.
3 Determine the nature and dimensions of the dilemma and seek consultation.
4 Generate possible courses of action.
5 Consider the possible consequences of all options and determine a course of action.
6 Evaluate the selected course of action.
7 Implement the course of action.

In light of the emphasis of this book on good and poor mind skills, the Bond and Corey models are rather too optimistic in implying that ethical decision-making is a rational process. As the saying goes: 'Who ever said that humans were rational?' Counselling trainees tend to bring different decision-making styles to ethical decisions: some avoid making them for as long as possible, others rush into making them, still others worry over every detail. In addition, even when trainees make decisions, they differ in their commitment to them and in their abilities to implement them skilfully. I now provide at least one example of how counselling trainees' poor skills can interfere with making decisions rationally for each of the mind skills of creating rules, perceptions, self-talk, visual images, explanations and expectations.

Counselling trainees may have demanding rules that interfere with rational thinking and communication: for example, 'I must never acknowledge an ethical lapse' or 'My supervisor must always approve of me.' Furthermore, sensitive ethical areas are fertile breeding grounds for false perceptions. For instance, controlling trainees may possess little insight into their ethical lapses in the area of client autonomy. Another example is that of culturally insensitive trainees failing to perceive both their insensitivity and its negative effects on their clients and on the counselling relationship.

Counselling trainees may use negative self-talk that increases their anxiety about facing, making and implementing decisions about ethical problems: for instance, their self-talk may heighten their anxiety rather than be calming and help them to stay focused on the task of rational decision-making. Trainees may also create visual images that increase their chances of deciding to act unethically: for instance imagining clients without their clothes.

In regard to creating explanations, counselling trainees are sometimes unwilling to own and admit their lapses and mistakes. In an article entitled 'Why can't we own our mistakes?', Roger Casemore, who chaired the British Association of Counselling and Psychotherapy's Complaints Committee, stated that many lengthy complaints procedures might have been avoided by counsellors acknowledging mistakes and perhaps even saying 'Sorry, I won't do it again' (Casemore, 1999). Clearly, it is easier to forgive minor rather than major mistakes and ethical lapses. Trainee expectations about the damage to themselves and to clients of any ethical lapses may be far off the mark. Those who either gratuitously give bad advice or in other ways act unethically may not anticipate the adverse consequences for their clients. When things go wrong or turn sour, clients may angrily blame their counsellors and even take them to court.

Counselling trainees should always be alert for how they may be turning what is outwardly a rational decision-making process into one that is less than completely rational because of their own needs and anxieties. The more they can successfully work on their own mental development both as persons and as counsellors, the more likely they are to work their way rationally through the ethical dilemmas that inevitably arise in counselling.

Activity 25.4 Making decisions about ethical issues and dilemmas

1 Critically discuss the strengths and weaknesses of:

- Bond's ethical problem-solving model;
- Corey and Corey's ethical decision-making model.

2 Which of the following factors might interfere with your making decisions about ethical issues and dilemmas rationally?

- your current style of making decisions (please specify);
- poor mind skills in one or more of the following areas:
  - creating rules
  - creating perceptions
  - creating self-talk
  - creating visual images
  - creating explanations
  - creating expectations
- any other factors (please specify).

3 What can you do now to improve your ability to make decisions wisely when faced with ethical issues and dilemmas in future?

diversity-sensitive counselling and helping 26

Chapter outcomes

By studying and doing the activities in this chapter you should:

- gain some awareness of the range of diversity issues in counselling and helping;
- understand some criticisms of mainstream counselling approaches;
- know about some goals for multicultural counselling;
- know about some approaches to multicultural counselling;
- know about some goals for gender-aware counselling;
- know about some approaches to gender-aware counselling; and
- understand how the lifeskills counselling model addresses issues of diversity in counselling.

This chapter looks at diversity-sensitive counselling and helping. Addressing the range of differences is much too vast a topic for a single chapter. Consequently, I choose to review issues connected with multicultural and gender-aware counselling as being particularly important and relevant to many clients. Over the past 30 to 40 years there has been a growing interest in diversity-sensitive counselling and helping. All counsellors, trainees and clients possess a mixture of different characteristics that they bring to the counselling process. They also have perceptions and evaluations of these different characteristics in themselves and others. There is no such thing as perfect counsellor–client matching, though there may be important similarities, for example regarding culture or race.

Not only do issues of diversity influence the counselling relationship, but there can also be special counselling needs and challenges attached to each of the different characteristics or areas. Furthermore, as Bond observes: 'One of the major current challenges for all British professional counselling organizations is the under-representation within their membership of the cultural diversity of the general population' (2000: 36). This state of affairs exists in countries like Australia and America as well. Box 26.1 indicates just some of the many areas of diversity in the practice of counselling and helping.

Box 26.1 Ten areas of diversity in counselling and helping

Culture. Ancestral origins in either the mainstream or in a minority group culture and, if the latter, one's degree of acculturation.

Race. Possessing distinctive physical characteristics according to a racial sub-grouping or being of mixed race.

Social class. Differences attached to such matters as income, educational attainment and occupational status.

Biological sex. Female or male.

Gender-role identity. Differences in feelings, thoughts and behaviour according to the social classification of attributes as 'feminine' or 'masculine'.

Marital status. Single, cohabiting, married, separated, divorced, remarried or widowed.

Sexual and affectionate orientation. Heterosexual, lesbian, gay or bisexual.

Physical disability. A deficiency in the structure or functioning of some part of the body.

Age. Childhood, adolescence, young adulthood, middle age, late middle age or old age.

Religion or philosophy. Christian, Hindu, Muslim, Buddhist or some other religious or secular belief system.

Some criticisms of traditional counselling approaches

Interest in diversity-sensitive counselling and helping has been stimulated by the perception that the main Western counselling and helping approaches either insufficiently or wrongly consider the special needs of different groups of clients. Counselling trainees should always take diversity and contextual considerations into account in how they relate to, assess and intervene with their clients.

Advocates of multicultural counselling assert that the Euro-American bias of these mainstream counselling approaches may cause Western-oriented counsellors to fail many of their actual and potential minority group clients (D'Ardenne and Mahtani, 1999; Sue et al., 1996; Sue and Sue, 1999). Counselling services are under-utilized by minority groups for reasons such as mistrust, perceived irrelevance and insensitivity to their cultural norms and personal meanings. Assessment may insufficiently take into account cultural differences in how clients communicate or in how specific behaviours are perceived. Some counsellors may fail to understand the chronic stresses attached to being in a cultural minority group. In addition, counsellors may not fully grasp the negative impact of racism, which for many Black clients is the most painful experience of their lives (Mohammed, 2000). Furthermore, counsellors may focus too much on dealing with individuals rather than dealing with them in the context of their families and community networks.

Counselling and helping approaches are also criticized for insufficiently taking into account the experiences and needs of women, although they are clearly not a minority group. To some extent, though not entirely, counselling theories assume unisex counsellors and clients. All the major theorists have been men, though some women have also made important contributions, for example Melanie Klein to psychodynamic therapy and Laura Perls to Gestalt therapy.

Central to the thinking of feminists is that men have used their positions of power to oppress women both inside and outside the home. Women are devalued because their capacities, including their sexuality, are viewed as inferior to those of men. However, boys and men as well as girls and women can be the victims of sex-role conditioning and attention needs to be paid to liberating each sex to reveal their full humanness.

Sexual orientation is another area in which some traditional therapeutic approaches have been criticized for being biased and insensitive. As recently as 1973, the American Psychiatric Association removed homosexuality as a diagnosable mental disorder. Since then there has been a gradual increase in gay affirmative counselling and helping which takes as its starting point a non-pathological view of lesbian, gay and bisexual counsellors and clients (Collins et al., 2001; Davies, 2000; Harrison, 2000).

There are special problems and issues attached to providing sensitive and relevant services to each of the client groupings identified in Box 26.1. This task is made more complex by the fact that all clients and counsellors possess numerous diverse characteristics and that each area of diversity can contain numerous sub-issues. Consequently, diversity-sensitive counselling needs to take into account the salient characteristics and issues in each unique client–counsellor relationship.

Multicultural counselling and helping

Culture can be defined as 'a patterned system of tradition derived norms influencing behaviour' (Spindler, 1963: 7). Cultural norms are processes in a constant state of flux, and there may be numerous sub-cultures within an overall mainstream culture. Culture encompasses thoughts, communications, actions, customs, beliefs, values and institutions. A colloquial definition of culture is 'the way we do things here'.

Culture and demography

Some indication of the importance of culture to contemporary counselling can be found in the demographic statistics of various countries. Demography is the study of population sizes, movements and trends, including those concerning ethnic minorities. In Britain, in 1999/2000, Caucasians formed 93.3 per cent of the total population of 56.9 million people. The overall ethnic minority population, comprising both those born abroad and those born in the UK, was estimated as 6.7 per cent or about 1 in 15 of the total population, up from 5.8 per cent or about 1 in 18 in 1995–96 (Haskey, 1997). In 1999–2000, the four largest ethnic minority groups were Indian, 1.7 per cent, Pakistani, 1.2 per cent, Black-Caribbean, 0.9 per cent, and Black African, 0.7 per cent (Tyrrell, 2001).

Australia is one of the most multicultural and, increasingly, multiracial countries in the world. In 2000, about 23 per cent or nearly a quarter of the population of just over 19 million was born overseas. In June 1997, of the overseas born, the two largest groupings were European, 55.8 per cent, and Asian, 22.7 per cent (Department of Foreign Affairs and Trade, 2000). There is a shift in migration patterns with, in 1995–96, nearly 40 per cent of settler arrivals being Asian born: 18.8 per cent from northeast Asia; 13.3 per cent from southeast Asia; and 7.8 per cent from southern Asia (Department of Immigration and Multicultural Affairs, 1997). Because they have settled in Australia over a shorter period of time than other immigrants, the Asian-born population is largely concentrated in the 20–44 age bracket (Weston et al., 2001). In the 1996 Australian census, 352,970 people identified themselves as of Aboriginal and Torres Strait Islander descent.

Like Australia, the United States is undergoing a marked change in its racial/ethnic population distribution. The 2000 census found that the US population was over 281.4 million, of whom 11.1 per cent were foreign born. The Black and Hispanic populations each formed about 13 per cent of the total population, the Asian population was just over 4 per cent, and the American Indian and Alaskan Native population was 1.5 per cent. Nearly 98 per cent of Americans answered that they came from only one race, with Whites forming three-quarters of the population (US Census Bureau, 2003). Demographic projections indicate that non-White will outnumber White persons some time between the years 2030 and 2050 (Sue and Sue, 1999).

Multicultural counselling goals

There are many different client groups for whom cultural considerations are important. These groupings include indigenous people, such as

Australian Aborigines and Torres Strait Islanders, first generation migrants, descendants of migrants at varying levels of assimilation to the mainstream culture, and members of the mainstream culture, among others.

Sometimes in the counselling literature the goals of multicultural counselling are simplified to that of how best to assist minority group members when faced with a hostile majority group culture. In reality, multicultural counselling is a much more complex and varied endeavour. Box 26.2 presents some goals, which may overlap, for working with clients for whom cultural issues play an important part.

Box 26.2 Ten goals for multicultural counselling

1. **Support.** Providing culture-sensitive support when migrants first arrive in their new home countries.
2. **Dealing with post-traumatic stress.** Offering specialized counselling for migrants suffering from post-traumatic stress disorders caused by their previous home country and refugee experiences.
3. **Acculturation and assimilation.** Helping clients to deal with the practical and psychological challenges of adjusting to a new country and culture.
4. **Coping with racism.** Providing clients with support and skills to deal with the inner wounds and outer circumstances of racism.
5. **Handling cross-cultural relationships.** Assisting clients with intergenerational and cross-cultural difficulties, for example value conflicts between migrant parents and their children; and negotiating differences in cross-cultural intimate relationships.
6. **Minority group consciousness-raising and liberation.** Encouraging clients to take pride in their culture and race and to liberate themselves from internalized negative stereotypes.
7. **Majority group consciousness-raising and liberation.** Assisting mainstream culture clients to relinquish negative aspects of their enculturation, such as a false sense of cultural and racial superiority.
8. **Avoiding further marginalization.** Resisting colluding when some minority group clients further marginalize themselves by unfairly 'demonizing' their host cultures at the same time as doing little positive to change their situations.
9. **Attaining higher levels of development.** Assisting clients to grow psychologically beyond the average for their culture. Visions of higher levels of development can differ by culture and also transcend culture in that they espouse universal values.
10. **Creating the good society.** Developing formal and informal norms within societies that are synergistic rather than antagonistic to developing the full human potential of all their members.

Multicultural counselling approaches

As may be seen from the goals listed in Box 26.2, there are many different considerations in how to conduct multicultural counselling. The issue of culturally relevant counselling can be addressed in at least three different ways: by making existing Euro-American counselling approaches more culture sensitive, by counsellors developing multicultural counselling competencies, and by using non-Western approaches to counselling. The future of culture-sensitive counselling should incorporate developments in all three of these broad approaches to it.

Making existing Euro-American counselling approaches more culture-sensitive

The following discussion addresses some issues in applying person-centred counselling and the cognitive-behavioural counselling approaches to minority group and mainstream culture clients. With mainstream culture clients, person-centred counsellors can use Rogerian empathy to help them to experience and explore their cultural and racial concerns. However, this will only happen in those instances where clients have sufficient awareness and interest to work on such issues. The person-centred concept of empathy can be expanded to include cultural empathy (Ridley and Lingle, 1996). Person-centred counsellors who see themselves and their clients as cultural beings can encourage non-Western clients to share their experiences by such methods as listening carefully for and responding to culturally relevant cues, and also by openly acknowledging that they are from a different culture and then asking their client's assistance in understanding the cultural context of their concerns. For example, Vicary and Andrews (2000) encouraged non-Aboriginal counsellors to discuss their limitations in terms of knowledge of Aboriginal culture, mention the probability that they may make errors, and request that the mistakes be identified by clients.

There are barriers to Western counsellors being perceived as empathic by ethnic minority clients (Laungani, 1999; Sue and Sue, 1999). Asian clients often want to perceive their counsellors as expert and expect more direction from them. Furthermore, Asian clients may be reluctant to talk about their problems outside of their families. Communication will be made even more difficult when clients and counsellors do not understand the meanings and nuances of one another's spoken and non-verbal communication. In addition, there is a distinct possibility that the Western counsellor will not understand the Asian client's cultural worldview, including the importance attached to family relationships, and will project parts of her/his own worldview on to the client.

The cognitive-behavioural counselling approaches provide another example of how it is possible to extend existing Euro-American approaches to become more culture-sensitive. Regarding rational emotive behaviour therapy, Ellis (1998) includes racial prejudice in his list of prejudice-related irrationalities. In REBT, clients' cultural and racial irrational beliefs and prejudices can be detected, disputed and, where appropriate, restated in preferential and rational terms. Similarly, in Beck's cognitive therapy, questioning by skilled counsellors can help clients to identify their underlying cultural and racial automatic thoughts, explore how realistic they are, and formulate more realistic thoughts and perceptions for the future.

Multicultural counselling competencies

An American approach to issues of culture and race in counselling has been to develop a statement of multicultural counselling competencies for culturally skilled counsellors (Sue et al., 1998). This statement is the work of a committee of the American Psychological Association's Division of Counselling Psychology. The committee saw multicultural counselling competencies as having three main dimensions: awareness of own assumptions, values and biases, understanding the worldview of the culturally different client, and developing appropriate strategies and techniques. Each dimension is divided into beliefs and attitudes, knowledge and skills. The United States' long history of serious, and often brutal, racial oppression provided one of the main contexts in which this statement was compiled. One of the statement's major assumptions was that of widespread and systematic cultural and racial oppression.

Awareness of own assumptions, values and biases

The attitudes held by culturally skilled counsellors include being sensitive to their own cultural heritage, being comfortable with the differences of clients from other cultures and races, and recognizing the limitations of their competence and expertise. Counsellors should know about their cultural and racial heritage and how this affects the counselling process, understand how oppression, racism and discrimination may affect them personally and in their work, and realize the impact of how they communicate on culturally different clients. Skills required include seeking out relevant educational and training experiences, actively understanding oneself as a cultural and racial being, and seeking an identity that transcends race.

Understanding the worldview of the culturally different client

Attitudes of culturally skilled counsellors include being aware of their negative emotional reactions and of the stereotypes and preconceived notions that they may hold of culturally and racially different groups.

Counsellors should know about the cultural experiences, heritage and historical background of any particular group with whom they work, acknowledge that culture and race can affect help-seeking behaviour, know how culture and race can influence assessment and the selection and implementation of counselling interventions, and be aware of the oppressive political and environmental influences impinging on the lives of ethnic and racial minorities. Skills include keeping up to date on research findings relevant to the psychological well-being of various ethnic and racial groups as well as being actively involved with minorities outside work settings to gain deeper insight into their perspectives.

Developing appropriate intervention strategies and techniques

Culturally skilled counsellors respect clients' religious and spiritual beliefs about physical and mental functioning, respect indigenous helping practices, and value bilingualism. Their knowledge base includes understanding how the culture-bound, class-bound and monolingual characteristics of counselling clash with the cultural values of various minority groups, being aware of institutional barriers to minority groups using helping services, knowing about the potential for bias in assessment instruments, and understanding minority group family structures, hierarchies, and community characteristics and resources. Skills include the ability to send and receive verbal and non-verbal communication accurately, interacting in the language requested by clients or making appropriate referrals, tailoring the counselling relationship and interventions to the clients' stage of cultural and racial identity development, and engaging in a variety of helping roles beyond those perceived as conventional for counsellors: see Box 26.3 (Atkinson et al., 1993; Sue et al., 1996).

Box 26.3 Additional roles for multicultural counsellors and helpers

1 **Adviser.** Advising clients how to solve or prevent problems and providing relevant information.
2 **Advocate.** Representing and speaking up for clients' best interests to other individuals, groups or organizations.
3 **Facilitator of indigenous support systems.** Knowing about and appropriately involving support systems, such as the client's extended family and community elders.
4 **Facilitator of indigenous healing systems.** Either referring clients to healers or, if sufficiently knowledgeable and skilled, actually using the indigenous healing methods.

5 **Consultant.** Working collegially with clients to impact or change a third party, including organizational change.
6 **Change agent.** Initiating and implementing action-oriented approaches to any changing social environments that are oppressing clients.

Non-Western approaches to counselling

Non-Western counselling approaches come from many cultures, for instance Asian and African. Such approaches may be the treatment of choice not only for some ethnic minority group clients, but also for some mainstream culture clients. In Asia, there is a long tradition of training the mind to foster interdependence, minimize suffering and create happiness. Meditation and Naikan therapy are two Asian approaches to counselling.

Meditation falls into two main categories: mindfulness of breathing or breath meditation and awareness or insight meditation. Breathing meditation consists of relaxed concentration on the flow of one's breathing, on the in-breaths and on the out-breaths. Breathing meditation may be performed sitting, standing, walking or reclining. Buddhist insight meditations include calmly becoming aware of the impermanence of whatever experiences and sensations arise and meditations that cultivate the four divine abodes of mind – loving kindness, compassion, sympathy and equanimity (Thitavanno, 2002). All meditation approaches require practice, with perseverance increasing the likelihood of better results.

Naikan therapy is a Japanese approach adapted from a more intensive Buddhist meditation practice (Reynolds, 1990). It is aimed at assisting clients to find meaning in their lives, recognize human interdependence, feel and show gratitude, and repair relationships. Naikan therapy assumes that narrowly focusing on oneself creates suffering both for oneself and others.

Clients are encouraged to establish a calm meditative state and then to reflect specifically on three things:

- what another person or other people have done for them;
- how much gratitude is due to them; and
- the difficulties they have caused others and how little they have demonstrated gratitude.

Naikan therapy can elicit various thoughts and feelings, for instance guilt and unworthiness. However, many clients also get in touch with kinder and more generous feelings towards their care givers. Clients may realize that, despite their weaknesses and failings, these people did look after and help them. Furthermore, they may start feeling very grateful to people in their pasts and want to make amends for their own inadequacies towards them.

Activity 26.1 Exploring multicultural counselling and helping

Part A: My culture and counselling

(a) From which ancestral culture or cultures are you?
(b) What distinctive values, and ways of thinking, communicating and acting, stemming from your ancestral culture(s), do you possess?

Part B: Goals for multicultural counselling and helping

Discuss the relevance of each of the following multicultural counselling and helping goals for working with either your current or your future clients.

- support;
- dealing with post-traumatic stress;
- acculturation and assimilation;
- coping with racism;
- handling cross-cultural relationships;
- minority group consciousness-raising and liberation;
- majority group consciousness-raising and liberation;
- avoiding further marginalization;
- attaining higher levels of development; and
- creating the good society.

Part C: Approaches to multicultural counselling and helping

Describe and critically discuss each of the following approaches to multicultural counselling and helping:

- making existing Euro-American counselling approaches more culture-sensitive;
- counsellors developing multicultural counselling competencies; and
- using non-Western approaches to counselling and helping.

Part D: Self-evaluation

What good and poor skills do you possess for counselling clients from different cultures? Please be specific.

Gender-aware counselling and helping

A major criticism of existing counselling and helping approaches is that they insufficiently address women's experience and issues. One way of looking at women's experience is in terms of the interaction of the social, the political and the personal. Here concepts like patriarchy, oppression and social action are important. Another way to look at women's experience is in terms of the particular challenges throughout the life span inherent in being a woman: for example, premenstrual tension, infertility and miscarriage, giving birth, post-natal depression, mothering, menopause and, frequently, outliving a spouse.

A further perspective is that of problems that specifically beset women in varying degrees. These problems include domestic violence, sexual harassment, sexual abuse, relentless pressure to be beautiful, anorexia, bulimia, rape, abortion, single parenting, attitudes that constrain career choice, workplace discrimination, and depression and exhaustion resulting from carrying a disproportionate share of work/family responsibilities (Greer, 1999).

Though formulated by men, existing counselling approaches may perhaps be insufficiently sensitive to men's as well as women's experience and issues. Men's life expectancy is five or six years lower than women's and this key issue could be highlighted and addressed more by both sexes. Related to this is the fact that boys and men commit suicide three to four times more frequently than girls and women (Biddulph, 1995; Browne, 2001a). Men are vulnerable to prostate cancer, a health problem that receives far less attention and resources than women's vulnerability to breast cancer. In addition, men are nine times as likely to be homeless as women, four times as likely to be drug addicts, three times as likely to be the victims of violence, and twice as likely to be unemployed (Browne, 2001a).

Psychological problems beset many boys and men. These problems include behavioural problems in school, hurt stemming from absent or neglectful fathers (sometimes called 'father hunger'), work-related stress, alcoholism, being physically violent, pressure to initiate relationships with the opposite sex, pressure to perform sexually (men cannot fake erections), and difficulty in showing tender feelings and vulnerability. Further problems include insufficient preparation for fatherhood, intimacy difficulties with same-sex friends, the expectations that they will be financially successful, loss of identity through unemployment, and loss of daily contact with children after a relationship break-up.

Many men are confused and threatened by challenges to adjust to the changes brought about in their partners by the women's movement. Since women easily outnumber men as counselling clients, another problem for men would seem to be their greater unwillingness to seek psychological assistance when experiencing difficulties themselves, thereby creating difficulties for others.

Gender-aware counselling goals

Where gender-role issues are involved, it is possible to state counselling goals for both sexes and for each sex. General goals include helping individual clients use their strengths and potential, make appropriate choices, remedy poor skills, and develop positive and flexible self-concepts. Counselling goals relating to gender roles can often involve both male and female partners: for example learning to deal with demand/ withdraw interaction patterns in marital conflict (Christensen and Heavy, 1993) and handling the numerous issues confronting dual career couples in a time of rapid technological and economic change (Fallon, 1997).

Counselling goals for women

Chaplin (1999) observes that women and others at the bottom of hierarchies usually have considerable experience of being put down and losing self-esteem. She continues: 'Feminist counselling aims instead to empower people and develop more self-confidence and control over their lives,' (1999: 8). Chester (1994) surveyed 140 Australians who considered themselves to be both feminists and counsellors, though just over 14 per cent did not consider themselves feminist counsellors as such. Participants were asked to choose, from a list of 26 characteristics, the ones they considered essential for feminist counsellors. Translating the essential characteristics into goals for feminist counselling, the two most essential goals were women valuing themselves on their own terms and women becoming free of sex-role stereotypes.

Statements of counselling goals that take women's sex and gender issues into account can focus both on women's life span issues and on problems that are much more commonly faced by women than men. For example, gender-aware and feminist counsellors can counsel mid-life women to cope with the menopause constructively (Huffman and Myers, 1999). In addition, suitably trained and qualified counsellors can help women address issues such as insufficient assertiveness, eating disorders, domestic violence and sexual harassment.

Counselling goals for men

Since considerably fewer men than women come for counselling, one broader goal for the profession in general may be to increase the number of men prepared to address their gender role and other problems in counselling. Men, like women, need to free themselves from limiting gender-role stereotypes and to develop more of their unique potential. Consequently, another counselling goal is, where appropriate, to make men aware of the extent to which their thoughts, feelings and behaviours have been and continue to be heavily determined by their past and current gender-role socialization.

Counselling goals for men can include addressing at least three of the four issues identified by the Gender Role Conflict Scale (O'Neill et al., 1986):

excessive need for success, power and competition, restrictive emotionality, and restrictive affectionate behaviour between men. Other counselling goals for men clients include stopping being physically violent both inside and outside of the home, dealing with work-related stress, overcoming tendencies to treat women as sexual objects, and developing better health care skills.

A consequence of women redefining their gender roles faster than men is that many men are inevitably put in positions of exploring, understanding and altering their own gender roles. Positive maleness – combining tenderness and toughness and treating women with respect and as equals – is a desirable outcome from this change process. Boys and men are likely to be more constructive and caring if encouraged to become confident in their manhood. They will be less inclined to seek to prove themselves all the time by pretending to be what they are not.

Gender-aware counselling approaches

The above discussion indicates that there are many goals for gender-aware counselling and helping. Here I present four overlapping approaches to women's and men's gender issues and problems: making existing counselling approaches more gender-sensitive, developing gender-relevant counselling competencies, feminist counselling, and men's counselling.

Making existing counselling approaches more gender-sensitive

Undoubtedly the rise of feminism and the start of a men's movement have already influenced many counsellors of both sexes to undertake counselling with a greater focus on healing psychological distress stemming from restricted gender-role socialization and sexism. Jung's analytical therapy emphasized the importance of the feminine much more than Freud's psychoanalysis. Jung acknowledged the importance of the mother archetype, which appears in numerous aspects (Jung, 1982). Jung saw people as psychologically bisexual, with men possessing an anima (the personification of the feminine nature in their unconscious) and women possessing an animus (the personification of the masculine nature in their unconscious). Jungian psychology can certainly provide a base on which to explore gender role issues at varying levels of consciousness (Schaverin, 1999).

Humanistic counselling approaches can also be adapted to deal with gender-role issues. For example, clients in person-centred counselling can in an emotional climate of safety and trust experience and explore their prior gender-role socialization and current gender-role issues and conflicts. The egalitarian quality of the relationship in person-centred counselling also challenges gender-based stereotypes.

The cognitive-behavioural approaches too lend themselves to focusing on gender-role issues. For instance, in rational emotive behaviour therapy, gender-related irrational beliefs can be detected, disputed and either discarded or restated more rationally. In cognitive therapy, counsellors and clients can identify and question the reality of gender-related automatic thoughts that confuse fact with inference. Afterwards, where necessary, counsellors can work with clients to replace previous sexist and self-oppressing automatic thoughts with conscious and realistic ones.

Gender-relevant counselling competencies

Earlier in this chapter, I presented a statement of multicultural counselling competencies (Sue et al., 1998). This statement can be adapted for gender-relevant counselling competencies which consist of three main dimensions: awareness of one's own assumptions, values and biases, understanding the worldview of the sex-different client, and developing appropriate strategies and techniques. Each dimension is divided into beliefs and attitudes, knowledge, and skills. The basic presumption in stating these competencies is that all counsellors and trainees need to address their own levels of gender awareness and their ability to offer gender-sensitive services. Clearly a commitment to developing these competencies demands a very high level of motivation.

Awareness of own assumptions, values and biases

The attitudes held by gender-skilled counsellors include being sensitive to their own gender heritage, being comfortable with differences that exist between them and clients of the other sex, and recognizing the limitations of their competence and expertise. Counsellors should know about their gender heritage and how this affects the counselling process, understand how sexist oppression and discrimination may affect them personally and in their work, and realize the impact of how they communicate on clients of the other sex. Skills include seeking out relevant educational and training experiences on gender-related factors in psychological wellness, actively understanding oneself as a gendered being and seeking an autonomous and appropriately flexible gender identity.

Understanding the worldview of the sex-different client

Attitudes of gender-skilled counsellors include being aware of their negative emotional reactions and of the stereotypes and preconceived notions that they may hold of clients of the other sex. Counsellors should know about the gender-related experiences, heritage and historical background of any particular group of men or women with whom they work, acknowledge that gender can affect help-seeking behaviour, know how gender can influence assessment and the selection and implementation of counselling interventions, and be aware of the oppressive political and environmental influences impinging on the lives of women and men. Skills include keeping up to date on research findings relevant to the psychological well-being of women and men as well as being actively involved with minority and other relevant groups outside work settings to gain deeper insight into their gender perspectives.

Developing appropriate intervention strategies and techniques

Counsellors' skills include the ability to send and receive verbal and non-verbal communication accurately, making appropriate referrals to other counsellors whatever their sex, tailoring the counselling relationship and interventions to take into account the gender-related dimensions of clients' problems, and engaging in a variety of helping roles beyond those conventional for counsellors, for example those of adviser, advocate, consultant and change agent.

Feminist counselling

Feminist counsellors subscribe to many different theoretical orientations (Chaplin, 1999; Chester, 1994). Feminist counselling is perhaps best described by the values or principles that have emerged from the joining of feminism with counselling. Box 26.4 describes five central principles (Ballou, 1996; Cheatham et al., 1997).

Box 26.4 Five central principles of feminist counselling

1 **Egalitarian relationships.** Feminist counsellors are extremely sensitive to issues of power and its distribution. They emphasize sharing power with clients and believe that hierarchical forms of power distribution are inappropriate. Disclosure of one's own experiences as a woman can be an important part of the counselling process.
2 **Pluralism.** Feminist theory acknowledges and values difference, including complex and multiple-level diversities. Respect for others, including their differences, is a basic tenet of feminist counselling.
3 **Working against oppression.** Feminist counsellors work against all forms of oppression: for instance, on the basis of sex, sexual/affectionate orientation, race, culture, religious belief, lifestyle choice, and physical disability.
4 **External emphasis.** External factors, such as social/political/economic structures, are crucial to shaping the views of women, how they see themselves and how others see them. Women as individuals are shaped by and interact with political, environmental, institutional and cultural factors.
5 **Valuing women's experiences.** This means relying on the actual experiences of women for descriptions of 'reality': grounding knowledge claimed about women on women's actual experience, valuing it highly rather than ignoring or discounting it and assuming men's experience to be normative.

What are some specific interventions in dealing with women clients? Often assertiveness training, gender role analysis and consciousness-raising are particularly appropriate for the needs of women. Chester (1994) asked her feminist counsellor sample whether they used any techniques or interventions related to their feminism. Ninety-one per cent of respondents replied in the affirmative. The most commonly cited interventions were challenging sex-role stereotypes and challenging patriarchal norms (each around 15 per cent), assertiveness training, strategies to encourage a sense of empowerment, and self-disclosure (each around 12 per cent). Needless to say, many women clients bring to counselling specific issues, such as procrastination, for which gender-related interventions can be, but are not always, irrelevant.

An issue in feminist counselling is whether and how to confront clients with issues of sexism. Counsellors may also need to help women clients to anticipate and to deal with the consequences of changing their gender role. One danger of bringing up issues of sexism too soon is that clients resist the explanation and do not see its relevance. The opposite is also possible in that clients simplistically latch on to a sexist oppression analysis of their situation, get extremely angry with their partners, and prematurely leave them rather than attempt to work through relationship issues.

Some feminist counsellors develop their own approaches to working with clients. For example, Jocelyn Chaplin (1999) has developed 'cognitive feminism'. Chaplin distinguishes between the masculine control model (in which opposites, such as mind–'masculine'–strong and body–'feminine'–vulnerable, are split hierarchically into superior and inferior constructs) and the feminine rhythm model. In the rhythm model there is flow and balancing between extremes, for instance alternating between joy and sorrow throughout a day. Each client needs to find her own unique rhythms and balance between her 'active' and 'resting' sides, her 'private' and 'public' sides, and her 'self-expression' and 'caring for others' sides.

Counselling in cognitive feminism starts with a trust-building mothering stage. Depending on the client, in varying degrees the counsellor acts as a container and a non-judgemental presence, and provides a space for emotionally letting go. The second stage involves focusing on specific issues, identifying themes and separating out the opposites – for example, the head must rule the heart. The third stage explores the past to understand where the opposites and inner hierarchies came from. The next stage involves dissolving the inner hierarchies, facing ambivalence and accepting opposites. Then counselling progresses to the last stage where clients make decisions and behave differently in the world. During this stage, assertiveness training helps many women express themselves more effectively, for instance by asking clearly for a change.

Men's counselling

More work is needed on counselling approaches to men's problems and issues. Many boys and men are suffering psychologically and need assistance to become confident and positive males. Virtually all of the negative behaviours towards women chronicled by Greer (1999) are symptomatic of men's psychological wounds and insufficient personal development rather than of their innate badness. Unfortunately, the behaviours of some wounded men, for instance aggression and violence, do little to generate sympathy for their underlying suffering and low self-esteem.

There needs to be a greater development of men's counselling to complement – and definitely not to compete against – responsible feminist counselling. At the time of writing, neither the British nor the Australian Psychological Society has an interest group focusing on the psychology of men to complement their psychology of women interest groups. Much of the existing literature on men's issues focuses on changing negative aspects of men's behaviour, such as curbing domestic violence and sexual abuse. There is a dearth of counselling books and articles advocating positive maleness and how to achieve it (for example, Biddulph, 1995). The American Psychological Association's recently inaugurated journal, *Psychology of Men and Masculinity* may go some way to redressing this deficiency.

Just as the men's movement can be seen as the missing half of the women's movement, men's counselling can be seen as the missing half of feminist counselling. With some adaptation, the five central principles of feminist counselling – egalitarian relationships, pluralism, working against oppression, external emphasis, and valuing the experience of one's own sex (see Box 26.4) – are highly relevant for men's counselling too. Many counsellors and counselling services probably need to become more user-friendly for males and skilled at working with the specific issues facing boys and men. They can then help these clients to celebrate, liberate and develop the fullness of their male humanity.

Activity 26.2 Exploring gender-aware counselling and helping

Part A: My gender-role identity

1 How do you describe yourself on the dimensions of 'masculinity' and 'femininity'?
2 Succinctly summarize your gender-role identity.

Part B: Goals for gender-aware counselling and helping

1 What are some special problems that girls and women bring to counselling?
2 What are some special problems that boys and men bring to counselling?
3 What are some goals for gender-aware counselling

- for both sexes;
- for girls and women; and
- for boys and men?

Part C: Approaches to gender-aware counselling and helping

Critically discuss each of the following approaches to gender-aware counselling and helping:

- making existing counselling approaches more gender-sensitive;
- counsellors developing gender-sensitive counselling and therapy competencies;
- feminist counselling; and
- men's counselling.

Part D: Self-evaluation

What good and poor skills do you possess for counselling clients of the other sex? Please be specific.

Using the lifeskills counselling model with diverse clients

Given the range of differences in actual and potential client populations, stating clear-cut guidelines about using the lifeskills counselling model with diverse clients becomes difficult. In many instances, counsellors and trainees will require special knowledge and skills to address adequately problems of specific populations. Ivey and his colleagues observe that, when translating the microskills model of counsellor training to different cultures, active involvement of people from the host culture is important (Ivey et al., 2001). Similarly, if the lifeskills counselling model is to be adapted sensitively to meet the needs of diverse client groupings, active involvement of representatives of these groupings is essential.

Though counselling trainees using the lifeskills model require flexibility in adapting it, this should not be at any price. Some values are of universal importance and transcend the interests of different cultures and interest groups: for example, benevolence, reverence for life and security (Schwartz, 1992). Counselling trainees should not attempt to be all things to all people. The approach contains some essential points such as the need for clients to accept responsibility for improving how they think and communicate/act, even in face of external adversities. In addition, trainees should accept realistic limitations in their abilities to deal with diverse groups of clients and, where appropriate, be prepared to refer clients to those better qualified to treat them. There is sometimes a risk of counselling becoming too fragmented when trainees focus on issues of diversity rather than on clients as whole persons. In addition, clients frequently possess poor skills that are either unconnected or only loosely connected with issues of diversity.

Despite the above qualifications, the lifeskills counselling model can be used in ways that show sensitivity to diverse client groupings. The following discussion briefly addresses some considerations in adapting it to take diversity into account.

Stage 1: The relating stage

Counselling trainees need to examine carefully the nature of the pre-counselling information they provide and where and how it is distributed. Where ethnic minority populations are involved, such as people from south Asia in Britain or people from north and southeast Asia in Australia, this information should sometimes be provided in their home languages as well as or instead of in English. Building and gaining trust is a critical factor. Therefore trainees may need to spend time in their local communities establishing their human and not just their professional credentials, as well as creating networks for obtaining clients.

When starting initial sessions, counselling trainees should pronounce the names of people from different minority groups correctly and introduce themselves in appropriate ways, for instance avoiding over-familiarity. Where relevant, trainees can solicit clients' assistance in helping them understand their minority group better, whether it is an overseas culture or a gay or a lesbian sub-culture.

Counselling trainees need to allow clients space to tell their stories in ways appropriate to their cultures and circumstances. Trainees should be sensitive to cultural differences in vocal and bodily communication. For example, Australian Aboriginal clients' listening or attending behaviour can involve 'vastly differing eye contact (relatively little eye contact, and occasional "sweeping" head to toe glance), a side by side conversational posture with a less assertive body language, a considerably softer vocal tone, and much less emphasis on direct, immediate verbal following' (Ivey et al., 2001: 15). Trainees should also be sensitive to differences in how questions are used in any specific minority groups with which they deal.

Stage 2: The understanding stage

Though the lifeskills counselling model has an individual focus, it takes into account the broader social, cultural, organizational and community factors that can create suffering. Minority group clients almost invariably require improved mind and communication/action skills to deal with other people's and societal shortcomings as well as their own. When conducting a reconnaissance with people from specific diverse populations, trainees can explore how being a member of that grouping may be creating problems or contributing to sustaining them.

Counselling trainees who regularly deal with specific minority groups should develop an extra sharpness in understanding the specific skills that clients from those groups usually need to improve. For example, physically disabled people as a group can be prone to certain demanding rules, for example, 'I must be the perfect physical specimen', and automatic perceptions, for example, 'She/he thinks less of me because of my disability.' Diversity-sensitive counsellors are aware of the poor mind skills that minority group members use to oppress themselves, as well as those they require for dealing with external oppression and discrimination. Though trainees should not jump to conclusions based on preconceptions, they also should check out whether any frequently found poor mind skills are present in individual clients.

When agreeing on shared analyses of clients' problems, counselling trainees need to consider how comfortable clients from different minority groups and cultures feel about their problems being broken down into the mind skills and communication/action skills they need to improve. If using the term 'skills' creates difficulties, trainees can consider adjusting their language. However, certain minority group clients are already primed to think in skills terms: for instance thinking and living skilfully are central to Buddhist psychology. Furthermore, many minority group clients are likely to appreciate that the lifeskills counselling model empowers them to deal with the specific problems that they face both as individuals and as members of their group.

Stage 3: The changing stage

Already I have mentioned that clients from minority groups may possess poor mind skills characteristic of their particular group. Where this is the case, counselling trainees should use appropriate interventions to help clients improve their skills. They can train clients in each of the six central mind skills – creating rules, perceptions, self-talk, visual images, explanations and expectations – in ways that help them to address internalized self-oppression. Trainees can also look for links between traditional approaches to mind training and teaching the six central mind skills. For example, the practice of Buddhist breathing meditation in either an upright or lotus position can be used as the entry point to working on mind skills such as disputing and replacing demanding rules.

When assisting clients from minority groups to improve their communication skills, counselling trainees always need to intervene in ways that encourage them to use verbal, vocal and bodily messages appropriate to the groupings in which they lead their lives. Trainees often need to help minority group clients communicate with the mainstream culture, including developing skills of affirming positive aspects of their identity and coping with negative comments. Trainees using the lifeskills counselling model can consider drawing on a range of interventions beyond counselling. Such interventions include facilitating the involvement of minority group support systems, advocacy on behalf of clients, and more broadly working as change agents to eliminate or modify oppressive organizational and social policies. Trainees, however, need to be cautious not to try too much too soon.

When helping clients to maintain their improved skills, counselling trainees need to be mindful that other minority group members can have agendas that conflict with those of the client. Sometimes clients require assistance in freeing themselves not only from oppressive mainstream culture norms, but also from oppressive minority group culture norms that could undermine their attempts to maintain their improved skills. Furthermore, trainees can assist minority group clients to understand that, when maintaining their skills, they need to guard against tendencies to blame either the mainstream or their minority group culture in unproductive ways. Instead they need to rise to the challenge of persevering in the use of their improved skills.

supervision 27

Chapter outcomes

By studying and doing the activities in this chapter you should:

- understand the importance of counsellors and helpers as practitioner-researchers monitoring and developing their skills;
- understand some forms of and functions of supervision;
- know about the importance of collaborative working relationships in supervision;
- know about various ways of preparing for and of presenting information in supervision; and
- know about the shadow side of supervision and what to avoid.

Introduction

Supervision literally means over-seeing. Supervisors oversee the actions or work of others; in this context the focus is on how well counselling students use essential counselling and helping skills. Fortune and Watts state: 'Counselling supervision is a space for practitioners to discuss their work with another professional with the purpose of providing support and consultation, with the aim of enhancing the counsellor's work with clients' (2000: 5). Carroll (1996) distinguishes between 'training supervision' and 'consultative supervision'. Training supervision is part of the ongoing training of trainees both on courses and afterwards in their probationary period prior to becoming accredited as counsellors. Consultative supervision is an egalitarian arrangement between one or more qualified counsellors who meet together for the purpose of improving the practice of at least one of them. The major emphasis here is on training supervision rather than on consultative supervision, though the two emphases overlap. Counsellor training courses must prepare trainees for supervision and ensure that they are able to reflect on themselves and how they work in supervision.

Contexts for supervision

There are two main contexts for supervisor–trainee contact in counsellor training: the placement agency in which the trainee counsels clients and the trainee's training course. Mearns (1997) observes that the term 'placement' comes from the social work domain whereby the course 'places' the trainee into a practice context and then maintains a parental oversight responsibility between the course member and agency. Critical issues for training courses are the availability of suitable placements, who is responsible for arranging or finding them, and negotiating appropriate lines of responsibility and communication between placement agencies and courses. Many counselling courses try to develop networks of placements that trainees can use on a regular basis (McCann, 1999). Many such placements are external to the training institution, but some may be on campus, for instance a student counselling service. Some courses, such as the University of East London in Britain and Swinburne University of Technology in Australia, run their own clinics to provide the public with counselling services and trainees with placement opportunities.

Mearns (1997) prefers the term 'counselling opportunities' to placements since person-centred courses often prefer an arrangement whereby trainees find their own sources of clients during training. Finding suitable placements or counselling opportunities can be difficult for trainees, especially those living in or attending courses outside of large population centres (Minikin, 2000). Training courses often have to settle for a mixture of course-found and trainee-found placements. To iron out administrative matters, it is good practice if training course placement tutors can hold three-way meetings between placement agencies and trainees. Ideally, there should be a written three-way agreement or contract identifying areas of responsibility between course, placement agency and trainee. If necessary, the contract should be extended to take into account supervisors external to the course. Izzard notes that it is all too easy for clinical responsibility to 'fall down the hole between supervisor, training course and placement' (2003: 38). Unfortunately, in the scramble to find placements, some serious compromises can be made in such matters as the compatibility of the course's theoretical orientation and that of an agency. Furthermore, some placements experience difficulty in providing a sufficient variety of suitable short-, medium- and longer-term clients.

There are numerous issues attached to training courses as contexts for supervision and only a few are discussed here. One issue is the relationship of the supervision sessions to the remainder of the course. Where possible, trainees require supervisors, whether they come from inside or outside the institution in which the course is lodged, who subscribe to the same theoretical orientation as that of the course's core model. It is also helpful if trainees can continue in a training group both prior to and accompanying supervision.

Another issue is that of how to integrate the evaluation of trainees' placement work into the overall evaluation required by the course. There is inevitably a role conflict when supervisors have to provide formal assessments of trainees' work at the same time as they are trying to establish trusting relationships in which trainees can gain confidence in their counselling ability and explore without defensiveness their good and poor use of counselling skills. In addition, of necessity, supervisors on training courses are often internal course staff, and therefore are in dual relationships with supervisees. Webb and Wheeler (1998), in a study of psychodynamic counsellors, found that supervisees were significantly better able to disclose sensitive issues regarding their clients if they were not trainees. One way to minimize the negative impact of these role conflicts is to grade trainees' placement work on a pass–fail basis. Another possibility – as at the University of East Anglia – is to have both group supervisions, conducted by internal staff members, and confidential individual supervisions, conducted by external supervisors. Where they are required, supervisor evaluations can be discussed with trainees prior to being submitted to the course authorities and courses can also solicit trainee self-evaluations. The main purposes of ongoing supervision are to improve trainees' skills and to protect clients. Therefore when supervisors have serious reservations about trainees' skills, this must be brought to trainees' attention as early as possible, both for clients' sake and to give trainees the chance to change before any end-of-semester or end-of-course assessments.

Formats for supervision

Supervision can take place either one-to-one, or with two or more trainees. Resources permitting, my preference, especially when trainees start seeing clients, is for individual supervision. Advantages of individual supervision include providing trainees with adequate time to be supervised thoroughly and the fact that trainees are more likely to discuss sensitive issues regarding clients and themselves than if supervised with others (Webb and Wheeler, 1998). Small group supervision also has some advantages: for example it gives trainees exposure to a greater range of clients and enables them to develop skills of discussing and receiving feedback on their work from peers as well as from their supervisor. A combination of individual supervision and trainees participating in counselling skills training groups has much to recommend it. Trainers can continue teaching trainees assessment skills and different interventions in a training group. Furthermore, trainees can share their experiences of working with clients in ways that may be beneficial for all concerned.

In addition, there are forms of consultative supervision. One format is that of one-to-one peer consultative supervision in which two counsellors provide support and supervision for one another by alternating the roles of superviser and supervisee. In peer group consultative supervision, three or more counsellors share the responsibility of providing one another with support and supervision. Trainees and trainee counsellors require training supervision prior to becoming accredited. However, they can also provide one another with consultative supervision. In reality, much consultative supervision takes place informally, with counsellors discussing clients and their reactions to them with trusted colleagues and those who have specialist knowledge.

Functions of supervision

The overriding goal of supervision is to aid trainees to think and communicate as effective counsellors and, in so doing, to develop the skills of being their own 'internal' supervisors. Box 27.1 lists some of the functions of supervision (Carroll, 1996; Fortune and Watts, 2000; Jacobs, 2001; King and Wheeler, 1999; Milne and James, 2000; Wosket, 2000). I start the list by stressing the importance of trainees thinking scientifically about their clients. Counsellors as practitioner-researchers search for evidence to support their work. Supervisors can encourage trainees to create hypotheses about what they do in counselling and then to monitor and evaluate the outcomes of their decisions. The process of supervision involves helping trainees, within a safe emotional climate, to question, question and question the adequacy of their performance and the thinking that precedes, accompanies and follows what they do. Such a questioning attitude requires humility and a reasonable absence of defensiveness for trainees to be able to identify, explore and own genuine strengths and also to be honest about the skills they need to improve. Supervisors can also encourage trainees to examine the research and professional literature for suggestions as to what interventions to use with which clients, under what circumstances. Needless to say, such literature should be examined critically rather than unquestioningly and trainees should never attempt any intervention for which they are inadequately prepared.

Box 27.1 Some functions of supervision

Overall goal: Developing trainees' skills of being their internal supervisors

Functions include:

1 Teaching trainees to think scientifically about the counselling process.
2 Providing a good service for clients.
3 Providing emotional support for trainees.
4 Being available in times of crisis.

5 Helping trainees to develop strong collaborative working relationships with clients.
6 Teaching trainees specific relationship, assessment and intervening skills.
7 Teaching trainees to apply the lifeskills counselling model flexibly and well with clients.
8 Developing trainees' skills of monitoring and evaluating their counselling practice.
9 Developing trainees' ability to integrate research findings into their counselling practice.
10 Encouraging trainees to be realistic about their own limitations and strengths and knowledgeable about the strengths of other counsellors.
11 Helping trainees to understand the importance of developing good professional and personal support networks.
12 Developing trainees' ethical awareness and ethical decision-making skills.
13 Developing trainees' awareness and skills for dealing with diverse clients.
14 Helping trainees to address tendencies to misperceive clients to meet their own needs.
15 Teaching trainees to address poor mind skills in relation to counselling and supervision.
16 Developing trainees' skills of using supervision time wisely.
17 Providing trainees with knowledge of opportunities for continuing professional and personal development.
18 Dealing with the formal administrative and evaluative aspects of supervision.

When trainees start counselling clients on placements and being supervised they are at the exciting stage of putting into real-life practice skills and learnings that they have acquired so far. This is the moment of truth towards which they and their trainers have been working. For many trainees, eager anticipation is tinged with apprehension that they are not good enough. Though some level of performance anxiety is realistic in beginning counsellors, trainees who have demanding and perfectionist rules create unhelpful levels of anxiety that can interfere with performance. Early on, supervisors may have to do some 'hand holding' as they help trainees to break the ice with real clients. Supervisors may need to assist trainees to examine poor mind skills contributing to performance anxiety. Throughout supervision, supervisors should provide emotional support for trainees in ways that encourage self-reliance and honest self-appraisal rather then dependence and a need for supervisor approval.

Supervisors can assist trainees to perform the joint tasks of providing good client services and improving their essential counselling skills by helping them to explore how well they are conducting each stage and phase of the lifeskills counselling model. To some extent the supervision process parallels the counselling process, in that supervisors should develop good collaborative working relationships with trainees to provide fertile contexts in which to monitor and improve their skills. In supervision, however, the emphasis is on improving the mind skills and the communication skills required for effective counselling rather than on managing personal problems. In a British study, both supervisors and supervisees rated creating a learning relationship as the most important of seven tasks of counselling supervision (Fortune and Watts, 2000).

Helping trainees to offer clients high quality counselling relationships is the primary task of supervision's early stages. Supervisors who model good relationship skills are invaluable sources of learning for trainees. It is critically important that supervisors assist trainees to develop a comfortable interviewing style that forms a sound base both for varying the nature of the counselling relationship, for instance by using skills such as questioning or challenging, and for using more technical skills and interventions.

Supervision should back up counselling skills training groups in teaching trainees about important aspects of practice. Trainees may wrongly think they are not up to handling some of the clients they counsel on their placements. In many instances, placement agencies will screen clients prior to referring them to trainees. However, this is not always the case and Mearns (1997), based on experience at the University of Strathclyde's free public Counselling Clinic, argues that resources spent on screening would be better diverted to supporting trainees as they work with challenging clients.

Supervisors should help trainees to gain a realistic acknowledgement of their strengths and limitations. Trainees need to develop knowledge and confidence about when they can take on difficult clients provided they have access to adequate support and supervision. Supervisors can also assist trainees to realize the importance of acknowledging other professionals' strengths. There is nothing shameful about referring clients to colleagues who have special areas of expertise, for instance in pain management or in overcoming drug addiction. Supervisors can help trainees realize the value of arranging in advance good support systems for such purposes as dealing with emergencies, medical considerations, clients with special problems and their own levels of stress and burnout.

Supervisors can also help trainees to understand the ethical dimensions of counselling, including issues connected with seeing clients in placement agencies and on counsellor training courses. Supervisors can address issues of diversity in supervisor–trainee relationships and assist trainees in gaining awareness and skills for dealing with clients whose personal characteristics differ from their own.

While supervision should have as its focus improving the trainees' counselling skills, the dividing line between supervision and personal counselling is not clear-cut. Trainees may bring past patterns of unhelpful thinking and communicating to both their counselling and their supervision relationships. Earlier, I mentioned trainees whose demanding rules create their own performance anxiety, which in turn makes them less effective with clients. Assisting trainees to identify, challenge and restate such demanding rules might be perceived as performing aspects of personal counselling within the supervisory relationship. Similarly, if supervisors and trainees become aware of sexism or cultural prejudice, such issues require addressing in supervision as well as, possibly, in personal counselling.

The supervision literature is full of references to counter-transference, the process by which counsellors and trainees distort how they perceive and behave towards clients to meet their own needs. For instance, trainees may at varying levels of awareness be encouraging dependency, sexual interest or even distance in some clients. Effective supervision helps trainees to identify, explore and address such distortions, at least insofar as they affect their work with clients. Supervisors should also identify and address their own counter-transference distortions towards their supervisees (Ladany et al., 2000).

Supervisors who adopt the lifeskills counselling model should definitely, as part of supervision, be assisting trainees to monitor the poor mind skills that they bring to and exhibit when counselling and not just allow them to focus on the poor mind and communication skills of clients. Some trainees require further personal counselling, a possibility that can also be explored within supervision.

Trainees need to learn how to get the most out of supervision, both when on training courses and afterwards. They need pointers to how they can improve their skills once supervision and the training course ends. Lastly, supervision helps smooth out administrative aspects related to trainees seeing clients in placement agencies and provides appropriate feedback about their progress to training courses.

Presenting material in supervision

Supervisors, counsellors and trainees who adopt a practitioner-researcher approach to their counselling work should ask themselves 'What is the most valid way of presenting what transpired in counselling sessions in supervisions?' In examining session content, there are at least three dimensions: (1) the observable dimension of the verbal, vocal and bodily communication of counsellor and client; (2) the private dimension of what was going on in the client's mind; and (3) the private dimension of what was going on in the counsellor's mind. However, examining the content of counselling sessions does not cover all relevant dimensions. Further dimensions include how each participant thought about and prepared for the session and also how the session influenced each participant afterwards.

Following are some methods whereby trainees can present, or attempt to present, counselling session content in supervision sessions. Some of these methods can be used in combination to add to the effectiveness of understanding what actually transpired.

Verbal report

Verbal reporting on its own relies entirely on memory, which will certainly be incomplete and will almost certainly be highly selective. The greater the period of time between sessions and supervision, the more invalid memory can become. When trainees are seeing other clients it can become difficult to remember exactly what happened with whom.

Process notes

Process notes, if written up immediately after counselling sessions and using a structured format, do not rely so heavily on memory. Such notes can act as an aid to memory during supervisions. The combination of process notes and verbal report, while still open to a high degree of invalidity, is probably more reliable then verbal report alone.

Transcripts

Transcripts of sessions are extremely time-consuming to prepare. One advantage is that they provide a valid record of counsellor–client verbal communication that can be examined to show how participants influenced one another and also to chart any progress during the course of the session, so far as these matters can be ascertained from written information.

Audiotaping

Audiotaping means that there is a valid record of all the verbal and vocal content of sessions. Another advantage is that supervisors can request or trainees can choose specific segments on which to focus. Audiotaping can be relatively unobtrusive when only a small microphone is visible to clients. By the time trainees start placements they should be comfortable with audiotaping their counselling sessions, which helps them to be more relaxed when asking clients' permission. It greatly assists supervision if trainees use high-quality recorders. As well as avoiding irritating background hiss, good recordings make it easier to understand quiet passages and different accents.

Videotaping

Videotaping has the great advantage of providing a valid record of body as well as verbal and vocal messages. Viewing videotapes of sessions is my preferred way of conducting supervisions. However, some placements may not be set up for videotaping, in which case audiotaping is the next best choice. A possible disadvantage of videotaping is that the machinery tends to be more obtrusive than for audiotaping.

Role-playing

Where videotaping is not available, role-playing can provide a way of finding out how trainees actually communicate with clients. The trainee can orient the supervisor to the client's role and then counsel the supervisor as 'client' in a way that resembles part of the actual session. Though there is some loss of validity, at least role-playing highlights the importance of the trainee's bodily communication.

Client feedback

Clients can provide feedback relevant to understanding what happened in trainees' counselling sessions in a number of ways. Supervisors and trainees should take note of and try to understand the reasons for single-session clients and for missed appointments. Towards the end of counselling sessions, trainees can ask their clients to provide feedback about the counselling relationship and procedures (Padesky and Greenberger, 1995). Clients can also fill out brief post-session questionnaires asking them for similar feedback (McMahon, 1999).

Though probably only feasible on a few occasions, clients can be asked to listen to tapes of sessions as part of supervision and to recall what they were thinking at the time of specific counsellor–client interactions. By such using interpersonal process recall methods (Kagan, 1975, 1984), supervisors, trainees and clients may discover great differences in how the participants perceived and processed certain interactions and situations at the time (Rennie, 1998).

Conducting supervision sessions

Counsellor training courses may orient trainees as to what to expect from supervision and how to make the most of it. In initial supervision sessions, trainees and supervisors may need to clarify details of their contract. Points for clarification can include how many times they meet, when, where, arrangements for getting in touch with one another between sessions, details of limitations on confidentiality, and evaluation requirements. Supervisors not previously known to trainees can introduce themselves, say a few words about their counselling and supervision experience, and answer queries. Supervisors can also ask trainees to introduce themselves and to evaluate their progress in developing counselling skills to date.

Supervision sessions can be broken down into three stages: preparation, the supervision session itself, and follow-up. In the preparation stage, trainees can do such things as write up and reflect on their session notes, go through audiotapes or videotapes selecting excerpts for presentation of their use of good and poor counselling skills, read up on possible interventions to use with clients, think about issues connected with differences between themselves and their clients, ponder ethical issues, and in other ways reflect upon how they can make the most of their supervision time.

Early in sessions, trainees and supervisors can establish session agendas. Sometimes, trainees only get one supervision hour for five or eight hours of client contact (Feltham, 2000a). Supervisors and trainees need to agree on how best to use the time, though not too rigidly since major issues may emerge during sessions. If taping is used, important decisions can be which tapes to present and, for those tapes chosen, which excerpts to review. When observing videotapes, a risk is that so much time is spent watching the first few minutes of a session that later work in sessions either receives insufficient or no attention. If trainees select tapes and tape excerpts, they may leave out important material. Dryden often addresses this issue by asking students to bring in all their tapes for him to make a 'lucky dip' (Dryden and Feltham, 1992).

In Chapter 15, I mentioned the need for counselling trainees to balance didactic and facilitative coaching skills with clients. Supervisors can balance similar skills with the trainees they supervise. Sometimes supervisors may wish to stop tapes to point something out to trainees. However, on many occasions, trainees should be the ones to choose which excerpts to present and when to stop tapes for discussion. Supervisors can facilitate trainees by focusing on their feelings and asking questions such as 'What were you feeling?' 'How did you experience that?' and 'Did you have any other feelings?' Further questions that supervisors might ask include: 'What was going on there?' 'What were you trying to do?' 'What skills were you using and how well were you using them?'

The content of supervision sessions comprises performing the functions already presented in Box 27.1. Within the context of good collaborative working relationships, supervisors develop trainees' skills of thinking scientifically about their counselling work so that they may become their own internal supervisors. Towards the end of a session both supervisors and trainees can review its main points and negotiate any specific homework or follow-up assignments.

The follow-up stage has two main goals: using improved skills discussed and worked on in supervision when counselling clients prior to the next supervision session; and carrying out specific homework assignments. For instance, supervisor and trainee may agree that the trainee should practice a specific intervention with another trainee before using it in a counselling session. A further assignment might be reading specific research references relevant to particular clients. Supervision homework assignments can also focus on trainees and not just on their clients. For example, trainees can agree to spend time challenging and restating any demanding rule or rules that contribute to performance anxiety.

The shadow side of supervision

Most supervisors work professionally and do their best to look after the interests of both supervisees and clients. However, just as counselling and counsellor training can be for better or worse, so can supervision. Some difficulties result from shortages of resources, both human and financial. For example, it may be difficult to find sufficient supervisors who match the theoretical orientation of a training course or good placements that provide trainees with a range of clients. Training courses always have limited funds to employ supervisors, thus making it difficult for trainees to receive a sufficient quantity of supervision.

Quality of supervision can also be a problem. Magnuson, Wilcoxen and Norem (2000) interviewed experienced counsellors to examine ineffective supervision practices and found six main characteristics of poor or 'lousy' supervision in three general spheres: organizational/administrative, technical/cognitive and relational/affective. The following are the six main characteristics that the authors identified:

- *unbalanced* in that supervision contained too much or too little of all the elements of the supervision experience;
- *developmentally inappropriate,* in that the changing developmental needs of supervisees were insufficiently taken into account;
- *intolerant of differences,* failing or unwilling to be flexible;
- *poor modelling of professional/personal attributes,* in that supervisors demonstrated what not to do, including sometimes unethical behaviour;

- *untrained,* in that supervisors were unprepared to manage boundaries, difficult issues and other interpersonal exchanges; and
- *professionally apathetic,* where supervisors lacked commitment to the counselling profession, supervisees and clients.

Some supervisors possess weak facilitation skills and thus create poor working relationships with trainees. The ideal supervision experience is one in which trainees can explore themselves as counsellors and improve their counselling skills within the context of affirming and accepting relationships. Good supervision requires a balance between being facilitative and encouraging and being didactic and helping to correct mistakes. Some supervisors err in the direction of being far too judgemental. Trainees can freeze when their supervisors seem always to be emphasizing what is wrong rather than helping them to own and develop their strengths. In addition to excessive criticism, other negative aspects of supervisory relationships include rigidity, stifling creativity, creating dependence, inattention to different trainees' learning styles, and absence of humour and fun. Further problems are caused by supervisors being insensitive to cultural and other differences, lazy, sloppy over time-keeping and availability, and abusing trainees in other ways, for instance by sexual harassment (Kaberry, 2000; Rapp, 2000).

Unfortunately some supervisors are poor in assisting trainees in the technical aspects of counselling, such as assessment and intervening. Supervisors who possess inadequate technical skills themselves are in a poor position to help trainees to improve their skills. Other supervisors may possess reasonably good technical skills, but are poor at imparting their knowledge and expertise.

What can trainees do when they feel that they have problems with their supervisors – such as someone with an inappropriate orientation or someone who is too judgemental? Sometimes wrongly matched trainees and supervisors struggle far longer than is necessary. Trainees should be able to discuss their difficulties with counselling course staff members responsible for supervision. Some difficulties can be resolved without changing supervisor. On other occasions, however, assuming that it is possible, changing supervisor may be the best solution.

Along with a few poor supervisors, there are also some poor supervisees. Some trainees are not prepared to work hard at achieving competence. Others have personal problems of such magnitude that possibly they should not be counselling clients at all until their own lives are in better shape. It is particularly hard to supervise trainees who are defensive and possess little insight into how their poor mind skills and communication skills interfere with their counselling. Some trainees are difficult to supervise because, to varying degrees, they know it all already.

A minority of trainees initiate and/or engage in unethical behaviour, whether with their clients or their supervisors.

Activity 27.1 Supervising and being supervised

Address the following:

1 What is the difference between training supervision and consultative supervision?
2 Turn to the list of functions of supervision in Box 27.1 and select the five most important functions for you at this stage of your development as a counsellor.
3 Critically discuss the advantages and disadvantages of each of the following ways of presenting material in supervision:

- verbal reports
- process notes
- transcripts
- audiotaping
- videotaping
- role-playing
- client feedback

4 What are the main characteristics of good supervisors?
5 What are the main characteristics of good supervisees?
6 Are you satisfied with the current supervision you are receiving and, if not, what if anything can you do to improve the situation?

personal counselling and continuing professional development 28

Chapter outcomes

By studying and doing the activity in this chapter you should:

- understand some issues surrounding receiving personal counselling;
- know about the movement towards mandatory continuing professional development and some approaches to it; and
- monitor and evaluate your counselling and helping skills.

Personal counselling and self-help

Counselling and helping trainees need to become their own best counsellors. If the counselling approach to which they subscribe helps clients to lead happier and more fulfilled lives, it seems logical to apply it to themselves. Trainees can work on becoming more human and compassionate both within and outside the context of training courses.

Personal counselling

Already I have suggested that good supervision involves elements of personal counselling as trainees address parts of themselves that have the potential to distort their counselling relationships. Supervisors using the lifeskills counselling model should encourage trainees to apply the model to themselves when it is relevant to how they counsel.

Some trainees will have been clients before embarking on counsellor training and may still be continuing in counselling. Legg (1999) cites three reasons why counselling trainees should consider undergoing therapy: personal growth, gaining empathic understanding of the client's position, and extending their experience of types of therapy. All three reasons are valid. Another reason is to gain a deeper understanding of how to apply the core counselling approach in which they are being trained. Some approaches, such as the psychoanalytic, require clienthood as part of training, so that trainees learn to deal with personal issues and to understand the approach more thoroughly. Other approaches, such as the person-centred, prefer personal counselling to be a matter of choice. As far as the lifeskills counselling approach is concerned, trainees should gain a better grasp of the model if they can address a specific problem or problem situation with a course of brief, focused training counselling.

Personal counselling can be very beneficial in working through blocks to being a happier, more fulfilled and compassionate person. In addition, trainees may address material in personal counselling related to their placements and supervisions, for instance fears about dealing with certain kinds of client and tendencies towards over-involvement or under-involvement. Trainees wishing to deal with past deprivations and current problems can also consider undertaking couples, family or group modes of counselling. Furthermore, participating in lifeskills training groups, focused for instance on assertiveness skills or managing stress skills, can help some trainees to become stronger and more skilled human beings.

The experience of being a client can improve a trainee's understanding of being in the client role. However, to gain a genuine understanding of the client's viewpoint, especially in regard to the processes of longer-term work, counselling should not simply be a training experience, but grounded in other motivations based on trainees' life experience, hopes and suffering.

The better trainees understand the client's role, the more compassionately they may be able to respond to clients' inevitable ambivalence about being in counselling. Because of their somewhat different emphases, trainees may also experience different aspects of their humanity by working with counsellors from different theoretical orientations. However, it is best to start with a firm grounding in one approach rather than to act like a magpie hopping from one approach to another.

An issue in counsellor training is whether undergoing personal counselling should be mandatory. Above I have presented some ways in which personal counselling might be beneficial. However, there is another side to the issue. Wilkins (2000) cites five areas of reservation about making personal counselling a criterion for the accreditation of counsellors: relevance, coercion, cost, defining the minimum length, and insufficient research evidence. Regarding relevance, counselling approaches differ in the importance they attach to trainees undergoing personal counselling. Regarding coercion, counselling will not necessarily be effective when in response to a bureaucratic demand. Forcing trainees to undergo a course of counselling also runs counter to the philosophy of an approach such as person-centred counselling. Regarding cost, adding the costs of personal counselling to the expense of training leads to elitism and discriminates against poorer trainees. Regarding the required length of counselling necessary, approaches differ on how long this should be – that is if they require it at all. Finally, regarding the research evidence for the effectiveness of personal counselling in enhancing counselling practice, some consider that the case has still to be proven.

Self-help

Counsellor training can provide trainees with the tools for improving their own functioning. The lifeskills counselling model advocated in this book is a self-helping model. As trainees understand and become more comfortable with the model they can adapt and apply it to problems and problem situations in their daily lives. Sometimes, this is best done systematically. For example, trainees can clear sufficient temporal, physical and psychological space within which to create a collaborative working relationship with themselves. Next they can clarify and expand their understanding of what is going on in problem situations. During this process they can identify unhelpful thoughts and communication/actions and translate these into specific mind skills and communication/action skills to improve. Then, applying some of the interventions described in this book to themselves, they can work to improve their skills.

As time goes by counselling trainees are likely to get wise to characteristic poor mind skills and communication/action skills they employ. They are then in a good position to cope with some problems quickly. For example, a trainee may develop skills at dissipating self-defeating anger through identifying, challenging and, if necessary, restating a demanding rule that was creating much of their anger. Trainees can also become adept at retrieving mistakes they make in their private lives by acknowledging them and using appropriate mind and communication skills to get back on track.

In addition to working on their own, trainees can be part of peer self-help groups and support networks. For example, members of women's groups, men's groups, gay and lesbian groups, and groups comprised of members of specific ethnic minorities can help one another to develop more of their humanity and to deal with personal, institutional and political oppression.

Continuing professional development (CPD)

Once trained and accredited, counsellors and helpers as practitioner-researchers cannot rest on their laurels. Instead they should assume responsibility for their continuing professional development (CPD). Since trainees on courses rather than accredited counsellors are the main audience for this book, this section on post-accreditation CPD is brief. In the past, counsellors were expected to be self-directed in arranging CPD rather than forced to undertake various activities. However, over the past decade or so, there has been a movement towards mandatory CPD. Undoubtedly, mandatory CPD requirements are now here to stay and will form a significant part of all counsellors' professional lives.

The activities that qualify for CPD eligibility vary according to the different counselling and helping professional associations and according to the divisions within them. Box 28.1 lists 10 types of activity that might count towards fulfilling counsellor CPD requirements. Other CPD activities might be either recommended by or negotiated with the relevant committees of the different professional associations.

Box 28.1 Ten types of CPD activity for counsellors and helpers

1. **Supervision** may be based on a consultative rather than a training model.
2. **Attendance on training courses** recognized by the professional association for CPD purposes.
3. **Attendance at workshops** recognized for CPD purposes.
4. **Presentation and/or attendance at conferences.** Conferences organized by the counsellor's professional association are especially likely to be eligible for CPD purposes.
5. **Watching videotapes and/or listening to audiotapes.** The professional association may maintain a library of videotapes and audiotapes that may be borrowed for CPD purposes.
6. **Reading** theoretical, research and professional books and articles.
7. **Personal psychological counselling** for professional purposes.
8. **Research.** Conducting applied research on counselling processes and outcomes and on providing counselling services.
9. **Publishing.** Writing books and articles for publication.
10. **Maintaining a log book** of CPD activities.

Various reasons motivate professional counselling and therapy associations to oblige accredited members to undertake CPD. One reason is to protect the public by trying to ensure that counsellors keep up to date with new developments in the field. Another reason is to help counsellors improve the levels of service that they offer to clients. Protecting the image of the profession with the media and the public is still another reason. In addition, the presence of mandatory CPD requirements may reassure legislators when the counselling and therapy professions seek to receive additional legal recognition, for instance through statutory regulation (Browne, 2001b).

Mandating CPD requirements can also have some drawbacks. It may seem a paradox that in a profession like counselling and helping that has autonomy and self-direction as central values, counsellors need to be forced to maintain and improve their skills. Furthermore, as in the case of the British Association for Counselling and Psychotherapy's supervision requirement, counsellors are given little choice in how they construct a PD programme that meets their individual needs and stages of professional experience and development (Feltham, 2000b; Wheeler, 2000). There is also no certainty that some of the weaker members of the counselling profession maintain and improve their skills just by going through the motions of fulfilling CPD requirements. Furthermore, this involves extra expenses, arguably discriminating against less well off counsellors and, in some instances, it may not be justified by what the counsellors receive in return.

There are also dangers that mandatory CPD requirements may be used as instruments of control by certain factions within professional associations who want to push their own narrow agendas. Though mandatory CPD is a fact of life, it is important that counsellors are vigilant in seeing that CPD requirements still allow individual counsellors much scope to choose and to undertake the activities that they think will best support their practice. Counsellors should beware of allowing their professional associations to adopt too much of a 'Nanny knows best' attitude. Challenging professional associations to produce research evidence to justify their CPD requirements is one way of resisting arbitrary decisions.

CPD and the new technologies

The above section is mainly based on conventional technologies. However, there are many ways in which technological developments may affect how CPD is conducted in future. Here I offer only a few possibilities. Professional counselling and helping associations may increasingly use the Internet to support practitioners and already, to some extent, are doing so. For instance, all of the Australian Psychological Society's ethical codes and guidelines for practice are available for downloading from the Internet (www.psychsociety.com.au), as is the British Psychological Society's *Code of Conduct for Psychologists* (www.bps.org.uk). Information about training courses and workshops eligible for CPD purposes can easily be found on the Internet. In addition, professional counselling associations can provide summaries on the Internet of research on specific problems and disorders. Furthermore, in conjunction with their authors and publishers, relevant counsellor manuals and client manuals might be available for downloading.

Developments in audiovisual technology could also be used for supervision and training purposes. For example, supervisions might be performed through visual link-ups in which supervisor and supervisee can see one another. A limitation here might be when the supervisee presents videotaped material from counselling sessions, though overcoming this limitation should not be insuperable. A more serious limitation might be a dilution of the quality of the supervisory relationship in the absence of genuine human contact.

Already, training material can be put on videotapes and CDs for playback. Furthermore, currently long-distance education and training takes place through television and other methods of relaying audiovisual images to groups of people. In time professional associations and other authorized bodies may offer visual training via the Internet in such areas as how to apply specific interventions and how to provide services for diverse client populations. In addition, psychological education packages for developing specific skills may become more widely available on the Internet for schools, colleges and the general public. However, teaching and demonstrating skills by means of audiovisual transmission can only go so far. In the final analysis, such training is best accompanied by real-life coached practice in the targeted skills. With too much reliance on the new technologies, there is a real danger of diluting the face-to-face personal relationships, here-and-now feedback, self-evaluation and discussion between trainers and learners.

Counsellors using the lifeskills counselling model and CPD

Counsellors and helpers using the lifeskills counselling model are lifelong learners who willingly engage in self-directed continuing professional development. As practitioner-researchers they constantly search for ways to improve how they provide services to clients. They evaluate the relationship and technical aspects of how they counsel as well as the outcomes for clients. They welcome input from others able to help them improve their skills whether through informal discussion with peers or more formal consultative and training supervisions.

When contemplating and undertaking professional development activities, lifeskills counsellors should focus on breadth as well as depth. By means of the CPD activities listed in Box 28.1, counsellors can broaden their expertise, including learning new interventions, extending the range of client problems with which they can work skilfully, gaining experience in how best to help diverse groups of clients, and working in different modes of counselling such as couples counselling and group interventions. Counsellors should remain open to learning from other counselling approaches, for instance improving their ability to offer counselling relationships through a better understanding of the person-centred approach or enabling clients to express their feelings more openly through Gestalt therapy interventions.

Lifeskills counsellors understand the importance of engaging in continuing personal as well as professional development. They understand that their ability to counsel successfully is influenced by maintaining their own mental well-being and avoiding staleness and burnout. Much of the time they use self-help, in which they monitor their own use of mind skills and communication/action skills and, where appropriate, make the necessary adjustments. However, sometimes they may seek the help of others, for instance when in crisis or facing important decisions. In addition, counsellors adopting the lifeskills counselling model should seek out different life experiences that provide valuable insights into what it means to be fully human.

Concluding comment

The purpose of skilled counselling is to create skilled clients. In this book I have tried to present students of counselling and helping, and trainers and supervisors too, with a lifeskills counselling model that can provide a framework for helping a wide range of clients. I have encouraged readers to be flexible in adapting the model to the particular circumstances of individual clients. I end now with a single-sentence summary of the book's main message:

> Counsellors and helpers using the lifeskills counselling model are practitioner-researchers who, within the context of accepting, affirming and collaborative working relationships, assist clients to improve specific mind skills and communication/action skills in order to manage current and future problems more effectively and thus to lead happier and more fulfilled lives.

Review activity

Monitoring and evaluating your counselling and helping skills

This final activity gives you the opportunity to review your counselling and helping skills for each stage and phase of the lifeskills counselling model. For each skills area, focus on both your mind skills and your communication/action skills. When focusing on your communication/action skills, remember to assess voice and body as well as verbal communication. For more information about specific skills areas please turn to the relevant chapters.

For each phase, list your good and poor skills in implementing the lifeskills counselling model.

Stage 1: Relating
Main task: Form a collaborative working relationship

Phase 1: Pre-counselling contact. Communicating with and providing information for clients prior to the first session.
Phase 2: Starting the initial session. Meeting, greeting and seating, making opening remarks, and encouraging clients to tell why they have come.
Phase 3: Facilitating client disclosure. Allowing clients space to reveal more about themselves and their problem(s) from their own perspective.

Stage 2: Understanding
Main task: Assess and agree on a shared analysis of the client's problem(s)

Phase 1: Reconnaissance. As necessary, conducting a broad review to identify the client's main problems and to collect information to understand her/him better.
Phase 2: Detecting and deciding. Collecting specific evidence to test ideas about possible poor skills and then reviewing all available information to suggest which skills might require improving.
Phase 3: Agreeing on a shared analysis of the client's problem(s). Arriving at a preliminary analysis of the client's problem(s) including, where appropriate, specifying mind skills and communication/action skills for improvement.

Stage 3: Changing
Main task: Achieve client change and the maintenance of change

Phase 1: Intervening. Helping clients to develop and implement strategies for managing current problems and improving relevant mind skills and communication/action skills for now and later.
Phase 2: Ending. Assisting clients to consolidate their skills for use afterwards and to plan how to maintain them when counselling ends.
Phase 3: Client self-helping. Clients, largely on their own, keep using their skills, monitoring their progress, retrieving lapses and, where possible, integrating their improved skills into their daily living (this phase relates to the client, not to the counsellor).

Final stocktaking

1. What are your main counselling skills strengths?
2. What are the main counselling skills areas in which you still need to work?
3. Refer back to the relevant chapters for suggestions on how to improve specific skills and develop and implement a plan to improve your essential counselling and helping skills.

references

Abramson, L. Y., Seligman, M. E. P. and Teasdale, J. D. (1978) Learned helplessness in humans: critique and reformulation. *Journal of Abnormal Psychology,* 87: 49–74.

Alberti, R. E. and Emmons, M. L. (2001) *Your Perfect Right: Assertiveness and Equality in Your Life and Relationships* (8th edn). Atascadero, CA: Impact Publishers.

American Psychiatric Association (2000) *Diagnostic and Statistical Manual of Mental Disorders* (DSM-IV-TR). Washington, DC: Author.

Argyle, M. (1999) *The Psychology of Interpersonal Behaviour* (5th edn). London: Penguin Books.

Arlow, J. A. (2005) Psychoanalysis. In R. J. Corsini and D. Wedding (eds) *Current Psychotherapies,* 7th edn. Belmont, CA: Wadsworth. pp. 15–51.

Atkinson, D. R., Thompson, C. E. and Grant, S. K. (1993) A three dimensional model for counseling racial/ethnic minorities. *The Counseling Psychologist,* 21: 257–77.

Australian Psychological Society (1996) *Guidelines for Psychotherapeutic Practice with Female Clients*. Melbourne: Author.

Australian Psychological Society (2002) *Code of Ethics*. Melbourne: Author.

Ballou, M. (1996) MCT theory and women. In D. W. Sue, A. E. Ivey and P. B. Pedersen (eds) *A Theory of Multicultural Counseling and Therapy*. Pacific Grove, CA: Brooks/Cole. pp. 236–46.

Bandura, A. (1986) *Social Foundations of Thought and Action: A Social Cognitive Theory*. Englewood Cliffs, NJ: Prentice-Hall.

Bandura, A. (1989) Human agency in social cognitive theory. *American Psychologist,* 44: 1175–84.

Bandura, A., Grusec, J. E. and Menlove, F. L. (1966) Observational learning as a function of symbolization and incentive set. *Child Development,* 37: 499–506.

Barlow, D. H., Levitt, J. T. and Bufka, L. F. (1999) The dissemination of empirically supported treatments: a view to the future. *Behaviour Research and Therapy,* 37: S147–62.

Barrett-Lennard, G. T. (1962) Dimensions of therapeutic response as causal factors in therapeutic change. *Psychological Monographs,* 76 (whole no. 562).

Barrett-Lennard, G. T. (1998) *Carl Rogers' Helping System: Journey & Substance*. London: Sage.

Bayne, R., Horton, I., Merry, T., Noyes, E. and McMahon, G. (1999) *The Counsellor's Handbook* (2nd edn). Cheltenham: Stanley Thornes.

Beck, A. T. (1976) *Cognitive Therapy and the Emotional Disorders*. New York: New American Library.

Beck, A. T. (1988) *Love Is Never Enough: How Couples Can Overcome Misunderstandings, Resolve Conflicts, and Solve Relationship Problems through Cognitive Therapy.* New York: Harper & Row.

Beck, A. T. (1991) Cognitive therapy: a 10-year retrospective. *American Psychologist,* 46: 368–75.

Beck, A. T. and Emery, G. (1985) *Anxiety Disorders and Phobias: A Cognitive Perspective*. New York: Basic Books.

Beck, A. T. and Weishaar, M. E. (2005) Cognitive therapy. In R. J. Corsini and D. Wedding (eds) *Current Psychotherapies,* 7th edn. Belmont, CA: Wadsworth. pp. 238–68.

Beck, A. T., Laude, R. and Bohnert, M. (1974) Ideational components of anxiety neurosis. *Archives of General Psychiatry,* 31: 319–25.

Beck, A. T., Rush, A. J., Shaw, B. F. and Emery, G. (1979) *Cognitive Therapy of Depression.* New York: John Wiley.

Beck, A. T., Epstein, N., Brown, G. and Steer, R. A. (1988) An inventory for measuring clinical anxiety: psychometric properties. *Journal of Consulting and Clinical Psychology,* 56: 893–7.

Beck, A. T., Freeman, A. et al. (1990) *Cognitive Therapy of Personality Disorders.* New York: Guilford Press.

Bernstein, D. (1988) *Put It Together, Put It Across: The Craft of Business Presentation.* London: Cassell.

Bernstein, D. A. and Borkovec, T. D. (1973) *Progressive Relaxation Training: A Manual for the Helping Professions.* Champaign, IL: Research Press.

Biddulph, S. (1995) *Manhood: An Action Plan for Changing Men's Lives* (2nd edn). Sydney: Finch Publishing.

Blatner, A. (2005) Psychodrama. In R. J. Corsini and D. Wedding (eds) *Current Psychotherapies,* 7th edn. Belmont, CA: Wadsworth. pp. 405–38.

Bond, T. (2000) *Standards and Ethics for Counselling in Practice* (2nd edn). London: Sage.

Bordin, E. S. (1979) The generalizability of the psychoanalytic concept of the working alliance. *Psychotherapy: Theory, Research and Practice,* 16: 252–60.

Borkovec, T. D. and Sides, J. K. (1979) Critical procedural variables related to the effects of progressive relaxation: a review. *Behaviour Research and Therapy,* 17: 119–25.

Brammer, L. M. and MacDonald, G. (2002) *The Helping Relationship: Process and Skills.* Boston: Pearson Allyn & Bacon.

British Association for Counselling and Psychotherapy (2002) *Ethical Framework for Good Practice in Counselling and Psychotherapy.* Rugby: Author.

British Psychological Society Division of Counselling Psychology (1998) *Guidelines for the Professional Practice of Counselling Psychology.* Leicester: British Psychological Society.

British Psychological Society Division of Counselling Psychology (2002) *Guidelines on Confidentiality and Record Keeping.* Leicester: British Psychological Society.

Browne, A. (2001a) Why aren't men interesting? *The Psychologist,* 11: 546–7.

Browne, S. (2001b) Regulation coming soon. *Counselling and Psychotherapy Journal,* 12(2): 4–5.

Bugental, J. F. T. (1981) *The Search for Authenticity.* New York: Irvington Publishers.

Carkhuff, R. R. (1987) *The Art of Helping* (6th edn). Amherst, MA: Human Resource Development Press.

Carroll, M. (1996) *Counselling Supervision: Theory, Skills and Practice.* London: Cassell.

Casemore, R. (1999) Why can't we own our mistakes? *Counselling,* 10: 94–6.

Cautela, J. (1967a) A Reinforcement Survey Schedule for use in therapy, training and research. *Psychological Reports,* 20: 1115–30.

Cautela, J. (1967b) Covert sensitization. *Psychological Reports,* 20: 459–68.

Cautela, J. R. (1976) The present status of covert modeling. *Journal of Behavior Therapy and Experimental Psychiatry,* 6: 323–6.

Chambless, D. L., Sanderson, W. C., Shoham, V., Bennet Johnson, S., Pope, K. S., Crits-Cristoph, P., Baker, M. J., Johnson, B., Woody, S. R., Sue, S., Beutler, L., Williams, D. A. and McCurry, S. (1996) An update on empirically validated therapies. *The Clinical Psychologist,* 49: 5–18.

Chambless, D. L., Baker, M. J., Baucom, D. H., Beutler, L. E., Calhoun, K. S., Crits-Christoph, P., Daiuto, A., DeRubeis, R., Detweiler, J., Haaga, D. A. F., Bennett Johnson, S., McCurry, S., Mueser, K. T., Pope, K. S., Sanderson, W. C., Shoham, V., Stickle, T., Williams D. A. and Woody, S. R. (1998) Update on empirically validated therapies. 2. *The Clinical Psychologist*, 51: 3–15.

Chaplin, J. (1999*) Feminist Counselling in Action* (2nd edn). London: Sage.

Cheatham, H., Ivey, A. E., Ivey, M. B., Pedersen, P., Rigazio-DiGillio, S., Simek-Morgan, L., and Sue, D. W. (1997) Multicultural counselling and therapy: 1 Metatheory – Taking theory into practice; 2 Integrative practice. In A. E. Ivey, M. B. Ivey and L. Simek-Downing (eds) *Counseling and Psychotherapy: A Multicultural Perspective*, 4th edn. Boston, MA: Allyn & Bacon. pp. 133–205.

Chester, A. (1994) Feminist counselling in Australia. MA (Women's Studies) thesis, University of Melbourne.

Christensen, A. and Heavy, C. L. (1993) Gender differences in marital conflict: the demand/withdraw interaction pattern. In S. Oskamp and M. Constanzo (eds*) Gender Issues in Contemporary Society*. Newbury Park, CA: Sage. pp. 113–41.

Clark, A. J. (1991) The identification and modification of defense mechanisms in counseling. *Journal of Counseling & Development,* 69: 231–6.

Collins, T., Kane, G. and Drever, P. (2001) Understanding homosexuality: working with gays, lesbians and bisexuals. *InPsych,* 23: 26–8.

Corey, G. (2000) *Theory and Practice of Counseling and Psychotherapy* (6th edn). Belmont, CA: Wadsworth.

Corey, M. S. and Corey, G. (2002) *Groups: Process and Practice* (6th edn). Pacific Grove, CA: Brooks/Cole.

Corey, M. S. and Corey, G. (2003) *Becoming a Helper* (4th edn). Belmont, CA: Wadsworth.

Cormier, S. and Nurius, P. S. (2002) *Interviewing and Change Strategies for Helpers: Fundamental Skills and Cognitive-Behavioral Interventions* (5th edn). Belmont, CA: Wadsworth.

Corsini, R. J. (2005) Introduction. In R. J. Corsini and D. Wedding (eds) *Current Psychotherapies,* 7th edn. Belmont, CA: Wadsworth. pp. 1–14.

Corsini, R. J. and Wedding, D. (eds) (2005) *Current Psychotherapies,* 7th edn. Belmont, CA: Wadsworth.

Daley, M. F. (1969) The 'reinforcement menu': finding effective reinforcers. In J. D. Krumboltz and C. E. Thoresen (eds) *Behavioral Counseling: Cases and Techniques*. New York: Holt, Rinehart & Winston. pp. 42–5.

D'Ardenne, P. and Mahtani, A. (1999) *Transcultural Counselling in Action* (2nd edn). London: Sage.

Davidson, F. (1988) *The Art of Executive Firing*. Melbourne: Information Australia.

Davies, D. (2000) Sexual orientation. In C. Feltham and I. Horton (eds) *Handbook of Counselling and Psychotherapy*. London: Sage. pp. 50–7.

Deffenbacher, J. L. and Suinn, R. M. (1988) Systematic desensitization and the reduction of anxiety. *The Counseling Psychologist,* 16: 9–30.

Deffenbacher, J. L., Oetting, E. R., Huff, M. E. and Thwaites, G. A. (1995) Fifteen month follow-up of social skills and cognitive-relaxation approaches to general anger reduction. *Journal of Counseling Psychology,* 42: 400–5.

Deffenbacher, J. L., Huff, M. E., Lynch, R. S., Oetting, E. R. and Salvatore, N. F. (2000) Characteristics and treatment of high-anger drivers. *Journal of Counseling Psychology*, 47: 5–17.

Department of Foreign Affairs and Trade (2000) *Australia in Brief 2000*. Canberra: Author.

Department of Immigration and Multicultural Affairs (1997) *Australia's Population Trends and Prospects 1996*. Canberra: Author.

Dolliver, R. H. (1991) Perls with Gloria re-viewed: Gestalt techniques and Perls' practices. *Journal of Counseling & Development*, 69: 299–304.

Donohoe, G. and Ricketts, T. (2000) Phobias. In C. Feltham and I. Horton (eds) *Handbook of Counselling and Psychotherapy*. London: Sage. pp. 494–501.

Dryden, W. (1991) *A Dialogue with Arnold Lazarus: 'It Depends'*. Milton Keynes: Open University Press.

Dryden, W. (ed.) (2002) *Handbook of Individual Therapy* (4th edn). London: Sage.

Dryden, W. and Feltham, C. (1992) *Brief Counselling: A Practical Guide for Beginning Practitioners*. Buckingham: Open University Press.

Edwards, C. E. and Murdoch, N. L. (1994) Characteristics of therapist self-disclosure in the counseling process. *Journal of Counseling & Development*, 72: 384–9.

Egan, G. (2002) *The Skilled Helper: A Problem-Management and Opportunity-Development Approach to Helping* (7th edn). Pacific Grove, CA: Brooks/Cole.

Egan, G. and Cowan, M. (1979) *People in Systems: A Model for Development in the Human-Service Professions and Education*. Pacific Grove, CA: Brooks/Cole.

Ekman, P. (1995) *Telling Lies: Clues to Deceit in the Marketplace, Politics, and Marriage*. London: Norton.

Ekman, P., Friesen, W. V. and Ellsworth, P. (1972) *Emotions in the Human Face*. New York: Pergamon Press.

Elliott, R. (1985) Helpful and nonhelpful events in brief counseling interviews: an empirical taxonomy. *Journal of Counseling Psychology*, 32: 307–22.

Ellis, A. (1977) *Anger: How to Live With and Without It*. New York: Lyle Stuart.

Ellis, A. (1998) The biological basis of irrationality. In A. Ellis and S. Blau (eds) *The Albert Ellis Reader*. Secaucus, NJ: Citadel. pp. 271–91.

Ellis, A. (1999) *How to Make Yourself Happy and Remarkably Less Disturbable*. Atascadero, CA: Impact.

Ellis, A. (2001) *Feeling Better, Getting Better, Staying Better: Profound Self-Help Therapy for Your Emotions*. Atascadero, CA: Impact.

Ellis, A. (2003) *Ask Albert Ellis? Straight Answers and Sound Advice from America's Best-Known Psychologist*. Atascadero, CA: Impact.

Ellis, A. (2005) Rational emotive behavior therapy. In R. J. Corsini and D. Wedding (eds) *Current Psychotherapies*, 7th edn. Belmont, CA: Wadsworth. pp. 166–201.

Ellis, A. and Crawford, T. (2000) *Making Intimate Connections: 7 Guidelines for Great Relationships and Better Communication*. Atascadero, CA: Impact.

Ellis, A. and Dryden, W. (1997) *The Practice of Rational Emotive Behaviour Therapy*. London: Free Association Books.

Ellis, A. and Harper, R. (1997) *A Guide to Rational Living*. North Hollywood, CA: Wilshire Books.

Ellis, A. and MacLaren, C. (1998) *Rational Emotive Behavior Therapy: A Therapist's Guide*. San Luis Obispo, CA: Impact.

Epps, J. and Kendall, P. C. (1995) Hostile attributional bias in adults. *Cognitive Therapy and Research*, 19: 159–78.

Fallon, B. (1997) The balance between paid work and home responsibilities: personal problem or corporate concern? *Australian Psychologist,* 32: 1–9.

Feltham, C. (2000a) Supervision. In C. Feltham and I. Horton (eds) *Handbook of Counselling and Psychotherapy.* London: Sage. pp. 718–20.

Feltham, C. (2000b) Counselling supervision: baselines, problems and possibilities. In B. Lawton and C. Feltham (eds) *Taking Supervision Forward: Enquiries and Trends in Counselling and Psychotherapy*. London: Sage. pp. 5–24.

Fischer, R. L. (1972) *Speak to Communicate: An Introduction to Speech.* Encino, CA: Dickenson.

Fortune, L. and Watts, M. (2000) Examining supervision: comparing the beliefs of those who deliver and those who receive. *Counselling Psychology Review,* 15: 5–15.

Frankl, V. E. (1963) *Man's Search for Meaning: An Introduction to Logotherapy.* New York: Washington Square Press.

Frankl, V. E. (1967) *Psychotherapy and Existentialism: Selected Papers on Logotherapy.* Harmondsworth, UK: Penguin.

Frankl, V. E. (1975) *The Unconscious God: Psychotherapy and Theology.* New York: Simon & Schuster.

Frankl, V. E. (1988) *The Will to Meaning: Foundations and Applications of Logotherapy*. New York: Meridian.

Frankland, A. (2003) Counselling psychology: the next ten years. In R. Woolfe, W. Dryden and S. Strawbridge (eds) *Handbook of Counselling Psychology* (2nd edn). London: Sage.

Freud, S. (1936) *The Problem of Anxiety*. New York: W. W. Norton.

Freudenberger, H. J. (1980) *Burnout: The High Cost of High Achievement.* London: Arrow Books.

Fromm, E. (1956) *The Art of Loving.* New York: Bantam Books.

Garrett, T. (1998) Sexual contact between patients and psychologists. *The Psychologist,* 11: 227–30.

Gazda, G. M., Ginter, E. J. and Horne, A. M. (2001) *Group Counseling and Group Psychotherapy: Theory and Application.* Needham Heights, MA: Allyn & Bacon.

Glaser, R. D. and Thorpe, J. S. (1986) Unethical intimacy: a survey of sexual contacts and advances between psychology educators and female graduate students. *American Psychologist,* 41: 42–51.

Glasser, W. (1984) *Control Theory: A New Explanation of How We Control Our Lives.* New York: Harper & Row.

Glasser, W. (1998) *Choice Theory: A New Psychology of Personal Freedom.* New York: HarperPerennial.

Glasser, W. and Wubbolding, R. (1995) Reality therapy. In R. J. Corsini and D. Wedding (eds) *Current Psychotherapies,* 5th edn. Itasca, IL: Peacock. pp. 293–321.

Goldfried, M. R. and Davison, G. C. (1976) *Clinical Behavior Therapy*. New York: Holt, Rinehart & Winston.

Gordon, T. (1970) *Parent Effectiveness Training: The Tested New Way to Raise Responsible Children*. New York: Wyden.

Greenberg, L. S., Rice, L. N. and Elliott, R. (1993) *Facilitating Emotional Change: The Moment by Moment Process*. New York: Guilford Press.

Greenberger, D. and Padesky, C. A. (1995) *Mind Over Mood: Change How You Feel by Changing the Way You Think*. New York: Guilford.

Greer, G. (1999) *The Whole Woman*. London: Anchor.

Hackman, A., Suraway, C. and Clark, D. M. (1998) Seeing yourself through others' eyes: a study of spontaneously occurring images in social phobia. *Behavioural and Cognitive Psychotherapy,* 26: 3–12.

Hall, E. T. (1966) *The Hidden Dimension*. New York: Doubleday.

Harrison, N. (2000) Gay affirmative therapy: a critical analysis of the literature. *British Journal of Guidance & Counselling,* 28: 37–53.

Haskey, J. (1997) Population review: (8) The ethnic minority and overseas-born population of Great Britain. *Population Trends,* 88: 13–30.

Heesacker, M. and Bradley, M. M. (1997) Beyond feelings: psychotherapy and emotion. *The Counseling Psychologist,* 25: 201–19.

Heesacker, M., Wester, S. R., Vogel, D. L., Wentzel, J. T., Mejia-Millan, C. M. and Goodholm, C. R. (1999) Gender-based emotional stereotyping. *Journal of Counseling Psychology,* 46: 483–95.

Heppner, P. P., Rogers, M. E. and Lee, L. (1984) Carl Rogers: reflections on his life. *Journal of Counseling & Development,* 63: 14–20.

Herlihy, B. and Corey, G. (1996) *ACA Ethical Standards Casebook* (5th edn). Alexandria, VA: American Counseling Association.

Ho, D. Y. F. (1995) Internalized culture, cultrocentrism, and transcendence. *The Counseling Psychologist,* 23(1): 4–24.

Huffman, S. B. and Myers, J. E. (1999) Counseling women in midlife: an integrative approach to menopause. *Journal of Counseling & Development,* 77: 258–66.

Ivey, A. E. (1987) Cultural intentionality: the core of effective helping. *Counselor Education and Supervision,* 26: 168–72.

Ivey, A., Rathman, D. and Colbert, R. D. (2001) Culturally sensitive microcounselling. *Australian Journal of Counselling Psychology,* 2: 14–21.

Izzard, S. (2003) Who is holding the baby? *Counselling and Psychotherapy Journal,* 14(5): 38–9.

Jacobs, M. (2001) Supervisors can change. *Counselling and Psychotherapy Journal,* 12(1): 26–7.

Jacobson, E. (1938) *Progressive Relaxation* (2nd edn). Chicago: University of Chicago Press.

Johnson, D. (2002) *Reaching Out: Interpersonal Effectiveness and Self-actualization* (8th edn). Boston: Pearson Allyn & Bacon.

Jung, C. G. (1966) *The Practice of Psychotherapy* (2nd edn). London: Routledge.

Jung, C. G. (1982) *Aspects of the Feminine*. London: Routledge.

Kaberry, S. (2000) Abuse in supervision. In B. Lawton and C. Feltham (eds) *Taking Supervision Forward: Enquiries and Trends in Counselling and Psychotherapy*. London: Sage. pp. 42–59.

Kagan, N. (1975) *Influencing Human Interaction*. Washington: American Personnel and Guidance Association.

Kagan, N. (1984) Interpersonal process recall: basic methods and recent research. In D. Larsen (ed.) *Teaching Psychological Skills*. Pacific Grove, CA: Brooks/Cole. pp. 261–9.

Kalodner, C. R. (1998) Systematic desensitization by Cynthia R. Kalodner. In S. Cormier and B. Cormier (eds) *Interviewing Strategies for Helpers: Fundamental Skills and Cognitive Behavioral Interventions,* 4th edn. Pacific Grove, CA: Brooks/Cole. pp. 497–529.

Kazdin, A. E. (1994) *Behavior Modification in Applied Settings* (5th edn). Pacific Grove, CA: Brooks/Cole.

Kelly, E. W. (1995) Counselor values: a national survey. *Journal of Counseling & Development,* 73: 648–53.

Kelly, G. A. (1955) *A Theory of Personality: The Psychology of Personal Constructs.* New York: W. W. Norton.

Kelly, J. A., Sikkema, K. J., Winett, R. A., Solomon, L. J., Roffman, R. A., Heckman, T. G., Stevenson, L. Y., Perry, M. J., Norman, A. D. and Desiderateo, L. J. (1995) Factors predicting continued high-risk behavior among gay men in small cities: psychological, behavioral, and demographic characteristics related to unsafe sex. *Journal of Consulting and Clinical Psychology,* 63: 101–7.

Kendall, P. C. and Hollon, S. D. (1989) Anxious self-talk: development of the anxious self-statements questionnaire (ASSQ). *Cognitive Therapy and Research,* 13: 81–93.

King, D. and Wheeler, S. (1999) The responsibilities of counsellor supervisors: a qualitative study. *British Journal of Guidance & Counselling,* 27: 215–29.

Knox, S., Hess, S.A., Peterson, D. A. and Hill, C. E. (1997) A qualitative analysis of client perceptions of the effects of helpful therapist disclosure in long-term therapy. *Journal of Counseling Psychology,* 44(3): 274–83.

Ladany, N., Constantine, M. G., Miller, K., Erickson, C. D. and Muse-Burke, J. L. (2000) Supervisor countertransference: a qualitative investigation into its identification and description. *Journal of Counseling Psychology,* 47: 102–15.

Laungani, P. (1999) Client or culture centred counselling. In S. Palmer and P. Laungani (eds) *Counselling in a Multicultural Society*. London: Sage. pp. 134–52.

Lazarus, A. A. (1984) *In the Mind's Eye*. New York: Guilford Press.

Lazarus, A. A. (1993) Tailoring the therapeutic relationship, or being an authentic chameleon. *Psychotherapy,* 30: 404–7.

Lazarus, A. A. (1997) *Brief but Comprehensive Psychotherapy: The Multimodal Way.* New York: Springer.

Lazarus, A. A. (2005a) Multimodal therapy. In R. J. Corsini and D. Wedding (eds) *Current Psychotherapies,* 7th edn. Belmont, CA: Wadsworth. pp. 337–71.

Lazarus, A. A. (2005b) The case of George. In D. Wedding and R. J. Corsini (eds) *Case Studies in Psychotherapy*, 4th edn. Belmont, CA: Wadsworth. pp. 177–87.

Legg, C. (1999) Getting the most out of personal therapy. In R. Bor and M. Watts (eds) *The Trainee Handbook: A Guide for Counselling and Therapy Trainees.* London; Sage. pp. 131–45.

Lenihan, G. and Kirk, W. G. (1990) Using student paraprofessionals in the treatment of eating disorders. *Journal of Counseling & Development,* 68: 332–5.

Lewinsohn, P. M., Munoz, R. F., Youngren, M. A. and Zeiss, A. M. (1986) *Control Your Depression* (rev. edn). New York: Prentice-Hall.

Lindsay, G. and Clarkson, P. (1999) Ethical dilemmas of psychotherapists. *The Psychologist,* 12: 182–5.

MacPhillamy, D. J. and Lewinsohn, P. M. (1971) *Pleasant Events Schedule.* Mimeograph, University of Oregon.

Magnuson, S., Wilcoxon, S. A. and Norem, K. (2000) A profile of lousy supervision: experienced counselors' perspectives. *Counselor Education and Supervision,* 39: 189–202.

Mahrer, A. R., Fairweather, D. R., Passey, S., Gingras, N. and Boulet, D. B. (1999) The promotion and use of strong feelings in psychotherapy. *Journal of Humanistic Psychology,* 39: 35–53.

Maslow, A. H. (1970) *Motivation and Personality* (2nd edn). New York: Harper & Row.

May, R. and Yalom, I. D. (2005) Existential psychotherapy. In R. J. Corsini and D. Wedding (eds) *Current Psychotherapies,* 7th edn. Belmont, CA: Wadsworth. pp. 269–98.

McCann, D. (1999) Supervision in primary care counselling. In R. Bor and D. McCann (eds) *The Practice of Counselling in Primary Care.* London: Sage. pp. 214–28.

McKay, M. and Fanning, P. (2000) *Self-Esteem: A Proven Program of Cognitive Techniques for Assessing, Improving, and Maintaining Your Self-Esteem.* Oakland, CA: New Harbinger Publications.

McMahon, G. (1999) Reflective practice. *Counselling,* 10: 193.

McNair, D. M., Lorr, M. and Droppleman, L. F. (1981) *EITS Manual for the Profile of Mood States.* San Diego, CA: Educational and Industrial Testing Service.

Mearns, D. (1997) *Person-Centred Counselling Training.* London: Sage.

Mearns, D. and Thorne, B. (1999) *Person-Centred Counselling in Action* (2nd edn). London: Sage.

Meichenbaum, D. H. (1977) *Cognitive-behavior Modification: An Integrative Approach.* New York: Plenum.

Meichenbaum, D. H. (1983) *Coping with Stress.* London: Century.

Meichenbaum, D. H. (1985) *Stress Inoculation Training.* New York: Pergamon Press.

Meichenbaum, D. H. (1986) Cognitive-behavior modification. In F. H. Kanfer and A. P. Goldstein (eds) *Helping People Change: A Textbook of Methods,* 3rd edn. New York: Pergamon Press. pp. 346–80.

Meichenbaum, D. H. and Deffenbacher, J. L. (1988) Stress inoculation training. *The Counseling Psychologist,* 16: 69–90.

Meltzoff, J. and Kornreich, M. (1970) *Research in Psychotherapy.* New York: Atherton.

Miller, R. (1999) The first session with a new client: five stages. In R. Bor and N. Watts (eds) *The Trainee Handbook: A Guidebook for Counselling and Psychotherapy Trainees.* London: Sage. pp. 146–67.

Milne, D. and James, I. (2000) A systematic review of effective cognitive-behavioural supervision. *British Journal of Clinical Psychology,* 39: 111–27.

MIMS (latest edition). Middlesex, England: Haymarket Publishing and Australian MIMS, 68 Alexandra Street, Crows Nest, Sydney, Australia.

Minikin, K. (2000) Placements. *Counselling,* 11: 638–9.

Mohammed, C. (2000) Race, culture and ethnicity. In C. Feltham and I. Horton (eds) *Handbook of Counselling and Psychotherapy.* London: Sage. pp. 62–70.

Morawetz, D. (1989) Behavioral self-help treatment for insomnia: a controlled evaluation. *Behavior Therapy,* 20: 365–79.

Moreno, Z. T. (1959) A survey of psychodramatic techniques. *Group Psychotherapy,* 12: 5–14.

Nelson-Jones, R. (2001) *Theory and Practice of Counselling & Therapy,* 3rd edn. London: Sage.

Nelson-Jones, R. (2004) *Cognitive Humanistic Therapy: Buddhism, Christianity and Being Fully Human.* London: Sage.

Nelson-Jones, R. and Cosolo, W. (1994) How to assess cancer patients' thinking skills. *Palliative Medicine,* 8: 115–21.

Novaco, R. (1977) Stress inoculation: a cognitive therapy for anger and its application to a case of depression. *Journal of Consulting and Clinical Psychology,* 45: 600–8.

O'Neill, J. M., Helms, B. J., Gable, R. K., David, L. and Wrightsman, L. S. (1986) Gender Role Conflict Scale: college men's fear of femininity. *Sex Roles,* 14: 335–50.

Padesky, C. A. and Greenberger, D. (1995) *Clinician's Guide to Mind Over Mood.* New York: Guilford.

Parrott, C. (1999) Doing therapy briefly in primary care: clinical applications. In R. Bor and D. McCann (eds) *The Practice of Primary Care.* London: Sage. pp. 148–71.

Patterson, C. H. (1974) *Relationship Counseling and Psychotherapy.* New York: Harper & Row.

Patterson, C. H. (1986) *Theories of Counseling and Psychotherapy* (4th edn). New York: Harper & Row.

Pattison, S. (1999) Are professional codes ethical? *Counselling,* 10: 374–80.

Pavio, S. C. and Greenberg, L. S. (1995) Resolving 'unfinished business': efficacy of experiential therapy using empty-chair dialogue. *Journal of Consulting and Clinical Psychology,* 63: 419–25.

Pease, A. (1981) *Body Language: How to Read Others' Thoughts by Their Gestures.* Sydney: Camel.

Perls, F. S. (1965) Gestalt therapy. In E. Shostrom (ed.) *Three Approaches to Psychotherapy.* Santa Ana: CA: Psychological Films.

Perls, F. S. (1973) *The Gestalt Approach and Eyewitness to Therapy.* New York: Bantam Books.

Perls, F. S., Hefferline, R. F. and Goodman, P. (1951) *Gestalt Therapy.* New York: Souvenir Press.

Perry, M. A. and Furukawa, M. J. (1986) Modeling methods. In F. H. Kanfer and A. P. Goldstein (eds) *Helping People Change: A Textbook of Methods,* 3rd edn. New York: Pergamon. pp. 66–110.

Poon, D., Nelson-Jones, R. and Caputi, P. (1993) Asian students' perceptions of culture-sensitive and culture-neutral counselling. *Australian Counselling Psychologist,* 9(1): 3–16.

Psychotherapy & Counselling Association of Australia (2001) *Ethical Guidelines.* Melbourne: Author.

Rapp, H. (2000) Working with difference: culturally competent supervision. In B. Lawton and C. Feltham (eds) *Taking Supervision Forward: Enquiries and Trends in Counselling and Psychotherapy.* London: Sage. pp. 93–112.

Raskin, N. J. and Rogers, C. R. (2005) Person-centred therapy. In R. J. Corsini and D. Wedding (eds) *Current Psychotherapies,* 7th edn. Belmont, CA: Wadsworth. pp. 130–65.

Rennie, D. (1998) *Person-Centred Counselling: An Experiential Approach.* London: Sage.

Rennie-Peyton, P. (1995) Bullying within organizations. *Counselling Psychology Review,* 10(4): 10–11.

Reynolds, D. (1990) Morita and Naikan therapies – similarities. *Journal of Morita Therapy,* 1: 159–63.

Ridley, C. R. and Lingle, D. W. (1996) Cultural empathy in multicultural counseling: a multidimensional process. In P. B. Pederson, J. G. Draguns, W. J. Lonner and T. E. Trimble (eds) *Counseling across Cultures* (4th edn). Thousand Oaks, CA: Sage. pp. 95–104.

Rogers, C. R. (1951) *Client-centered Therapy.* Boston: Houghton Miflin.

Rogers, C. R. (1957) The necessary and sufficient conditions of therapeutic personality change. *Journal of Consulting Psychology,* 21: 95–103.

Rogers, C. R. (1959) A theory of therapy, personality and interpersonal relationships as developed in the client-centered framework. In S. Koch (ed.) *Psychology: A Study of Science* (Study no. 1, Vol. 3, pp. 184–256). New York: McGraw-Hill.
Rogers, C. R. (1961) *On Becoming a Person: A Therapist's View of Psychotherapy*. Boston, MA: Houghton Miflin.
Rogers, C. R. (1962) The interpersonal relationship: the core of guidance. *Harvard Educational Review,* 32: 416–29.
Rogers, C. R. (1975) Empathic: an unappreciated way of being. *The Counseling Psychologist,* 5(2): 2–10.

Schaverin, J. (1999) Jung, the transference and the psychological feminine. In I. B. Seu and M. C. Hennan (eds) *Feminism & Psychotherapy: Reflections on Contemporary Theories and Practices*. London: Sage. pp. 172–88.
Schwartz, S. H. (1992) Universals in the content and structure of values: theoretical advances and empirical tests in 20 countries. In M. Zanna (ed.) *Advances in Experimental Social Psychology*. New York: Academic Press. Vol. 25, pp. 1–65.
Seligman, M. E. P. (1991) *Learned Optimism*. Milsons Point, NSW: Random House Australia.
Selye, H. (1974) *Stress without Distress*. Sevenoaks, UK: Hodder & Stoughton.
Sexton, J. (1999) Counselling and the use of psychotropic medication. In R. Bor and D. McCann (eds) *The Practice of Counselling in Primary Care*. London: Sage. pp. 184–200.
Sexton, J. and Legg, C. (1999) Psychopharmacology: a primer. In R. Bor and M. Watts (eds) *The Trainee Handbook: A Guide for Counselling and Psychotherapy Trainees*. London: Sage. pp. 201–18.
Sharpley, C. F. and Sagris, A. (1995) When does counsellor forward lean influence client-perceived rapport? *British Journal of Guidance & Counselling,* 23: 387–94.
Sichel, J. and Ellis, A. (1984) *RET Self-help Form*. New York: Institute for Rational-Emotive Therapy.
Simone, D. H., McCarthy, P. and Skay, C. L. (1998) An investigation of client and counselor variables that influence the likelihood of counselor self-disclosure. *Journal of Counseling & Development,* 76: 174–82.
Skinner, B. F. (1953) *Science and Human Behavior*. New York: Macmillan.
Skinner, B. F. (1969) *Contingencies of Reinforcement*. New York: Appleton-Century-Crofts.
Spindler, G. D. (1963) *Education and Culture: Anthropological Approaches*. New York. Holt, Rinehart & Winston.
Strong, S. R. (1978). Social psychological approach to psychotherapy research. In S. L. Garfield and A. A. Bergin (eds) *Handbook of Psychotherapy and Behavior Change: An Empirical Analysis*. New York: Wiley. pp. 101–35.
Strong, S. R., Welsh, J. A., Cocoran, J. L. and Hoyt, W. T. (1992) Social psychology and counseling psychology: the history, products, and promise of an interface. *Journal of Counseling Psychology,* 39: 139–57.
Strong, S. R., Yoder, B. and Cocoran, J. (1995) Counseling: a social process for constructing personal powers. *The Counseling Psychologist,* 23: 374–84.
Stuart, R. B. (1980) *Helping Couples Change: A Social Learning Approach to Marital Therapy*. New York: Guilford Press.
Sue, S. and Sue, D. (1999) *Counseling the Culturally Different: Theory and Practice* (3rd edn). New York: John Wiley.
Sue, S. and Zane, N. (1987) The role of culture and cultural techniques in psychotherapy. *American Psychologist,* 42: 37–45.

Sue, D. W., Ivey, A. E. and Pederson, P. B. (1996) *A Theory of Multicultural Counseling & Therapy*. Pacific Grove, CA: Brooks/Cole.

Sue, D. W., Carter, R. T., Casas, J. M., Fouad, N. A., Ivey, A. E., Jensen, M., LaFromboise, T., Manese, J. E., Ponterotto, J. G. and Vazquez-Nutall, E. (1998) *Multicultural Counseling Competencies: Individual and Organizational Development.* London: Sage.

Sullivan, H. S. (1953) *The Interpersonal Theory of Psychiatry.* New York: W. W. Norton.

Sullivan, H. S. (1954) *The Psychiatric Interview.* New York: W. W. Norton.

Task Force on Promotion and Dissemination of Psychological Procedures (1995) Training in and dissemination of empirically-validated psychological treatments. *The Clinical Psychologist,* 48: 3–23.

Tasto, D. L. and Hinkle, J. E. (1973) Muscle relaxation for tension headaches. *Behaviour Research and Therapy,* 11: 347–9.

Teyber, E. (2000) *Interpersonal Process in Psychotherapy* (4th edn). Pacific Grove, CA: Brooks/Cole.

Thitavanno, P. (2002) *A Buddhist Way of Mental Training* (2nd edn). Bangkok: Chuan Printing Press.

Thoresen, C. E. and Mahoney, M. J. (1974) *Behavioral Self-control.* New York: Holt, Rinehart & Winston.

Tyler, L. (1961) *The Work of the Counselor* (2nd edn). New York: Appleton-Century-Crofts.

Tyrrell, K. (ed.) (2001) *Annual Abstract of Statistics: 2001 Edition United Kingdom.* London: Stationery Office.

United Kingdom Council for Psychotherapy (2003) *Ethical Requirements for Member Organizations.* London: Author.

US Census Bureau (2003) *Census 2000 Briefs.* www.census.gov

Vicary, D. and Andrews. H. (2000) Developing a culturally appropriate psychotherapeutic approach with indigenous Australians. *Australian Psychologist,* 35: 181–5.

Wampold, B. E., Lichtenberg, J. W. and Waelher, C. A. (2002) Principles of empirically supported interventions in counseling psychology. *The Counseling Psychologist,* 30: 197–217.

Watkins, C. E. (1990) The effects of counselor self-disclosure: a research review. *The Counseling Psychologist,* 18: 477–500.

Watson, D. L. and Tharp, R. G. (2001) *Self-directed Behavior: Self-modification for Personal Adjustment* (8th edn). Belmont, CA: Wadsworth.

Webb, A. and Wheeler, S. (1998) How honest do counsellors dare to be in the supervisory relationship? An exploratory study. *British Journal of Guidance & Counselling,* 26: 509–24.

Weinstein, N. D. (1980) Unrealistic optimism about future events. *Journal of Personality and Social Psychology,* 39: 806–20.

Weinstein, N. D. (1984) Why it won't happen to me: perceptions of risk factors and susceptibility. *Health Psychology,* 3: 431–57.

Weston, R., Qu, L. and Soriano, G. (2001) *Ageing yet Diverse: The Changing Shape of Australia's Population. Australian Family Briefing No. 10.* Melbourne: Australian Institute of Family Studies.

Wheeler, S. (2000) Supervision and mature professional counsellors. In B. Lawton and C. Feltham (eds) *Taking Supervision Forward: Enquiries and Trends in Counselling and Psychotherapy*. London: Sage. pp. 204–6.

Wilkins, P. (2000) Personal therapy. In C. Feltham and I. Horton (eds) *Handbook of Counselling and Psychotherapy*. London: Sage. pp. 721–3.

Wilson, G. T. (2005) Behavior therapy. In R. Corsini and D. Wedding (eds) *Current Psychotherapies*, 7th edn. Belmont, CA: Wadsworth. pp. 202–37.

Wolpe, J. E. (1958) *Psychotherapy by Reciprocal Inhibition*. Stanford, CA: Stanford University Press.

Wolpe, J. E. (1990) *The Practice of Behavior Therapy* (4th edn). New York: Pergamon Press.

Wolpe, J. E. and Wolpe, D. (1988) *Life Without Fear: Anxiety and Its Cure*. Oakland, CA: New Harbinger Publications.

Wosket, V. (2000) Clinical supervision. In C. Feltham and I. Horton (eds) *Handbook of Counselling and Psychotherapy*. London: Sage. pp. 201–8.

Yalom, I. D. (1980) *Existential Psychotherapy*. New York: Basic Books.

Yalom, I. D. (1989) *Love's Executioner: and Other Tales of Psychotherapy*. London: Bloomsbury.

Yalom, I. D. (1995) *The Theory and Practice of Group Psychotherapy* (4th edn). New York: Basic Books.

Yalom, I. D. (2001) *The Gift of Therapy: Reflections on Being a Therapist*. London: Piatkus.

name index

subject index